BATTLE
OF THE BULGE

The Stackpole Military History Series

THE AMERICAN CIVIL WAR
Cavalry Raids of the Civil War
Ghost, Thunderbolt, and Wizard
Pickett's Charge
Witness to Gettysburg

WORLD WAR I
Doughboy War

WORLD WAR II
After D-Day
Armor Battles of the Waffen-SS, 1943–45
Armoured Guardsmen
Army of the West
Australian Commandos
The B-24 in China
Backwater War
The Battle of Sicily
Battle of the Bulge, Vol. 1
Battle of the Bulge, Vol. 2
Beyond the Beachhead
Beyond Stalingrad
The Brandenburger Commandos
The Brigade
Bringing the Thunder
The Canadian Army and the Normandy Campaign
Coast Watching in World War II
Colossal Cracks
A Dangerous Assignment
D-Day Deception
D-Day to Berlin
Destination Normandy
Dive Bomber!
A Drop Too Many
Eagles of the Third Reich
Eastern Front Combat
Exit Rommel
Fist from the Sky
Flying American Combat Aircraft of World War II
Forging the Thunderbolt
Fortress France
The German Defeat in the East, 1944–45

German Order of Battle, Vol. 1
German Order of Battle, Vol. 2
German Order of Battle, Vol. 3
The Germans in Normandy
Germany's Panzer Arm in World War II
GI Ingenuity
Goodwood
The Great Ships
Grenadiers
Hitler's Nemesis
Infantry Aces
Iron Arm
Iron Knights
Kampfgruppe Peiper at the Battle of the Bulge
The Key to the Bulge
Kursk
Luftwaffe Aces
Luftwaffe Fighter Ace
Massacre at Tobruk
Mechanized Juggernaut or Military Anachronism?
Messerschmitts over Sicily
Michael Wittmann, Vol. 1
Michael Wittmann, Vol. 2
Mountain Warriors
The Nazi Rocketeers
No Holding Back
On the Canal
Operation Mercury
Packs On!
Panzer Aces
Panzer Aces II
Panzer Commanders of the Western Front
Panzer Gunner
The Panzer Legions
Panzers in Normandy
Panzers in Winter
The Path to Blitzkrieg
Penalty Strike
Red Road from Stalingrad
Red Star under the Baltic
Retreat to the Reich
Rommel's Desert Commanders
Rommel's Desert War
Rommel's Lieutenants
The Savage Sky
The Siegfried Line

A Soldier in the Cockpit
Soviet Blitzkrieg
Stalin's Keys to Victory
Surviving Bataan and Beyond
T-34 in Action
Tank Tactics
Tigers in the Mud
Triumphant Fox
The 12th SS, Vol. 1
The 12th SS, Vol. 2
Twilight of the Gods
The War against Rommel's Supply Lines
War in the Aegean
Wolfpack Warriors
Zhukov at the Oder

THE COLD WAR / VIETNAM
Cyclops in the Jungle
Expendable Warriors
Flying American Combat Aircraft: The Cold War
Here There Are Tigers
Land with No Sun
Phantom Reflections
Street without Joy
Through the Valley

WARS OF THE MIDDLE EAST
Never-Ending Conflict

GENERAL MILITARY HISTORY
Carriers in Combat
Cavalry from Hoof to Track
Desert Battles
Guerrilla Warfare
Ranger Dawn
Sieges

BATTLE OF THE BULGE

Volume One:
The Losheim Gap / Holding the Line

Hans Wijers

STACKPOLE BOOKS

Copyright © 2009 by Hans Wijers

Published in 2009 by
STACKPOLE BOOKS
5067 Ritter Road
Mechanicsburg, PA 17055
www.stackpolebooks.com

All rights reserved, including the right to reproduce this book or portions thereof in any form or by any means, electronic or mechanical, including photocopying, recording, or by any information storage and retrieval system, without permission in writing from the publisher. All inquiries should be addressed to Stackpole Books.

Cover design by Tracy Patterson

Library of Congress Cataloging-in-Publication Data

Wijers, Hans J.
 Battle of the Bulge / Hans Wijers.
     v. cm. — (Stackpole military history series)
 Includes index.
 Contents: v. 1. The Losheim Gap/Holding the line.
 ISBN 978-0-8117-3592-6
 1. Ardennes, Battle of the, 1944–1945. I. Title.
 D756.5.A7W55 2009
 940.54'219348—dc22
                            2009011932

Contents

Book One: The Losheim Gap

    Foreword to Book One 2
    Introduction to Book One 4
Chapter 1   The German Plan of Attack 5
Chapter 2   U.S. Defensive Positions at the Losheim Gap 22
Chapter 3   The Germans Attack 40
Chapter 4   The Defense of Buchholz Station 52
Chapter 5   The German Assault against the
                  Losheimergraben Crossroads 64
Chapter 6   The Hilltop at Lanzerath 74
Chapter 7   Evening with the 1st Battalion, 394th Infantry 88
Chapter 8   The 277th Volksgrenadier Division Attacks 93
Chapter 9   Losheimergraben Is Lost 115
Chapter 10 Nemesis at Honsfeld 128
Chapter 11 The 254th Engineers Block the Road 150
Chapter 12 Withdrawal toward Elsenborn 167
Chapter 13 The 277th Volksgrenadier Division
                  Continues Its Attack 199
Chapter 14 Conclusion to Book One 211

Book Two: Holding the Line

    Foreword to Book Two 214
    Introduction to Book Two 217
Chapter 1   The German Plan of Attack 218
Chapter 2   American Defensive Positions 235
Chapter 3   Situation on the Southern Flank of the
                  2nd Infantry Division 255

Chapter 4	The Germans Attack 269
Chapter 5	The Battle at Höfen, 16–18 December 295
Chapter 6	The Withdrawal of the 2nd Infantry Division Begins 307
Chapter 7	The Fight for Krinkelt-Rocherath, 17 December ... 318
Chapter 8	The Second Attempt to Seize Krinkelt-Rocherath, 18 December 352
Chapter 9	Withdrawal toward Elsenborn 377
Chapter 10	Conclusion to Book Two 393

Sources 396
Acknowledgments 398

BOOK ONE

The Losheim Gap

Foreword to Book One

The Battle of the Bulge, the greatest battle ever fought by the U.S. Army, was not just one battle. It was hundreds of battles, some of battalion size and some of squad size and smaller. This book is the sum of many stories of many different battles—stories by individual men of the infantry, artillery, engineers, and others, by leaders of squads, platoons, companies, battalions, and even divisions and armies.

The varied topography of the Ardennes greatly influenced the pattern of the soldiers' experiences. Thick forest of tall trees, sparse areas of shorter trees (mortar positions), snowy fields, muddy trails, hills and valleys, log-covered foxholes, uncovered holes, shallow holes in ground too frozen to dig into—all contributed to the different actions at the individual places of combat as well as the perception of the combatants. These terrain features, while allowing some secrecy and protection for the German troop movements, posed much difficulty for advancing any appreciable distances. The same features also provided for well-prepared defensive positions for the early part of the action, positions that were held in many places by the American defenders although there were wide gaps between small units, mostly outposts. The difficulty of the terrain and the inability of the attacking units to perform reconnaissance, plus the fog that was to have been an advantage for surprise, combined to create great confusion for the attackers. The confusion that helped stymie the German advance of large units also initially confused the American commanders so that the magnitude of the attack could not be accurately determined.

While there were many bits of intelligence sent back from the front lines prior to that fateful day, there was a mindset in the higher levels that the Germans were running out of steam and that the thinly held Ardennes front was ideal for breaking in two inexperienced divisions and refitting two well-worn ones. The fact that the surprise attack did not follow Hitler's plan at the north shoulder is revealed in the many stories in this book, stories that show the lack of in-depth leadership on the German side, while showing individual entrepreneurship among many Americans, even when there were only two or three engaged. The many actions of this scale afforded precious

Foreword to Book One

time for reinforcements to be brought into the area and effectively blunted the main thrust of the German offensive.

Although I have not met the author personally, I've grown to know him through our correspondence over a period of more than a year. Hans Wijers has impressed me with his investigative energy and his deep passion for learning all he can about the events of this important piece of history. His presentation of the many stories, colored by interviews of participants from both sides, adds interesting highlights to the already large volume of writings on this battle.

B. O. Wilkins Jr.
K Company, 393rd Infantry
Houston, Texas

Introduction to Book One

The following work describes the fighting at the Losheim Gap, which was part of the sector of the 99th Infantry Division starting on 16 December, and as the retreat of these American troops to Elsenborn. It is based on official U.S. Army documents, together with the combat interviews of the 99th Infantry Division and its supporting troops and the after-action reports. These are completed by the testimony of several members of the units who fought in this area. Documents and testimony from the German side are also included.

This book describes actions fought at Losheimergraben, Lanzerath, Krinkelt, Buchholz Station, Mürringen, Wirtzfeld, Elsenborn Ridge, and other places starting on 16 December 1944. This book describes a part of the Battle of the Bulge fought at the northern shoulder, where the main thrust of the German offensive was halted.

Panthers of a tank battalion concealed in the snow-covered wood of Schmidtheimerwald (Eifel). The rugged and heavily wooded terrain of the Eifel, which was almost impenetrable to Allied air reconnaissance, decisively contributed to the surprise of the German offensive in the Ardennes. U.S. ARMY

CHAPTER 1

The German Plan of Attack

SCRAPING THE LAST RESERVES

Hitler had planned a surprise attack at the end of 1944 in the Ardennes, a sector weakly held by the Americans. According to the plan of attack, Army Group B (*Heeresgruppe B*) under Field Marshal Walter Model was to break through the thin American defensive lines and rapidly drive through to Antwerp. Having done this, the Germans could trap those Allied forces that at this time were menacing northwest Germany. The offensive was to be carried out by the 6th SS Panzer Army, the 5th Panzer Army, and the 7th Army.

The most important task, the taking of Antwerp, was given to the 6th SS Panzer Army, which had been concentrated in the sector north of the Schnee-Eifel. This sector was limited by natural barriers on two sides. In the south were the imposing peaks of the mountains that generally run from northwest to southeast. They stood nearly at right angles on the route of the planned attack. To the north, on the Belgian border, was the desolate plateau of Hautes Fagnes with its immense forests and rough terrain. In general, it was unsuitable for operations by armored divisions, though the close proximity of the Meuse River improved the situation somewhat. This was the area chosen for the 6th SS Panzer Army's advance.

THE 277TH VOLKSGRENADIER DIVISION
UNDER COL. WILHELM VIEBIG

The rebuilding of the division had been in progress since September 1944 in the Neuhäusel area of Hungary, using the remains of the 277th Infantry Division—2,500 men of which had escaped from the cauldron of Falaise in Normandy—and the remaining parts of the 574th Volksgrenadier Division. Rebuilding had to be finished by late October. The transport of the division toward the Eifel started on 2 November 1944. By 10 November, only about a third of the transports had arrived in the division's disembarkation area (Kall, Blankenheim, Jünkerath-Hillesheim).

The transportation sequence was completely disrupted by the repeated bombing of the Vienna area and the railroads in southern and western

Model, Rundstedt, and Krebs during one of the meetings in November 1944 discussing the plan of attack. HANS WIJERS

Germany. The 277th Logistics Regiment did not arrive in Ahrdorf until 13 November, and detraining could not take place until the next night. The division was ordered by the LXXIV Army Corps under General Straube to relieve the 347th Infantry Division on the Siegfried Line in a hurry. This relief took place by sector as the units of the 277th Volksgrenadier Division arrived, and this led to a mixing up of units, which had to be cleared up by a time-consuming reorganization.

The 277th Volksgrenadier Division held its positions without noticing anything important until around 13 December, when it grew suspicious about the numerous patrols by American artillery observers. But the men in the Siegfried Line bunkers had strict orders not to make any attacks. The regiments of the 277th now had positions in bunkers along the Höfen–Alzen–Monschauer Forest (Wahlerscheid)–Udenbreth line. On 13 December, the U.S. V Corps opened its attack to seize the Roer River dams. Units of the 2nd Infantry Division and the 99th Infantry Division began the offensive in the Wahlerscheid-Schleiden sector, but they gained only partial success. By the evening of the fifteenth, they had seized six bunkers in the area of the Forsthaus Wahlerscheid, which they later had to give up.

The 277th's sector at first was about thirty-eight kilometers long and ran from the Forsthaus Wahlerscheid in the north to Losheim in the south. The mission was to cover and defend the first line of the Siegfried Line. The

Wilhelm Viebig.

grenadier regiments were lined up from right to left—990th, 991st, and 989th—and they entered operations that way. When the battle for the Hürtgen Forest made necessary an expansion of the division's area toward the north (the Huppenbroich area), the 989th Grenadier Regiment was relocated to the right flank, and its sector on the left flank was taken over by the 18th Volksgrenadier Division under Major General Hoffmann-Schönborn. The southern limit of the 277th Volksgrenadier Division ran one kilometer south of Udenbreth. Its neighbor on the right was the 272nd Volksgrenadier Division under Col. Georg Kossmala (later Maj. Gen. Eugen König).

The divisional command post was located first in Schmidtheim, then in Krekel. The regimental command posts from north to south were located as follows: east of Rohren (989th Grenadier Regiment), west of Schleiden (990th Grenadier Regiment), and south of Reifferscheid (991st Grenadier Regiment). The division's fusilier company and two companies of the tank destroyer battalion (assault guns and antiaircraft tanks) were standing by in the Sistig area.

The so-called "static" units, with limited fighting value, were not counted. Scouting, reconnaissance, communications, and security determined events on both sides of the front line. Patrols by reconnaissance and assault troops as well as artillery harassing fire broke the relative quiet; the initiative lay mostly with the enemy, the untested U.S. 99th Infantry Division. In this way, the 277th Volksgrenadier could train its newly formed units close to the front line and become accustomed to operations there.

Until 13 December, the Americans recognized no signs that the situation was about to change. In its sector, the indications of the coming operation grew, however. Battery positions of German artillery units were established, and artillery staffs conducted feverish reconnaissance activity. Several companies had to receive training in attacks in the forest. That the orders for this came from the highest authority was made clear when the commander of Army Group B, Field Marshal Walter Model, thoroughly reviewed such an exercise of the division's fusilier company in person.

Expectant tension enveloped the constantly tested 277th. This was diminished somewhat in early December 1944 when the commander, Colonel Viebig, and the chief of staff, General Staff Lt. Col. Freiherr von Wangenheim, were briefed by the commanding general of the I SS Panzer Corps, SS Lt. Gen. Hermann Priess, at the command post in Schmidtheim about the plans for the attack and the objectives to be achieved by the 277th Volksgrenadier Division.

German soldiers of the Wehrmacht equipped with machine guns and a *panzerfaust* leave their West Wall bunkers in the Monschauer Forest to prepare for the attack.
HANS WIJERS

The German Plan of Attack

OPERATIONS OF THE 277TH VOLKSGRENADIER DIVISION BEFORE THE OFFENSIVE

In December 1944, the LXVII Army Corps under Lt. Gen. Otto Hitzfeld was lined up on the first line of the Siegfried Line or in the bunkers of the Siegfried Line in the area south of Vossenach and Udenbreth. The northern sector of the so-called Corps Monschau was taken over by the 272nd Volksgrenadier Division under Maj. Gen. Eugen König and the southernmost sector by the 277th Volksgrenadier. The common division boundary ran four kilometers northeast of Monschau. The regiments of the 277th had been positioned from north to south in the Höfen, Alzen, Monschau Forest (Wahlerscheid), and Udenbreth sectors as follows: the 989th, 990th, and 991st Grenadier Regiments.

The regimental sectors had to be expanded toward the north in order to make a larger concentration of German forces in the Hürtgen Forest possible. However, the division had not taken part in the fighting of November 1944. In the Wahlerscheid area, the 991st Grenadier Regiment had been hit by an American attack, which was part of a larger operation that the U.S. V Corps undertook on the Monschau-Schleiden road in the direction of the Roer dams between 13 and 16 December. The American opponents—parts of the 2nd U.S. Infantry Division and the 99th U.S. Infantry Division (the 1st and 2nd Battalions of the 395th Infantry Regiment and the 2nd Battalion of the 393rd Infantry Regiment)—gained local advantages. According to information from the commander of the 99th U.S. Infantry Division, the 2nd Battalion of the 393rd Infantry had by the evening of 15 December been able to capture six bunkers in the vicinity of the Wahlerscheid forestry house, as well as the mouth of the wood tracks from the Rocherath-Krinkelt area toward the Monschau-Schleiden road. It also took a number of prisoners.

This surely also was the result of the late arrival of the 326th Volksgrenadier Division in the Konzen-Wahlerscheid area. This delay also slowed down the move of the regiments of the 277th Volksgrenadier Division toward the southern sector between Hollerath—more specifically, the Hollerath Knee in the road from Losheim to Hellenthal and Udenbreth—to prepare for the attack of 16 December. As the 277th Volksgrenadier Division joined the I SS Panzer Corps on arrival in its starting locations, this corps now bordered on the LXVII Army Corps, which now consisted of the 326th and 272nd Volksgrenadier Divisions (north of Konzen).

Furthermore, on 16 December 1944, the 326th Field Replacement Battalion managed to reestablish the course of the front line near Wahlerscheid and to proceed to the Schwalm Valley northeast of Elsenborn, following the withdrawing opponents. The 272nd took no part in this attack.

THE MISSION OF THE 277TH VOLKSGRENADIER DIVISION AT THE START OF THE OFFENSIVE

The 277th Volksgrenadier Division had the job of opening up Advance Routes A and C in its own sector. Advance Route A ran from the Hollerath Knee over an unhardened forest trail to Rocherath in the German-speaking part of Belgium and continued from there, via Krinkelt and Wirtzfeld, to Elsenborn and then continued via Sourbrodt to Hockal. Advance Route C began near Neuhof in the vicinity of Udenbreth and ran to Losheimergraben via the Reich Road and then via Büllingen toward Waimes, Malmedy, and Stavelot. Advance Route B was identical to Advance Route C until it forked off between Weisser Stein southwest of Udenbreth and Losheimergraben, from which it continued, via Mürringen, Bütgenbach, and Belair, in the direction of Francorchamps.

In the corps sector and in the 6th SS Panzer Army area, Advance Route C was best suited to a quick advance, especially in the winter conditions in the Eifel. In order to open up Route A and B/C for a bold, energetic advance of the 12th SS Panzer Division *Hitlerjugend*, commanded by Standartenführer Hugo Kraas, the 277th Volksgrenadier Division formed two attack groups. The main effort lay with the leftmost group, which had to free Route B/C. For this purpose, the 990th Grenadier Regiment was reinforced with the division Füsilier Company with five platoons and an engineer company.

The experienced commander, Lt. Col. Josef Bremm, bearer of the Oak Leaves to the Knight's Cross of the Iron Cross, deployed his units during the night of 16 December in the Siegfried Line bunkers around Udenbreth. The objective was Krinkelt. The rightmost group consisted of the 989th Grenadier Regiment, commanded by General Staff Col. Georg Fieger, plus an engineer company and parts of the 277th Tank Destroyer Battalion. The regiment stood by in the Siegfried Line bunkers around Hollerath and was to attack from the Hollerath Knee, cross the Jansbach stream, and take Rocherath.

The 991st Grenadier Regiment under Lt. Col. O. Jaquet took up its starting positions around Ramscheid between both combat groups and slightly to the rear. It was the reserve with orders to reinforce either the leftmost or rightmost attack group as the situation demanded after the Reich Road between the Hollerath Knee and Weisser Stein had been opened. The three grenadier regiments had each been organized into two battalions of four companies each, as well as an infantry gun and a tank destroyer company.

The mood of the troops was good; despite the drawbacks of the night march and the insufficient briefing on the situation and the terrain, they were confident they could overthrow the opponent, the U.S. 99th Infantry Division, of which they did not have a high estimate, and attain the objectives of the attack. That units of the U.S. 2nd Infantry Division had taken part in

The German Plan of Attack

Soldiers of the Waffen-SS inside their bunkers waiting for the start of the attack. HANS WIJERS

the American attacks on 13–15 December in the area north of Wahlerscheid and that an intervention by this division therefore had to be taken into account were unknown on the German side.

Because of the strict secrecy of the preparations of the offensive, the enemy positions, operations, and organization could not be sufficiently reconnoitered or scouted. The possibilities of penetrating the dense and thickly snowed woods in front of and behind the Reich Road from Hollerath to Weisser Stein in a depth of four kilometers in icy and cold weather, or even in a thaw, and using the narrow, unhardened forest trails for the advance on Rocherath and Krinkelt could only be guessed at, but not estimated. These difficulties were all too well known to the division commander and his chief of staff, Lieutenant Colonel of the General Staff Horst Freiherr von Wangenheim. Their main concern was whether it would be possible to knock out or interdict the strong enemy artillery positions in the Rocherath-Krinkelt area.

Viebig received orders for their attack on 16 December. The 277th Volksgrenadier Division of the 6th SS Panzer Army had to seize the roads from Hollerath Knee toward Rocherath and the road from Krinkelt to Wirzfeld and Elsenborn (Route A and C). These roads had to be kept open for the 12th SS Panzer Division *Hitlerjugend*. On the left side of the attack group was the 990th Regiment under Lt. Col. Josef Bremm. They were heavily reinforced with parts of the fusilier company and parts of the division's pioneer unit because they had the most difficult task—seizing Krinkelt. On the right was the 989th Regiment under Col. Georg Fieger. They had their positions in the area of Hollerath (West Wall bunkers). Their objective was to seize Rocherath. To do so, they had to attack through Hollerath Knee and the Jansbach (a small stream in the Krinkelter woods). In the center was the 991st Regiment under Lt. Col. O. Jacquet, largely in the area of Ramscheid. They were to hold in reserve, and when the International Highway was captured, they could be called to reinforce the left or the right group.

The three regiments were supported by the division artillery (the 277th Artillery Regiment under Major Kienzler) and by *nebelwerfer* and heavy *mörser* of the independent Volksartillery Corps. One tank battalion of the 12th SS Panzer Division was attached to the 277th Volksgrenadier Division during the opening hours of the attack.

THE 12TH VOLKSGRENADIER DIVISION UNDER MAJ. GEN. GERHARD ENGEL

The Losheimergraben Crossroads, which gave access to the route to Malmédy, the only road suitable for a quick advance of German armor in the region, had an extraordinary importance. The task of capturing the Losheimergraben Crossroads and opening up the road to Malmédy had been given to the 12th Volksgrenadier Division, commanded by Maj. Gen. Gerhard Engel. This division was below strength. Since September, the 12th Division had been in action virtually without pause in bloody combat in the Aachen sector. It was only during the night of 2–3 December that the last elements of the division were relieved from the front to assemble in the area north of the Eifel, in the sector of Tondorf-Engelgau-Zingsheim-Nettersheim-Marmagen-Schmidtheim-Blankenheim-Mülheim. The last elements of the division arrived on the morning of 4 December.

The division had been weakened by the preceding combat. Generally speaking, infantry units had no more than one-third of their authorized strength, and the batteries on average had no more than three guns. Furthermore, they also had lost over half of their forward observers. Nearly 90 percent of all automatic weapons had been lost, and the same was true of the heavy infantry weapons (mortars, infantry, and antitank guns). The antitank battalion had only six assault guns at its disposal, instead of the twenty they were supposed to have, and these were only partially operational due to various technical problems.

The German Plan of Attack

October 1944. Part of the officer corps of the 12th Volksgrenadier. In the center Gen. Maj. Gerhard Engel (with the long pants). HANS J. WIJERS/H. ZEPLIEN

On 11 December, General Engel received the orders for the attack. His division, as the first wave of attack of the 6th SS Panzer Army, was to pierce the thin American lines at Losheimergraben and open a breach in the enemy lines to permit the advance of the tanks of the 12th SS Panzer Division. The division was to advance down the Losheim-Bütgenbach-Malmédy axis prior to turning north toward Verviers. Once there the division was to take up defensive positions in order to protect the right flank of the 6th SS Panzer Army.

Engel decided to launch the attack with two attack groups located on both sides of Road No. 32, leading from Losheim to Bütgenbach: on the right was the 48th Grenadier Regiment of Col. Wilhelm Osterhold and on the left was the 27th Fusilier Regiment of Lt. Col. Heinz-Georg Lemm. The 89th Grenadier Regiment of Lt. Col. Gerhard Lemcke and the 12th Fusilier Battalion were kept in reserve. The first objective of the attack was to take the crossroads at Losheimergraben and to reach the western edge of the wide forest. If this was achieved quickly, the attack was to continue as soon as possible to take the high ground that dominates Hünningen and Mürringen. If not, then the assault groups were to reorganize at the west edge of the forest and take the heights in a prepared assault. With the taking of Hünningen and Mürringen, the positions of the American artillery would have been reached, and with that the breakthrough of the American lines would be complete.

To exploit this breakthrough of American lines, a motorized assault group of an advance detachment under Maj. Günther Holz, commander of the antitank battalion, stood by on the Kronenburg-Hallschlag road. Advance Detachment Holz consisted of an antitank battalion, reinforced by one company of the 12th Fusilier Battalion and pioneers loaded onto trucks. The 12th Volksgrenadier Division busied itself with completing and reorganizing it units. In an unhoped-for manner, the division received 3,500 replacements; 500 were experienced men who returned from various hospitals, which permitted the ranks to be fleshed out a bit. Half of the men came from depots and were green, having received only rudimentary training. With regard to the resupply

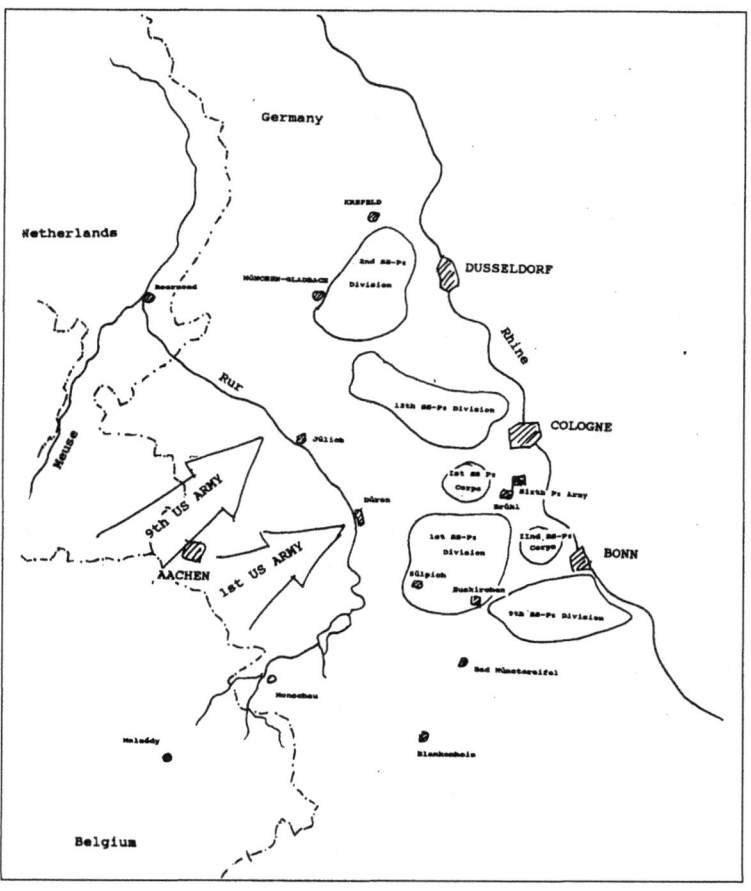

Troop dispositions before the Battle of the Bulge, November 1944.

The German Plan of Attack

and the handing out of light weapons to the division, all went relatively well. With regard to antitank weapons, many problems were encountered. Despite all the promises of higher command authorities, the fourteen missing assault guns were never delivered to the division.

It was not until 13 December that the commanders of the 12th Division learned that the date of Operation *Herbstnebel* ("Autumn Fog") was set for 16 December. For the first phase of the offensive, the breakthrough of the enemy lines, the division was attached to the I SS Panzer Corps. During the nights of 14–15 and 15–16 December, the troops of the division advanced to the start positions under conditions of great secrecy. During the last night, the assault elements took up their attack positions, which were generally located in the fortified strongpoints of the Siegfried Line west of Scheidt and Frauenkron.

KAMPFGRUPPE PEIPER UNDER WAFFEN-SS COL. JOACHIM PEIPER

This battle group, the 1st SS Panzer Regiment of the 1st SS Panzer Division, was badly mangled after the heavy fighting in Normandy and the retreat through France. The 1st SS Panzer Division came to its rest area in Minden (Westfalen) and had two months to reorganize its troops. The division received about 3,500 new combat troops, bringing the division up to full strength of 22,000 men. The division also received new material, mostly coming directly from the assembly line. However, the regiment was supposed to have one battalion of Mark IV and one battalion of Panther tanks. Not having enough tanks, Joachim Peiper organized one battalion with a mixture of two companies of Mark IV and two companies of Panther tanks. To compensate for the shortage of tanks, the regiment was further reinforced with a battalion of Tiger tanks which had formerly been corps armor. Therefore, the regiment finally consisted of one battalion of mixed Panther and Mark IV tanks, one battalion of Tiger tanks, and one battalion of SS personnel without tanks. Prior to coming to Westfalen, the division had about fifty tanks. They received about 200 additional tanks during the period of reequipment.

About three weeks before the Ardennes offensive, the unit was moved into army reserve twelve kilometers east of Düren, north of Euskirchen. On 13 December, the division was given a detailed march order issued by I SS Panzer Corps. No mention of the impending offensive was contained in this order; nothing was mentioned except the route of march and the assembly area. The division moved out at 1900 hours on 13 December and had disappeared into the woods in their assembly area by 1000 on 14 December. They assembled in the area of Marmegen-Blankenheimerdorf-Schmidtheim. Advance elements of the division were in Dahlem.

Joachim Peiper.

PLANS AND PREPARATIONS FOR THE OFFENSIVE

The division also had the 9th Parachute Regiment of the 3rd Fallschirmjäger Division (they got stuck following the start of the offensive). In addition, at the beginning of the offensive, special Skorzeny units of the 150th Panzer Brigade were attached. Each combat team had such a group. A group consisted of 500 men, twenty M-4 Sherman tanks, a few German tanks, thirty two-and-a-half-ton trucks, and thirty to fifty jeeps. Much of the equipment had been captured during the invasion and had stayed with various units up until October 1944, when a general order was issued to turn in all captured equipment. The route of advance for the 1st SS Panzer Division was as follows: Schmidtheim-Dahlem-Kronenburg-Hallschlag-Scheid-Losheim-Losheimergraben-Hünningen-Honsfeld-Hepscheid-Möderscheid-Schoppen-Ondenval-Thirimont-Ligneuville-Pont-Trois Ponts-Werbo-mont-Guffet-Seny-Tinlot-Stree-Huy.

Kampfgruppe Peiper in the center was to have the primary role in the offensive. It was not to bother about its flanks but was to drive rapidly to the Meuse River, making full use of the element of surprise.

THE 150TH PANZER BRIGADE UNDER OTTO SKORZENY

The 150th Panzer Brigade moved into the Ardennes area on 14 December 1944 in the neighborhood of Münstereifel. The brigade had moved into the area mostly at night, and the tanks were always kept deep in the woods dur-

The German Plan of Attack

Otto Skorzeny.

ing the day. The soldiers were not allowed to go into towns in the area, nor were any men sent to the front lines prior to the attack.

Skorzeny considered it much more important to conceal their movements than to risk betraying the offensive by conducting reconnaissance. On the afternoon of 16 December 1944, the brigade moved out, and from there the combat groups moved in behind the attacking divisions. The units were placed at the rear of the leading elements of the divisions to which they were assigned, and the plan was that they were to move around the divisions on side roads once the objective, Hohe Venn, was reached. Around the first of December 1944, all of the officers of the brigade were given this outline of the plans. It was not until 10 December that even the group commanders were aware of the actual plans for the attack.

The organization was composed of two main groups, the Commando Unit and the 150th Panzer Brigade. The Commando Unit was composed of English-speaking men who had been withdrawn from various units in the armed forces. Skorzeny received about 600 men initially, and from these he picked 150 of the best. All were equipped with American jeeps and uniforms. The highest American rank they used was that of colonel; they did not disguise anyone as an American general officer. The Commando Unit was divided as follows:

    a. Demolition Groups. These were composed of five to six men in each group whose job was to blow bridges and munition and gasoline dumps.

b. Reconnaissance Groups. These units, with three to four men, were to reconnoiter in depth east and west of the Meuse River to spot enemy tank, artillery, and other unit movements. Some of these groups were equipped with radios with which they were to send back information of these movements. They were also instructed to give false commands to units they met, to reverse road signs, to remove minefield signs, and to put white strips in streets with no mines so that the enemy force would believe the roads were blocked.

c. "Lead" Commandos. These groups, of three to four men, primarily were to disrupt the enemy command by cutting telephone wires, wrecking radio stations, and giving false commands. They were to work closely with the attacking divisions.

The 150th Panzer Brigade was composed of two tank groups and one infantry combat group, each with its own small combat staff. The total composition of the 150th Panzer Brigade was as follows:

Staff and a signal company

Three small combat staffs

Two signal companies from the army (200 men)

Two battalions of Kampfgrupe 200, which was a parachute unit from the German Air Force (800 men)

One company of *Jagd Verband Mitte* (a special unit organized initially to hunt and fight partisans in occupied countries) (175 men)

Two companies of the 600th FS Battalion, which was a special infantry battalion (350 men)

Two tank companies from the army (240 men)

Two panzer grenadier companies (350 men)

Two companies of heavy mortars from the army (200 men)

Two antitank companies from the army (200 men)

One pioneer (engineer) company (100 men)

Three vehicle repair companies (75 men)

All of these companies were somewhat weaker than a regular army unit. The two tank companies each had twelve tanks, half of which were either Sherman or Mark II tanks and the other half Panther tanks. In the panzer grenadier companies, two or three of the half-tracks were American and the other ten or twelve were German.

The following is a sample organization of one of the tank combat groups:

A small staff

A platoon of signalmen

One company of tanks

The German Plan of Attack

Three companies of infantry (120–150 men each) made up of two companies of Kampfgruppe 200 and one company of *Jagd Verband Mitte* or the 600th FS Battalion
Two platoons of heavy (120-millimeter) mortars
Two antitank platoons
Two platoons of panzer grenadiers
One platoon of engineers
One vehicle repair group

Both tank groups were based on this organization, as was the infantry group (except that the latter had no tanks). The mission of the brigade was to seize undamaged at least two Meuse River bridges from among the Amay, Huy, or Andenne. The action was to be initiated when the panzer units of the panzer divisions reached the Hohe Venn, roughly on a line running northeast and southwest from Spa. At that time, the troops were to move forward at night and reach their objective six hours later. It was originally planned that the attack would reach the Hohe Venn on the first day and that they would move out that night. The plan could be carried out only when the area of the Hohe Venn had been reached, because it was necessary to move forward with complete surprise and without having to fight. The three groups were then to move on parallel routes toward the three bridges. Radio communication was to be used between groups in order that they might shift if resistance were encountered.

THE 3RD FALLSCHIRMJÄGER DIVISION
UNDER MAJ. GEN. WALTER WADEHN

This division was hastily rebuilt in the Netherlands from battered remnants of the 3rd Fallschirmjäger (Paratroop) Division, which had escaped from France. It was mainly filled up with excess *Luftwaffe* personnel, and both men and officers alike were woefully inexperienced. In November, OB West committed the division near Aachen, where it encountered the American drive through the northeastern fringes of the Hürtgen Forest.

Although the paratroopers succeeded in stopping the American drive, they paid dearly for their inexperience. As the target date for the offensive approached, the division was still locked in bitter fighting near Düren, and it proved almost impossible to extricate it. On 10 December, only one regiment, the 9th Fallschirmjäger Regiment, had been relieved. On 14 December, after forced night marches, the regiment arrived in the assigned assembly area at Schüller, a village near the town of Stadkyll.

The combat strength of the 9th Fallschirmjäger Regiment had been considerably diminished by the previous fighting. The three battalions that constituted the regiment had an average strength of only 450 men. It was not

Walter Wadehn.

until the night of 13–14 December, that the remaining two regiments could be extricated from the lines near Düren. Both were exhausted and had taken a severe beating. Upon release of the 3rd Fallschirmjäger Division, the Fifteenth Army reported that it was incapable of any offensive action for some days at least. In an effort to transfer the troops of the division as quickly as possible to the zone of attack, a part of one regiment was hastily loaded into lorries borrowed from the I SS Panzer Corps and, while leaving its heavy infantry weapons behind, was transported to the concentration zone. The other elements, the heavy infantry weapons included, were to move on foot to the assigned zone, where they arrived in the evening of the sixteenth, too late to take part in the initial phase of the offensive. Personnel strength of the 3rd Fallschirmjäger Division was estimated at approximately 75 percent of authorization. The division lacked the support of self-propelled guns.

The 3rd Fallschirmjäger Division, forming the left wing in the initial disposition for the attack, had a zone of advance roughly following the southern shoulder of the road to Honsfeld (Advance Route D). The division went into combat with two groups: on the right was the 9th Fallschirmjäger Regiment taking a route via Berterath-Lanzerath-Honsfeld-Hepscheid toward Schoppen, and on the left was the 8th Fallschirmjäger Regiment that moved via Krewinkel-Manderfeld-Holzheim-Wereth toward Eibertingen.

The area selected for the breakthrough attempt comprised the north half of the U.S. 14th Cavalry Group sector and took in most of the gap between the cavalry and the 99th Division to its north. In the first hours of

The German Plan of Attack

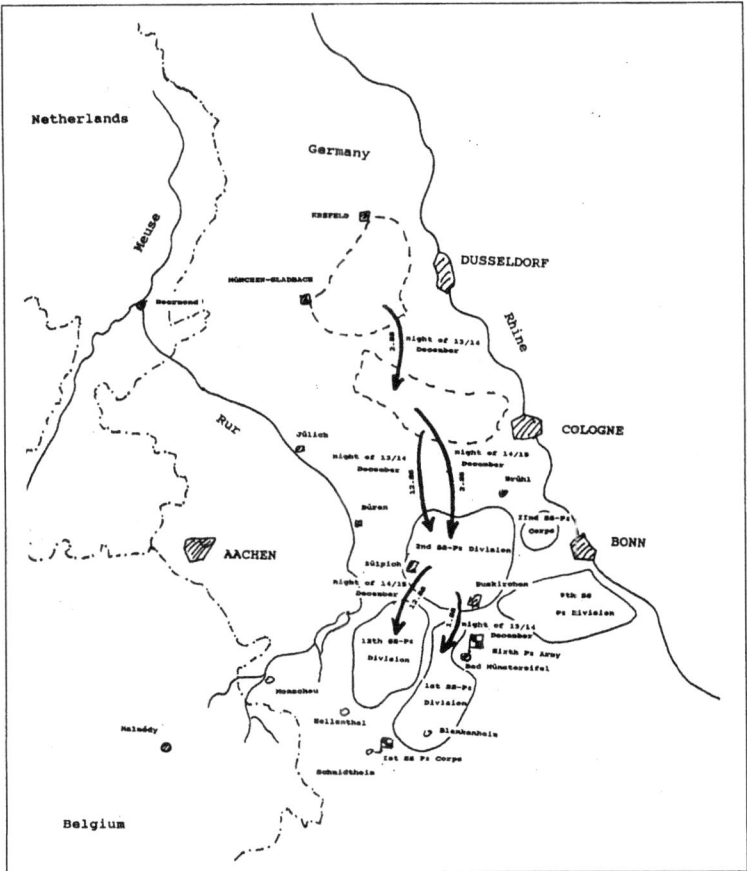

The 6th SS Panzer Army moves into the Eifel, 13–16 December 1944.

the advance, then, the 3rd Fallschirmjäger Division would be striking against the 14th Cavalry Group in the Krewinkel-Berterath area. But the final objective of the 3rd Fallschirmjäger's attack was ten miles to the northwest—the line Schoppen-Eibertingen on Route D. The 3rd's axis thus extended through the right of the 99th Division.

CHAPTER 2

U.S. Defensive Positions at the Losheim Gap

THE 99TH INFANTRY DIVISION

The 99th Infantry Division, an untried and inexperienced infantry division commanded by Maj. Gen. Walter E. Lauer, arrived on the continent in November 1944. It began taking over a broad defensive position in the southern part of the V Corps' (Gen. Leonard Gerow) sector from the 9th Infantry Division on 9 November.

The division assumed responsibility for the defense of a position roughly twenty miles wide. It extended from Monschau in the north to a point near Losheim in the south. General Lauer stated that he had "refused" (not accepted responsibility for actual occupation) several thousand yards of terrain on his right flank, which would have included the town of Losheim. His reason was simply that he felt it would overstretch his already thinly spread line. Instead, he turned his flank to the southwest.

The boundary between the V and VIII Corps was the 99th's right (south) boundary. South of this boundary, the area was thinly held by elements of the 14th Cavalry Group (Task Force X). They were charged with the responsibility for maintaining physical contact by means of hourly lateral visiting patrols. From that time until 13 December 1944, when the division launched an attack with the 395th Regimental Combat Team in conjunction with the 2nd Division, its main activities consisted of improving positions and patrolling. The German counteroffensive caught the division completely by surprise.

As part of the normal precautions against attack, General Lauer had defensive positions dug several thousands yards to the rear of the front lines. One of these positions was an area of some 5,500 yards on the high ground east and south of the towns of Mürringen and Hünningen. Other defensive positions were constructed on the high ground west and northwest of Wirzfeld.

The forward positions of the 393rd and 394th Infantry Regiments were in the thick woods. This area, all part of the Monschau Forest, is as densely

Walter Lauer.

wooded in many places as was the Hürtgen Forest. It is an area pitted with rocky gorges, small streams, abrupt hills, and an extremely limited road net. The routes to the forward positions, with the exception of the one main road running southeast of Losheim, consisted of narrow, rutted firebreak trails.

During most of the period prior to 16 December, these routes were quagmires of mud. Drainage was almost impossible because these trails were lower than the ground immediately around them. Even the corduroy log base on the route leading to the command post of the 2nd Battalion, 394th Infantry, which had been built originally by the 9th Division engineers, did little to help. It did make movement possible by providing a firm base. But this was covered by a sea of knee-deep mud. Vehicular movement was slow and torturous. Visibility was limited to 100–150 yards maximum. Fields of fire were equally limited and poor. Fire lanes for automatic weapons would not be cleared for any great distance without cutting down trees and thereby disclosing the position.

It was clearly recognized that the Germans could infiltrate and penetrate these poor and thinly held positions. General Lauer emphasized this latter point, stating that the Germans could probably shove an entire battalion through the line at any number of places. However, until the German counteroffensive was well under way, the general and his staff felt that at the most, the only effort that the Germans could make would be a limited attack by one or two battalions or possibly a regiment. Further, this effort would be merely a reaction to the attack to the Roer. There was no suspicion of an enemy buildup.

Three roads were of primary importance in the division's area of concern. In the north, a main paved road led from Höfen through the Monschau Forest, then divided as it emerged on the eastern edge (this fork beyond the forest would have some tactical importance). A second road ran laterally behind the division center and right flank, leaving the Höfen road at the tiny village of Wahlerscheid, continuing south through the twin hamlets of Rocherath and Krinkelt, then intersecting a main east-west road at Büllingen. This paved highway entered the division zone from the east at Losheimergraben and ran west to Malmédy by way of Büllingen and Bütgenbach. As a result, despite the poverty of roads inside the forest belt where the forward positions of the 99th Division lay, the division sector could be entered from the east along roads tapping either flank.

From 8 December on, the 99th Division had been preparing for its first commitment in a large-scale operation, repairing roads, laying additional telephone wire, and shifting its guns for the V Corps' attack toward the Roer dams. In addition, a new supply road was constructed from the Krinkelt area to the sector held by the 395th Infantry. The 2nd Infantry Division was to pass through the 99th, and then a regimental combat team of the 99th would attack, covering the southern flank of the 2nd Division advance. As

The road from Eupen toward Sourbrodt as seen in winter 1999. HANS WIJERS

The road from Eupen to Sourbrodt in 1944.
U.S. ARMY

scheduled, the 2nd Division passed through the 99th Division on 13 December, beginning its attack on a narrow front toward Dreiborn, located on the northern fork of the Höfen road beyond the Monschau Forest.

The dispositions of the 99th Division were as follows. On the north flank, the 3rd Battalion, 395th Infantry, occupied the Höfen area, with the 38th Cavalry Squadron on its left and the 99th Reconnaissance Troop on the right. The ground here was open and rolling. The 3rd Battalion was well dug in and possessed good fields of fire. Next in line to the south, the 2nd Division was making its attack on a thrust line running northeastward, its supply route following the section of the Höfen road, which ran through the forest to the fork. The remaining two battalions of the 395th Infantry plus the 2nd Battalion, 393rd Infantry, formed the combat team attacking on the right of the 2nd Division. The 99th Division defensive front resumed to the south, in turn, by the 3rd Battalion and 1st Battalion of the 393rd Infantry and by the 394th Infantry. Conforming to the wooded contour, the defensive line of the 99th Division south of the attacking columns occupied a slight salient bellying out from the flanks.

THE 393RD INFANTRY REGIMENT
The 393rd Infantry Regiment under Lt. Col. Jean D. Scott relieved the 39th Regiment of the 9th Infantry Division on 11 November 1944. Between 13 November and 11 December, A Company was attached to the 395th Infantry. Service and HQ Companies were in Krinkelt, and antitank platoons were attached to the battalions, with the antitank company's headquarters also in Krinkelt. Cannon Company established positions just northeast of the town behind the reserve battalion area. The 393rd Infantry was in the line on 16 December with the 3rd Battalion on the left and the 1st Battalion on the right. The 2nd Battalion was attached to the 395th Infantry in the attack toward the Roer dams, protecting its right flank.

THE 394TH INFANTRY REGIMENT
The fateful position of Col. Don Riley's 394th Regiment would bring against it the main effort of the I SS Panzer Corps and, indeed, that of the 6th SS Panzer Army. Two roads ran obliquely through the regimental area. One, a main road, intersected the north-south International Highway (and the forward line held by the 394th) at Losheimergraben and continued northwestward through Büllingen and Bütgenbach to Malmédy. The other, a secondary road but generally passable in winter, branched from the International Highway north of Lanzerath and curved west through Buchholz, Honsfeld, Schoppen, and Faymonville, roughly paralleling the main road to the north.

Before the German counteroffensive, the 394th held a defensive sector with the 1st Battalion on the right, the 2nd Battalion on the left, and the 3rd Battalion (under Maj. Norman Moore) in regimental—and also division—reserve. The regimental Intelligence and Reconnaissance Platoon was on high ground on the extreme right flank covering the road from Lanzerath.

The regiment had moved into the line and, with the exception of infrequent patrols and slight artillery activity, had an extremely quiet part of the front. The men had improved their living conditions and had elaborate huts and a rest center at Honsfeld. No one in the regiment had any idea that a German buildup was going on opposite them. The regiment was occupying an extremely large front line—about 5,500 meters—and there was a big gap between the 394th and Task Force X (14th Cavalry Group) on its right. The Losheimergraben Crossroads was guarded by a single American battalion, the 1st Battalion of the 394th Infantry Regiment, commanded by Lt. Col. Robert H. Douglas. The battalion had entrenched itself beyond the crossroads in the surrounding forests.

THE 394TH INFANTRY'S INTELLIGENCE AND RECONNAISSANCE PLATOON AT LANZERATH

The Intelligence and Reconnaissance (I & R) Platoon, commanded by Lt. Lyle Bouck Jr., plus eighteen men of the 394th Infantry and four members of the forward observer party from C Battery, 371st Field Artillery, occupied an area on a hilltop overlooking the village of Lanzerath. They had moved into this position on 10 December, taking over the dugouts prepared by the men of the 2nd Division, which had pulled out earlier. Lyle Bouck's men added fortifications to the dugouts, heavy logs that would later prove to be life savers.

In sworn testimony to Congress in 1981, Pvt. G. Vernon Leopold gave a very accurate and detailed report of the situation of the platoon prior to the battle (starting 10 December, when the platoon took over the positions prepared by the 2nd Infantry Division): "I was a member of the I & R Platoon of the 394th Infantry Regiment under leadership of Lt. Lyle Bouck Jr. On 10 December 1944, the 2nd Infantry Division was pulled out of the line to our regiment's immediate south to prepare for the mission of attacking the Roer River dams to our north. Our I & R Platoon was 'temporarily' moved into the resulting gap with orders to investigate and report any observed enemy activity. Equipped with M1 rifles, automatic carbines, a jeep-mounted .50-caliber machine gun, two Browning automatic rifles (BARs), mortars, antitank bazookas, and grenades, we were placed into well-concealed positions on a wooded crest of a ridge which overlooked a clear slope down to and beyond a road which connected Lanzerath to our right and immediately south, and

U.S. Defensive Positions at the Losheim Gap

Vernon Leopold.

Losheim somewhere off to our left and north. Weatherwise, bitter cold interspersed with periods of snowfall prevailed throughout.

"During the ensuing five days, we improved and added to these positions, which, in effect, became bunkers with easterly-facing firing slits, reinforced and covered with logs and dirt, and rendered virtually indistinguishable from the surrounding terrain by a blanket of snow several inches in depth. We also dug out and constructed a similarly reinforced position for our jeep which had a .50-caliber machine gun and our two-way radio mounted on it. To afford warnings of possible enemy infiltrators, we strung out a network of trip wires to which we attached empty cans containing rocks. From this position various squads of the platoon fanned out intermittently in day and night patrols in search of enemy activity, occasionally using a building in the hamlet of Lanzerath as a forward outpost.

"As a radio operator fluent in German, my task included the scanning, interpreting and recording of German field communications. During the nights we stood guard in groups of two men per bunker serving three-hour shifts. Those of us not on guard, patrol or otherwise occupied would rest in a log cabin constructed approximately 390 to 400 feet back. We kept in touch with regimental headquarters in Hünningen by means of our field telephones backed up by our jeep-mounted radio which was my job to operate. Also, twice daily Private Oakley would drive in food, supplies and mail from headquarters by jeep.

"For the first three days, we saw and heard very little combat activity. However, during the night of 14 December, artillery fire became heavy to our north, where, so we were told, the 2nd and 99th Division Combat Teams were launching their attacks to the Roer River dams east of the German-Belgian border. More significantly, however, one of our platoon's night patrols reported having sighted and heard tanks and heavy equipment moving around some distance behind the German lines, and we promptly reported this information to regimental headquarters.

"During the early afternoon of 15 December, after we had lost one man from the outpost because of trenchfoot contracted by him during the previous night, Lt. Bouck ordered me to report to the regimental aid station in Hünningen in order to receive treatment for frostbite. Therefore, I cannot describe the events which began twelve to sixteen hours after I left our outpost—more particularly, the defensive effort by the nineteen members of my platoon which held back the German onslaught for the critical twelve hours for which the platoon was highly decorated in 1982."

THE SITUATION OF THE 3RD BATTALION, 394TH INFANTRY, AT BUCHHOLZ STATION

HQ Company of the 3rd Battalion was established at Buchholz on the morning of 16 December 1944. L Company was directly to the east with its platoons on both sides of the railroad track at Losheimergraben. The 1st Platoon was west of the railroad, the 2nd on its left and the 3rd Platoon in support. The Weapons Platoon and one squad of mortars were attached to the 3rd Platoon. L Company's headquarters was located in the railroad station. M Company, minus one platoon, was northeast of L while K was on

L Company headquarters at Buchholz Station, facing southeast. N. COLONERUS/HANS WIJERS

both sides of the road. A tank destroyer platoon—possibly the 801st—and one platoon of B Company, 324th Engineers, were attached to the battalion, while the 371st Field Artillery Battalion was in position to give direct support. No one was on the battalion's right except Task Force X, which was supposed to patrol 5,000 yards laterally and make reports every hour. On the left was the 1st Battalion of the 394th Infantry under Major Clayton.

Bob Mitsch of L Company, 394th Infantry, remembers: "Initially, we occupied positions in a forest area known as the Ardennes. Activity was limited to various patrols and outpost duty. After some time up front where our lines were thinly strung out, we were placed in somewhat of a reserve position. I recall our squad, or at least certain members of that squad, was in a rather narrow building perhaps three or so stories tall and near a railroad track when the Battle of the Bulge began. In that building, we enjoyed the luxury of receiving a long overdue haircut from one of the squad members (Don Rucker). At this time, our company was located in the Buchholz sector area."

Bob Mitsch.

Clifford McDaniel.

S/Sgt. Clifford McDaniel, also of L, gives the following account: "Company L of the 394th Infantry regiment moved into front line positions in the Ardennes Forest of Belgium on or about 14 November 1944. Our initial positions were to the left (northward) from Losheimergraben up the International Highway thence to the immediate right facing Germany. From then until about 10 December, we generally worked in the snow and cold at improving our positions and striving at creating more comfortable surroundings. Combat patrols were conducted across no-man's-land into enemy positions. The company commander was Capt. Allen Ferguson, whereas the assistant company commander was 1st Lt. Neal Brown. My platoon sergeant was T/Sgt. Ken Lewis, and my squad leader was S/Sgt. Glen E. Burcholtz, presently of Dayton, Ohio. I recall three separate combat patrols. On the first, PFC Jack W. Rowland of Seattle was a fatality and a Lieutenant Radkowski was injured. Within a few days, the second combat patrol went out. My only recall of this patrol is that S/Sgt. Glen E. Burcholtz was injured by a land mine (he lost an arm and a leg), thus leaving us. I was not a member of either of the first two patrols but did participate in the third. It was led by Captain Ferguson. This patrol had crossed a snow-covered valley and entered into the edge of a forest moving forward. Suddenly an enemy machine gun opened fire on us. My recall is that Captain Ferguson was killed and another member, who was a survivor of the Battle for Guadalcanal, also died.

"Company Headquarters and the first platoon were quartered in the Buchholz railway station. The remaining three platoons were quartered in a multi-storied building below and to the right of the station. I took this to be a residence as there were jars of jellies, etc. in a closet. Others, however, say it was a tavern. Having hot meals brought up by the kitchen and enjoying the luxuries of a warm building for sleeping was beyond description!! On 15 December, we had a normal day. Evening meal was brought up as per schedule followed by that wonderful, restful night of secure, peaceful sleep. Little did we suspect that all this would end within a few hours and we would depart on a trip that would be our hell!"

Since the battalion was in a defensive sector, it did not run patrols between 13 and 16 December and therefore had no inkling from prisoners' reports of any enemy buildup to the east or south. No information had come from higher echelons regarding enemy preparations, and as a matter of fact, the reports on the night of 15 December had indicated that enemy artillery along the front consisted only of two horse-drawn artillery pieces. Because one of the rifle companies and a machine-gun detachment of L Company had been sent as a reserve for the 395th Infantry's attack, Moore had only two rifle companies. The battalion was about eighty-five men under strength so that it consisted at the beginning of approximately 730 to 740 men.

U.S. Defensive Positions at the Losheim Gap

Cpl. Max Lehmann of I Company, 394th Infantry, recounts: "I think that to understand the events shortly before, during and until the bulge was closed, you must understand that we were in a state of confusion and without much of a leadership. I can only relate as to what I was confronted with. To start with, on 12 or 14 December, we were taken off of line and were on reserve alert. We were alerted on the late afternoon of 15 December that a sister regiment, the 395th, was on attack in a part of the Siegfried Line and had encountered fire against them by the Germans and wanted a back up. We were trucked a short distance and it was very near dark. We unloaded from the trucks and were ordered to march in single file into the woods with a flank scouting on both our sides. My foxhole buddy was ordered to break the snow about ten to fifteen yards on our right flank; this he did, and we very well forgot him.

"Now to back this up a bit, around 13 December, I came down with the runs, and it was hard to control my bowels, and it was so bad that when we were told to take a break, I dropped my pants and tried to pass my stool, but it was only a watered down amount and you would strain to pass more and then we were ordered to resume our march. It was so cold that the liquid around the rear end that you could not clean had frozen and you pulled up your trousers and went on with the march. Of course the frozen liquid had

Max Lehman
(on right).

thawed out and what a mess I had. The only thing was, I was not the only one with this problem. It was far worse than anything the Germans could do to me—at this time anyway."

THE LOSHEIMERGRABEN CROSSROADS

Since 10 December, the 1st Battalion of Lt. Col. Robert H. Douglas occupied the crossroads of Losheimergraben. The companies of the battalion found themselves in defensive positions in the dark and dusky woods east and southeast of the crossroads. A Company, under the command of 1st Lt. Willard S. Clarke, was positioned on the right in the woods north of the railway line. Facing south, the company placed two platoons, while the third platoon held a camp southeast of the crossroads. The company command post was located near the crossroads. In the center of the 1st Battalion's positions was B Company under Capt. Sidney A. Gooch (until 15 December). One platoon of heavy machine guns from D Company was in position in both A and B Companies' sectors.

S/Sgt. Harold P. Mann of the antitank platoon, HQ Company, 1st Battalion, remembers: "There was really no start; we had been fighting German patrols since we moved into position, and at night, we could hear the Germans getting ready for something. Captain Gooch, commander of A Company, with the men from his outpost, came running by my gun position and told me that he was being attacked in force. I had a direct line to corps artillery and immediately notified them. They pulled all heavy guns into position and nothing else happened. On the sixteenth, I was called to 394th headquarters and reported what had happened; as a result, he was court-martialed and shipped out."

The 1st and 3rd Platoons of B Company were located well forward to the east of the crossroads; the 2nd Platoon occupied a supporting position. The 1st Platoon of 2nd Lt. Chester F. Lubick was located on the right, across the main road, barring access from Losheim itself. 57-millimeter antitank guns, in place along the road, reinforced the defense. An advance detail of one squad, reinforced with a light machine gun, guarded the destroyed bridge on the railway line north of Losheim. On the left flank of B Company, the 3rd Platoon of 1st Lt. Robert E. McClothlin was located in the woods. When Lieutenant McClothlin was killed by a shell before 16 December, Sgt. Nick Machnik took command of the platoon for the time being. The platoon had dug in on a wooded slope which descends toward the valley of the Kyll. The platoon maintained a weak contact with Capt. James A. Graham Jr.'s C Company, which was on the left on the other side of the valley of the Kyll.

U.S. Defensive Positions at the Losheim Gap

Harold Mann.

Robert W. Jones, a scout with the 2nd Platoon, C Company, 394th Regiment, recounts: "C Company was deployed in a wooded area that appeared to be a hunting resort. We were spread over a wide area. Most of the men were in two-man fox holes. I was billeted in what was probably a hunting cabin. Action was limited. We periodically checked our outposts."

Every morning, four or five men of the 3rd Platoon made their way across the valley of the Kyll toward the positions of C Company. During the afternoon Captain Graham sent out a patrol of a few men. Booby-traps and mines had been placed in the valley to prevent the enemy from using it as an avenue of approach. The men of the 3rd Platoon nicknamed their positions in the dark woods "Creepy Corner," which illustrates that the combatants were well aware of their isolation in this spot.

S/Sgt. George Ballinger, machine-gun section leader of B Company's Weapons Platoon, remembers: "We were on the extreme left flank of B Company's position facing a shallow ravine that extended from the road down to our position. I think it may have been 500 or 600 yards or more. There was a long gap between B Company and C Company on our left. I had come up to this area a few days ahead of the main body of B Company. We were in the process of relieving the 9th Infantry Division, and I was to familiarize myself with the machine-gun positions they had constructed so that the transition would go more smoothly. It was the 9th Division people who called the left flank the 'Creepy Corner' because of the heavy patrolling the Germans were

"Creepy Corner," with dugouts still visible in 1998. HANS WIJERS

doing through the gap between our units. It was seldom referred to by that name except for those of us in that immediate area."

The forward positions and the artillery observation posts were located east of the forest edge, giving the men a good view of Losheim, located lower down in the valley on top of a hillock and on the ground to the southeast which the Germans held. The command post of the 1st Battalion had been installed south of Route No. 32 from Losheimergraben to Büllingen, and it was situated 700 meters from the crossroads, where a small road led to the village and the station of Buchholz. A heavy machine-gun platoon was located in the sectors of A and B Companies. The 81-millimeter mortar platoon was located in an open space south of the crossroads of Losheimergraben. The three antitank guns (57-millimeter) of the 1st Battalion were located along the roads leading to the crossroads. They had been reinforced by the 1st Platoon of the Anti-Tank Company of the 394th Regiment, commanded by 1st Lt. Gifford E. Benson. Platoon Benson consisted of three ten-man squads and three 57-millimeter antitank guns.

The road bridges that crossed the railroad leading in the directions of Losheim and Lanzerath had been blown up by the Germans during their retreat to the Siegfried Line in September 1944. Only the footbridge on the rural road in the direction of Hüllscheid was still intact and practicable, but halfway up the road, it degenerated into a muddy forest trail before it joined the road from Lanzerath to Losheimergraben south of the crossroads. On

15 December, an engineer team prepared the narrow bridge for destruction, and during the night, they placed 1,500 pounds of TNT on the surface of the bridge. But its destruction could not take place until an order was given by the regiment. In any event, this order was never given.

On the left, the 1st Battalion of the 394th was in contact with the 2nd Battalion of Lt. Col. Philip Wertheimer, which continued the front line of the 99th Infantry Division in the forests to the north. The right flank of the 1st Battalion, southeast of the crossroads, represented the division boundary of the 99th Infantry Division. The righthand neighbor was the 106th Infantry Division, recently arrived and not yet used to war conditions. That division had concentrated the mass of its troops on the long top of the Schnee-Eifel, leaving the terrain of the upper valley of the Our to be occupied by a single troop of mechanized cavalry (14th Cavalry Group). With a link this weak, the right flank of the 99th Infantry Division for all intents and purposes was in the air. For this reason the 99th Division placed its only divisional reserve, the 3rd Battalion of the 394th Regiment, at Buchholz Station. The presence of this reserve battalion, southeast and not far from Losheimergraben, had an important influence on the defense of the crossroads. The terrain between Losheimergraben and Lanzerath, where the nearest cavalry troops were located, was watched by patrols of the Intelligence and Reconnaissance

Aerial view of Losheim. The railroad bridge is clearly visible. DICK BYERS

Platoon of the 394th Regiment. This platoon had put an outpost at the edge of the woods, just north of Lanzerath. Several deep gorges and valleys, where streams gurgled, led to the interior of the 1st Battalion positions.

In the sector of B and C Companies, a valley split from the east to a large forest trail. Part of B Company found itself on the left (to the north) of the road. On 16 December, a German assault group, making use of this access, made an important breakthrough. East of the 1st Battalion positions, three or four other valleys wound their way through its defenses. Furthermore, the presence of multiple foxholes in the woods, which had been abandoned by earlier American troops, had an unfortunate effect on orientation in a defensive battle.

According to Arthur Mings of A Company, 394th Infantry, "A Company was on the right flank of the 1st Battalion. We didn't know that two companies of the 3rd Battalion were held in reserve on our right rear at Buchholz Station. We dug a second line of defense around Hünningen on Thanksgiving Day. A Company's line of defense was from the Losheim-Losheimergraben road south and east of the crossroads parallel to the Lanzerath road. We slept in cabins south of the Losheim-Losheimergraben road. My squad was in the first cabin south of this road. On the night of 14 December, my squad was on the east side of the railroad bridge. When we were relieved on the morning of the fifteenth on our way back to the cabins, we dug a line of defense west of the railroad bridge on the south side of the road, the line of foxholes running east-to-west. The Germans used them against us on 16 December."

Arthur Mings.

The 1st Battalion did not have enough men to occupy all these positions. In the attacks that followed, in several cases the Germans occupied these protected positions in order to force the defenders out of their entrenchments.

THE POSITIONS AT THE INTERNATIONAL HIGHWAY

On 13 December, the 3rd Battalion, 393rd Infantry, was deployed in the left sector of the regimental front, with the 1st Battalion, 393rd, on its right, and the 2nd Battalion (part of the 395th Regimental Combat Team) on its left. Its positions ran generally parallel to the International Highway along the Belgian-German border and then bent westward on the southwest slope of the Olef Bach Creek. K Company was on the right, L Company on the left, and I Company in the center to attack Rath Hill.

PFC Jack Pricket of L Company, 3rd Battalion, 393rd Infantry, tells his story: "L Company arrived on the front at Krinkelt-Rotherath about 10 November 1944. Our commander was Capt. Paul V. Fogleman, and our executive officer was Roland Neudecker. L Company entered the front line with close to 200 men. We relieved the 9th Infantry Division, a veteran division that had been in combat for a few months.

"Other officers of L Company at the time of the Bulge were 1st Lt. Egbert Oliver, 1st Platoon; 2nd Lt. Peter Jenkisson, 2nd Platoon; 2nd Lt. Richard Burns, 3rd Platoon; 1st Lt. Charles F. McNulty, 4th Platoon. The NCOs were almost all from the midwest, east, and southern part of the United States. They were what I would call the blue-collar, hard-working men of the United States. I was among a group of college boys who started their

Jack Pricket.

army service by being sent back to college for a year in the Army Specialized Training Program (ASTP). The army during World War II gave priority to all other branches of the army and sent the rest of the available manpower into the infantry. When we were transferred into the 99th, we made up from one third to one half of the infantry riflemen and other frontline troops.

"My foxhole buddy was Leslie M. Miller, a young married man from Dallas, whom I met at Huntsville, Texas, during our ASTP session at Sam Houston State. When we were transferred to the 99th, we were lucky to get assigned to the same company. We became best friends and hoped to stay together and somehow live through the war. We planned to go to college together after the war.

"After a short stay in England, we crossed the channel on an LST and landed at Le Havre, France. The place was almost destroyed from bombs and shelling. On shore we met a convoy of trucks. I asked one of the black drivers where they were going to take us. He said if you are infantry, you are going straight to the front. The second day we were at Aubel, Belgium. After a short time we reached the front.

"The next month consisted of getting used to being shelled if we made too much noise going back to get food, being wet and cold all the time, trying to sleep with water dropping on our faces, etc. I was sent back to Krinkelt to regimental headquarters with several others to get a shower. The headquarters stallions were SOBs, and I was glad to get back up to the front. Les and I worked hard to keep our feet dry as we started losing people from trench foot. The captain of M Company was killed by a mortar shell. Others were lost from mines, artillery, accidents, sickness, patrol shoot outs, etc. A few self-inflicted wounds and battle fatigue occurred. Even though this was a quiet front, people still died.

Former aid station at the Heartbreak Crossroads.
PIERRE CONSTANCE

U.S. Defensive Positions at the Losheim Gap

"Around 10 December, we were moved off the front and went into battalion reserve defensive positions. These were foxholes well dug in and covered with logs and dirt. We heard rumors that we were going to attack in several days. Some talked like they were ready for action. Les and I had talked a lot to each other that we should never volunteer, it could get you killed. The new position was on the north side of the road, about 100 yards west of Olef Creek. It was nice to be off the front and eat hot meals, especially hot cakes. One of our officers wanted Les and me to dig him a new fox hole. Fogleman put a stop to that kind of BS.

"On 15 December, we moved out early in the morning, crossed Olef Creek, and marched north at the base of Rath Hill. The narrow trail was covered with snow and ice, with tracks from vehicles that had been on it before us. Several jeeps were in our column, and after we had gone about a half mile, one of the jeeps hit a mine. Rath Hill was fairly steep, with trees and about six inches of snow. We stopped and were told that we would attack up the hill. Several days before, we had received several replacements who had been transferred from the air corps. Our platoon Sergeant told one of the new men that he would go out as the point man. The kid said, 'Hell no, I'm not going first; I don't know anything about this; you are just trying to get me killed.' I heard myself say, 'Hell, I'll go out as point,' but I did tell the kid that within a week he would know as much as we did, and if he refused to do what he was asked, I would shoot him myself. Miller told me I was stupid for doing this. Anyway, I led our platoon up the hill, slipping and sliding with my BAR (Browning automatic rifle). We were lucky, with only minor firing on the left side of the hill away from my position. It was beginning to get cold. We moved close to the edge of the forest and were told to start digging in.

"We didn't know it, but our little attack was just to trick the Germans into thinking that this was an enlargement of the offensive that . . . had started on 13 December against Wahlerscheid and the West Wall. The 395th Infantry (two battalions) and the 2nd Battalion of the 393rd Infantry of the 99th Division were being heavily blooded on the right flank of the 2nd Infantry Division's attack. The 2nd Infantry also was taking heavy casualties. We were about to really get into the war."

CHAPTER 3

The Germans Attack

THE OPENING HOURS: "ALL HELL BROKE LOOSE"
The 12th Volksgrenadier Division, regarded by the 6th SS Panzer Army staff as the best of the infantry divisions, had as its axis of attack the Büllingen road (Route C); its immediate objective was the crossroads point of departure for the westward highway at Losheimergraben and the opening beyond the thick Gerolstein Forest. The ultimate objective for the 12th Division's attack was the attainment of a line at Nidrum and Weywertz, eight miles beyond the American front, at which point the division was to face north as part of the infantry cordon covering the 6th SS Panzer Army's flank.

Helmut Stiegeler, 12th Engineer Battalion, 12th Volksgrenadier Division, remembers: "It was 15 December 1944. After a night march, our engineer unit had been directed to a wood somewhere in the Eifel early in the morning. There was snow, and it was very cold. We saw human habitation nowhere. No one knew exactly where we were, and for the moment, no one cared. Because of enemy air reconnaissance, we could move only within the woods in the daytime. We had to avoid anything that could draw the attention of the Yanks to our positions. We could not make fires to warm ourselves by. Truly not an ideal place to spend a longer time.

"The day went by, and by the evening, there was hot food. Rice with peaches. That was a true feast for many. A little later the message spread that all were to prepare to march. Every squad received a bottle of schnaps, which was put in our light pack. Even before darkness fell, the column started to move. We were ordered to proceed in the 'goose march.' Nearly without making a sound, one after another we marched down the road. Because of the solid snow cover, the night was not as dark, and one could see the men in front of him quite clearly. There always was a short break when the point men were looking for the right road. The villages through which we marched lay peaceful in the December night. Perhaps a dog barked here and there. Or people were talking and looking at the passing soldiers while standing by the walls of the houses. Perhaps out of an imperfectly blacked-out window, a vague light shone out. With all these sights,

The Germans Attack

Helmut Stiegeler.

most of our thoughts were of being home in warm houses with our families. But we continued on.

"Suddenly, we met soldiers in snow shirts. On the other side of the road stood an assault gun, also painted white. Then we understood that we were nearing the front line. Our objective was a bunker in the West Wall. We did not arrive there until 2300 hours and had long been expected. In the moist damp rooms, there first was a well-deserved rest. My comrades were not enthusiastic, as our bottle of schnaps had fallen out of my pack in a jump over a ditch and shattered on the ground. By the shine of the so-called 'Hindenburg lights,' a squad was ordered to clear a tank obstacle. We were guided past a line of 'dragon's teeth' of the West Wall down to the road that leads from Hallschlag to the Belgian Büllingen. This road had been blocked by steel girders, and behind it was a deep antitank ditch.

"Our order was to make the road usable by the morning. Then for the first time it became clear to us that an attack by our side was imminent. With pickaxe and shovels we began clearing the site. But the earth had frozen so solid that we could only achieve little. Throughout the night units of the 3rd Parachute Division passed us by on their way to their starting positions. By morning I was sent back to the bunker to collect explosives to clear the obstacles.

German soldiers at a crossroads.

"On the return journey—it must have been about 0530 hours—something happened, which I remember vividly to this day: in the rear area behind our front line all of a sudden it became bright. As far as one could see, our searchlights were shining up to the skies. And the artillery and rocket artillery opened fire from all barrels. For the first time in my life I heard such a horrible noise. Until I understood what was happening, I first threw myself down between these dragons' teeth. And then I rejoined my squad as quickly as possible. So the inferno had begun. Soon we had to conclude that we could not carry out our task in time. Already we saw ambulances come down with wounded soldiers. It was said that the rocket artillery had fired short. Our group was given a talking to and then was moved off from this position."

On Saturday, 16 December, at 0530 hours in the morning, under the artificial lighting of searchlights, the Germans launched their offensive. An artillery barrage of guns, mortars, and rocket launchers of all calibers fell down on the Losheimergraben Crossroads. This first thunderclap of the massed German guns and rocket launchers was initially thought by outposts of the U.S. 394th Infantry to be "outgoing mail"—i.e., fire from friendly guns—but in a matter of minutes, the entire regimental area was aware that something unusual had occurred. Intelligence reports had located only two horse-drawn artillery pieces opposite one of the American line battalions; after a bombardment of an hour and five minutes, the battalion's executive officer reported, "They sure worked those horses to death." But until the German infantry were actually sighted moving through the trees, the Americans believed that the Germans were simply feinting in response to the 2nd and 99th Divisions' attack up north. Along with the rest of the 99th, the line troops of the 394th had profited from the quiet on this front to improve their positions with log roofing, so casualties during the early-morning bar-

The Germans Attack

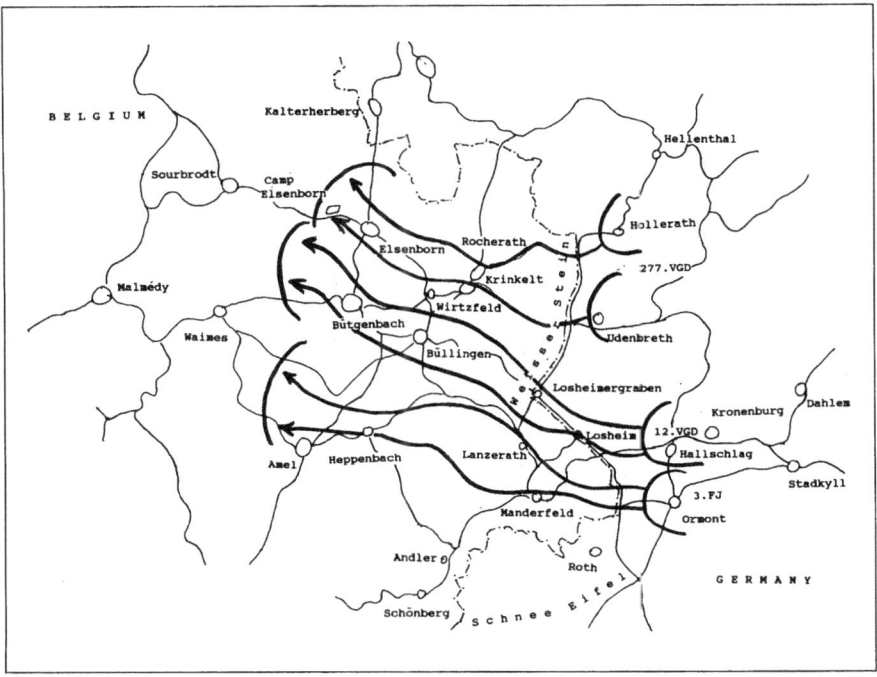

The German offensive.

rage were few. Until 0715 hours, the 1st Battalion of the 394th Infantry was rocked by the German artillery.

S/Sgt John Hilliard of C Company, 394th Infantry, remembers: "It was the best-fed artillery barrage of the war, and I am sure that none of us has any desire to experience it again. Smoke and fire were everywhere, the tops of the trees were hit, and the tree trunks were flying in all directions. The Germans were busy with firing a rolling barrage below us, the shells hitting the ground in front of our positions. The enemy gunners elevated their guns with each salvo, and in this way moved the zone of the bombardment on top of our position and behind it. They repeated this tactic without stopping and every time they hit their mark. The intensive and continuous barrage dealt a terrible blow to the nervous system and hindered an individual from acting in a reasonable manner. Several of our men went mad and left their shelters in order to get killed or mutilated."

B Company's positions were also hit by the artillery, resulting in numerous losses. According to S/Sgt George Ballinger, squad leader of the machine-gun squad of the 4th (Weapons) Platoon of B Company, 394th Infantry, "The German artillery began falling in our position at about 0530 hours and lasted with

Members of *Luftwaffe* flak units bring heavily camouflaged searchlights to the front line. HANS WIJERS

few lulls until daylight. When one exploded very close, it seemed as if my body was being compressed and my vision distorted as if my eyes were being squeezed out. It only lasted a second, then everything would be normal again. We had several wounded, but our platoon commander, Lt. Charles E. Butter, was killed and several others were wounded by direct hits on their shelters. He was on our extreme right, very near the road."

Charles Kent continues the story: "When the barrage started, I was in a foxhole with Bill Sears, the rifle squad leader, and I was his assistant. After the barrage lifted for a while, I checked the other foxholes of our squad. We only had one man with a slight scratch for a wound. Before too long a German scout showed up in front of us. We didn't shoot so he wouldn't have any information about us. He withdrew shortly and our squad had no further contact with the Germans until late that afternoon."

Meanwhile, thanks to their well dug-in and dispersed positions, the GIs of the 1st Battalion, 394th Regiment, suffered relatively few losses. But the artillery bombardment wreaked havoc on the telephone communications network. The advance positions were isolated from their companies, which in turn were isolated from the battalion.

In his memoirs, PFC Devon A. Lewis of HQ Company, 1st Battalion, 394th Infantry, writes: "The command post was close to our cabin where the commanding officer and other officers were inside trying to map out a way to protect our position and defend it. This is where I last saw 1st Lt. Dewey

The Germans Attack 45

A German soldier inspects ammunition.

Charles Kent.

Plankers, as he was cold and his combat jacket was torn and bloody. He must have been in a helluva battle! Next to the command post was a large tent which the medics used as a hospital and aid station. The casualties were heavy, and they were bringing in the wounded and the near dead. They worked very hard to try to help them with their wounds. They were bringing in wounded German soldiers and Americans alike. We went back into our cabins and tried to protect ourselves from the heavy shelling and shrapnel. In the medic tent they had so many dead Germans that they were putting the bodies on top of one another. It was hell!"

Lt. Col. Robert H. Douglas, commander of the 1st Battalion, 394th Infantry, recalls: "I remember well having visited all company command posts at the front in order to see how they had held themselves during the bombardment. I asked Capt. James A. Graham of C Company, a big Texan, what he did during the bombardment: 'Hell, colonel, I stayed here in the shelter until it was finished; it would not have been any use to have my head shot off.' One of the first losses of 16 December was a new telephone line to the frontline positions which had just been erected. It was shameful to see

Shells of the six-barrel *Nebelwerfer* ("Screaming Meemy") can still be found in the woods formerly occupied by C Company. HANS WIJERS

the lines of bright copper, which had recently been strung up with such alacrity between standing poles, lying on the ground, mixed up and half uncovered. Communications with the frontline units nevertheless was maintained, thanks to the heroic efforts of the communications platoon. During my visits to the units, I was told that the mortar platoon of D Company of Capt. John S. Sandiland was subjected to a strong attack, and that I would do better to return to my command post in order to exercise my command from there."

Sgt. Peter Gacki, a forward observer for C Battery, 371st Field Artillery, describes the scene at Lanzerath: "We were awakened by an artillery barrage early in the morning of the sixteenth. We were in contact with the battery and I don't remember what our orders were, but when we began to get ready to leave, we found that the tank destroyer company had already left town. . . . While I was loading the jeep, I was singing a part of 'O Tannenbaum.' I seem to recall a woman made some remark about my singing. Guess it was strange considering the circumstances, but we didn't feel any sense of urgency at that time. We left some food and a package I had received from home. As far as I know, we were the last to leave town. We started back to the battery, and then stopped to help the I & R [Intelligence and Reconnaissance] Platoon. I guess we stayed too long."

Lt. Lyle Bouck Jr., commander of the Intelligence and Reconnaissance Platoon of the 394th Infantry at Lanzerath, remembers: "In the early-morning hours of 16 December, concentrated artillery fire came into our area. In front of the area, in back of the area, all around us. We were protected by the logs, so we didn't have any casualties. But it was a nerve-racking experience for a couple of hours. I called the regimental commander. I said,

The Germans Attack

'The TDs [tank destroyers] have pulled out. What should we do?' He said, 'You stay!'" Bouck and two men, T/Sgt. William Slape and Pvt. John Creger, moved down the hill to the village to see what the Germans were doing in the wake of the artillery. They moved to the second story of a house that afforded them a view to the east.

According to PFC Jack Pricket of L Company, 3rd Battalion, 393rd Infantry, at the International Highway: "Our digging in was very hard, and by dark we were only deep enough to barely be covered if we laid down side by side. The only food we had with us was a can of C rations and several chocolate D bars, which was like concentrated candy. We dug for a while, and the wind and cold got worse. We tried to take turns being on guard, but our feet begin to really hurt. We couldn't sleep so we took our shoes off and took turns sticking our feet under the other guy's armpit. It wasn't easy, but it helped some. A few weeks earlier we had received rubber overshoes. I think they kept our feet wet, and when I took the shoes off my feet, I could not get them back on. I put on three pairs of socks, and just wore the overshoes. We relapsed into a slumber, and it was still dark when all hell broke loose. We heard many big guns firing and it became almost a constant roar, trees were being hit and shell fragments were all around. This did not last long in our area but the intensity of firing kept up. At times several very big, big shells came over, like freight trains up in the air. This lasted for a while and almost became silent, with just occasional firing. We could see our people milling around for some time."

Willis Sellhorn of K Company, 393rd Infantry, remembers: "We were in the edge of the forest along the International Highway on the right flank of K Company which was the right flank of the battalion. I think I was in the first squad of the first platoon, but I am not sure. As a replacement, I had not been there long enough to get acquainted with many people. On the front you just didn't go about 'socializing.' The squad was split in half, with half here with the squad leader and the other half several hundred yards to the right with the assistant squad leader. We had wet army overcoats that weighed about a ton and wet shoes, so we were not really equipped for winter warfare. Everyone had foot trouble, some worse than others. We were spread too thin to be much defense, but that is the way it was. Then came 16 December 1944. It sounded like the sky was falling as we scrambled out of our sleeping hole toward the outpost hole. I saw a mortar round explode about ten feet in front of me, and I couldn't understand how I was unhurt, but I was and I dove into our fire point. It was deeper than our sleeping huts, so it had water in the bottom, but it still wasn't deep enough for me to feel comfortable. Those *Nebelwerfer* 'screaming meemies' sounded like they were aimed right at me."

The fortified bunkers in the area of Losheimergraben. They are still visible today.
HANS WIJERS

Sgt. B. Wilkins, a member of 2nd Platoon, K Company, 393rd Infantry, describes what he saw: "John McCauley had the last watch of the night in our lookout position. I was asleep in our hole. Mac came to wake me and tell me something was weird, and I'd better take a look. We went to the lookout and saw the entire front bathed in floodlights from the German side. Then the artillery barrage began, and many shells landed in the trees behind us. We were in the open, in front of the tree line, but since we were down in a ravine, we had some natural protection, even though the lookout position was open to our rear. Mac suddenly said, 'I'm hit, I'm hit!' He'd been hit in his left buttocks, so we took his pants down to check. There was no evidence of a wound, so we checked his pants and found a piece of shrapnel embedded in his wallet."

The first indication of further enemy activity came immediately after the barrage had lifted, when an American jeep, driven by Germans, came northwest up the road from Losheim. It was observed by the antitank gun crew, including PFC Carl Combs, which was in position about fifty yards north of the road. The jeep halted almost under the nose of the gun, which did not fire, then turned around and went back to the south. It returned about five minutes later leading an assault gun up the road. (The after-action report mentions a Tiger, but the 12th Volksgrenadier Division didn't have any Tigers. The only "tanks" they had were the assault guns.) As the assault gun

The Germans Attack

came almost opposite the antitank gun, the gun crew opened fire on the tank. The first round knocked off a track, a second round penetrated the hull, and the third round set the tank on fire. The German crew bailed out and took up firing positions around the tank, where they opened up on the antitank gun crew with small arms. The jeep, which had continued up the road, was knocked out by small-arms fire from the men of B Company astride the road.

PFC Carl Combs, assistant squad leader of the 1st Squad, 1st Platoon, B Company, 394th Infantry, describes what happened: "My hole partner was Fred Robertson, another good Okie. Our hole was approximately 50 to 100 yards left of the Losheim road covering a 57-millimeter gun set up at the edge of the road. We had cleared some good firing lanes to our front. Shortly after the opening barrage, German infantry showed up to our front, and we opened fire, getting quite a few. After three or four such incidents, a tank [assault gun] moved up the road, and at close range the 57 knocked it out. It was quite a sight with its ammo exploding. The infantry activity picked up after that for quite a while."

Immediately after this, the first indications of a German attack arrived at the command post of the 1st Battalion, 394th Regiment. Germans were discovered by the men of A Company. At about ten o'clock, the observation post of the mortar platoon reported that a group of enemy infantry was advancing west through the mist along the railroad toward Honsfeld. It was estimated the group included 300 or 400 men. This force probably had

Carl Combs.

German soldiers of Advance Detachment Holz looking at a map shortly before the Battle of the Bulge. They have an amphibious jeep with them. LUTZ KONETZNY

The Germans attack through the woods at Losheimergraben as shot by the German Signal Corps. HANS WIJERS

The Germans Attack

reached the railroad while using a stream bed starting in Hüllscheid. Although the forward positions of A Company south of the railway line were driven in one after another, the Germans, ignoring the rest of the 1st Battalion, continued to advance west following the railroad in the direction of Buchholz. There the Germans ran into the companies of the 3rd Battalion.

CHAPTER 4

The Defense of Buchholz Station

Charles Dodson, 3rd Battalion headquarters, 394th Infantry, remembers his experiences: "I joined the 99th Infantry Division in its activation in December, 1942, and was assigned as company mail clerk and worked in the supply room as armorer. After extensive training we finally arrived in Aubel, Belgium, on 11 November 1944. There we grouped together and began to take over 82nd Airborne's positions. There was quite a bit of snow on the ground that was becoming slushy. I was placed with the kitchen truck and a supply trailer. We were told that we were two miles behind the front line. This was, as I understood, around the Losheimergraben area in dense woods. After three or four days, word came down for all the 394th's kitchens to move back eight miles. I think the 3rd Battalion's kitchen took over a house in Honsfeld. On 16 December 1944, I did not know then but have learned since that the 3rd Battalion was in reserve for some R & R with some movie star to visit us. But the night of 15 December, the kitchen had word to prepare a hot breakfast for the company the next morning. However, early in the morning some heavy artillery came in, casting doubt on what to do. I had assembled the mail by platoons; the cooks went ahead and prepared a hot breakfast (eggs, meat, hash browns, and coffee). About daybreak, the artillery slowed, and word was received about daylight to begin the food and mail to the command post of the 3rd Battalion headquarters. We loaded up a three-quarter-ton truck, ending up in the Buchholz railroad station area.

"The mermite containers were set up in a line, and I believe the headquarters platoon started through the line when all hell broke loose. A barrage of mortar and 88s—it was awesome. Everybody ran for the basement of the house. The cooks, myself, and members of the headquarters platoon stayed there for quite a while. Finally, a lull came. The cooks and I went out to check on the truck. We found holes in the tarp, but all the tires were up, so we loaded the food, and I gave some of the fellows the mail, and we took off to our quarters. On returning, we were told to load up. We were moving out."

On the morning of 16 December between 0530 and 0700 hours, the enemy opened up with an artillery preparation lasting an hour and five minutes. Afterward, Major Clayton remarked dryly that the battalion concluded

The Defense of Buchholz Station

Wesley J. Simmons (left), with Lieutenant Kaplan.
JOHN DUFALLA/HANS WIJERS

that the Germans "sure worked those horses to death" (referring to the two pieces of horse-drawn artillery mentioned earlier). It was presumed that this was friendly fire.

Capt. Wesley J. Simmons, commander of K Company, 394th Infantry, recalls: "At 0530 hours on 16 December 1944, the men of K Company, 394th Infantry, were awakened by the loud bursting of artillery fire. The rounds seemed to be landing near the front line, and it was thought that they were 105s, and that the Germans were catching 'hell' early in the morning. In a few seconds the bursts became much louder, and it was thought that they were 155s, and that the Germans were really getting a big dose of it now. Suddenly the rounds were landing in the company area, and not until then was it realized that 'that stuff' had been coming in and not going out. By 0535 hours, everyone in the company area was stirring. At about that moment the company commander's attention was called to an unfortunate incident which occured in the 3rd Platoon area. Two antitank men, whose organization was unknown to anyone in K Company, had been shot, one killed instantly and the other in critical condition. Hasty investigation revealed that their antitank gun had been located at the road junction just west of Losheimergraben for over a week, but they had never bothered to dig any defensive positions. When the shells started landing around them, they abandoned their gun and started running wildly for any cover they might find. In their impulsive move to safety, they ran into the 3rd Platoon's area of K Company, oblivious to the several calls to halt, and tore off the cover of one of the foxholes. They were, of course, the instant target of one of the foxhole occupants."

According to 1st Lt. Neil Brown, commander of L Company, 3rd Battalion, 394th Infantry, "On the morning of 16 December, probably somewhere around 0500, I was stretched out on the floor, on what I believe is the east end of the Buchholz Station, when 1st Sgt. Elmer P. Klug and I and one or two others were awakened by the sound of distant artillery fire. Recalling the earlier conversations with Major Moore, about the Ruhr River dams, I assumed that this artillery fire was friendly and was battlefield preparation fire for our own troops, and I paid no more attention to it."

The barrage along the regimental front lasted for ninety minutes. It was concentrated mainly on the Losheimergraben area and falling on the 1st and 3rd Battalion areas. There were no casualties in K Company as most of the artillery fire in this area had resulted in tree bursts, and all positions had been constructed with overhead cover during the previous week. The 3rd Battalion (Maj. Norman A. Moore), to the south and west of the 1st Battalion position at Losheimergraben, first encountered the enemy. About 0745 hours, L Company, at the Buchholz station, had taken advantage of the lull in the shelling and was just lining up for breakfast when figures were seen approaching through the fog. A platoon of about 40–50 men (probably from Lanzerath) came marching along the track in a column of twos straight up the railroad toward the station in which L Company headquarters was located. First thought to be friendly troops, the Germans were almost at the station before recognition brought on a fusillade of American bullets.

1st Lt. Neil Brown continues his story: "Later the same morning, at exactly five minutes after 0700—by both of the wrist watches I carried—I looked out of the window down-track from the Buchholz Station, and noticed soldiers walking alongside of the railroad tracks, it seems to me almost at the distant curve in the track. Our chow line had just been set up behind the Buchholz Station, and some of the soldiers from the platoon that was behind the station were in line about to eat. Because I knew that Sergeant Klug had set up a schedule for each of the platoons to walk into the station to be fed, instead of carrying the food to the platoons, upon seeing these soldiers coming down the railroad tracks, I turned to 1st Sgt. Elmer P. Klug, and said, 'Klug, that 1st Platoon is coming in early for their breakfast. What the hell's going on?' Klug came alongside me to the window, which as I remember was at least breast high to the lower sill of the window, and peer-

The Defense of Buchholz Station

ing and squinting and looking down that railroad track, he said to me, at about the same time it was also clear to me, '1st Platoon, my ass, those are Germans!' With no hesitation, and with no direction, Klug grabbed his carbine, which he had hung from the wall to our backs inside that station, and out the door he left, and around the corner of the station, he headed down that railroad track on a dead high run.

"As I said, Klug ran as hard as he could run down that railroad track, toward the approaching German soldiers who were walking in two columns, along either side of the railroad. I watched this entire procedure while I talked on the telephone to the Battalion HQ. When Klug got within about 50 or 75 yards from the lead people in the German columns, in a voice that I could clearly hear inside the Buchholz Station, he yelled a thunderous, 'Halt!' And believe me, every one of those German soldiers stopped. I watched the third German in what was my righthand column turn and start yelling orders in German to those soldiers, and at that time 1st Sgt. Elmer P. Klug shot that soldier in the back and dropped him cold. Klug turned, crouched, and ran back toward the station room, and when he could regain his breath inside, he told me that there were between twenty-five and fifty, in his judgement, in this group; he wasn't quite sure because they had scattered after this German soldier, who was the third one back, had turned around and started barking directions to the people. Some of these German soldiers got into, I believe, a couple of empty railroad cars that were on a siding in the yard, and at least one climbed to the top of a water tower in the railroad yard.

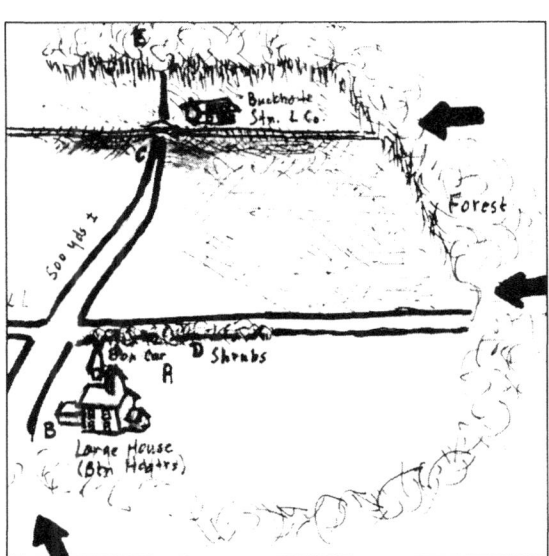

Sketch by Don Wallace showing battalion headquarters and, in the background, Buchholz Station.

"Klug left the front of the railroad station and went around to where the mess line was set up, and told them to pack up the chow line and get it out of there; and he then mustered the platoon that was preparing to eat into service along the left side of the station. At about the time these people started a move forward in the direction of the dispersed German troops, artillery in great abundance came down on the station, and the area to the right and left of the station, and to the front of the station, strongly to the right. The glass in the front end of the station was immediatly blown out, and automatic weapon fire came through the shattered window. I stood up once to look around, down track and a bullet went under the left edge of my helmet, alongside the left side of my neck, and struck the brick wall behind me and caused a little brick dust and mortar to go down the back of my shirt.

"Now, to go back to the story a little bit, while Klug was out in front on his one-man challenge, I had the battalion headquarters on the line, and told them we had German soldiers in our area, and that we didn't know how many or where they had come from, and that we were trying to protect ourselves and deal with the situation. The response from battalion headquarters was that I was to keep them informed. The battalion headquarters soon knew that we had some serious problems in the vicinity, because the artillery fire was also in the edge of the area where the battalion command post was located. Major Moore caused the battalion staff to put together a perimeter defense around the battalion headquarters during this short interval. I don't know how much of a time interval there was, exactly, but I know it was after the wire had been blown out, and after Lieutenant Zuber had restored wire communication with the battalion, and while we were still receiving artillery fire in the railroad yard, although of less intensity than at the outset. Major Moore called me to tell me that I was to assemble my company and report to Colonel Douglas in the 1st Battalion area, that he had heard from regiment and regiment had heard from the division headquarters, and that whatever was going on in my area was nothing but a small patrol, and that the main thrust of a German operation was on the highway in Colonel Douglas's area, and that Moore had been directed to cause whatever troops he had still under his control to be placed at the discretion of Colonel Douglas to help him. But I heard this message as we were right in the middle of a fire fight, and I told him that we were occupied, and that as soon as I could gather up the people and disengage, I would report to him.

"In the meantime, the platoon that I had thought was coming in to breakfast too early reported to me that they were out of ammunition. I never found out what they were shooting at. Sergeant Klug told me that he would see what he could do about taking care of the ammunition problem, and I remember that a squad from the platoon that had been preparing to eat breakfast behind the station volunteered to carry a resupply of ammunition to the left of the railroad tracks and forward to the platoon that told me they were out of supplies. I also remember that as that squad ran by the left corner of Buchholz Station, dispersed just a few yards apart, carrying ammunition with some two-man loads, an artillery shell lit right in the middle of them, destroying some.

"Over a period of more than an hour, we received artillery fire in and around the station, punctuated by small-arms fire, and a few times by automatic weapons fire. We weren't very effective because we couldn't clearly figure out where the fire was coming from, and if anyone moved around the station, fire from someplace seemed to develop. I know that some German soldiers climbed into at least two boxcars, and I guess that occasionally some fire was coming from those boxcars. I know that at least one soldier made an attempt to climb into that water tower in the railroad yard. We had a lot of artillery fire in and around the area, and I was of the opinion that it was directed by someone who knew that it was important to keep that railroad station under fire and minimize movement in and around that building. The artillery fire developed on the station so rapidly following the dispersal of the German soldiers by Klug, that I was of the opinion that someone in that group had called for the artillery fire because they could see what was happening as a result of whatever activity was going on inside the station."

The first platoon in the building to the west of the railroad track now opened fire, while Lt. Neil Brown and the headquarters company began shooting from inside the railroad station.

Capt. Wesley J. Simmons, commander of K Company, 394th Infantry, remembers: "At about 0820 hours, a messenger from the battalion command post made his way to the area of Company K and relayed the message that the battalion commander, Major (later Lieutenant Colonel) Moore, wanted one rifle platoon and the weapons platoon to rush to his headquarters area. The commander of Company K immediately took down the 1st Platoon, led by Lieutenant Spencer, and the weapons platoon, led by Lieutenant Ralston, to Forest Buchholz Station."

Lt. Dick Ralston, Weapons Platoon, K Company, 394th Infantry, details his actions: "That afternoon [morning], I took my weapons platoon of K Company, 394th, from the company area on the road that ran parallel to the front, where we were in regimental reserve, over to the right (facing the front) to Buchholz Station. We got there a little before dusk. There was no time, I guess, to move out into positions because it became pitch black

Dick Ralston.

shortly. We were all in a little wooded area a short distance from the station. We dug and dug for hours in the shale and dirt to gain depressions deep enough to get a horizontal body out of sight."

Information received at that time revealed that enemy troops had been spotted approaching down the railroad tracks toward the prepared positions of L Company, so that the company had pulled in their outposts in order to obtain more surprise fire. As the two platoons of K Company reached Forsthaus Buchholz Station at about 0912 hours, they became involved in a firefight as L Company engaged the enemy when they came within 200 yards. While this initial firing was taking place, the 1st Platoon went into positions on the high ground to the right front of the battalion command post and just to the right of L Company. The light machine-gun section of the weapons platoon set up within the 1st Platoon area, and the 60-millimeter mortars went into defilade behind the 1st Platoon on the reverse slope.

Pvt. William Bray, L Company, 394th Infantry, was pinned down between the railroad tracks for a couple of hours. "We had started down the tracks when the sniper in the water tower down the line began shooting at us, and then the Germans in the box car began shooting. My buddy was shot in the knee, and we had to drag him back to the station depot. . . . When the firing began that morning, my platoon was in the old farmhouse (maybe it was sort of an inn) near the depot."

Cpl. George F. Bodnar recollects: "At this point in the fighting, the Germans began to shell the L Company command post. One man, Private Rude,

The Defense of Buchholz Station

Modern-day view of Buchholz Station coming down the road from Lanzerath (facing north). On the right is the house Bill Bray and his platoon were in during the shooting. HANS WIJERS

was hit. Five men were in the supply room at the left end of the railroad station when it received a direct hit. A shell fragment bounced off my bandoleer and killed a medical corpsman, Pvt. Joe Ryan, who was struck in the head. Pvt. Joe Genovino said, 'The hell with this,' and we all piled out of the room into a concrete shelter outside where we stayed for about a half hour until the shelling was over. The company commander, Lieutenant Brown, and the supply sergeant crowded into the cellar with us and stayed there until about 1200 when we were directed to move to a house nearby. Artillery and mortar shells were still falling at this time. Altogether we received about forty rounds on the command post from artillery in the woods to the west."

1st Lt. Neil Brown picks up his story: "During these first artillery blasts, a soldier in the company command post with me and with Bodnar and with Klug received a shrapnel wound in his back three or four inches long and close to his spinal column. I thought the guy was dying. I opened my first aid packet while cradling the phone between my shoulders, trying to figure out what battalion was trying to tell me, and I stuffed a bandage in that wound to stop the bleeding. It was quite a while before the fire settled down enough for us to move that soldier out of the front of Buchholz Station toward the back of the station where he could later be evacuated. I'm not sure whatever happened to him."

According to PFC Don Wallace, L Company, 394th Infantry, "Sometime after the initial battle when the German advance broke down, there was an artillery barrage laid on L Company and the 3rd Battalion headquarters. We had dug slit trenches in the yard, but scampered into a box car (it was low to the ground without its wheels) instead, and without thinking. The barrage lasted a while, and the noise was shattering and ceaseless. No shell ever hit the box car directly, but it was very scary when I realized during the barrage that I should be in my foxhole. In examining the box car afterward, we noted that shrapnel had torn through the box car, leaving gaping holes all along its side down to less than two feet above ground level. The yard was full of holes from artillery explosions. Again I felt lucky. During the day on the sixteenth, I carried messages from the farmhouse down the road to Buchholz Station. Once in a while a single artillery round would be lobbed in. These were not part of any barrage, but played psychological havoc with their suddenness. There was absolutely no warning. On one of my trips to the station, I was within about twenty feet of the railroad overpass, when one of those shells exploded on top of the overpass. The concussion tore my helmet off and knocked me to the ground. When I realized that I was okay, I thought about how lucky I was!"

The Germans scattered, heading for the boxcars outside the station, or they sought shelter in ditches along the right-of-way, and a close-quarters firefight began. A Browning automatic rifle caught one when he was about 100 yards away. Cpl. George F. Bodnar, aided by Private Claypool, got four direct hits with a bazooka on the railroad car, but he was unable to check and see what damage had been done. The 1st Platoon then went down the track and fired into the woods on the right of the railroad.

L Company's position was exposed to artillery fire because the railroad station was elevated. One platoon was now placed to the west of the track, a second was placed to the front of the railroad station near a cut, and the 3rd Platoon was placed astride the railroad track. Two mortars were set up to fire into positions behind the railroad car in which the Germans had hidden. A 37-millimeter antitank gun of the 801st Tank Destroyer Battalion placed direct fire on the railroad car while a tank destroyer was brought up to fire six rounds of 3-inch shells directly into it.

1st Lt. Neil Brown continues: "Elmer Klug was aware of the bazooka fiasco, and he asked me if I had any objection to turning S/Sgt. Savino Travalini loose on the boxcars and the water tower. He had known Travalini a long time, and knew that Travalini was in our area, and theoretically under our control as part of the intended division reserve. I, of course, had no objection and in no time Klug had the arrangements made, how I'm not sure, to get Travalini in there. I remember Travalini, and I believe two sol-

The Defense of Buchholz Station

diers, with a jeep and an antitank gun, rolling up from the rear and from the south of the station. Methodically turning the jeep around and unhooking the gun, totally oblivious of any danger from his exposed position, and preparing the gun for fire, he unloaded several direct hits into the boxcars, and at least one into the water tower, after which he loaded up his gun and pulled away. I do not recall any German resistance expressed in any way while Travalini and his people were involved in this firing."

When the firing began during the morning of 16 December, the attack was reported to battalion headquarters. Notice was given to Lt. Robert E. Martin, commander of the antitank platoon, in the old beer tavern to the west of the railroad. Martin took three men and went forward to previously prepared positions near the edge of the woods in which the Germans had taken cover. He succeeded in advancing from these positions 250 yards into the woods where he suddenly ran upon a reinforced platoon of Germans "standing around." Unable to withdraw, Martin and his men opened fire with their M1s and got nine or ten of the enemy. The firing was heard by T/Sgt. Savino Travalini who took a runner and joined the party, helping to cover its withdrawal. Martin now got his antitank squads and the A & P men and deployed them in the woods. Lt. John W. Higgins, A & P Platoon leader, attempted to reach Martin but was killed by a sniper in the woods. Thinking that the lieutenant was still alive, a medical corpsman and three members of Higgins's platoon evacuated his body under fire to the aid station 200 yards southwest of the railroad station.

Forsthaus Buchholz Station, HQ, 3rd Battalion, 394 Infantry Picture taken shortly before the war. N. COLONERUS/BUCHHOLZ (B)/ARCHIVE HANS. J. WIJERS

A running firefight continued between 0800 and 1100 hours. A machine gun in a water tower "beat the hell out of us," according to Lieutenant Clements of L Company. Another machine gun about 400 yards south of the railroad station pinned down the antitank platoon of Tech Sergeant Travalini. He proceeded to crawl up the side of the road and knock out the gun with a hand grenade. Later in the action, Travalini discovered that the enemy was near the roundhouse about 300 yards southeast of the L Company command post. Private First Class Dalton ran across exposed ground to fire a bazooka several times into the roundhouse. This usually flushed out some of the enemy, and as they came into view, Travalini picked up his M1 and fired into them. For his work during this action, he was promoted to second lieutenant. During the fight, Tech 5 Janecke was wounded as he ran back and forth bringing ammunition to members of his platoon. He was awarded the Bronze Star for his activity. During the morning, M Company's mortars fired 300 rounds of ammunition in support of L Company.

After the Travalini episode, there was a quiet spell during which 1st Sergeant Klug counted a few Germans who were dead and got some of his own men evacuated. It was during this lull that someone got to the dead soldier whom Klug had shot shortly after 0700 hours in the morning and recovered a dispatch case containing, among other things, a map with an overlay and a copy of Rundstedt's field order. The contents were stripped out of the dispatch case so that Elmer Klug might retain that case as a souvenir. 1st Lt. Neil Brown reported the contents to battalion headquarters immediately and was told to bring it to the headquarters as soon as he could.

No further action occurred for about one hour, when suddenly a very heavy large-caliber mortar barrage fell on the battalion command post at Forsthaus Buchholz Station and caused several casualties. It also destroyed the battalion switchboard and telephone communication with regiment, but communication to all companies was still available by emergency means. Shortly after the heavy attack on L Company, K Company in its entirety went into position on the commanding terrain about 400 yards south of the battalion command post and blocked the road leading from German-held territory to Honsfeld, which was to the northwest of the 3rd Battalion and on the alternate route to Bütgenbach and Vervier. At about 1100 hours, K Company was heavily attacked by an estimated two companies of enemy troops, and though Germans came within 100 yards of the positions, they failed to penetrate and, after about three-quarters of an hour, withdrew.

By noon, the Germans had been repelled, leaving behind about seventy-five dead. L Company had suffered twenty-five or thirty casualties; K Company suffered three casualties (one killed and two wounded). The attacks on the 3rd Battalion indicated that the enemy would continue his advances

The Defense of Buchholz Station

until he succeeded in making a pentration. Word received from the 1st Battalion, 394th Infantry, revealed that although the enemy had penetrated their area in several places, they were still maintaining their original positions for the most part. The enemy would soon be rushing unopposed through the gap on K Company's right flank, for there was a distance of several hundred yards to the next friendly unit. It was very likely that the troops around Forsthaus Buchholz Station would soon be completely surrounded. Reinforcements could not be expected as the 3rd Battalion was not only the regimental reserve but also the division reserve, and they were completely engaged.

At about 1445 hours on 16 December, the 3rd Battalion headquarters withdrew to the position occupied by K Company the previous evening. At 1500 hours, the 2nd Platoon of K Company moved over to the left of the 1st Platoon and took positions astride the road to Lanzerath and the railroad. L Company then withdrew to the area previously occupied by I Company before they were attached to the 3rd Battalion, 393rd Infantry. The 3rd Platoon of K Company shifted its positions behind the 1st Platoon and had the same mission.

About 1645 hours, as soon as dusk would permit, K Company sent the 3rd Squad of the 3rd Platoon as a patrol down the Lanzerath road to seek information about the enemy. The patrol returned around 1800 hours and reported that they patroled the area for about 500 yards and had encountered no enemy but heard tank movements on the Lanzerath-Losheimergraben road. This information was relayed to battalion headquarters. At this time, orders were received to leave two rifle platoons in the present position to defend the area in the vicinity of Forsthaus Buchholz Station. The remaining rifle platoon and the weapons platoon of K Company, along with two rifle platoons from L Company under the command of the commander of K Company, were attached to the 1st Battalion to reinforce their defense. 1st Lt. Joseph P. Rose, executive officer of K Company, remained with the 1st and 2nd Platoons in the vicinity of Forsthaus Buchholz Station.

CHAPTER 5

The German Assault against the Losheimergraben Crossroads

During the morning, the powerful German combat force, which had been repulsed by the defenders of 3rd Battalion at Buchholz Station, searched for a road through the northeast and was approaching the command post of Lt. Willard W. Clark, the commander of A Company, 394th Infantry. Another group of German soldiers of the 2nd Company, 27th Fusilier Regiment, had moved out of Losheim in the direction of Losheimergraben. They followed the railroad to the railroad bridge and went down to the small road leading towards Buchholz. There they took a small firebreak to the north, where they bumped into the defenders of A Company.

Sgt. Hubert Eggert of the 27th Fusilier Regiment, 12th Volksgrenadier Division, recalls: "The rest was of short duration. At five o'clock in the morning the tension was released in a horrible bombardment of half an hour by our artillery and heavy rocket artillery units. My god, it was like bygone years. As infantrymen we had to shout at each other to make ourselves heard. Now our hour struck. We march and are amazed that we can take the road so quietly and without any trouble, and later pass a forester's house. But we haven't reached our starting position yet, and finally we reach the road bridge that crosses the railroad from Hallschlag-Stadtkyll to Buchholz. Before we reach the bridge we leave the road, down to the railroad tracks and up again into the woods (Hochwald). Lieutenant Kirsten and I show the platoons to their positions, about a distance of thirty meters parallel to the road from Prüm to Büllingen. Apart from two or three platoon commanders who are organizing their groups, all lie in cover when suddenly a rifle shot wounds Lieutenant Reimann. A sergeant takes over command of the platoon. A little later the same situation occurs; again a platoon commander, a sergeant major, is wounded. That platoon is also taken over by a sergeant. Now we switch immediately, and at about fifty meters we make out a well-camouflaged pile of earth, which must be the point. A private first class immediately accepts the challenge with a *Panzerfaust*, and lo and behold, a white handkerchief on

Hubert Eggert.

a stick is shown. In they come with their hands raised, and they are our first prisoners here in our standby position.

"Today I sadly no longer know what time the X-hour was and our attack rolled forward. First we passed through the woods well spread out on a narrow forest track until we reached a wood of very beautiful beeches. Our artillery was firing, and guess what happens, they fired short and straight into the treetops with a strong shrapnel effect. The consequences: two men of the company are mortally wounded, among whom was the medic sergeant. We have to go on, and now reach the lovely high wood. And exactly here the Yanks could have positioned a trap. To the left of us there is a meadow, about 200 meters long. Next to it is a plantation of young firs on the slope; we have a short meeting and decide to cross the meadow by groups and jump toward the firs. That succeeds without losses, as the Americans are only waking up now. They probably are firing with a fixed machine gun as much as they can. But the thick tree trunks hold off a lot, but we nevertheless suffer losses. All of a sudden the firing stops, and we hear a car driving off. Immediately we pursue. The Americans had positioned a so-called picket with a machine gun here."

Sgt. William Kirkbride of the 1st Platoon of the antitank company was one of the first men who discovered the incoming Germans. "We were at a T-shaped crossroads from which the central leg led east in the direction of Hüllscheid. It was a beautiful asphalted road of the same quality of the major international road known as the International Highway. During the first few weeks we had been located on the eastern side of the road. Subsequently, we moved to the western side and buried our 57-millimeter cannon facing the south and east. Our mission was to deny the crossroads to enemy tanks. Early in the morning of 16 December, we were bombarded by the artillery until 0700 hours. A Company, on the other side of the firebreak north of us, had several men killed by these shells as their dug-outs had not been completed. They did not have logs on top of their holes.

"At about eight in the morning, Angelo Esultante and I were outside, having guard duty on our gun, when a patrol of eighteen men broke from the woods about 100 yards southeast of us, and they ran straight along their side of the big road in order to take cover in the ditch along the road. A few among them opened fire as they ran, and it was to these shots that we owed our lives. We jumped behind the gun's steel shield and thought about what we were supposed to do now. Their appearance had surprised us completely. We had been told that the front lines were two miles ahead of us and we did not suspect an enemy offensive was taking place. Angelo and I retired on a hidden forest track, just behind our gun, and subsequently we headed west in order to warn the rest of the gunners, who were still in their dug-outs. They had heard the German shots and had taken up defensive positions.

On this dirt road—seen here looking toward Hüllscheid—Sgt. William Kirkbride of the 1st Platoon of the antitank company discovered the incoming Germans. HANS WIJERS

"A ten-man antitank gun crew consisted of four men armed with pistols, four with carbines, and two with M1 rifles. So, effectively we only had six men capable of doing battle, and from that we decided to retreat farther back in the zone of A Company. When we were in the A Company zone, the Germans were hot on our heels. Fortunately, A Company had a vigilant BAR gunner who spotted us arriving through the firebreak. He opened fire with his weapon at several inches from us, firing over our heads, and with a single burst he killed the first three Germans who were arriving in pursuit; they were really close. One of them was a very young officer in a new-looking uniform. The next carried an MG42 machine gun, and the third carried several belts of machine-gun ammunition slung about his body."

The noncombatant personnel of the A Company command post established an improvised position about 100 meters south of the command post and slowed down all advances by the enemy. On hearing the noise of battle from the command post, 1st Sgt. Lyle O. Frank, who at this time was rejoining the company to which he belonged (A Company), ordered the three men who accompanied him to deploy and to open fire while advancing. They advanced into the enemy flank. Surprised by this audacious action, the German, thinking that it was a far greater force than the four GIs, withdrew east in disorder. Subsequently two squads of A Company, who had just left their positions to the south, arrived to retake the command post and struck the withdrawing Germans in the flank.

Meanwhile, the Germans were pushing straight towards the positions of the 81-millimeter mortar platoon. The mortars, well dug in, had open fields of fire in the direction of German territory. The withdrawing Germans, pressed by troops of A Company, arrived directly into the rear of the mortar positions. Immediately, confused combat developed in the woods. The chief of the mortar platoon, 1st Lt. John W. Vaughan, deployed one of his mortar squads and a squad from A Company to beat back the Germans. The Volksgrenadiers did not advance north to the Losheimergraben Crossroads, which still was being worked over by the German heavy artillery, but infiltrated towards the east, towards the positions of the mortar platoon. While several Germans were killed by Lieutenant Vaughan's men, the mortars continued to fire missions for 1st Battalion. After the German force had crossed the positions of the mortar platoon, they turned and deployed themselves about 100 meters southeast of the position. It was clear that the Germans had noted the mortars and had turned in order to neutralize them. As they approached, Lieutenant Vaughan made his mortars fire almost vertically. The mortar rounds exploded twenty-five meters or less from his own positions. The German attack failed with heavy losses, and the rest of the troops

Modern-day view of the the positions of 1st Lt. John W. Vaughan. Behind the barn were the 81-millimeter mortars of D Company. HANS WIJERS

took off to the east. Capt. John S. Sandiland, commander of D Company, estimated that the German casualties were seventy-five men wounded or killed in this skirmish. Among the victims were the commander of the 1st Fusilier Battalion of the 27th Regiment, Maj. Klaus Breger. On his body, according to Arthur Mings of A Company, the GIs found a copy of Field Marshal Rundstedt's order of the day, which gave the scope of the German attack. About a dozen Germans were captured as well.

The main attack against the Losheimergraben Crossroads was carried out by the 48th Grenadier Regiment of Col. William Osterhold from the direction of Frauenkron. From the start of the offensive, the attack launched by the regiment ran into obstacles and problems and the grenadiers of the 48th Regiment lost much time in getting to the crossroads. The 1st Battalion of the 48th Regiment marched at the head, with the 2nd Battalion in reserve. Osterhold "had no idea of the location of the American positions. We had not been informed and had been forbidden to carry out reconnaissance. We had to stay in Kronenberg until night fell, and then we were directed west in the direction of Losheimergraben. That was all! I never took part in an attack that was worse prepared."

Osterhold continues: "We found the wires of the booby traps. When the young Volksgrenadiers learned about these wires, they began to cut them in

William Osterhold.
KAMERADSCHAFT
FUSILIER RGT. 27/M.
STEGLICH

two, without making any distinction. Doing this, they also cut the communication wires of the artillery. No more communication with the artillery! This is why so many men of the battalion were killed by our own artillery. Respecting the time table, the German artillery bombarded the woods to the east of Losheimergraben and began to shell the 1st Battalion. Half of the shells exploded in the treetops, hitting the troops sheltering below with shrapnel splinters and bits of wood. During this avalanche of shells, two-thirds of the battalion was put out of action. The battalion commander, Maj. Siegfried Moldenhauer, was severely wounded a few paces from me. The survivors were completely occupied with treating and evacuating the wounded."

With the point battalion out of action, Osterhold ordered the 2nd Battalion, which had been held in reserve, to start moving and to continue the attack on the crossroads. But this took much time. In order not to demoralize the soldiers of the 2nd Battalion, the attack went south of the route followed by the 1st Battalion. With all the delays in the execution of this attack, it was around midnight before the Volksgrenadiers reached the first American positions. Despite the great delay with regard to the timetable, the assault struck like lightning. Violent and confused combat was fought in the woods. In the wooded terrain, the visibility and the fields of fire were limited to a few meters. In a short time both platoons of B Company were swamped.

The 3rd Platoon of Sgt. Mick Machnik was completely overrun; the 1st Platoon of Lieutenant Lubick was surrounded in the woods to the east of Losheimergraben.

Staff Sergeant Ballinger of B Company, 394th Infantry, takes up the story: "It was a cold, damp, misty morning with a heavy snow lying on the ground. There was absolute silence as we waited for the attack to come. It came, but not the way we expected. From behind a tree came six German soldiers. They were walking very slowly straight toward us. They were in the exact center of the field of fire of a machine gun we had. George Boggs was the machine gunner. He wanted to begin firing right away, but I could see that there were others coming, so I told Boggs to wait until I told him to fire. Those in the rear caught up to the first six, and they stood in a close group talking to each other. They seemed to be unaware of us. Finally, one of them placed the tripod on the ground, and another put a machine gun on it. They were sixty yards or less away. One of them dropped to his knees behind the machine gun, so I told Boggs to fire. He fired a long burst, and all of the Germans fell. That seemed to be the signal for everyone in the area to fire, and now the noise of the machine-gun and rifle fire was deafening.

"The Germans had taken cover in the ravine and were laying down heavy fire from there. PFC Alphonse M. Sito, who was to the right of our shelter, said that the majority of German fire came from our right flank. Our only machine gun was not in a position to sweep that far to the right. There was a BAR team, instead of a machine-gun team, to cover this sector. After a moment Sito said that the Germans had broken through and would arrive from our rear. He told us the BAR team had been eliminated. A minute later, Private Clarkson, who was in the hole with Sito, told us that Sito had been killed. D Company had a heavy machine gun at a hundred yards or so to our right area. We could hear them firing for a while, then there was no firing at all except for the Germans."

Shortly afterwards, the Germans opened up on Ballinger's positions with intensive fire from automatic weapons. Ballinger goes on: "It seemed as if all their firepower was now being concentrated on our position. Our shelter and machine-gun pit had been dug down and covered with logs and dirt. The logs were disintegrating under steady machine guns and rifle fire, which was coming so low we couldn't get our heads off the floor. Throughout all this time a German medic was out in front of us attending the wounded, paying no attention to us or all the bullets so close to him. He was attending a German who had fallen about fifteen feet from our dugout. He looked at us and shook his fist. None of us ever took a shot at him. By now it was impossible for any of us to return fire. We decided it would be best for us to surrender. We decided to bury all our letters and money. We attached a white undershirt to a machine-gun cleaning rod and pushed it out of the shelter opening. Immediately all the firing stopped, and the Germans shouted at us to come out. There were four of us in the shelter and three in the machine-gun pit. As far as I know, we were the last resistance of B Company, all the others having been killed, wounded, or captured, with the exception of those who were lucky enough to have gotten out. From the time the battle started to the moment we surrendered was no more than an hour."

In the dense forests, the men of B Company had resisted as well as they could. During the afternoon, confused fighting took place in various small islands of resistance. According to PFC Robert Muyres of the 3rd Platoon, B Company, 394th Infantry, "When the Germans attacked, I was in a foxhole with S/Sgt. Ernest F. Davidson. After a while, our hole was strafed by machine-gun fire. Davidson was killed, and I was lightly wounded in the arm and wounded more seriously in the leg. Shortly afterwards, I was hit by the explosion of a *Panzerfaust* that reached my foxhole, and I lost consciousness. Later, when I recovered consciousness, I saw four German soldiers pass, carrying a fifth who had been seriously wounded. I asked them to help me. One answered that they would come back to search for me. I didn't really believe them. Very shortly afterwards, the four men returned, their comrade having died, and they carried me to a first-aid post."

William Sears, another member of the 3rd Platoon, remembers: "Thomas and Sams were on our left, in the BAR dugout. Thomas had been hit in the stomach by a machine pistol. The last time I saw him, he didn't have a chance. The Germans did not permit me to help him, so I think he was still there. I was taken prisoner shortly before nightfall."

S/Sgt. James F. Murray, whose squad was completely destroyed, took up the weapon of his BAR man, who had been mortally wounded several seconds earlier, and threw himself on the enemy with his last clip of ammunition. He was shot down a few paces from the Germans. The heavy machine-gun section was eliminated. The leader of the section, T/Sgt. Eddie Dolenc, with a complete disregard for security, had set up his machine gun outside its prepared position, which had a limited field of fire, and so he set it up in a shellhole.

Dolenc opened fire with his gun, killing or wounding a great number of Germans and forcing the attackers to retire. During a lull in the firing, he ordered his comrades to rejoin their platoon, while he alone stayed in his precarious position. The last that was seen of his action was that he was serving his weapon alone, while twenty to twenty-five dead Germans were lying in front of his position like a tapestry. Not being able to fire in all directions, Eddie Dolenc succumbed to the numbers and was take captive. But his action prevented an advance by the Volksgrenadiers long enough to give the survivors of B Company time to retire and for reinforcements of C Company to come up for support. Visibility was poor in this wooded area. Fields of fire for rifles and automatic weapons were about as limited as visibility, 50 or 100 yards or so. At about 1300 hours, one platoon of C Company was ordered to attack to the south with the mission of limiting the penetration of B Company's position.

Robert W. Jones, a scout in the 2nd Platoon, C Company, 394th Infantry, describes what happened: "We were subjected to a severe artillery attack. I later learned that our outposts had been overrun and were thus not able to alert us. This was our initiation into battle; our first expierence of seeing friends with whom we had formed strong attachments being killed and wounded. When the artillery eased, we learned that B Company to our right had taken the brunt of the attack. We were sent to reinforce their position."

The 48th Grenadier Regiment also struck part of C Company, which was located on the other side of the Kyll valley. As S/Sgt. John Hilliard of 3rd Platoon, C Company, remembers it, "We heard several loud explosions in our forward defenses, which consisted of obstacles and barbed wire. The German engineers had pushed an explosive tube under the wire and blown a passage through. The German infantry flowed into the breach, and we opened fire and killed several of them. But when the entire company opened fire, the Germans turned and saved themselves. We continued to fire as they carried out their rapid retreat, killing even more."

Hensil S. Cohron writes: "In the early-morning hours of 16 December, the Germans threw in an artillery barrage for two to three hours. The weather was so foggy you could hardly see a person in front of you; there was also a heavy snowfall. After the barrage ended, we were served a breakfast of pancakes and coffee. (We did not know that this would be the last food we would get until 28 or 29 December.) The group to our left was wiped out, and sixteen of us were sent over to try to cover this area. The morning was filled with the clatter of tanks, mortar fire, and all kinds of gunfire. The sergeant in charge of our group told us we must keep moving, or we would be killed. The fighting was very vicious; we kept losing men and picking up other Americans also lost in the fog. We ended up in the custom houses on the Losheim road in front of Losheimergraben, evidently in the Losheim Gap."

By mid-day, the situation of B Company was getting desperate. At about 1300 hours, the 2nd Platoon of C Company, commanded by 1st Lt. Dewey A. Plankers, received an order to launch an attack to the south in order to reduce the enemy breakthrough in the sector of B Company. S/Sgt. Mel J. Weidner, a member of the 2nd Platoon, recalls: "Our platoon ran into fierce resistance on the way. We holed up in a defensive position, while the remains of B Company retired and reorganized on a new defensive line. They had been hit hard, that was sure, and they had many men killed and wounded. But the Germans had paid a heavy toll for this, because we saw more German bodies than American ones."

Somewhat later, the 3rd Platoon of C Company also received orders to prepare a counterattack and throw back the farthest extent of the German penetration. According to Staff Sergeant Hilliard of the 3rd Platoon, "We silently descended into the ravine and headed towards the B Company sector. We passed it and ended up at the edge of Losheimergraben. We progressed along the edge of the village, meeting only limited resistance until the moment we reached the east-west road (toward Losheim). Two squads deployed in an extended Indian file on both sides of the road, while the third squad deployed around the crossroads in order to provide support for the other two squads and to prevent an enemy from approaching the crossroads. As we were moving in a wooded area, all hell broke loose. The fire was instinctive and intense; undoubtedly it came from an infantry unit that was bigger than ours and too strong for the two squads that faced it. We retreated to one part of the wooded area where we could not be seen by the enemy and awaited the night which was falling rapidly by now. We found ourselves on some high ground overlooking, and to the south of, Losheimergraben, and we observed the village."

Despite fierce combat that lasted until the fall of night, the GIs were not able to throw back the attackers. But the Volksgrenadiers of the 48th Grenadier Regiment were not able to gain any ground either. At dusk, two platoons of C Company and the remains of B Company found themselves near the Losheimergraben Crossroads. The men of the 2nd Platoon of Lieutenant Plankers dug themselves in at the small group of buildings east of the crossroads. The 3rd Platoon, including Staff Sergeant Hilliard, took up positions in the buildings at the crossroads.

CHAPTER 6

The Hilltop at Lanzerath

The activities of the 394th's Intelligence and Reconnaissance Platoon prior to 16 December 1944 must be understood. When the position was occupied on 10 December, Platoon Sgt. William Slape and radio operator James Fort established telephone and radio communications with the 14th Cavalry (in Lanzerath), the 1st Battalion (in Losheimergraben), and the 394th Regiment (in Hünnigen). Slape then worked with squad leaders Sgt. George Redmond and Sgt. William Dustman in placing their squads for good observation and effective fields of fire. In turn, the assistant squad leaders, Cpl. Sam Jenkins and Cpl. Aubrey McGehee, worked with their men to relocate and improve the fortified two- and three-man foxholes. They placed rows of ten- to twelve-inch pine logs in Alpine fashion over the tops of these bunkers. Bill Tsakanikas prepared a position for the platoon command post in a log hut to the rear of the area and improved a foxhole to accommodate three people. The platoon perimeter was ringed with hand grenades, with wires attached to the pins and running to respective foxholes. The assigned positions of the men, from left to right, were Aubrey McGehee, Jordan Robinson, and James Silvola (outside the woods in the field near some logs or stumps) with observation and cover of the road junction. Inside the edge of the woods were, from left to right, George Redmond, Louis Kalil, Bob Adams, Risto Milosevich, Carlos Fernandez, Joseph McConnell, William Dustman, Clifford Fansher, Bob Baasch, Sam Jenkins, and Robert Preston. William Slape and John Creger were located in the front center. Tsakanikas, Vernon Leopold, James Fort, and Lyle Bouck were in the log shack, with two foxholes outside.

German PFC Rudi Frühbeisser, 9th Infantry, 3rd Fallschirmjäger Division, wrote an account of this costly attack on the defensive positions at Lanzerath. It shows how hard his unit was hit by the defenders of the hilltop looking over the road. "6 o'clock! All of a sudden this hellish spectacle stops! There is the order: 'Attack!' We go in at the double! Suddenly the enemy territory in front of us is bathed in a milky-white light. Hundreds of searchlights are used to create an artificial moonlight. The company is advancing steadily. We old men have been continually waiting for it. Now it should begin! All of

The Hilltop at Lanzerath

Aerial view of Lanzerath. DICK BYERS

a sudden we reach a road which is at right angles to us. One man shouts that this is the road which forms the Belgian border. We continue to advance, pass another small road and close in on a height. We reach the small hamlet of Hergersberg. To our right in front of us, tank engines are roaring on a road. Now we have reached the main road. To our right the large Belgian customs house is standing by the side of the street. When the road is twisting its way down into a valley, there is a big explosion in front of us. To the side of the road a tank has run over a mine (one of the mines laid by the German troops when they were retreating earlier).

"So the road that forks off to the right and which we'll have to take is mined. Now we can use the break and study the map with the chief. So now we are lying by the road that is coming from Losheimergraben and is leading towards Manderfeld. Our first objective should be the small village of Hüllscheid, that is lying on the hill slope behind a mill. Slowly dawn creeps up. A squad of Sergeant Major Kuhlbach's platoon advances on the road to provide cover. We see no Yanks. Now we have passed the mill, after a signal has come in from forward troops. To our right the road from Losheimergraben is coming down. So forward on our left. By a row of high firs we proceed with caution. Suddenly a heavy machine gun opens up!"

Mortar fire rained down on the village. Officer Cadet Herbert Vogt, who was hunkering down next to Frühbeisser, was shot in the neck. Frühbeisser

Rudi Frühbeisser.

quickly pulled him into the house opposite. The round must have gone straight through the throat, thought Frühbeisser, who already had some experience with wounds. An antitank gun must have shot straight through the house. Rubble and stones flew through the air. Squad leader Private First Class Lassek was hit mortally. The sergeant medic of the first company was also killed. Captain Schiffke, the 1st Company commander, sent some men into the foremost house, as there was a better view from there. They spotted a Yank up in a big tree in the woods. A rifle grenade fired at him, and the American tumbled out of the tree. The 2nd Battalion attacked the village of Merlscheid from Backelsberg, which lay behind Hüllscheid. Again and again one could hear the high barking of an antitank gun firing into the village. According to the map it should have been higher up at the crossroads, which on the right runs towards Lanzerath and on the left towards Hasenvenn. After a while the men succeeded in making their way forward and found the signalers with their radios lying by the side of the road. They belonged to the signals platoon of the 2nd Battalion. Five of them have been killed, the others severely wounded. Here the runner of the staff of the 1st Battalion, Cpl. Peter Heidkamp, got it in his right hand. However, he passed his orders on to the company commander. Sergeant Major Schega of the 1st Company with his squad managed to break through a wall into a house. From there they knocked out an American machine gun. They continued and after a few shots reached Merlscheid safely.

"Yanks really must have lived here," Frühbeiser says. "Food stands around on tables everywhere. We capture American weapons, ammunition, and equipment. The first American cigarettes are smoked in this battle. A squad from the 15th Company, which is located in a house in Hüllscheid, takes a direct hit. Private Mittelmann, Corporal First Class Hermann, and Corporals Conrad, Wittig, and Pfau are killed straightaway. Private Eder is killed by a shell from an infantry gun. In Merlscheid, Private Hildebrand of the 14th Company, shot through the head by an infantry gun, is killed outright. The 2nd Battalion now has crossed the road leading to Lanzerath. The 1st Battalion from Merlscheid is approaching Lanzerath via a small road."

The snow covered the field to the front of the I&R Platoon, 394th Infantry, and extended 200 yards down to the first house in Lanzerath. The field was bisected by a farm fence about four feet high, creating a main line of resistance. The two- and three-man foxhole bunkers were covered with six- to eight-inch pine logs. The interlocking fields of fire created a final protective line measuring up to Fort Benning's "school solution." The .50-caliber machine gun mounted on the jeep was in a defilade position. Fresh snow had fallen several times and camouflaged the position beyond detection. A bitter cold had temperatures ranging from the teens at night to the twenties and low thirties during the day. Snow was two to four inches deep in the fields and drifting. The sharp wind gusted from the north and forced a freezing fog to roll into and out of the platoon area.

Lt. Warren Springer of the 371st Field Artillery describes the situation: "On 15 December 1944, Peter Gacki, Willard Wibben, Billy Queen, and I were in a house on the east side of the road in Lanzerath that served as our base and observation post. I don't remember anyone else being in the house on that day or the next. On the second floor of the house, there was a window that provided a good view of Losheim and the Schnee Eiffel area. Sandbags were in place against the wall just below the level of the window ledge. A BC scope was in place to aid in observation of the enemy area. During the

View of the farmhouse (left), the small road leading up to the fields, and the hilltop. The church is at below right.

This house was the command post of the observation party of the 371st Field Artillery in December 1944. PETER GACKI/J. WIJERS

morning on the fifteenth, we spotted a man riding into Lanzerath on a bicycle. I questioned him, and he said he had come into the village to pick up some shoes he had left with a cousin so that they could be repaired. Somehow his story didn't seem quite right, so I took him to a building diagonally across the street where there were a number of our troops. I don't remember if they were part of the tank destroyer group or some of the I&R Platoon. I wanted to see if any of them had seen the suspect around before. As I remember, the person in charge of the group said he would have a couple of his men take the suspect back to Battalion S-2 for questioning."

Lt. Lyle Bouck Jr., commander of the I&R Platoon remembers: "Suddenly, without warning, a barrage of artillery registered at about 0500 hours and continued until about 0700 hours. The artillery was relentless and frightening, but not devastating. Much landed short, wide, and long of our position, and mostly tree bursts. At any rate, our well-protected cover prevented casualties. The telephone lines were out, but the one radio allowed us to report to the regiment. Kriz told us that regiment and the entire front had received the same artillery. He suggested some forward patrol action, and to maintain contact. As a patrol was being prepared, three jeeps and several trucks (the 801st Tank Destroyer Battalion in Lanzerath) came up the road, turned left at the platoon left flank, and headed for Buchholz Station. This information was reported to regiment. 1st Lt. Ed Buenger (the 394th's assistant S-2) explained this to Kriz and Riley. We were directed to get someone into the village and try to determine what was happening. Slape and Creger went into Lanzerath and occupied the command post vacated by the tank destroyers. As Slape went forward, he took a field phone; he and Creger ran a new wire for contact.

"The next hour or so, nothing happened. Then Slape reported what appeared to be a column of troops marching toward Lanzerath. This was reported to regiment, and I asked permission to withdraw and engage in a delaying action. Kriz said to remain in position and some reinforcements would come from the 3rd Battalion. Slape called again and said some Germans were in the house (downstairs) and he and Creger wanted help. I sent McGehee, Silvola, and Robinson across the road, told them to creep along the ditch, get close to the second house on the left, open fire, and see if they could release Slape and Creger. Sak went forward to the point foxhole and Fort monitored the radio. In the meantime, Slape and Creger slipped out of the house, into a barn, under some cows, and out the other side, into the woods. While they circled north in the draw and woods, McGehee, Silvola, and Robinson closed into the village and engaged in a fire fight and wiped out what they described as platoon in size. At this time, Sak reported seeing a young girl come out of the corner house, on the right, and talk to the German soldiers, pointing north. When this happened, Risto Milosevich and I crept out the rear of the platoon position, crossed the road to Buchholz, and entered a group of sapling pines (five to six feet tall) in hopes of locating or learning something of Slape, Creger, McGehee, Silvola, Robinson. The entire platoon was firing for a short time, then suddenly Slape and Creger appeared in the small trees with Risto and me. Slape was crouched forward and moaning; he told of falling as he slipped while running across the road (from Lanzerath to Losheimergraben). As he ran following Creger, the Germans fired upon him with an automatic weapon, and shot the heel of his shoe off. Later, we learned, he had fractured two ribs in the incident which caused him pain."

Frühbeisser continues his story: "A loud single explosion. Captain Schiffke has been hit in his arm. A medic sergeant major quickly bandages his chief. He got a grazing wound on the upper arm. Now the 1st, 2nd, and 3rd Companies have run into opposition. Weapons specialist Private First Class Federowski is hit. And PFC Willi Kölker also is wounded by a round in the upper thigh. Private First Class Bradel from Vienna is killed. The 2nd Battalion also has got engaged in combat. There the commander of the 6th Company, Captain Theetz, falls. A machine-gun crew consisting of Lance Corporal Hoffmann, Private First Class Ollermann, and Private Jähring all are mortally hit by headshots while lying at their gun. Platoon commander Sgt. Otto Pleie,

Lyle Bouck.

who is a veteran of Normandy, takes a round in the shoulder. Within the 4th Company of First Leutenant Grau, platoon commander Sergeant Ilk and Private First Class Weishäupel are hit. Private First Class Klein, the tank killer squad leader, and Private Noak both fall with head shots."

Lt. Lyle Bouck picks up his description: "The four of us crept across Buchholz road and back into the rear of the platoon position. All of this movement was accomplished without exposure, because we were below the crest of the hill. Slape was not aware of McGehee's fate. McGehee, Silvola, and Robinson all described later how they were cut off from the platoon and traveled north to reach the lst Battalion to try to get some help (not knowing help would not come, as all units were having the same problems as we). In their movement north, they had to negotiate the deep railroad cut (thirty to forty feet deep) containing the tracks running from Losheim to Buchholz Station. At this time, they were in another fire fight with a battalion of German troops wearing 'white' to blend in with the snow. Robinson was badly wounded, the calf of his right leg was ripped open. Silvola was wounded severely in the left elbow. They were trapped on the north bank of the railroad cut and captured at gun point. I told Slape and Creger to get into McGehee's vacated hole. As they crept forward to do so, the first attack by the Germans was made on our position. This may have been two platoons, storming up the snow-covered slope, trying to get over a fence, and to our position."

Frühbeisser continues: "The 2nd Company is carrying out a storming attack on a small section of wood 300 meters left of the street. During the attack, platoon commander Sgt 1st Class Karl Quator and Corporal Fischer, as well as Privates Rench and Roth as well as Private Heube are killed. Platoon commander Sergeant P is wounded. The 1st Company cannot proceed. The fir forest is strongly mined. Some now try to clear the mines. Our old Private First Class Winter, who was in Russia with General Meindl, is slightly wounded in his arm. Winter was an orator in the Nazi Party, and one man jokingly teases him, 'So, Hans, you with your golden party membership badge, are impervious to more than a scratch?' And, as if he really is invulnerable, he walks back to the street in order to get bandaged by the medic, Sergeant Otto."

Lt. Warren Springer of the 371st Field Artillery remembers his experience: "Although there had been some increase in activity both during the day and night in the area around Losheim before 16 December, it hardly prepared us for the intensity of the enemy artillery barrage that opened up around 0530 on that morning. This continued for more than an hour. The area in front of our observation post was blackened by a concentration of artillery shells that had fallen short by about fifty yards. The concentrated pattern made it clear that the enemy knew that the house was used as an observation post. I remembered the man we had questioned the previous day and suspected that he or someone else had passed on information on our location.

"When the barrage lifted we watched from our command post window for signs of enemy approaching, but none appeared. I went outside to check the road and saw the tank destroyer group pulling out. I stopped one of the vehicles and was told a strong German force was advancing up the road. I called the fire direction center, told them of the situation and asked for artillery fire on the road 200 yards south of our observation post. They told me they could not do anything at that time because they were under small-arms attack. A short time later two or three men appeared in a jeep and said they were on their way to a prepared defense position and advised us to go with them since the Germans were right behind them. I was glad that artillery fire had not been delivered when I requested it because these men might have been casualties. I had been under the impression from the tank destroyer group that they were the last ones out. We followed the men a short distance north on the Lanzerath road, turned left and followed a trail up to the prepared position. There were several foxholes or dugouts in the area. Each one was surrounded and covered with logs and dirt. There were narrow openings in front for firing and an entrance in back. The I&R Platoon, commanded by Lieutenant Bouck, was already in place. Bouck—or one of his men—directed Gacki, Wibben, and me to one of the dugouts and asked Billy Queen to join two or three of his men in one of the other dugouts. I think these men were the same ones who led us to the position.

"Lieutenant Bouck asked me if I could bring in some artillery fire. I told him I would try, but they were under attack back in the rear area and might not be able to respond. I did get through on the radio and asked for artillery fire in front of our position. I was told they would try to give us artillery support as soon as possible, but reinforcements were out of the question. A short time later some rounds came in to our right front. I asked for a correction to bring the fire directly in front of the position and also asked that they drop some fire on the Lanzerath road in the vicinity of our observation post in the house we had occupied to prevent enemy reinforcements, particularly armored vehicles, from coming from that direction.

"A few more rounds came in, but they were still too far to the right, and I asked for a further correction. Just then there was a loud crash just in back of our dugout and the noise of shattered glass. At that point my radio went dead. I don't know if it was a mortar shell or machine-gun fire that hit our jeep, but I knew that was the end of communication with our firing batteries.

"No further artillery fire landed in our immediate area. I thought I heard artillery fire landing at the other location where I had requested fire, namely down the Lanzerath road about 200 yards from the house we had used as an observation post. I cautiously stuck my head and shoulders out of the entrance on the rear aspect of our dugout to see where the shells were landing, but I could only judge from the sound because my vision in that direction was obstructed. At that point some twigs started dropping from an overhanging tree branch just in back of our dugout. I realized the twigs were being clipped off by bullets, so like a turtle, I quickly pulled back into the dugout.

"I waited for more artillery fire to be dropped in our area, but that didn't happen. When our radio communication was interrupted so abruptly, back at fire direction center they may have thought that we had been captured and would be exposed to any fire landing in our area."

The 3rd Company of Captain Woitschek stopped in the left part of the village. Frübeisser continues his story: "Here, there is snow lying on the heights and so the paratroopers in their mottled smocks really stand out. When the 3rd Company continues to close with the houses, platoon commander Sergeant Major Schiele stumbles and does not get up anymore. When somebody turns him over, he concludes, 'Headshot!' Corporals Mayer and Schmidt have been wounded less severely. The call 'Medic!' goes out. Medic Corporal Matthieu walks to the wounded. He is clearly recognizable with the red cross on his chest. A red cross flag hangs from his back pack on a metal rod. Suddenly, as he is treating the wounded, there is a shot, and he grasps his face and keels over. Another headshot. Then medic Corporal Schmidt runs out to help, and he also is hit in the head."

Lyle Bouck resumes his account: "Sometime in mid-afternoon, a second attack was made and repelled, but left its mark on the I&R Platoon. While I was giving information to Lieutenant Buenger on the radio during a lull, small-arms fire from a sniper shot the transmitter out of my hand. I was not wounded. Kalil was struck in the face with a rifle grenade that failed to detonate. As the grenade fell to the floor of the foxhole, Kalil was stunned. His face was lacerated, his jaw and cheekbone fractured, his teeth imbedded into the roof of his mouth. Redmond used two first-aid kits and bandaged Kalil in an expert manner. About this time, the Germans presented a white flag and another with a red cross indicating a desire to tend to their wounded. While they where accomplishing this, Milosevich detected a helper leaning over a wounded soldier and appeared to be talking into a communications device. Soon mortar fire landed behind our location, a few rounds fell short. At this time, Milosevich put the 'imposter' out of action.

"The communications were out, ammunition was running low, the wounded increasing, and apprehension running high. I told Sak to get Slape, Dustman, and Redmond. Our evaluation was not impressive. We realized heavy fighting was taking place north of us at 1st Battalion and to the northwest where 3rd Battalion was in reserve at Buchholz Station. (Later, of course, we learned it was the German 12th Volksgrenadier Division battling the 1st Battalion and the same unit reaching Buchholz Station by way of the railroad cut.) This meant that we were cut off and could only retreat on foot. I told Slape to send Jenkins and Preston back to regiment or 3rd Battalion to tell them our problem, and that we would hold as long as possible. Also, that we planned to withdraw under the cover of darkness and, if possible, get some help. Jenkins and Preston made it back to regiment, but not until 18 December. The headquarters was no longer in Hünningen, having to withdraw to Elsenborn. Jenkins and Preston, out of ammunition, were captured the following day at the point of a bayonet in a hayloft. A third attack was directed on the platoon later in the afternoon; this was also repelled. During this attack, Sak jumped up on the jeep and was firing the .50 caliber until I told him to get down and take cover. Moments later, Slape manned the .50 caliber and was firing when automatic enemy fire hit the breech and rendered the machine gun inoperable. As dusk approached, thoughts were directed toward getting out on foot, leaving the foxholes that had offered security to us for the entire day. Our ammo was not out, but it was low.

"All of a sudden, and no one knows from what direction, our entire platoon was infiltrated with Germans. Some firing, screaming, and running.

Sak, who earlier had been firing the .50-caliber machine gun on the jeep, leaned out of the rear of our emplacement and emptied his last clip of ammo at three Germans running toward the foxhole vacated by Jenkins and Preston. I leaned out for a moment and unloaded by last full extended clip at two Germans about twenty yards away. As I ducked back into the hole, automatic small-arms fire ripped into our emplacement. Sak and I were now helpless and sure we had been located by the Germans. Just then, the end of a burp gun barrel pointed into our hole. As I leaned to the right, I pushed Sak to the left. A burst of five or six rounds exploded, and Sak slumped to the floor of the foxhole. I found myself reaching down to help him, as I did I was aware that I was being aided by two Germans lifting Sak. We got him out of the hole, the growing dusk made vision limited, but the severity of Sak's wounding was evident when the Germans shined a flashlight on him. He had been struck along the right side of his face. Everything from the right side of his nose to his right ear was missing. His right eyeball hanging from the socket.

"At this time, everything seemed quiet, with small amounts of sporadic rifle fire. A voice asked calmly, 'Who is the Commandant?' I informed him it was 'me.' He wanted to know what my men were going to do. I told him I would call them from their positions if he would have his men stop firing. This was accomplished and we were searched. Then I was told to help two German guards escort Sak down the hill. As we walked around and over bodies, one guard stopped us and wanted to know if we had been at St. Lô. I told him, 'Nein,' and he muttered something like 'Mein Kamerad.'

"We were taken into a small café in Lanzerath and placed on a bench just inside and to the right of the door. Others in the I&R were ordered to help carry German wounded into the village. As Sak sat on my left side (seeming to pass out and come to), I wondered how long he could last (due to the severity of the wound and the constant blood loss). The paper bandages used by the Germans were poor by our standards. Kalil was brought in. Redmond's wound wrapping was excellent (so good I didn't know who he was). I could only see his nose and one eye. Slape, Milosevich, and I discussed the possibility of breaking out the back door (during the confusion in the room). We agreed we could never bring Sak and Kalil with us, so the decision was to stay.

"Activity increased as the night passed. Shortly after a clock on the wall struck 'midnight,' considerable excitement took place. A group of panzer officers stormed into the café, making demands and issuing lengthy orders. They placed a map against a wall by sticking two bayonets into the map. With light of lanterns they pointed, talked, screamed and stalked about as different officers came into and out of the room. The rumble and churn of tanks could be heard through the remainder of the night. Artillery fell in the area

The house in Lanzerath (Café Palm) where Lyle Bouck and his men were brought. Late that evening, Peiper came to this house to question the POWs. HANS WIJERS

Some of the men of the 371st Field Artillery. Standing fifth from left is Billy Queen. First on left in the middle row is Peter Gacki. Fourth from left in the front row is Dick Byers. PETER GACKI

through the night, but none hit the café. As dawn approached, I was instructed to place Sak on the floor with the other wounded. He still had his wallet and a small bible. I removed a picture of his girlfriend (Chloe) from his wallet, placed the picture and the bible on his chest and said a few words of prayer, and told him I pledged that we would see each other back in the States. I told him we were being separated now, and placed the picture back in his wallet and put it and his bible in his field jacket pocket, and said, 'Good-bye.' He could not speak, but I am certain he heard me, because he squeezed my hand."

Sgt. Peter Gacki recalls, "After we had been searched, Wibben and I had to help carry a wounded German back to Lanzerath. We later learned that Cpl. Billy Queen, who had gone to another foxhole, had been wounded and died (in January, Cleon Janos, a member of another C Battery forward observer party, found the body of Billy Queen where he had died earlier). Corporal Queen was the only one of the eighteen men that died in that battle. We were kept at Lanzerath that night, then began our journey to a POW camp."

PFC Rudi Frühbeisser picks up his narrative: "With this, the battle for Lanzerath has come to an end. At the 2nd Battalion, where the fight flares up once again, seven men are killed. According to the map we are stuck in the Büllinger Forest. In front of us the roads forks. On the right it leads to Losheimergraben, on the left it leads to the small railway station of Buchholz. One guy jokingly says that the commander of the 3rd Battalion, Captain Buchholz, has taken his own railway station with him for good measure. Until dusk we remain lying at the edge of the woods. Opposite the street to our right there is a small plantation of young fir trees. Well, there could be a surprise lying in wait for us there. With five men and Sergeant Kühlbach we manage to cross the street. When nothing happens, the entire company follows. Spread out we continue. As precaution everyone is walking in the ditches on both sides of the street, which at this point is a sort of drainage ditch and therefore is deep.

"The rising full moon shines brightly. The company is getting forward well. After a kilometer, a fork to the right between the fir trees in the snow can be made out. According to the map it should be the road leading to the station. All of a sudden we take fire from a wood to our right. It is a good thing that we all were in the ditch and that probably only our heads were visible. Bright red explosive bullets howl over our heads. The machine gun is less than ten meters in front of us. A hand grenade would be useless in the thick forest. So we all turn about and, as well as possible, we hasten back. After about a hundred meters everybody crosses to the other side of the street. In a lightly planted wood we remain lying down. Immediately our machine guns take up position and a small front is established. Everyone remains lying in a covering position. Now we learn that squad leader Private First Class Lenz is missing. No one is able to say where he has gone. Some want to walk back the same road again to look for him, but the chief forbids it. Some say that when the machine gun opened up, Private First Class Lenz had jumped into the woods. Following orders the company then has to withdraw to Lanzerath. In the first four houses the paras make themselves as comfortable as possible. Sentries are posted, and the houses are secured. After about two hours a sentry comes rushing into the cellar and shouts: 'Captain, there is a shape crawling towards us in the roadside ditch!' Immediately Sergeant Kühlbach and three men are sent out. Correct, there is a shape creeping towards the houses very slowly.

"'We'll capture him,' the sergeant says. Now we see in the moonlight that the shape is one of our paratroopers. Great is our joy, when we see that it is the missing PFC Karl Lenz. In the cellar, Lenz reports, 'When the machine gun opened up, it only took me a few jumps to be into the woods. The firing flashes made it easy for me to make out its location exactly. I remained standing behind a thick tree and observed. When the machine gun finally stopped firing, I noticed to my horror that I was alone in the woods. A few steps in front of me I could hear the Yanks whisper. I also understood something that sounded like 'dead man'! So they thought I had been killed. After a while both Americans left their pit. I was determined to sell my skin as expensively as possible. My finger already was on the trigger of my submachine gun. But suddenly both Yanks retreated into the forest. I waited a bit more and then ran as well as possible back to the street and continued in the ditch. Now I didn't know where the company had gone. Suddenly I noticed a large number of footprints which had crossed the street in the snow. So the company had withdrawn. Then I crawled on till I reached Lanzerath.'

"The company commander also is happy that everything has turned out so well. According to a report from battalion staff, we had captured eight men from the U.S. 14th Cavalry Group, a large amount of war booty, among which were several jeeps. The losses in the battalion are supposed to be sixteen killed, sixty-three wounded, and thirteen missing. The night is quiet."

CHAPTER 7

Evening with the 1st Battalion, 394th Infantry

Isolated in the woods east of the crossroads, the situation of B Company, 1st Battalion, 394th Infantry, was becoming desperate. At dusk the commander of the 1st Platoon, 2nd Lt. Chester F. Lubick, facing a useless fight, was forced to surrender what remained of his platoon in order to avoid extra losses among his men. Several GIs refused to surrender and succeeded in fleeing into the dark and regaining the Losheimergraben Crossroads.

Among those who escaped was Sgt. Carl W. Combs of the 1st Platoon: "When it got dark in the woods, Sergeant Kilber arrived at our position and told us Lieutenant Lubick wanted to surrender to the enemy. He asked us if we, too, wanted to capitulate. We answered 'no' because we thought that the Germans did not have much chance of finding us in the forest, where one could not see anything beyond three meters. Private Youngblood, who occupied the next shell scrape, joined us. On the way to the rear, we also received Larry Dobler, our BAR gunner, and together we marched through the woods to the crossroads. There we were able to rejoin fifty to sixty men of the 1st Battalion."

Danny Dalyai, another member of B Company, reports: "Finally, at dusk, we withdrew towards the buildings that were located about 700 meters to the rear. While withdrawing we were shelled by a well-fed barrage and two men in our group were mortally wounded by explosions"

PFC Devon A. Lewis of the 1st Battalion's HQ Company describes his experience: "Our antitank crew held our position all day on 16 December until very late in the evening. It was decided by our squad leader, a sergeant (S/Sgt H. P. Mann), to withdraw to a safer positions. We were almost surrounded. We first had to destroy our 57-millimeter antitank gun and also our three-quarter-ton truck. As we withdrew late that evening, I saw for the first time our dead American soldiers lying in the snow. It was a very sad, shocking feeling. We had a jeep and trailer, so Sergeant Haggerty and Ferrairi, a jeep driver, got the jeep started and two of our message-center personnel got into the jeep also. I laid flat on the trailer top. We pulled out from the woods onto the Losheimergraben and Losheim road. Our jeep driver got mixed up in his direction and turned toward Losheim and as he did so, the German soldiers were coming up this road, shouting, 'Heil, Hitler!' and shooting at us with burp guns and rifles. As we continued to withdraw to a safer area, we found a few abandoned foxholes that we occupied till early the following morning."

The majority of the men of B Company did not succeed in making their escapes. About seventy men were captured, many of them wounded. Among them was William Sears of the 3rd Platoon. He recollects: "The Germans had overrun all the positions of our platoon. What misery! All our foxholes were occupied by killed or wounded soldiers. I met up with Lieutenant Lubick, Goldman, and Schlenz, the last an old member of B Company who transferred to D Company. The poor lad had been hit by a round in the belly. During that night we proceeded a distance of about thirteen kilometers to the rear, passing our observation positions and farther on ascending and crossing the top of a hill where 'dragons' teeth' of the Siegfried Line were located. We arrived in a village, where we were interrogated. Those in need of medical aid were taken to an aid station. Goldman, Blaird, Tobin, and myself were taken to a first-aid post where the medics tried to treat our wounds, but they were lacking everything. What a mess!"

A Company held on to its positions south and southeast of the crossroads. But nevertheless the outpost south of the railroad was isolated by the Germans. PFC D. C. Wylie reports: "Our squad, with platoon S/Sgt. Arthur B. Jones was on the other side of the bridge on the railroad tracks in outpost duty. The artillery fire of the German Army began to rain down on us before dawn. Shortly after dawn, patrols began to scout out our positions, apparently having the idea in their heads to blow up the bridge. We also had

An American encampment.

emplaced explosives to blow up the bridge but neither side had finished the work. In the morning Staff Sergeant Jones sent Sergeant Francis U. Swift to the rear in order to seeks reinforcements, but he never returned. We exchanged fire during the entire day and the afternoon. We were bombarded by our own mortars. By dusk we had practically run out of munitions and the troops on the terrain concentrated the fire of light weapons on our position. At about that time, we received even more shellfire, this from the enemy. After dusk, Staff Sergeant Jones gave the order to surrender. PFC Ray Nahayama lit a starshell and equipped himself with a white flag. Tracers swept over his head. Nahayama threw himself on the ground and lit another starshell. The firing stopped and German soldiers arrived to take us prisoner. Our captors were very young, probably soldiers of less than twenty years old who spoke good English. After our capture, artillery fire passed overhead towards the American positions. After having been taken behind the lines, we again were under fire from the American artillery and mortars."

As the clarity of day subsided, the German pressure began to let up and finally ceased completely. This clearly is reflected in the severe losses suffered throughout the day by the Volksgrenadiers.

PFC Charles C. Kent of B Company, who was able to escape to the crossroads of Losheimergraben, reports: "Later that night, I took a patrol into B Company's sector. Our nightly patrol left the house on the side of the wood, advanced past the house destroyed by bombs and between the next two houses and subsequently turned right. We followed the route from Losheim to Losheimergraben until we arrived at our own foxholes; subsequently we marched north towards a open spot in the woods. We found no one. Then we moved to the log huts of B Company. The Christmas mail had arrived on that day. We filled our pockets with sweets and cigarettes and we brought them to Losheimergraben, where they were more than welcome. I doubt whether anyone had eaten anything that day."

This respite permitted the Americans to catch their breath and reorganize themselves in their new positions as much as possible. In one attempt to maintain a coherent defense, the commander of the 394th Regiment, Lt. Col. Donald Riley, on the evening of 16 December, ordered the 3rd Battalion to face south in the woods to the north of the railroad. In this way a semicircular defense was set up by both battalions. In the evening the command post of the 3rd Battalion rejoined the one of the 1st Battalion at about 250 meters southeast of the road junction. Patrols of A Company maintained a liaison with the 3rd Battalion. Two platoons of K Company, the 1st Platoon of 2nd Lt. Charles N. Spencer and the 2nd Platoon of 2nd Lt. Ray Thibadeaux, remained in position at Buchholz Railroad Station.

Evening with the 1st Battalion, 394th Infantry

A modern-day view of the snowy forest. HANS WIJERS

To reinforce the crossroads, Riley provisionally attached the equivalent of one company to the 1st Battalion. This force, composed of two platoons of K and L Companies and under the orders of Capt. Wesley J Simmons, commander of K Company, dug themselves in on the high ground north of the crossroads in order to give greater depth to the defenses of B Company. But it took more time to organize a defense line in the somber and icy forests. The men of Captain Simmons did not have tools to dig themselves into the frozen ground. These had been abandoned or lost during the preceding combat.

Capt. Wesley J. Simmons remembers: "Information was received about 1945 hours from Lt. Col. Robert H. Douglas, battalion commander, that the 1st Battalion had been hit hard and had suffered many casualties, and although they were still holding their original positions, they expected another full-scale attack before daylight. At 2100 hours on 16 December, we took up a defensive position about 600 yards north of Losheimergraben. Most of the men of K Company had not eaten since the evening meal on 15 December, and ammunition was running very low. These conditions were reported to 1st Battalion headquarters, but a resupply of neither food or ammunition was received. The men spent most of the night digging in and familiarizing themselves with their positions. At about 2400 hours, we heard over our radio (SCR 300) that Lieutenant Rose had reported tanks, with infantry aboard, overrunning his position at Forest Buchholz Station and that he was destroying his radio."

According to John Dufalla of K Company, "We were ordered to split. The headquarters and 1st and 2nd Platoons were ordered to Buchholz Station. The 3rd and 4th Platoons were ordered to an unknown destination to reinforce the 1st Battalion, which was then under attack from infantry with tank [assault gun] support."

In taking these measures, Douglas left the entire right flank of the defense of the crossroads largely open. In the woods north of Buchholz and at the railroad station, only four platoons of infantry were left to block the German assault.

CHAPTER 8

The 277th Volksgrenadier Division Attacks

THE AMERICAN DEFENSE LINE AT THE INTERNATIONAL HIGHWAY IS HIT

On the left flank in the area of the 1st and 3rd Battalions of the 393rd Infantry, the German 277th Volksgrenadier Division struck the Americans along the International Highway early in the morning of 16 December. At about 0530 hours, a tremendous artillery barrage shattered the regimental front. Regiment was immediately notified of this by the battalions, and shortly afterwards, according to Major Schmierer, the regimental S-3, they received notice from the 1st and 3rd that they were being attacked. The artillery preparation had raised hell with wire communications, and they were forced to depend almost exclusively on radio right from the start. The story seemed to be that the Germans had hit between the two battalions and had surrounded K Company on the 3rd Battalion's right flank and driven back B Company on the 1st Battalion's left flank. Both battalion commanders reported that they believed they could hang on, and Maj. Matthew Legler, commander of the 1st Battalion, said he was going to counterattack with A Company in the rear of B Company's sector in order to restore B's positions. To give the 3rd Battalion some help, I Company of the 394th Infantry was obtained later in the day, and shoved in behind the battalion's sector, and the company commander was given the order to attack to relieve the battalion.

Lt. Wingolf Scherer of the 277th Volksgrenadier Division quotes diary of a lieutenant in the reserves who commanded the infantry gun platoon (5th Platoon) of the divisional fusilier company: "5th Platoon marches up to the (foremost) artillery positions. 0530 hours massive bombardment of the artillery—lighting up of the searchlights. The fusilier company attacks on the road Neuhof-Krinkelt (axis B); 12th SS Panzer Division *Hitlerjugend* awaits the opening—but from Heilige (Captain Heilige is commander of the fusilier company) there is no report. Skorzeny's brigade is waiting in American vehicles and uniforms."

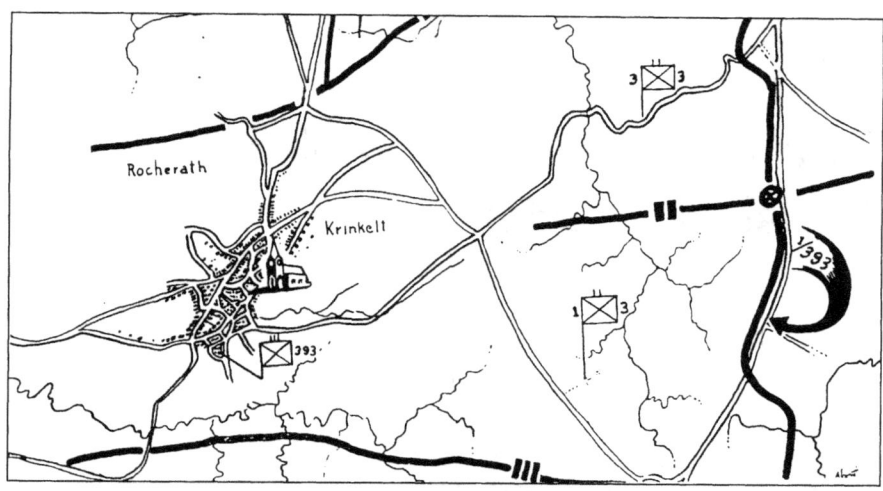

Krinkelt-Rocherath and vicinity.

The left group under Lieutenant Colonel Bremm, advancing with great speed south of the area on the Neuhof-Reich road (International Highway), ran into positions that had hardly been touched by the artillery bombardment. These were defended energetically by B and C Companies of the 1st Battalion of the 393rd Infantry Regiment, commanded by Maj. Matthew Legler, with A Company shoved in between both and G Company of the 2nd Battalion of the 394th Infantry Regiment located to the south of it.

Capt. Lawrence H. Duffin, the 1st Battalion's S-3, describes what happened: "Shortly after the barrage, enemy riflemen supported by automatic weapons attacked both flanks of the battalion front. This initial attack was repulsed with only a few casualties reported among the battalion troops. At approximately 0800, the enemy again attacked in force, this time using successive waves of infantry. The artillery forward observers estimated an almost continuous artillery barrage in front of our lines. Our own mortars and machine guns fired their final protective lines. Both frontline companies reported numerous dead piled up immediately in front of their positions, but at approximately 0830 hours, C Company reported an enemy breakthrough on their right flank."

Scherer remembers: "The battles in the light of the searchlights and the bleak light of the morning became man-to-man fighting, as the American infantrymen, apart from the snipers, often opened up with automatic weapons at a short distance. The unclarity of the snow-covered countryside furthermore hindered the attacker in a quick orientation of where he was and in gaining an overview of the enemy line. The surprise effect benefited the German fusiliers and grenadiers for only a short time. High losses were

Wingolf Scherer.

incurred, especially among the officers. The fusilier company ran into the left wing of the 2nd Battalion of the 394th and was pinned down by fierce artillery fire at about 0800 hours. The three assault guns that had been assigned to Lieutenant Colonel Bremm in the renewed attack were not able to make much headway either because of artillery fire on the G Company positions, and had to withdraw to Neuhof. The fusiliers that had penetrated the G Company sector were either killed or captured. In the end, the fusilier company took up a hedgehog position near the mouth of the street; communications failed; Weisser Stein could not be reached.

"The battalions of the 990th Grenadier Regiment crossed the Reich road and penetrated into the positions on the right wing of the 1st Battalion of the 393rd. In the woods they could not make enough progress in the face of the continual and increasing resistance, which very soon was supported by the mobile artillery of the 99th Division. The fighting spirit of the inexperienced American infantrymen—called 'Battle Babies' by Lauer—and the unexpectedly small result of the first attack had their consequences for the attackers. Nevertheless, they fought with toughness and determination. In hindsight, the situation by 1100 hours was like this: The last encircled platoon of B Company of the opponents had put up a bitter resistance and then had been freed by A Company; the German counterattack failed to penetrate whilst gaining little ground. The strongly attacked C Company had been replaced by a platoon from the antitank company and members of the staff because of lack of any other reserves. Here the American resistance stabilized as well. For Bremm, it was difficult to get an overview of the entire situation. Even in the late afternoon an attempt by a scouting party to reestablish communications with the fusilier company failed. Nevertheless, this much had become clear by midday: The attack needed flanking support by the 991st Grenadier Regiment if it was to get moving again."

T/Sgt. Bernard Nawrocki of B Company, 393rd Infantry, recalls: "The artillery barrage was intense, and the Jerries came in close behind it and seemed to be all around the platoon command post before anyone could do much. They swarmed into the area. The platoon on our right was overrun. Some of the men in the 2nd Platoon were being killed, wounded, and captured. The Germans even got up close enough to throw grenades into the log huts of some of the men and kill their occupants. The Germans, under cover of the artillery, had worked them close to the RJ [road junction] and had knocked out two machine guns of the 2nd Section, 1st Platoon, D Company, under Sgt. Thomas Panian, which were located there. They fired rockets [*Panzerfaust* or *Panzerschreck*] at them, the first one knocking out one machine gun and the next getting the second."

When his platoon was hit, 1st Lt. Charles Kingsley sent a messenger back to the company command post to tell them the situation and to ask for help, but when that runner was slow in returning, Nawrocki was sent back. There he told the company commander what had happened, but there was no help available. Things were chaotic, and 1st Lt. H. Rembold, the weapons platoon leader, told him that the mortar of the 1st Squad had been captured and that the other squads were in trouble.

The Germans were coming right through the positions, and when the right platoon fell, Nawrocki's platoon was sent back to the left and somewhat shattered. He couldn't get back to the platoon command post, so he tried to help organize some assistance around the company command post. He was joined by S/Sgt. Albert Brainard, 1st Platoon guide, and a Sergeant Malone, also from the 1st Platoon, both of whom fell back before the rush of the Germans without being cut off. Somebody gathered up the kitchen crew—some seven or eight cooks and helpers and the mess sergeant—and they came under Nawrocki's control. He took them forward through some scrub pines to the 3rd Platoon, where they offered themselves to Lieutenant Jones, the platoon leader, but he said he was in good shape and didn't need them. Nawrocki took the cooks back to the company command post.

Nawrocki continues: "About noon, I saw A Company's commander, Capt. Joseph Jameson, deploying and pushing the enemy back. He was moving his men forward, and I was with my group on his left. We then spread out in a line of skirmishers, and we made contact with A Company. I strung

The 277th Volksgrenadier Division Attacks

a roll of wire from the end of my rifle and laid it to one of the forward observation posts and then went back and stayed with Lieutenant Jones. Shortly afterwards, Sgt. Nick Sink, who was manning the observation post, reported back that the Germans were massing in the draw south of Miescheid and called for time fire from the artillery. When this came, it broke up the enemy action and sent them back screaming. The wounded could be heard hollering for hours, and later a couple of German litter teams went out and picked up what looked like a number of bodies."

Lt. Wingolf Scherer picks up his story: "The division sent the reserve regiment in a southwesterly direction to help the right wing of the 990th Grenadier Regiment to advance. On the open Miescheider Heath, the regiment was fired on in the flank by K Company of the 3rd Battalion of the 393rd (which had taken positions to the north of the adjoining B Company to the west of the Reich road), and then it was literally shattered by concentrated artillery fire. Serious losses—which were estimated for the first day of the attack to be about 350 killed and 580 wounded by the regimental doctor, Ed Bantz—were mainly caused by snipers, which had taken positions in the trees and opened fire at short distances by surprise. According to Ziak, it also was a problem that soldiers who had overrun enemy positions looted the rich plunder in food and luxuries (like chocolate and cigarettes) to quench their hunger."

The situation of the 3rd Battalion was as follows: The German artillery scattered their shells in the company areas, in the command post area, and in the rear areas; they thoroughly saturated their targets and wrecked the communications system. By 0600 hours, wire contact with all the rifle companies was out, and within the next half hour, wire contact, which had been established after the first wire went out, was lost with K Company. The only wire that stayed in was to L Company, and it, in turn, was able to keep contact with its mortars. Under these conditions, the situation was unclear at battalion headquarters, but finally, after repeated tries, the battalion got through to K Company's command post for a few minutes by using the artillery forward observer's radio. This link didn't last long, but it lasted long enough to reveal the situation as it was there.

Scherer continues: "The rightmost assault group, the 989th Grenadier Regiment, moved forward from its starting positions in the area of the 'Hollerath Knee' on both sides of the forest track to Rocherath-Krinkelt in a southwesterly direction. It ran into K and I Companies of the 3rd Battalion of the 393rd Regiment, whose headquarters was located close to this road just in front of the Jansbach. The last elements of the 989th Grenadier Regiment had arrived by 0400 hours. (The regiment was relieved in the Siegfried Line bunkers west of Schleiden in the night from 14 to 15 December 1944).

"Colonel Fieger had positioned his regiment on a small but deep frontage. The 1st Battalion was to be followed by the 2nd. The 1st Battalion was able to penetrate the woods quickly; but soon the operation of heavy infantry weapons no longer was possible, as the location of the front line could not be made out. Due to the conditions of the soil and the paths, it was nearly impossible to bring up the infantry guns (7.5 centimeters) and heavy mortars (12 centimeters) of the heavy companies (4th, 8th, and 13th). Because of technical difficulties, the communications equipment widely failed. The advance into the dense, completely unknown woods soon led to fragmented man-to-man fights that caused severe losses. (Both battalion commanders were lost this way.)

"The enemy put up a tough resistance. His well-camouflaged resistance nests, which often could not even be made out at close distance in the woods . . . again and again slowed down the attack. The 2nd Battalion was now slotted in on the right of the 1st Battalion in order to gain a wider punch and to start up the advance again."

The right half of K Company had been hit and overrun, and the rest of the company was surrounded. The Germans had moved in closely behind their artillery barrage and had fallen upon the 1st Platoon, under the command of 2nd Lt. Joseph F. Dougherty, and the 2nd Platoon, under T/Sgt. Paul Phifer, as well as the 1st Machine Gun Platoon of M Company, under 1st Lt. Joseph W. Mallon, which had its positions in that part of the K Company front. This information came back at about 0800 hours, and when the radio failed, it was all that was known. However, Capt. Stephen K. Plume, K Company's commander, managed to get his executive officer and another officer, his supply sergeant, and several other men back to the rear to give a more complete picture of his situation. They passed on the news that one man from M Company's machine-gun platoon, which was supporting K Company's right flank, had escaped and reported to Plume that he saw no one surrender, but that the whole right flank had been swallowed up in the first rush of the Germans. Every men was reported killed or captured.

PFC Frank J. Smollon, a BAR man in the 2nd Platoon, K Company, 393rd Infantry, describes what happened: "The riflemen of most companies of the 99th Infantry Division were positioned on outpost duty on the German/Belgium border on the east edge of the Ardennes Forest from the first week of November 1944 to 16 December 1944. Each post was manned by three or four men. These posts were from 100 to 300 yards apart. We were on the front in no-man's-land; there was no line. You know it was cold when more than half of these men were replaced due to frozen feet. In the dark hours of the morning of 16 December, German troops came across the Siegfried Line through minefields to our front. Our foxholes were on the

The 277th Volksgrenadier Division Attacks

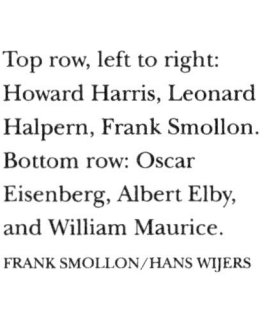

Top row, left to right: Howard Harris, Leonard Halpern, Frank Smollon. Bottom row: Oscar Eisenberg, Albert Elby, and William Maurice.
FRANK SMOLLON/HANS WIJERS

reverse side of a rise. Unbeknownst to us, scores of enemy troops were within thirty feet of our position. After an hour and a half of artillery fire, dawn appeared over the horizon, the artillery fire ceased, and the German advance began. Staff Sergeant Smith told us to hold fire as he pulled a pin from a grenade. They were down and around and behind us before we ever knew what was going on. Sarge was trying to put the pin back in the grenade when the Germans jumped in his foxhole. That grenade did not go off and probably saved our lives. The four of us were taken prisoner within seconds. Our position did not provide for a route of retreat since we were out on an elevated spit of land and cut off. Our rear and both flanks were steep slopes. I now know how a school of fish must feel when a net is thrown over them."

Sgt. B. O. Wilkins of the 2nd Platoon, K Company, 393rd Infantry, takes up the story: "We began to hear rifle fire to our right and to our rear, but could not see who was firing (we were in a ravine in front of the trees). I decided to go to the platoon command post and find out what was going on (we had no communication with anyone). Mac and I went back to our sleeping hole to get our own rifles; the BAR was in the lookout hole. As I was coming out of our hole (Mac was still in it, the passage was large enough for only one person), I noticed we were about to be attacked from our right, where the trees began their projection out to the highway, and where our ravine

B. O. Wilkins.

flattened out and was no longer apparent. A German crew was attempting to launch a *Panzerfaust* at our hole, assuming it was a type of bunker, I suppose. I fired three rounds at them, which broke up the attack. In the trees behind us, the firing began to subside, and a voice told us to surrender. Since we still didn't know the situation, and could not see who was back there, we didn't respond. We heard the demand to surrender again, and from our position, we could see one of our groups in the clump of trees north of us, just east of the ravine, coming out of the trees with their hands on their helmets.

"After we decided to surrender, I asked if anyone had a white handkerchief; no one did. I got out my dirty, brown checked handkerchief and tied it to the muzzle of my rifle and began to wave it. Finally, some Germans appeared from the trees and motioned us up to the top of the ravine. As I approached the German officer, he motioned to my chest and yelled something I didn't understand. I then realized that I had four grenades hanging in my field jacket pockets, so I gingerly removed them.

"Back in the trees, enemy soldiers were standing in a line, shoulder to shoulder, as far as I could see; there were that many. I've later learned that two entire regiments of the 277th German Volksgrenadier Division were attacking K Company: the 989th at the north end and the 991st at the south end of our position between us and our 1st Battalion. I asked the officer if I could return to my hole to get my overcoat, and he allowed me to under guard. I got my coat and Mac's and filled my field jacket pockets with packages of pipe tobacco. On coming out of the hole, I met our first-aid man,

Harvey Stockwell, who said that a wounded German (possibly the recipient of one of my shots) needed a shot of morphine, but the German sergeant wouldn't let him give it to him. I went to the officer, now propped up in our lookout hole eating the sugared dates Harris's mother had sent him for Christmas, who agreed to Stockwell giving the soldier a shot. I couldn't find Mac to give him his overcoat, so I gave it to Stockwell, who was shivering."

2nd Lt. Joseph F. Dougherty of the 1st Platoon, K Company, 393rd Infantry, says: "All communication was knocked out by the barrage, and upon losing one squad and having the enemy in the woods to my rear, I contacted the company commander by runner suggesting that the 1st Platoon be allowed to withdraw from its dug-in positions and move to the vicinity of the company command post in order to face the new threat from the right flank. I believe the other platoons also contacted the commander by runner at this time. My suggestion was approved an upon the return of my runner, I took my two remaining squads and attached weapons and moved them to the position in rear of the company command post. At this position, the company commander joined me. Soon after getting into position, we were attacked by enemy troops emerging from the short pines."

"1st Platoon remnants, including myself, had a fire fight with the encircling Germans well behind the 2nd Platoon. During the engagement, the commander consulted me as to the various courses of action left open. He decided it would be impossible to withdraw from the position. As men ran out of ammunition, they were allowed to go as individuals to try and get back to the battalion command post. A short while later, the commander talked with me again about surrendering. He made the decision to surrender about 1030, and it was fifteen to thirty minutes later that I succeeded in having my men and the enemy cease firing. I walked forward, contacted the enemy, received their instructions, and came back and got the remainder of my platoon that were in walking condition, and they were about ten in number. I gave them their instructions, formed them up in a single file, and turned them over to the enemy. We were not allowed to carry our wounded or dead. The commander came along with my men.

"[After we were captured] I was in the pillbox the first night. We were turning the hand-operated blower since oxygen went so low. . . . Plume, myself, Lt. Joseph Mallon, M Company's machine-gun platoon, and Lieutenant Dettor (the 3rd Platoon's commander) were separated out the next morning and walked to a nearby farmhouse and locked in a basement. We were interrogated many times over the next several days and ate cabbage. They deduced we knew nothing about the U.S. First Army except our own local positions, which was true. They were looking for information on armored divisions, particularly the 9th Armored."

Pvt. David Thompson of the 1st Platoon, K Company, 393rd Infantry, remembers his experience: "December 16, 1944, was quite a day. . . . From our outpost foxhole, Al Knegendorf and I were able to see one dead German a few feet away and lots of others attacking the main line, effectively cutting us off. As the five or six of us attempted to crawl back to K Company, we were intercepted by thrity-five or so well-armed enemy. Discretion proved the better part of valor and we surrendered. I carried that BAR all that way [to Belgium] and got to fire only a few rounds in combat."

PFC Don W. Rader, a member of the 1st Platoon of K Company, 393rd Infantry, recalls: "We were awakened by an artillery barrage that lasted nearly two hours. When it first started, I thought it was our own artillery dropping short rounds; but when the barrage stopped, German soldiers in great numbers crossed the International Highway to the right of our outpost position into other squads of our own K Company.

"We didn't fire initially, and were not attacked in the initial onslaught; however, Sgt. Langford thought Germans were in the forest behind us, and ordered us to be quiet till he could go to the company command post as the artillery had already knocked out all communications. [He] returned in a few minutes and led us to the command post which had once been a woodcutter's cabin.

"We were greeted by Captain Plume and radio operator Sgt. Warrick. My first observation of Captain Plume was the way he was dressed. He apparently had been in his sleeping bag during the artillery barrage and ensuing infantry attack, and had just slipped on his combat boots and leather jacket over his silk pajamas. He addressed Sergeant Langford, 'Sergeant, we're surrounded; you'd just as well surrender.' And to that, Langford said, 'Captain Plume, you can go straight to hell; we're getting out of here.' So with that, Langford led us west, leaving both men standing at the command post.

"The man next to me was a young man named Green; I believe he was killed later. Within a short time, I could see soldiers coming from the CP area in the front. As they came closer, I could see only their legs as they came down the hill, and then their whole body. They were speaking German.

"I grew up in a German community that spoke German, and I could recognize it immediately and fired. As soon as I fired, a voice came from the mortar positions saying not to fire anymore as they were our own men. This scared me, but in a short time, whoever called out could see that they were Germans wearing GI overcoats, probably taken from prisoners. A battle ensued during which Lieutenant Holloway was killed—probably from a burp gun blast in his throat.

"The mortar men did a fantastic job of firing at close range. I heard later that they took their barrels out of their base plate and held the barrels

The 277th Volksgrenadier Division Attacks

more straight up in order to do damage at close range. With our few rifles and two mortars, we dispersed the Germans and they retreated back up the hill."

"After some close fighting, orders were passed down to withdraw west toward Krinkelt. I took off like everyone else; I overtook an antitank officer who had a gun near where we had been the day before."

Headed to Krinkelt, they passed 2nd Division troops digging in a defense line. Entering Krinkelt they encountered traffic jams and shells falling everywhere. Rader hitched a ride on a Cannon Company truck, finally arriving at Elsenborn.

PFC Elton Kerbo, a sniper in the 2nd Platoon of K Company shared an outpost with Smollon, Mudra, and Smith. He describes being captured: "We were taken to the pillboxes and searched. I had a picture postcard of a commode with Hitler's picture in the pot. I was afraid that I had had it, but the German smiled and said, 'Roosevelt.' They then took our overcoats and overshoes."

PFC William Mudra remembers the last moments before surrendering: "My squad occupied the two outposts on the left flank of platoon. There were four men on one and six on the other (one man had gone back to division about a week before as an interpreter and the other, who had acted as assistant BAR man, was being used at the command post). So squad strength was only ten. The nearest outposts were 500 yards or so to either side of us. I was on the four-man post together with S/Sgt. Charles L. Smith (the squad leader) and PFC Elton Kerbo and PFC Frank Smollon (BAR man). The outpost consisted of two dugouts and a listening station where we stood watch; our phone was at the latter. . . . On 15 December, the enemy stirred things up a bit by throwing a few shells at us but we didn't think much of it. A burp gun which had been firing spasmodically into mid-platoon also increased its fire. Sometime during the night our phone went dead.

"At 4:30 in the morning, I came off my last watch. Staff Sergeant Smith took over; I gave him my wrist watch. It had been quiet except for a spurt now and then from the burp gun. I crawled into the dugout with Smollon and prepared to get a little sleep. [It seemed] I had just settled down when all of a sudden the Jerries opened up with 88s. Their shelling soon reached a deafening crescendo. We had to stick in the dugout and 'sweat it out.' Sometime after dawn, about three hours later, the barrage stopped as suddenly as it had begun. There were a few minutes of silence, then [Smollon], who was nearest the entrance, said he heard a sound outside. He poked his head out in order to see over the top of the dugout. 'They're here!' The Jerries were almost directly on top of us. I couldn't say with certainty just how many were about us, perhaps twenty; each one was armed with an automatic weapon.

They immediately spotted Smollon. We had little choice but to accept capture. Our disadvantage had been the location of the outpost. We were just 50 yards or so below the crest of a reverse slope (about half that distance was inside the forest line)."

2nd Lt. Robert Dettor of K Company's 3rd Platoon was in the same command post area as the 2nd Platoon. He wrote in his diary: "0540–0640: Artillery concentration on position. Artillery reported to company command post. Last conversation with command post. I reported sound of tank motors. 0640–1230: Small-arms firefight. Sent runner to company command post for reinforcements. Runner returned, stating no reinforcements, stay on position, and continue fighting. Communications to command post and outposts cut. No contact with men except those in foxholes in immediate vicinity. Sergeant Phifer, Sergeant Sutorka, myself fighting from same emplacement. Sergeant Sutorka moved to foxhole on right to cover flank. Sergeant Phifer covering right flank and rear.

"I ordered to destroy all letters, situation map site. Map burned by Stan Colby, runner, at my command post. Corporal Gardner reported left flank cut off by German infantry. German troops to rear. Heavy machine gun to front seen captured. Private Hunter dropped back to my foxhole to state that heavy machine gun to front had fallen. Sergeant Sutorka yelled over grenade being thrown at my foxhole. Hunter hit by grenade. Sergeant Phifer wounded in shoulder by rifle bullet. Enemy closing within twenty feet of foxhole. Took last report of ammunition. Sergeant Seifner had one clip left; I had four rounds. Burp gun to left rear firing at my foxhole hitting Hunter; I believe Hunter was dead. After first wound, Hunter had continued fighting. Sergeant Phifer reported he was almost out of ammunition early in fire fight. Ordered runner to throw box of D bars (chocolate) to my foxhole, which I distributed to men in immediate vicinity—last American food. At approximately 12:30 P.M., position overrun. German medics treated German wounded during firefight—carried pistols. I believed I would be shot. Ordered out of foxhole and kicked by German soldier."

K Company was left with part of one rifle platoon and two of its mortar squads. Its machine-gun section and one mortar squad had been overrun. Plume had tried to counterattack to the positions held by his 2nd and 3rd Platoons but met such stiff resistance that he was forced to fall back to the area around his company command post. There he held on while the Germans (the 989th Grenadier Regiment), who apparently had come down the road from Hollerath, swept on around his positions to the west.

Meanwhile, when the battalion commander, Lt. Col. Jack G. Allen, learned that K Company was in such a desperate situation, he ordered the

The 277th Volksgrenadier Division Attacks

battalion reserve, L Company's 2nd Platoon, under 2nd Lt. Peter Jenkisson, to withdraw to the original battalion reserve position behind K Company. This order was given at about 0815. The platoon reached its positions at about 0900, in the vicinity of the kitchen and supply sections. Just about this time then, as they were starting to dig in and prepare for a defense, they were hit hard by a large enemy force of infantry which had apparently crashed through from the east. The platoon was caught at a disadvantage and was shot up badly, disorganized, and suffered what were estimated at about 25 percent casualties. As soon as he found out about this new threat, Allen immediately ordered the rest of L Company to move over to assist the mauled 2nd Platoon in the same place. Previously, not knowing the full extent of the enemy strength, he had left both I and L Companies in their original positions on the left. He knew, however, from radio messages sent by regiment—with whom he had managed to maintain contact—that the situation in his immediate sector was grave since B Company of the 1st Battalion on his right had also been hit and overrun.

PFC Jack Pricket of L Company describes the situation: "Our sergeants passed the word that we were going back to the battalion headquarters area which was under attack. Miller and I talked some, wondering what fate had in store for us; we knew our misery and animal-like life was probably going to get much worse. Les reminded me that we had both promised not to take any unnecessary risks. We were both scared. We were in much better shape than many in our platoon, because we tried to take care of our bodies as best we could. I was raised on a farm in Oklahoma, and we went hunting as kids; we spent all day walking the hills and creeks. Les and I both were among the top shooters in the battalion. Infantry combat is not for country, or a cause; it is first of all for your buddies, your comrades, even the bastards you have in your company or battalion; after all, they are your own bastards. It is for pride, to show that you have what it takes when all is on the line, even your life, if need be. Scared? Afraid? You damned well better believe we were. But you have to overcome that if you hope to stay alive.

"We crossed Olef Creek almost directly after we came down from Rath Hill. We reached our old reserve positions we had just left on the fifteenth. Many of the foxholes had direct hits and were totally destroyed. Our hole was one of those that was hit. God was with us. We had scouts out in front and on both sides. We turned right, parallel to the trail from Krinkelt, about 100 to 150 yards off it. In some places you could see the trail through the trees. We assumed a more combat formation with full squads on each flank. My squad was sent out to the left, toward the trail. That would be where the Huns would most likely be coming from. The main body of the company advanced toward the old reserve position headquarters. We were to advance slowly to protect our flank.

"The company was soon out of our sight; we moved slowly when bullets came flying through our area. The sounds of a fire fight, apparently involving our company, raged for a few minutes, and we could hear the screams of people who were hit. When the bullets had started hitting in our area, we all hit the ground. We were spread out 5 to 10 yards apart; I could not see Miller or anyone. No one was talking; I was in an old foxhole; in about 5 minutes I crawled out and got behind a tree. I raised up to look, and my light field pack knocked my helmet down over my eyes. I finally adjusted it so I could see. More bullets came flying through; I asked Miller if he could see where they were coming from; he said he could not tell. Another big fire fight started, and then big shells landed in the area toward the main company area. One man started screaming; it went on, and on, and on. I later learned that this was a rocket, or several rockets that hit the old command post of L Company. Captain Fogleman had a fragment hit in the calf of his leg. T/Sgt. Alfred J. Sivertsen was killed, and 1st Sgt. Jack H. Mesarvey's leg was almost severed. A German doctor completed amputating the leg. A few others were wounded."

The Germans were pushing very aggressively against this part of the front, and it was not long before they had worked in as far as the area in front of M Company's command post, which was 200 yards to the east of the battalion command post, just across a dirt trail which ran in a general northwest-southeast direction between the two command post. The Germans had hit and folded back K Company and were on the command post front by about 0915 or 0930. By this time, the relieving platoon from L Company had been hit, too, and had retreated to the west side of this dirt trail. Every available man—mortar men, cooks, and headquarters personnel—had been thrown in front of the positions and all were fighting desperately. The situation was greatly confused, but the defenders fired their small arms and mortars at point-blank range, effectively holding the enemy off, although he infiltrated around both flanks and continued moving to the rear.

Thus, by the time the remainder of L Company came up, the Germans had pushed on through and around the position, and in effect, had isolated it. To relieve the beleaguered force, the two L Company platoons had to fight their way to them, establishing contact by about 1015. But the Germans were determined to press on to the west in this sector, and it was only about fifteen minutes later that they again hit the position, this time from the flanks. A fire fight started, and they tried to hold out; but apparently, feeling that his forces were too far out on a limb, and realizing that his best defense lay in closely-knit force, the battalion commander ordered this group to drop back to form a defense line around the battalion command post. Then, with the assistance of artillery and mortar fire support, the Germans were held off until about 1100.

PFC Jack Pricket recalls: "In the firefight, L Company killed a number of Germans and captured fourteen. Talking to friends that were there, we also rescued several GIs that had been captured. We pulled in from the flank and walked through the area of the fight. Close to the trail we had to crawl to stay out of sight of Germans who were now on both ends of the Schwarzenbruch trail. I nearly crawled right over three dead Germans. They looked very young, but they were trying to kill us. They looked like wax, not real. As we crossed the trail we were staring at clerks, runners and other battalion people who normally never had to fight. They had a blank look, what came to be called the '1,000-yard stare.' They look at you but don't see you. We didn't think about it, but we probably had the same stare. A lot of men and boys had died today, and more would before this is over. We passed the thin line of foxholes and down the side trail to the battalion headquarters area where we were sent east about 100–150 yards and told to start digging. Being that close to the 3rd Battalion command post, we almost felt like the 'Palace Guard.'"

At about 1100 hours, Lieutenant Colonel Allen decided to pull in his I Company, which was still too far out to the north. He ordered them to move to the west first and then to try to enter the original battalion reserve position formerly occupied by L Company's 2nd Platoon from the north. This would pull all his companies closer together and establish a perimeter defense.

The I Company commander wasted no time in complying and promptly started his company moving out in a column of platoons, in the order of 1st, 2nd, 3rd and Weapons. They had just about reached the draw when the leading elements were fired upon, and the column was stopped. One of the leading scouts was killed and the other wounded. The rest of the 1st Platoon was pinned down by small-arms fire. The remainder of the company took cover.

PFC Gilbert Clift, a scout in I Company tells his story: "In my platoon were Andy Andrews, Merrell Richardson, and Norris Northington, all of whom had been at Huntsville [ASTP]. I was a rifleman in a squad of twelve people, with three squads to a platoon. We used the buddy system, and because of the snow, rain, poor footwear, and living twenty-four hours a day outdoors, my buddy got trench foot and pneumonia and went off to the hospital. Our sleeping accommodations were a four-by-seven log-covered pit three feet deep, reminding me of the cave in Winfield. Our boots, leggings, gloves, and overcoat were grossly inadequate. My replacement buddy was a cook—or so he said—and kept saying he shouldn't be up on the front line.

As I was fixing him a place in our hole, a shot rang out. He had put his rifle down on his shoe and shot through the foot. Off he went to limp the rest of his life.

"You may not have ever thought of hearing the call of nature while in the woods in zero-degree weather day after day. It's not pleasant. I was then given a slightly built eighteen-year-old Catholic boy from Pittsburgh named Joe Piechowiak. He was nice but quiet. We had been together four or five days when the Battle of the Bulge started. Early before dawn on 16 December, a terrific artillery barrage started and lasted for about two hours. From our position on the front line we couldn't tell which way the shells were going. All we could hear was the whistling of shells overhead. About midmorning we were told to withdraw from our position and pull back to regroup with others. The first sergeant said we had lost contact with the company (L Company) on our right. Radios were out. He pointed to me and said, 'You're first scout,' and to my buddy, 'You're second scout.' 'Go that-a-way—we'll follow.'

"We hadn't gone far when rifle shots sang past us. We hit the ground. I managed to slide into a shallow foxhole, and Joe, my buddy, got behind a tree. Snow was about a foot deep and crusty. I realized my hole wasn't that much protection from rifle fire, only visually. Like we always did on maneuvers, I said, 'Flank them to the left,' as I could see I was facing a squad of ten or twelve Germans thirty or forty yards away behind some fallen trees. I would raise up and fire three or four shots and duck back down. I heard Joe cry out and start to say his rosary. I realized that the only shots from my side were mine. The Germans were throwing concussion grenades at my position and sooner or later would get one close to me. I thought of the only phrase I could recall, in German, and hollered out, 'Hilfen sie mir'—'Help me.' They approached, my hands went up, and that was the end of my soldiering. They removed my helmet, an indication I was out of the game, and my watch and led me to a log house where ten men from L Company were held.

"I had completed my mission. I'd found part of L Company, and they were prisoners. I learned later that my buddy Joe was killed."

When this was reported to battalion, Allen ordered the I Company commander to pull back, cover the withdrawal of the 1st Platoon with fire from the next platoon in line, and then to swing the whole company around to the west again, and attempt to come in close behind the battalion command post as the reserve. This was done. The company worked its way to the assigned position, which was in the rear of the command post, and was held as a mobile reserve. In moving down originally, it had come though parts of the same area where L Company had run into its fight earlier, only to find no

Germans there; and the presumption was that the Germans had continued on to the west, leaving their rear exposed. But, when they did run into the Germans, it was on the left flank and left rear of the command post. This indicated that the enemy might be trying to outflank the whole position.

At 1400, regiment informed Allen that he was going to be reinforced with I Company of the 394th Infantry, and he was told to send guides to help this outfit reach his position. This was done. The guides went to the RJ, where they met the men of the 393rd and led them through the woods to the 3rd Battalion sector, arriving about 1600. But before I Company of the 394th arrived, the enemy had renewed his attack in front of M Company. It was necessary to put two platoons of I Company into this line to help hold off the new threat. The company fared pretty well, but it was 6 to 8 percent understrength and so was not the strongest possible help.

When this thrust was stopped, the enemy settled down for the day. The colonel organized his companies in a tight, all-round defense of the command post area, with a hodge-podge from the battalion and company headquarters (A&P platoon, the cooks, the antitank platoon) holding on part of the perimeter, with I and L Companies tied in with them. K Company was in the rear of the area, and I Company was in reserve immediately around the command post. All of them dug in.

PFC Jack Pricket picks up the story: "We heard that the kitchen crew had been ambushed near Olef creek by the Germans. Word soon spread that K Company had been just about destroyed. At first only eleven came back. Forty plus did make it back, with tales of wounded being shot and/or bayoneted. Digging was again very hard with the tiny shovels that we had. We did go at it because we had seen what was needed. The field that we were in was not great for defense because of the tree stumps and trash on the ground. A person could crawl almost to our foxhole before we might see him! We checked for ammo and only found a few clips. Every one was running low on ammo. The situation for 3rd Battalion on the evening of the sixteenth was as follows: K was left with two officers and forty-five men. L lost Captain Fogleman and Lt. Charles McNulty and Lt. Richard Burns to wounds along with twenty men. I retained all its officers and 150 men. M Company lost one weapons platoon plus Lt. Joseph Mallon, leaving M with ninety officers and men. L Company was placed into the perimeter defense, with two platoons right next to the main trail back to Krinkelt. Lieutenant Burns's 3rd Platoon was west of the trail to 3rd Battalion headquarters, curving back toward Olef Creek.

"Across the battalion trail was Lieutenant Oliver's platoon, with one squad (McGarity's) along the Krinkelt trail, facing north like most of Burns's squads. The next squad of Oliver was facing east at ninety degrees to McGarity, with the next platoon of L facing east, just south of Oliver. Lieutenant Jenkisson had this platoon. I was in this platoon about 100 to 150 yards east of battalion headquarters. This positioning, especially those squads on the trail toward Krinkelt, would have to face German armor without any means of defense except for a few bazookas. Another problem was that not all the foxholes were dug deep enough to offer real protection, plus being too close to the trail. Regardless, this is where these squads had to make their stand on the seventeenth. Not many got any sleep on the night of the sixteenth."

Lt. Wingolf Scherer of the 990th Grenadier Regiment of the 277th Volksgrenadier Regiment describes what the Germans were experiencing: "By the afternoon the point troops had reached the Jansbach, but were not able to cross it. (Between Dreiherrenwald and Wolferst the Jansbach runs roughly parallel to the 'Reich' road and flows into the Olef stream). The 1st Panzer Corps attached the 1st Panzergrenadier Battalion of the 25th Panzergrenadier Regiment of the SS Panzer Division *Hitlerjugend* to the 277th Volksgrenadier Division to open up advance axis A across the Jansbach in the direction of Rocherath-Krinkelt and to expand the penetration into a breakthrough. By 1230 hours, the battalion, under command of SS Capt. A. Ott, entered the fray. The grenadier companies advanced on Rocherath south of the forest track; all too soon the heavy weapons and vehicles remained bogged down in the completely muddied roads. After crossing the Olef by 1730 hours, the west edge of the woods was reached. Here fire from security parties of the 393rd out of Rocherath set in. The battalion commander—out of touch with the 989th Grenadier Regiment—tried in vain to get orders. As the enemy was slowly feeling its way forward against the battalion, Ott decided to withdraw, which, according to Kurt Meyer, took place in the early-morning hours of the seventeenth."

There were no more attempts by the Germans for the rest of that day or night after about 1630 hours. The 3rd Battalion, 393rd Infantry, had managed to get its mortars set up and had tied in with the artillery. Every time the Germans made a suspicious move, or appeared to be gathering for anything which might resemble an attack or a raid, the suspected areas were peppered with shells. The enemy responded with desultory and sporadic mortar fire, but none of it was of more than a harrying nature.

When night fell, it was possible to start evaluating the results of the day's actions. The enemy had hit the battalion very hard, but had paid a high price. The battalion's lines had been bent back and one of its companies almost destroyed. The others had been heavily engaged. The present positions were in pretty good shape. M Company, before folding back, reported that its machine guns had piled up 200 to 300 German dead in front of its positions and had caused so many casualties that the screaming of the German wounded could be heard throughout the day and into the night.

The day's fighting left K Company with only two officers and forty-five enlisted men. One enlisted man of K Company managed to hide out until after dark. He then worked his way back to the battalion command post, where he reported that Captain Plume had been captured and that the platoon leaders were killed. During the afternoon, 1st Lt. Felix W. Salmaggi, who had been executive officer of I Company, was placed in command of K Company. The company's two remaining original officers, 1st Lt. John W. Fisher, the executive officer, and Lieutenant Dickman remained with it. L Company that night was left with three officers and 130 men. It had started with a full complement of officers and 165 enlisted men. The reshuffling of command affected them, too, since Capt. Paul V. Fogleman, the L Company commander, was seriously wounded, and the two platoon leaders, 1st Lt. Charles McNulty of the 4th Platoon and 2nd Lt. Richard Burn of the 3rd Platoon, were wounded. After Fogleman had been hit, 1st Lt. Rolland K. Neudecker, the executive officer, took over.

I Company, under Capt. William B. Coke, was in good shape with about 150 enlisted men and all of its officers. M Company had lost practically all of its machine-gun platoon, including the commander, 1st Lt. Joseph W. Mallon, who was missing in action as a result of the Germans overrunning K Company's positions, where Mallon had his guns sited. M Company had about ninety men and the rest of the officers left. Headquarters Company had lost five missing and seven wounded, but it still had all of its officers.

During the afternoon, I Company had captured two prisoners. L Company had taken fourteen others. Some of these were killed and wounded by German artillery and mortar fire as they were being taken back to the rear. McElroy, the 3rd Battalion's S-3, said that although they were not positive of the exact situation on their flanks during the sixteenth, information obtained from these prisoners revealed that a general attack was being made all along the line by the Germans.

Despite the earlier report that none of the men of K Company had gotten out, McElroy said that several of these men drifted in to the battalion later on, and still others rejoined at Elsenborn, having fought with other units along the way. Thus it is evident that some of the men of the battalion straggled back when they were first hit by the Germans on the morning of the sixteenth. Then, at about 1900 that night, regiment issued orders for the battalion to be prepared to attack the following morning with the mission of restoring the original K Company position. At the same time regiment warned that they must be prepared for possible further enemy attacks with an estimated force of about two battalions of infantry in their sector. With that in mind the battalion commander went ahead with his plans to make the attack in the morning, while trying not to weaken or endanger his present positions. During the night, it had generally been quiet at the front. In an unspoken agreement, medics from both sides recovered wounded at the area of the Reich road.

In the morning, the fighting flared up again. After I Company of the 394th had reinforced the encircled 3rd Battalion of the 393rd in the afternoon of the previous day, it launched an attack at 0800 toward the west and was able to open its supply road back to Rocherath.

SITUATION AT THE FRONT LINE IN THE SECTOR OF THE 99TH INFANTRY DIVISION

After a few initial successes on the morning of the sixteenth, the Germans' attack in the wooded and rolling terrain got stuck in the sector of Buchholz Station and the Dreiherrenwald. The advance did not proceed according to the plans of the German strategists. By midday, none of the planned Rollbahnen had been opened for the SS panzer divisions of the I SS Panzer Corps, which had been kept in reserve for just such an event. By 1400 hours, I SS Panzer Corps decided to send in a battalion of the 12th SS Panzer Division *Hitlerjugend* on the right of the 277th Volksgrenadier Division's sector, in the forest of Dreiherrenwald, where the Volksgrenadiers were to breach the American defenses.

Until nightfall, bitter fighting continued, but the German troops managed to gain little ground. That evening, the 12th SS was ordered to exploit the breach in the Dreiherrenwald and to renew the attack using tanks as early as possible the next morning. The lack of bridges on the railroad track, leading through a deep cut in the ground, was the main cause why the battle in this southern sector remained an affair for infantrymen.

The two grenadier regiments had seen their combat strength whittled down significantly during the first day and they reorganized during the night. Under pressure by his superiors, who demanded a quick advance, General Engel of the 12th Volksgrenadier Division decided to continue the attack with an unchanged combat formation. The 48th Grenadier Regiment of Colonel Osterhold was to continue with a frontal assault while the 27th Fusilier Regiment of Lt. Col. Heinz-Georg Lemm was to advance to the south of the crossroads in the direction of Hünningen. The 89th Grenadier Regiment under Col. Gerhard Lemcke was to deploy farther to the front in the woods of Gerolstein, east of Frauenkron, in order to support the attacks

The 277th Volksgrenadier Division Attacks 113

Heinz-Georg Lemm. KAMERAD-SCHAFT FUSILIER RGT. 27/M. STEGLICH

by the 48th Grenadier Regiment. During this time, the sappers of the 12th Engineer Battalion worked without pause to build a bridge crossing the Losheim railroad cut. The motorized force of Maj. Günther Holz stood by to intervene as soon as the engineers finished their work.

By daylight on 17 December, the Americans held a fairly continuous but thinly manned front with the 1st Battalion of the 394th Infantry around Losheimergraben, part of the 3rd Battalion west of the village, and the 1st Battalion of the 23rd Infantry (2nd Infantry Division) holding the exposed right-flank position in Hünningen. On the first day of the offensive, the soldiers of the 12th Volksgrenadier Division did not manage to break into the defense of Losheimergraben Crossroads. Farther south, the German assault had struck furiously at the weak force of the 14th Cavalry Group, which had been attached to the U.S. 106th Infantry Division.

The cavalry group was driven off, and contact between the 99th and 106th Divisions was broken. At noon on the sixteenth, the Germans decided to exploit this success by launching the armored combat group of the 1st SS Panzer Division—*Kampfgruppe Peiper* under Jochen Peiper. Because of bottlenecks and tailbacks on the roads—which were not designed for military convoys—the head of Peiper's column did not reach the battlefield until midnight. After a short stop at Lanzerath, Peiper advanced along the Lanzerath-Honsfeld road.

In the night, the menacing roar of the tanks was clearly audible to the defenders of Losheimergraben. Before dawn, at about five o'clock, the column of tanks and other vehicles reached Buchholz Station. Not able to do anything to oppose these mastodons that appeared all of a sudden out of the murk, the defenders of Buchholz Station fled into the woods and impotently watched the column pass on the road in the direction of Honsfeld. Had they continued, the Germans could have completely overrun Losheimergraben. Luckily for the Americans, they did not.

CHAPTER 9

Losheimergraben Is Lost

On the morning of 17 December, the 12th Volksgrenadier Division renewed its attack on the defenses of the Losheimergraben Crossroads. The main German attack came up the road and draws from Buchholz Station, after having come north from Lanzerath. In a southerly direction, the 27th Fusilier Regiment advanced on foot toward Buchholz while profiting from every dip in the terrain—an advance that had not been foreseen by the Americans. Contrary to what had been supposed, L and K Companies of the 3rd Battalion—each reduced in strength to about fifty men—were located a bit farther to the west. A powerful German assault group managed to infiltrate the gap between the 1st and 3rd Battalions, and reached the main route from Losheimergraben to Büllingen. Other elements pushed farther forward in the direction of the two battalion command posts, which were unprotected by any friendly troops to their front (south) or west.

All available men at the 3rd Battalion command post were organized into a hasty defensive position. By about 1100 hours, Lieutenant Colonel Douglas informed the regimental commander over the SCR radio—the only means of communications usable during the fighting—that he had one squad consisting of some A Company headquarters personnel and a few miscellaneous riflemen left as his battalion maneuvering force. No orders had as yet been received for the battalions to withdraw; although by this time, elements of the German attacking force were considerably west and north of these positions, and had attacked Büllingen and were driving on toward Dom Bütgenbach.

At about noon, the Germans, heavily armed with automatic weapons, advanced to about 100 meters from Colonel Douglas's command post. A little earlier Colonel Douglas, accompanied by Capt. John S. Sandiland, had left the battalion to check on the situation. On the north side of the road and about 100 yards southeast, the regiment's antitank company was attempting to pull out of a bivouac area onto the road to withdraw. They were receiving direct small arms and automatic weapons fire from Germans who had infiltrated to the main road not more than 100 yards southeast of the antitank company's bivouac area.

Sgt. William Kirkbride of the antitank company describes the situation: "In the dawn of 17 December, we heard the noise of a new action all around us, tanks were moving south of our location and behind us. The commander of B Company crossed to our position, coming from the front. He told us the front had been completely broken through, and he had been the only one that got out of his command post. Our telephone was out of order, and we were in need of new orders. Our staff sergeant returned, and he decided to go to the command post of our platoon commander to get orders and information. About noon, we took our Dodge 6 x 6 and moved north towards Losheimergraben, where we turned right and right again, and we parked between two houses. Nearly fifteen boys of various units were already there. Together with our squad that was about twenty-five men. When we went into the cellar of the customs house there was a very young looking boy lying down with his face on the earth, in the uniform of a second lieutenant. Nobody knew who he was. The others said he did not want to talk to anyone, and they thought he was upset. I sat down on the floor and talked quietly into his ear. He turned his head and looked at me but did not say a word. He neither wept nor trembled; he simply looked at me for a moment. Once I had verified that he had not been physically wounded nor was in a state of shock, I decided to leave him alone as he was in no condition to lead us. We established a defensive perimeter and waited. No one seemed to know what to do."

The battalion command posts were being overrun. As the colonel and Captain Sandiland left the command post, they met the battalion S-2, 1st Lt. George A. Reynolds, who was returning from the regimental command post in Hünningen with orders for withdrawal. He had been sent up earlier in the morning, taking with him Douglas's plan for withdrawal in the event it should become necessary. The battalion was ordered to withdraw and take up the previously prepared dug-in positions in an area around Hünningen and Mürringen covering a front of some 5,500 yards. This position was well known to the men in the battalion since they had helped to prepare it.

The 1st Battalion, 394th Infantry, began to retreat to Mürringen by 1530 hours. To the east, at the crossroads itself, the remains of the 1st Battalion were still engaged in fierce combat, as they had been since dawn. Lieutenant Colonel Douglas decided to warn his men in person and so went to the crossroads.

S/Sgt. Carl W. Combs of B Company, who was inside one of the buildings at the crossroads, reports: "Lieutenant Colonel Douglas ordered a retreat in order to try to reach Hünningen. At the same moment Douglas arrived, PFC James A. Cutter entered the house in search of extra munitions, and Douglas asked him and his ammo server to cover the retreat with their bazooka and afterwards catch up with the main force. Jim and I shook hands before he returned to the other side of the road, losing his .45 pistol in the road. I thought he was killed when he stopped to recover it slowly and with caution. It was the last time I saw him."

While this action was going on northwest of Losheimergraben, a composite force under 1st Lt. Dewey A. Plankers was holding solidly onto the crossroads at the town itself, denying this important road junction to the Germans. His force consisted of about two half-strength platoons of C Company (the ones which had been sent on the previous afternoon to pinch off the penetration into B Company), the fifteen remaining men of B Company, the crew of one knocked-out regimental antitank gun, a few jeep drivers whose vehicles had been knocked out by the enemy barrage, and a few wire men—for a total of about fifty men.

Earlier in the morning, this composite force had been holding dug-in positions about 200 yards southeast of Losheimergraben. These positions were hit at about daylight (0700 hours) from the front and the left flank where the Germans had infiltrated into the salient created the previous day in the B Company sector. This initial German force was estimated at approximately 100 men and was considered to be a strong combat patrol sent to probe the line. After a sharp fight, this force was driven back to the southeast. Another force then struck around to the west of these positions, hitting A Company's positions and the 3rd Battalion.

Staff Sergeant Hilliard, who was in the cellar of the building just east of the crossroads, takes up the story: "We hugged the walls of the cellar while the shells of their artillery struck the walls of the ground floor and shook the walls of the cellar; this, together with the shock of the explosions, followed by the fire and smoke, were so intense that they were hardly bearable. The German gunners continued their artillery fire and increased its volume and power while we tried to protect ourselves as well as possible in the cellar of the building. The firing stopped as suddenly as it started, and we knew that they had come to mount the assault. Suddenly, shouts and cries were audible in the German positions; at that moment the enemy stood up in the snow and advanced, in great number, in our direction. Those in the first rank were clothed in white camouflage for the snow. The attack came in from all sides, even from the wooded area. Their machine guns fired without ceasing from the woods, and their projectiles crashed through the windows and exploded behind us. When at length the German infantry closed for the attack, we were able to distinguish certain faces. Many among them looked as young, clean, and strong as the majority of us. Our men opened fire, and when they reached our crossfire, they stopped in their tracks, spread their arms and fell backwards onto the frozen soil. We have beaten off the attackers, wave after wave. Our losses turned out to be four men, but their losses must have been counted in tens."

At about midday, the Germans advanced to make contact again. An assault force of about a reinforced company, supported by assault guns, attacked the men of Lieutenant Plankers. This was the motorized battalion, under Maj. Günther Holz, of the 12th Volksgrenadier Division, which finally had crossed the railroad at Losheim. Holz's unit had been on standby since the morning of 16 December. Major Holz was dismissed to take charge of his unit. Everything having been discussed, the general dismissed his officers. In the meantime, a report had come from Captain Meyer that the first echelon had passed the jam. The combat formation was begun. Three Sturmgeschütze with accompanying infantry took over the point followed by two double-barrelled 2-centimeter guns of the flak company. Behind them the small command staff followed, accompanied by its dispatch riders, then the main force, in which are included the signals unit to maintain contact between the division and the units, and finally for all eventualities, a small rearguard to secure the tankers and ammunition vehicles. The tension among these men was at its highest; X-hour had come. The hours passed, and still no decision had been forced. Holz's unit stood without doing anything, the point had driven through Losheim and stopped at the edge of the wood. The short winter's day came to an end; it became cold, but there was no possibility of getting cover anywhere. The noise of battle disappeared almost completely.

Günther Holz.
F. RIESER

According to Major Holz, "The silence of the enemy artillery in our sector was amazing; until then it had barely intervened in the battle. The fear of large-scale attacks by the American air force had proven unfounded until now as well. In the morning we had witnessed large aerial battles in the distance, but it was sadly seen that the enemy was superior, and our fighters suffered heavy losses. As the day wore on the low clouds became so dense that we had nothing to fear anymore.

"The night seemed endless, but passed in the end. The dawn found the soldiers frozen through and tired, but far from downcast. The noise of battle rose again, very strongly behind us on the left flank. In front of us on the street, nothing could be spotted of the enemy. The young platoon commander of the 2nd Assault Gun Company came up with his boss, Lieutenant Schäfer, and asked permission to carry out a reconnaissance of a piece of road towards Losheimergraben with one tank and an infantry escort. He got his permission, but was only allowed to advance to the next curve in the forest road, escorted by an infantry group and followed by the second Sturmgeschütz. We observed the ride on a long straight part of the road and saw that the assault gun drove into the curve. At the same moment the hard detonation of an antitank gun sounded, a strong explosion followed and clouds rose up, at the same time machine guns stuttered. The commander and Lieutenant Schäfer drove up quickly, the tank was afire, ammunition was cooking off, and of the crew only the lieutenant had managed to get out of the hatch and was lying on the street severely wounded. Also the escorting infantry, led by an officer, had been shot up, the lieutenant and some of his men had fallen, the rest were wounded. The second assault gun had halted immediately. Under cover of its fire we succeeded in recovering the wounded. We had run into the second defense line of the enemy."

Alarmed by the noise of battle, the commander of the 48th Infantry Regiment, Lieutenant Colonel Osterhold, had come forward. Next to the street, under the cover of trees, a further operation plan was drawn up. But first the American positions had to be reconnoitered thoroughly. Both the regimental commander and Osterhold decided to reconnoiter for themselves. On the right side they worked themselves forward through the ditch. From here, in the woods to the right, enemy bunkers could be made out. To the left of the road a bunker with a big firing slit could be made out. Both commanders returned unhurt to the waiting company commanders. The decision was made to attack the rightmost bunker first with a platoon of the 48th Infantry Regiment. The men advanced carefully from the flank and rear to the position and were able to overwhelm the opponents. The bunker with the dangerous antitank gun was in now in German hands.

Major Holz recalls: "In the meantime, the enemy from another position had spotted our location and opened fire with mortars. The shells exploded overhead in the treetops. Lieutenant Schäfer crumpled without a sound, a splinter had penetrated his steel helmet and killed him. Three officers and several brave NCOs and soldiers lost in less than an hour; that was hard. The infantry was now sent against the left bunker determinedly. As the enemy on the right had been knocked out, the company commander with a strong group advanced quickly on the right; beyond it the ground sloped down sharply. We quickly crossed the street and were in the rear of the bunker. The first lieutenant, an old veteran of Russia, quietly and secure of himself, crawled up to the bunker and around it until he reached the slit, his hand grenade ready for throwing. A sure throw, a muffled explosion, and the bunker had been knocked out. From the road we could observe this brave action at a short distance."

The crew of the American antitank gun managed to escape, blasting themselves out through the enemy troops, and managed to rejoin the defenders in the immediate vicinity of the Losheimergraben Crossroads.

Holz continues his story: "Now the vehicles immediately were brought forward, a new point was formed and we assembled. Lieutenant Colonel Osterhold wanted to accompany us in his jeep for a while. We advanced without any incidents, until the woods opened up on the left and showed a group of houses: Losheimergraben. In the meantime, along the street we also

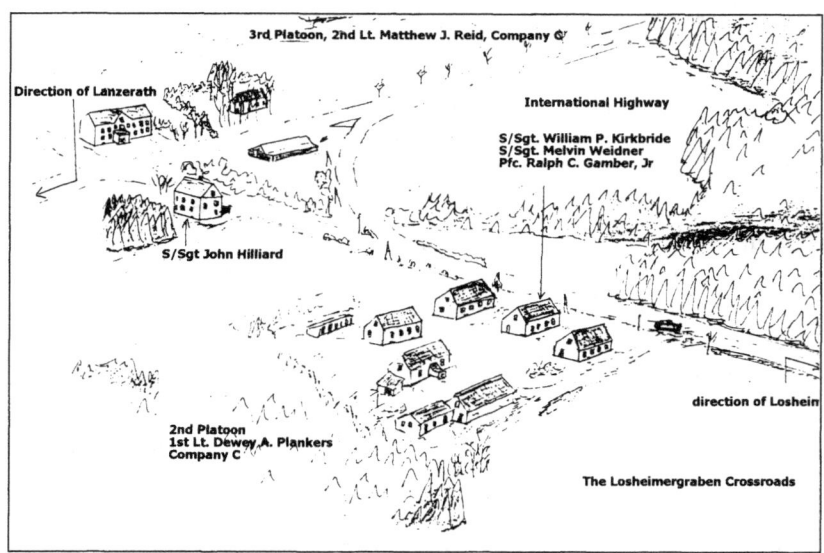

Drawing showing locations of American soldiers. F. RIESER

found the abandoned mortar position; the enemy had abandoned his weapons. Our vehicles had hardly left the cover of the woods when they were taken under machine gun fire from the houses on the left. With the binoculars it could be barely made out that some cellars had been fortified and had firing slits instead of windows. The 2-centimenter guns were brought up and opened fire, and in direct fire on the firing slits all enemy weapons were knocked out in a matter of minutes. The assault guns advanced; the first one had nearly reached the group of houses close to the road when the driver spotted a thick belt of mines that blocked the entire width of the road. The assault gun stopped; at the same moment, an antitank gun [actually a bazooka] fired from one of the first houses, where the cellars likewise had been converted to concrete bunkers. The assault gun received several hits; one track was destroyed, but it did not take fire. The men succeeded to get out of the vehicle safely and to take cover in the ditch beside the road. To the right of the street there still were woods. As the Americans had not secured them, our infantry advanced determinedly under the cover of trees, arrived on the flank of the fortifications and broke all resistance by destroying them. But still the open mine belt lay on the road and stopped any further advance. Sadly, we did not have any engineers at our disposal. Lieutenant Colonel Osterhold quickly exchanged glances with Major Holz, then both each lifted a mine, carefully checked if it were booby trapped, and carried it to the ditch. Quickly, they went to the next one, even if the heart was beating in the throat, and soon the mine belt had been cleared up."

The second attack on Plankers's position began at about 1100 hours with at least three assault guns and an infantry force estimated to be a reinforced rifle company, possibly armored infantry. The composite force under Plankers withdrew after a sharp fight to the shelter of the buildings in Losheimergraben, because twenty men of the force lacked effective weapons. They had pistols, but rifles and carbines were needed. Plankers radioed back on his radio an urgent request for additional weapons and ammunition. Carbines, M1s, and any other available small arms weapons were piled onto the sole available jeep, which belonged to the chaplain. His driver, an assistant, and an infantryman, Cpl. Frederick S. Cornell, drove the jeep forward voluntarily under intense small-arms fire all the way into town, delivering the much needed weapons to Plankers's group. This was at about 1130 or 1200. Very shortly afterward, the defenders discovered the first assault gun, coming from the direction of Losheim.

According to Robert W. Jones, a scout in the 2nd Platoon of C Company, "We were deployed in a row of houses in a large open area with a single road leading to a heavy stand of trees. The initial attack was led by assault guns. Two of our men managed to destroy one assault gun and disable another. However, that was not enough. Under cover of the assault gun, the German infantry advanced and lobbed concussion grenades."

The Germans approached the building occupied by S/Sgt. Melvin J. Weidner, who remembers: "The Germans bypassed the crossroads by the sectors of A and B Companies until about the afternoon, when a tank [assault gun] approached our building. We only had one bazooka and eight rounds at our disposal, but none of us knew how to serve the weapon. I had been to the rear several days to transport munitions, and on that occasion I had fired a bazooka once. Therefore I took the weapon and said that I needed an assistant. One man, whom we called 'Pap' because he was forty-eight years old [S/Sgt. William P. Kirkbride of the antitank company], answered that he would help me. Pap took the weapon while I loaded it with a round and pressed the trigger. I told him to aim over tank tracks, so it would hit between the tracks. I don't know whether the first round hit the tank . . . at least it hit it? We fired a second round, and a cloud of smoke appeared through all the openings of the tank. When the crew bailed out of the tank, they were fired on by the other people. Subsequently, we fired at the following tank, but it stayed at the edge of the forest outside the range of our weapon."

The German assault guns did not approach the crossroads during most of the afternoon, because of bazooka fire. Instead, they sat off from the town beyond bazooka range, and shelled all the buildings from which any sign of fight was shown. The small town was virtually leveled. Plankers and his men took shelter in the basement of the blasted buildings. The German pressure grew more and more, and the situation for the Americans became more and more awkward. Despite everything, the small band of men under Lieutenant Plankers retained their positions. The fighting lasted until dusk.

Staff Sergeant Hilliard recalls: "Thanks to ditches and undulations in the rolling terrain, German infantry had managed to infiltrate near us. From there they used their machine guns at short distance, and thanks to the high number of machine pistols that were firing, we had trouble making out their individual locations. At one time the enemy stood up in the powdery snow and charged us. Their voices were strong, angry and grated on our nerves while they approached. Every man by now knew that no help would be arriving, but they never lost their hope and did not think about having to abandon their positions. Every man held on to his place with bayonets fixed, firing his rifle with deadly precision into the enemy ranks as they advanced. They threw their hand grenades through window openings on the first floor, and only one German managed to reach our positions, where he was killed with a bayonet."

The destroyed command post of D Company, 394th Infantry, on the road to Lanzerath. RAPHAEL D'AMIGO

After the Germans had overrun the command posts of the 1st and 3rd Battalions, the defensive coordination of the Americans became impossible. Therefore, in the afternoon, platoons of the various companies were operating independently of each other. The platoons of A Company continued the fight during the entire day in the woods south of the crossroads, and they did not begin to retreat until night set in. So the remains of A Company, under command of 1st Lt. Willard W. Clark, carved themselves a path through the woods and reached Hünningen, which was defended by the 23rd Infantry Regiment of the U.S. 2nd Infantry Division.

The company of Capt. Wesley J. Simmons ran into tremendous difficulties at about midday, when the survivors of the 1st Battalion began to retreat under enemy pressure. During the morning, two platoons of L Company were detached in order to be engaged in their old sector of Buchholz Station. With the troops that remained with Captain Simmons, an infantry platoon of only eighteen healthy men and a heavy weapons platoon, he had to defend a line of over 700 meters long. In the beginning of the afternoon, a company of German infantry ran into the troops of Captain Simmons. While completely running out of their reserve of mortar shells, Simmons's men managed to throw back the attackers. After this, Simmons retired his men about 100 meters in order to shorten his front line. Between 1400 and 1500 hours, his position underwent a severe bombardment by German artillery and mortars. Later, Simmons retired his troops once more. Indefatigably he tried to contact the battalion command post, but no messages reached their destination. Since shortly before, the field kitchen had withdrawn to Mürringen, Simmons judged it a good idea to retire to this village. It was during this move that he learned that a general withdrawal was being carried out.

According to Simmons, "K Company was not notified of the plans for the withdrawal of the 1st Battalion; in fact no information had been received from the 1st Battalion since the evening before. At about 1030 hours, troops could be seen withdrawing on either side of our position. It was learned eventually that they were elements of A and B Companies, and that they were withdrawing but didn't know where they were going. We discovered that during the night, 1st Battalion had changed their radio call signs and had not included K Company. Whenever attempts were made to contact them on our SCR 300 radio, no one would answer, and radio traffic would cease for long periods of time.

"At about 1300 hours K Company was attacked by an estimated two companies of infantry. The enemy was pinned down by automatic and mortar fire for about seven minutes, at the end of which time all of our mortar ammunition and most of our ball ammunition had been exhausted. Simultaneously, enemy mortar fire began landing in our area, and the Germans began rushing our position. We withdrew with only a few minor casualties for a distance of about 300 yards where a hasty defense was again resumed. The trees in this location had been planted in rows which afforded good firing lanes from which each man of K Company fired a final volley at the enemy as he came within close range. At this time it was necessary to abandon our mortars in order to withdraw quickly and to aid those who were wounded.

"We were unable to comprehend at this time the intensity of this attack by the Germans, which has now gone down in history as the 'Battle of the Bulge,' and we decided to withdraw to the north and northwest though a thick forest to Krinkelt in an effort to contact other friendly forces and to obtain a resupply of ammunition and food."

At 1730 hours, the German assault guns, still numbering no more than three or four, moved up the road into the town. One pulled along side of the building and stuck its muzzle towards an opening into the basement which housed Plankers and several men. The assault gun fired point-blank into the basement with armor-piercing ammunition. Apparently, they had run out of high explosive. At this point, Plankers heard over his radio that the 2nd Battalion of the 394th Infantry to his northeast was withdrawing. He attempted to contact A Company on his right (west), but he was not able to reach them. Since it was almost dark, he decided to withdraw to the prepared positions

Raymond Wenzel.

around Hünningen and Mürringen. Under enemy small-arms fire, he went from building to building, alerting his men of the plan to withdraw, led them to a covered position west of the town and formed a combat patrol (at this point he had roughly twenty men left). The patrol fought its way through groups of Germans in the dark, all the way back into Mürringen. The patrol reached friendly defensive positions by 2300 hours on 17 December.

PFC Raymond Wenzel of C Company, 394th Infantry, remembers: "The Germans began to close in. I was firing out of an upstairs window along with my sergeant I see tanks and infantry coming up the road from the east, and in no time they had us pinned down. I saw a tank put its barrel into the second story window in the house to my right and let go a blast. About the same time, soldiers were hollering to me and my sergeant, Lu Oram, 'Alles raus (everybody out).' I said, 'Let's stay hidden until they go away.' 'No,' he said, 'drop your rifle. We're going out.' As we got about thirty feet from the building, I turned and saw a tank [assault gun] let go a blast into the window I was firing from. This is when I got some shrapnel in my leg and hand. At around 5:00 P.M., I was taken across the road to be searched. We were interrogated, and they took my watch and overshoes. Lu got a rifle butt aside of his head as he tried to kill a German. They took him away, and I never saw him again until fifty-one years later. I was put under guard in one of the buildings."

At dusk, the buildings around the Losheimergraben Crossroads were mopped up by the Volksgrenadiers. The last GIs finally surrendered to the Germans, who were threatening to blow up the buildings with explosives.

After the war, Osterhold recalled: "When we finally had managed to get some fire support, we crossed the road and reached the first customs post. We were being shot at from the cellars. There were also hand grenades which were thrown at us. First we reorganized ourselves, and subsequently we only fired at the windows, and the American fire stopped. First I tried to ask the Americans to surrender, but I did not get any reply. Finally, I cried, 'I want to talk with your commander. I warn you not to shoot me. Can you come out?' Subsequently, I entered the building; everyone was in the cellar. I had several men with me, and I went down into the cellar, where I talked to a second lieutenant [Matthew J. Reid of the 3rd Platoon of C Company]. I told him that he did not have any chance, and I emphasized he had to give up the fight. I promised them that they could keep their personal belongings and food. The lieutenant accepted and surrendered. Looking around myself, I discovered a young American crouching on the ground with a hand grenade with the pin out. The GI had already thrown the pin away into the dark cellar. I helped him find the missing pin. Having found it, he managed to put the pin in place and we both sighed in relief. In the cellar, there was about a platoon, with two wounded. The Americans marched off, the wounded being evacuated later in vehicles."

A little farther to the west, the building occupied by Staff Sergeant Hilliard and his men was also occupied by the Germans. As Hilliard remembers it, "The Germans came in from all sides, shouting and firing. We held ourselves ready, bayonets fixed, as the Germans penetrated the building and started throwing offensive hand grenades through openings and the windows. The offensive grenades either killed you or stunned you into a state of shock." Making a move toward a German with his bayonet, Hilliard fell. Someone had hit him with a rifle butt. When he came to, he saw three Germans carry his other comrades out of the building. It was nearly black when the Germans stood him up and led him to rejoin the rest of the platoon. After reaching them, Hilliard lay down on the ground of another building and fainted again.

One of the prisoners, S/Sgt. William Kirkbride of the antitank company, recalls: "We were all gathered in one of the supply cellars in the ground. There was a very young guard with us during that night. He told us he was seventeen years old, and that his job was to guard us and subsequently guide us to the rear. At about noon on 18 December, we left for Germany on the road through the valley. At this moment there were about a hundred of us. Our small group passed a burned tank. We were able to look inside, as it had been pushed into a small hollow and the top hatches were wide open. The interior was completely burned out. After the first four or five kilometers, we passed long columns of Germans going to the front. They had some of the

Losheimergraben Is Lost

worst equipment we had ever seen: tanks towing other tanks, tanks pulling buses without engines, buses and trucks with the red cross everywhere loaded with troops and ammunition. We finally felt somewhat better, because their rolling material seemed so bad."

Meanwhile, Lieutenant Colonel Douglas and Captain Sandiland, having received the order to withdraw, went north through the woods towards the corduroy east-west road which ran from Mürringen to the 2nd Battalion command post. For part of the way, they were chased by a small German patrol which fired several times but missed. The sole means of maintaining contact was over the SCR 300 radio they carried. Douglas's jeep had been destroyed by a direct hit of enemy artillery fire. Regiment could not be contacted on radio, but contact was maintained with A and C Companies. At about 1630 hours, Douglas arrived at the command post of the 2nd Battalion of the 394th Regiment at the moment it began moving toward Elsenborn. By radio, Douglas ordered the mortar platoon of D Company to withdraw to the command post.

CHAPTER 10

Nemesis at Honsfeld

KAMPFGRUPPE PEIPER REACHES LANZERATH

Since the early-morning hours of 16 December, Lt. Col. Jochen Peiper remained at the 12th Volksgrenadier Division command post with Engel in order to follow the progress of the fighting around Losheimergraben. He hoped to learn when he could give the attack order to his panzer group, *Kampfgruppe Peiper* after the units of the 12th Volksgrenadier Division—the 48th Infantry Regiment and the 27th Fuselier Regiment—had broken through the American defensive line.

At 1600 hours, he received orders from the I SS Panzer Corps to advance his *kampfgruppe* to Losheim and, from there, try to reach the Losheimergraben area for an eventual commitment to combat. Upon reaching the railroad viaduct one kilometer west of Scheid, Peiper realized that the bridging elements of the 12th Volksgrenadier Division's engineer battalion were unable to restore the blown bridge because of the loss of a truck with important bridging parts. (The bridges had been blown by the Germans in their previous retreat from this area.) In order to lose no time, Peiper decided to go around the bridging site. The panzer group left the road, skidded and slid down the railroad embankment, crossed the tracks and regained the road on the far side of the railroad. The group then drove to the road junction with Reich Road 421 and proceeded on that road in the direction of Losheimergraben. There, Peiper received an order to turn to Hüllscheid, march to Lanzerath in order to support the 3rd Fallschirmjäger Division's 9th Regiment, and continue his advance toward Honsfeld, bypassing Losheimergraben to the west because the 12th Volksgrenadier Division was still fighting against American resistance.

Lt. Col. Werner Sternebeck, commander of the advance units (the 6th and 9th Companies of the 1st Panzer Regiment) of *Kampfgruppe Peiper*, remembers: "Immediately west of Losheim, the first Panzer V drove into a minefield and was lost for the rest of the operation. After engineers removed the mines, the advance was cautiously continued. In the meantime, the sun had set. Uncertainly increased, we still saw nothing of the enemy. There was another explosion and the second Panzer V drove into the next minefield, approximately 500 meters west of Losheim. Again the mines had to be removed. This took a lot of time. Our two Panthers, which were thought of as battering rams, were lost for the rest of the deployment without having made any contact with the enemy. Immediately southeast of Merlscheid at an open road obstacle, my panzer jumped and came to a stand-still after a detonation. Now it was also lost. I climbed into 2nd Lieutenant Asmussen's panzer. The advance was again delayed. The panzer had to be pulled from the road obstacle and mines had to be removed."

These mines were not laid by U.S. troops but were still "German property" laid down when the German troops were moving back to the West Wall in October. Now, without taking care of these obstacles, *Kampfgruppe Peiper* already was crippled. Before reaching Lanzerath, Peiper lost more vehicles. Because the time schedule was much more important than some armored vehicles, he decided to used his half-tracks to detonate the mines by just rolling over them. That way he lost about five or seven half-tracks which could be repaired. Peiper reached Lanzerath shortly before midnight.

PFC Rudi Frühbeisser of the 9th Infantry Regiment of the 3rd Fallschirmjäger Division describes what he saw: "At dawn a giant tank stopped in front of the only inn[Café Palm] in Lanzerath. It is a King Tiger. Its commander is Lt. Col. Jochen Peiper, who is in command of an armored combat group. A serious difference of opinion arises between him and our regimental commander, Colonel [Helmuth von] Hoffmann. Our regimental commander, who has been a colonel in the General Staff for years, does not hide his opinions. The SS man wants to take our 1st Battalion with him

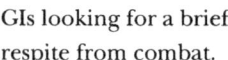
GIs looking for a brief respite from combat.

Helmuth
von Hoffmann.
KAMERADSCHAFT 3.
FALLSCHIRMJÄGER DIVI-
SION/R. ODENDAHL

permanently on his advance. Our regimental commander, however, only agrees to let his paratroops sit on the tanks for security as far as the passage through the forest of Büllingen."

Peiper takes up the story: "It was pitch dark, no shots rang out, and I had the disgusted impression that the whole front had gone to bed instead of waging war. Some way or other, I was conducted to the command post of the 9th Regiment, 3rd Fallschirmjäger Division. The room I had entered was full of soldiers, mostly officers, a great number of them wounded. The commanding officer, a full colonel without any combat experience, who had just skimmed out from the Ministry of the *Luftwaffe*, briefed me to the effect that the forest between Lanzerath and Honsfeld was full of pillboxes, snipers and other obstacles. Three probing attacks had been repelled, and a prepared attack could not be launched until after daybreak. I asked him if he had personally reconnoitered this American position in the woods, and he replied that he had received the information from one of the battalion commanders. I asked the battalion commander, and he said that he had got the information from a captain in his battalion. I called the captain, and he averred that he had not personally seen the American forces, but it had been 'reported to him.' At this point I became very angry and ordered the parachute regiment to give me one battalion, and I would lead the breakthrough."

Sgt. Dick Byers, a forward observer with C Battery of the American 371st Field Artillery, recalls his experience: "After dark on the evening of 16 December, I was part of the forward observation party sent up to replace the captured group and support what was left of the 3rd Battalion around Buchholz Station. All but two platoons of K Company, 394th Infantry, had been withdrawn from Buchholz and sent north. This was on the extreme south end of the 99th line. There was now nothing between us and the faltering 106th Infantry Division except *Kampfgruppe Peiper* with the surviving paratroopers. Wittingly or not, we were the sacrificial 'trip wire' for the right flank of the 99th Infantry Division on Rollbahn D. Lt. Harold Mayer, Sgt. Curtis Fletcher, and I made up the new party. We pulled our jeep off the road and backed it into a barn attached to a farmhouse which is now the house of the forrester Colonerus. It is across the road from Buchholz Station inside the bend in the Lanzerath-Honsfeld road. The barn is parallel to the section of the road running east and west while the house is parallel to the north-south section. Together, they form an L. Two other sides of the quadrangle are formed by stone sheds and walls with gates. These structures form an enclosed courtyard with a large gate opening to the west. Outside of the gate is a small woods growing along the road to the west.

This is the house Dick Byers entered late on the evening of 16 December. COLONERUS (B)/J. WIJERS

"Some members of the 1st and 2nd Platoon of K Company, 394th Infantry, were dug in on the side of the woods away from the road. From their holes they could see Buchholz Station and the road from Lanzerath. The rest of those few K Company men and their aid station were in the farmhouse basement where we joined them for the night. A single Coleman lantern and individual flashlights lit the low-vaulted basement. Fletcher and I split off from the lieutenant and spread our bedrolls in another room. From midnight to one o'clock I stood guard with an infantryman on the porch of the house. We took turns ducking into the house to warm up with a cigarette. It was a quite, cold night. We heard nothing from the station across the road and tracks, but we could clearly hear the SS panzer troops shouting back and forth, the racing of tank engines, the squeal of bogie wheels and the grinding of tanks as they worked *Kampfgruppe Peiper* around the hills from Losheim over Lanzerath and on toward us. I commented to the infantryman that their undisciplined noise sounded like a bunch of quartermaster troops on Louisiana maneuvers."

Jochen Peiper resumes his account: "I went to an adjacent house that meanwhile had been fixed up as my command post, and I issued orders for an attack on Honsfeld. Tanks with mounted infantry (paratroops were to use the road, preceded by a half-track company, led by 1st Lieutenant Preuss. Meanwhile, on each side of the road, one parachute company was to clear the underbrush and to protect the flanks. I ordered my troops to deploy and be ready to attack at 0400 hours. After this conference at about 0100 hours, I organized the attack as follows: Two Panther tanks lead the column as the point, followed by a series of armored half-tracks and then a mixture of Pan-

Dick Byers, shortly before the war.
MRS. DICK BYERS

ther and M4 tanks. This regrouping and preparations consumed much time, as it was extremely dark and the officers had difficulties to find their men in the houses."

The situation at the end of 16 December and in the early-morning hours of 17 December at the Buchholz Station was as follows: On the morning of 17 December, HQ Platoon and the 1st and 2nd Platoons of K Company were located west of the highway and the railroad north of the railroad station. The company commander, with the 3rd and the 4th Platoons, was on the east flank of the regiment with two platoons of L Company. The 2nd Battalion was to the right. These forces were located near the crossroads of the Losheimergraben-California road. At 0500 hours, enemy tanks and infantry began to move along the road toward Honsfeld by the railroad station. Estimates were made of twenty-five to thirty tanks, twenty-eight truck loads of infantry, and two battalions of foot troops in this movement. As they passed the troops of K Company, they sprayed their positions and succeeded in destroying entirely all troops there from headquarters and the 1st Platoon plus part of the 2nd Platoon. A total of sixty men were lost in the attack which took place between 0530 and 0730 hours. The tanks and infantry then continued on their way to Honsfeld.

Sgt. Dick Byers continues: "The K Company men quickly and quietly left the basement to man the positions. Fletcher and I slept through the tense whispering, shuffling and clinking. On the way out one of the men shook me and whispered, urgently, 'Get up! There's a tank outside!' I mumbled something, rolled over and went back to sleep. Fletcher never stirred. An injured infantryman lay near us. He had been badly shaken up by a near miss of an artillery shell and was in shock. He sensed everyone leaving and began calling out, 'Wha's goin' on? Wha's goin' on?' Lieutenant Mayer had been told that we were roused so he went upstairs out into the courtyard looking for us. When the courtyard cleared and we weren't there, he went back down into the cellar. He found Fletcher and me still lying there, sound asleep. He really woke us up! We grabbed our coats and helmets, buckled on our pistol belts and headed for the stairs.

"Once outside in the pitch blackness of the courtyard, we pulled on our galoshes, and after a hasty conference, we headed for the back door of the barn, thinking to use our radio in the jeep to call for artillery fire on the bend in the road where the tanks were slowing down. As we opened the back door of the barn we saw three German paratroopers coming up the driveway. We could see them silhouetted against the white snow, but they couldn't see us with the black courtyard behind us. Since they appeared to be armed with Schmeissers and had the backing and support of an entire panzer battle group, we decided not to argue for possession of the radio. We took off

Modern view of the wooded area across the street where Dick Byers and Lieutenant Mayer went. HANS WIJERS

through the side gate into the patch of pine woods running parallel to the road. In the woods things were noisy and confused. I only remember certain sights and sounds. Lieutenant Mayer had an SCR-536 handie-talkie which was picking up the Germans broadcasting in too-perfect English, 'Come in, come in, come in. Danger, danger, danger. We are launching a strong attack. Come in, come in, anyone on this channel?' No one responded, knowing they were using a captured radio in an attempt to locate us in the dark. This shouldn't have been very hard, because they were now around the house and on the road while we were only a few yards away in the still darker woods. Over the roar and smell of the tank engines we could hear the shouts of the paratroopers as they guided the tank commanders around the bend. Fletcher had not taken the time to buckle his galoshes before going out of the gate and they were snagging. Without saying anything to us, he knelt down to buckle them as we went on. He was captured before he finished the task. The paratroopers came through the gate and took him from behind.

"We wandered around in the woods, between the road and the infantry dugouts. A couple of times the lieutenant approached a hole, saying in a tense, stilted voice, 'Don't shoot, men. This is Lieutenant Mayer of C Battery, 371st. Don't shoot, men.' Then he remembered to use the password and said, 'Armor.' Only then could we see the two gun barrels, aimed between our eyes, move down out of the way as the countersign 'Knight' came back.

We felt alone and vulnerable without holes to go into or adequate weapons. Eventually, I decided this wasn't getting us anywhere, because we couldn't function as artillerymen without our radio, and we weren't going to be much help as infantry against paratroopers and tanks armed only with .45-caliber pistols. Further, my pistol hand was paralyzed from gripping it so tightly that my fingertips were permanently embossed on the butt.

"I suggested to the lieutenant that I knew the way to our gun position via trails, and we should try to get back there to get another jeep and radio so we could get on with our job. He accepted my suggestion and followed as I headed north toward the road. There was a steady stream of German tanks, half-tracks and paratroopers on the road which was lined with big, low-limbed pines. We ducked under a sagging pine into the roadside ditch and waited for a break in the convoy. Paratroopers trudged by just above our heads. When a break came we dashed across the road, dove into the ditch on the other side, then crawled under the trees to the edge of a field. Across the field we found the railroad track from Buchholz to Honsfeld. We followed it west a short distance, then headed north to Hünningen."

Meanwhile, in the farmhouse, Pvt. Nolan Williams of K Company, 394th Infantry, and his sergeant had come in from a patrol and gone to sleep on the first floor. A blast outside showered them with glass, so they decided to head for the cellar. According to Williams, "I slung my rifle across my chest, Jungle Jim–style, tucked a box of K rations inside my shirt, and carefully picked up my new overshoes. I had been without any until just the day before. As I started down the stairs behind another figure, I heard German being spoken in the cellar. My first thought was that someone was interrogating a prisoner, but when other voices answered in German I put my hand on the helmet of the figure in front of me, pulled his head over close and whispered to him, 'Sarge, there are Jerries in the basement!' I suddenly realized that the helmet he wore had no netting and was the wrong shape. Just then a German officer came to the foot of the stairs with a flashlight and said in English, 'Hands up, boys. The war is over.' I will never forget the saucer-sized eyes of the young German. He must have been as frightened as I was. I said, 'Like hell it is!' and shoved the young German down the stairs on top of the officer and bolted up for the door. A German soldier stood in the doorway to the courtyard. I'm sure that soldier still wonders what hit him. I hit him with my overshoes and ran over him like a freight train. I then dropped one of the galoshes and seriously considered going back after it, they were that precious. As I dashed through the courtyard to the back door of the barn, I saw the glow of a wristwatch dial and unslung my rifle, ready to fight. Then I realized, it was the odometer of a jeep. Hearing footsteps pounding after me, I got ready to club my pursuer, but it was the sergeant. We went down the driveway past an empty German half-track and escaped across the road."

Sergeant Byers recounts: "There were few survivors from the K Company platoons to tell the story, so one can only guess that they were as awed as we were by our first encounter with a panzer column and held their fire thinking it would end soon. Just after we left the woods by Buchholz Farm, some GI opened fire. Peiper's flak panzers mounting a cannon and quadruple 20-millimeters responded by mowing down those woods and destroying what was left of K Company. An officer in the cellar of Buchholz Station had radioed a count of all of the armor passing by, but his message was lost or ignored. So much for the 'trip wire' warning."

"CAMP MAXEY" IS OVERRUN

Honsfeld was the rest center of the 99th Infantry Division and was occupied by a variety of troops. A USO show with Marlene Dietrich was supposed to take place on 16 December, but Sepp Dietrich and parts of his 6th SS Panzer Army came instead.

PFC Rex Whitehead, a member of H Company, 394th Infantry, offers this account: "On 15 December 1944, I was sniffed out by someone in charge of sending men 'back' to have a shower. Have never put this in print before, but I was a bit miffed to have been chosen, for I had a shower just before we left England about 3 November when the order came down to wear jockey longs. It was not the first time someone had pulled 'rank' on me, and I felt they were unjustified. After all, the weather had been cool, and in Idaho the mothers during this season 'sewed' their kid into longjohns.

"Now, moving along, I left the positions we had in Germany and went a few hundred yards west to Belgium with guys with strange names like Fleck, Waters, Foley, Boocher, and Smith to a small village of Honsfeld, which had been named 'Camp Maxey'. It had a portable shower setup we were to use. Plus, Foley and Boocher were to stay an extra day, because their feet looked like trench feet should—bad. The shower would not work that evening, but they did give us a change of clothes, which helped somewhat. I have tried that trick since, and it still does not work real well. But we did get to sleep in a building for the first time in over a month, and a movie was shown. The sound did not work, which surprised no one, and did not matter for those present supplied the words, and would guess they were funnier than the real ones. I slept on a table in the Rec Hall, for there was no room on the floor. That was after a good chat with Smitty the Medic, who had become my friend in the barracks at Maxey, but now with the machine-gun platoons. Early the next morning there was a loud noise, reported as a buzz bomb that

Nemesis at Honsfeld

This is the house a bit north of the beer tavern, shown shortly after the war. Here in the back was where the portable showers were set up. HANS WIJERS

had been shot down, and some shingles were lost from the roof. I think it was artillery after all the study of the Bulge, but really does not matter—at least as to which side's artillery.

"The next morning rumors said 'something' was going on at the front (three miles east), and they even told all the medics to assemble to leave, including Smitty. We were scheduled to leave in the morning, but hoped that whatever was going on would continue, for Marlene Dietrich would be at the Rec Hall about noon to present a program. As the day wore on, it was a typical army day, with nuthin' going on until afternoon when rumors said things were happening, such as Marlene would not be there, and the trucks we were to go back in were delayed. They appeared just before dark, and by that time we were aware things were screwed up, but that surprised no one—with or without trench foot. When we got on the trucks, Foley and Boocher, who had another day of rear-area living promised, debated what to do, for the stories were things were 'not good.' They decided to stay their promised one-more-day. 'What the hell—we can walk back tomorrow of we have to.' It was dark as we left on the trucks, and those two guys were captured before daylight the next morning. The rest of us went back to the front line positions where it was safe. I have made good decisions all my life—before and after that day in Honsfeld."

Two platoons of the 801st Tank Destroyer Battalion had been sent in by General Lauer to Honsfeld to hold the road. Every platoon consisted of three towed 3-inch guns. The were placed just outside Honsfeld. Two protected the road from Lanzerath coming in to Honsfeld, and one protected the road that came from Holzheim. During the night, a few towed guns from the 612th Tank Destroyer Battalion were added to the defenses.

At approximately 2100 hours on 16 December, B Company of the 612th Tank Destroyer Battalion was alerted for movement by the 23rd Infantry Regiment and told to be prepared to move on the road to Büllingen. They arrived at the IP during the night. Here they spent an hour before a messenger came from 23rd Infantry Regiment stating the company would move on the road to Büllingen. While en route, the company commander received conflicting orders from 23rd Regimental Combat Team. The first order stated that B Company was to report to an engineer officer in Büllingen. The second order received by a messenger a few minutes later stated that he would report to a tank destroyer officer instead. This certainly was confusing, but the company continued to move as ordered along the designated route. The vigorous reconnais-sance previously conducted by the company paid dividends, otherwise the move would have been extremely difficult.

At 0130 hours on 17 December, the company arrived at its designated location, where it was met by the antitank officer of the 99th Infantry Division and a company commander from the 801st Tank Destroyer Battalion. The antitank officer stated that B Company's mission was to protect the right flank of the 99th Infantry Division from armored attack. One platoon would go into an assembly area nearby and at dawn would take up a defensive position covering the road leading north from St. Vith. The reinforced company, minus one platoon, was to proceed to Honsfeld under the guidance of the 801st Tank Destroyer company commander. In the Honsfeld area, the company would employ one platoon south of town at dawn, while holding the other platoon in mobile reserve within the town. B Company, minus one platoon, moved into Honsfeld without incident. The company commander of the 801st Tank Destroyer Battalion, whose unit had been in the area for some time, ordered the company commander of B Company of the 612th Tank Destroyer Battalion to bed his men for the night, and stated that at dawn he would direct the company to its position.

In addition, A Troop, 32nd Cavalry Reconnaissance Squadron, arrived in Honsfeld late in that evening. A Troop of the 32nd and remnants of the 18th Cavalry Reconnaissance Squadron were disposed along the Herresbach-Andler-Holzheim line. This position was known as "delay position #1," and the 32nd reported to group headquarters at Meyerode that it was in this position at 1600 hours on 16 December. At 1700 hours, the remnants of the 18th Squadron (G Troop, E Troop, and F Company) moved from Holzheim-Honsfeld-Heppenbach to Wereth. Thus, the 32nd was left to hold delay position #1.

At 2115 hours, A Troop of the 32nd notified squadron headquarters that it had no left flak protection and that it was moving to Honsfeld. In Honsfeld, A Troop found a captain, who was director of the 99th Infantry Division's rest camp, organizing the defense of the town. A few rounds of artillery were falling in the town. A Troop was to defend the town's center, while members of infantry and tank destroyer units were placed on the outskirts to defend the approaches of the town to the south and southeast. The 99th officer asked the troop commander, 1st Lieutenant Reppa, to provide some foot patrols to the south and southeast at first light. Reppa said that he would provide them if orders from his squadron did not prevent it.

At around 0500 hours on the seventeenth, tanks were heard generally in front by the men of the 801st Tank Destroyer Battalion, who had their guns just outside protecting the road coming in from Lanzerath. Sergeant Gallagher of the 1st Reconnaissance Platoon, who was acting as outpost for 3rd Platoon of A Company, was sent out to investigate and found two American light tanks with English-speaking personnel. But, still suspicious, they started to investigate further and were taken prisoner. These were elements of Skorzeny's unit, which was mixed with *Kampfgruppe Peiper*.

German paratroopers sitting on the rear of a King Tiger. The veteran soldier sitting on the tank and exchanging a cigarette is Sepp Reiner, one of the few who survived. U.S. ARMY

Sgt. Walter Wittlinger of the 3rd Fallschirmjäger Division's 9th Regiment describes the situation: "It still was night on 17 December, and the order 'Onto the tanks—mount up!' came. I myself was sitting on a King Tiger. Now the 2nd Battalion was the point of the attack. After Lanzerath, we turned left. We drove through the Buchholz Forest with occasional short halts. We did not dismount. Also we felt well protected. It was nicely warm on the tank, and we did not have to walk. But if we had known what was waiting for us, we would not have been so careless. For us there was no contact with the enemy. I still remember the forestry house and the sawmill near Buchholz Station very well. We drove on, still mounted on the tanks. During a slow ride as we drove into the village of Honsfeld, we saw light in the houses. In the streets jeeps and trucks were parked. In many jeeps the ignition keys were still in them, and the red lights were still burning. As we found out later, we had driven straight into a rest area of an American unit.

"At the time we wondered why the Americans did not stir. Probably they were surprised by the tank noise. To this day I can still see the many bundles of telephone cables. Certainly the Americans will have passed the report that German tanks have driven into Honsfeld to the rear. Roughly near the cemetery we dismounted from our tanks. The tank unit drove on, apparently in the direction of Liege [?]. Together with Major Taubert, 1st Lieutenant Gutermann, and several comrades, we entered a nearby farm. Day had begun. Here we found two soldiers in German Army uniforms with a radio. One soldier was sitting on a machine, like a bicycle, as it was used in earlier days, and was pedaling away to generate electricity for the radio. At the time I gave no thought about the presence of both radiomen. I can remember very well what I asked one of the signalers: what had he passed along over the radio, and he answered: 'We are jammed by Americans, he is on our frequency, we cannot get through.' I said: 'And the standby frequency?' 'Yes, here as well there is no connection anymore, as we are being jammed by the Americans.' Later on, and even today I still doubt the identity of those signalers. After all, how did signalers in Army uniform get here to Honsfeld? After all, our unit was the first to get into Honsfeld. Likewise I cannot remember that army signalers belonged to our unit. After all, we had our own signalers. Both signalers spoke perfect German. Of course I cannot prove that they were not Germans. 1st Lieutenant Gutermann also experienced this, and now, as I recently learned, he has passed away.

"The orders were to move from house to house and capture the Americans present. But this order had come much too late. It became clear that it was not very easy to execute. The Americans put up a tough resistance. And again, there was a sniper who fired at everything within his field of fire. It was not possible to recover a man seriously wounded with a headshot, as the

Men of *Kampfgruppe Peiper* who followed the leading elements into Honsfeld. U.S. ARMY

sniper prevented this. Even when a medic wanted to recover the wounded man, he was fired on by the sniper as well. Because of this there were several losses. The medics clearly were recognizable by Red Cross flags, a Red Cross on the helmet, a Red Cross armlet and Red Cross sheets on the front and back. But this action did not happen every day. Only when we had found out where the sniper stuck and captured him, the wounded man could be recovered. We were lucky that the SS came up with more tanks and supported our unit in this battle. Who knows how many losses we would have suffered otherwise. An antiaircraft tank with a four-barreled gun (SS) shot down a fighter-bomber."

Sergeant Gallagher, a member of the 1st Reconnaissance Platoon of the 801st Tank Destroyer Battalion, recalls: "When I returned from the battalion command post at around 0300 hours, I met elements of the 18th Cavalry moving back. I was told that we should not fire on tanks, unless we could identify them. At around 0515, a column of tanks came up the road and stopped. I and another member of our platoon moved forward to see if it was the 18th Cavalry. As we walked toward the lead tank, I was struck on my head. My buddy could escape, but I was taken to the rear of the column and questioned by an English-speaking officer. The officer told me we were surrounded and I should surrender our troops (this officer knew I was with the tank destroyers!). I agreed to walk back and surrender our section. When I walked back, I heard vehicles everywhere, so I told the German escort I was unable to find my section. We then walked back toward the tank. Then I saw the opportunity to make a break for the open field, and I escaped, under heavy small-arms fire. I then escaped and reached friendly lines and reported all this to the S-3 of the engineer battalion. By that time, the Germans had already entered Honsfeld and captured nearly all."

Throughout the hours of darkness, American traffic poured through Honsfeld, most of it going to the north and northwest. These motor columns were using "cats-eye" headlights, and frequently were preceded by a soldier guiding the vehicles with a flashlight. It was a very dark night. At about 0500 on 17 December, Sergeant Creel, commander of an armored car that had been positioned to defend the center of the town from attack from the southeast, saw a figure with a flashlight guiding a tank by Creel's vehicle. As the tank came abreast of the armored car, Creel saw a large swastika on the side of the tank; at that same moment, heavy small-arms fire began 100 yards down the road from the car.

In the furor that followed, Creel observed that enemy tanks were firing into the building that had housed the command post of the elements defending the town, and that the infantry and tank destroyer troops stationed at the southeastern approach to the town came streaming back along the road in disorder. Creel's car had a trailer attached to its rear. This prevented his car from firing at the enemy. The three companies of troops in that area were evacuated, and the men hurried to join 2nd Lt. John V. Harmon's platoon which was in position in the western sector of the town. By the time the men had reached there via the backyards and alleys, the impetus of the enemy attack had carried the enemy armor around his position, and Harmon directed the men to withdraw. He was convinced the town had been overrun with enemy armor. Split into two groups, Sgt. John S. Catanese and Lieutneant Harmon led eighteen- and fourteen-man groups, respectively, out of Honsfeld. Moving westward and cross-country, these remnants of A Troop rejoined the group at Mirfeld.

1st Lt. Werner Sternebeck remembers: "At approximately 0430 hours, we reached Honsfeld. In town, standing on the right side of the road in our direction, was an armored column (tanks, half-tracks, jeeps)—a reconnaissance unit. Since I thought it was a unit from *Einsatzgruppe Greif*, I stopped next to the column to make contact. I dismounted from my panzer and climbed onto the other and looked for the 'Z' designation on the turret. Unfortunately, my search was in vain; I was standing next to the enemy—who was sleeping. My next reaction was to climb back into my panzer, beat a quick retreat to the northwestern exit from the town, and report the presence of the enemy to the panzer battalion."

Karl Wortmann of the 1st SS Panzer Division tells his story: "I was in the Ardennes offensive from the first day to the last, and I was a tank commander

Karl Wortmann.

and commander of a half-platoon in a newly raised armored antiaircraft company. We partially had 3.7-centimeter antiaircraft guns on Panzer IV chassis [the so-called *Möbelwagen*] as well as 2-centimeter flak guns [*Wirbelwind*], partially mounted on the Panzer IVs. Our first tank platoon was a mixed one; we had four tanks, two *Möbelwagens*, and two *Wirbelwinds*.

"At the start of the Ardennes offensive, which really kicked off on 17 December 1944, we drove well at the front of the column. We had been divided into marching columns by platoons. On the stretch from Lanzerath to Buchholz Station, we suffered fierce enemy fire for a brief moment. The enemy had withdrawn to Buchholz Station. Our column split up before the village of Honsfeld. Part of the main street through the village was very narrow and had a lot of curves. In it both our tanks and a *Möbelwagen* were knocked out at close range from the entrance of a house. The third and fourth tanks were *Wirbelwinds*. I controlled the third tank. I noticed the flame from the barrel of the enemy antitank gun. With a few bursts of fire I knocked out the antitank gun. The two *Möbelwagens*, which had been hit, were no longer capable of continuing. Some of the crews were severely wounded. In the next house the Yanks were firing from the higher floors into the armored personnel carriers that followed us and which had open tops. The fight was short but fierce. My tank continued to drive to the exit of the village and remained standing there. I went back to our two knocked-out tanks to find out what happened. Both tanks and crews were total write-offs. I returned again to our *Wirbelwinds*. My comrades told me that by now they were standing opposite the cemetery, and that they had seen something move behind the tombstones. It was a combat unit of 'Skorzeny,' a group of German troops that operated in American uniform. That was the German detachment 'Greif,' which had been trained for several months for this operation and which were to render us many good services later. The fighter-bomber attack at Buchholz Station lasted only a short while and was driven off by our four antiaircraft tanks which at that time were still operational. The kills of the two *Möbelwagens* followed later directly in the village of Honsfeld. From Honsfeld Cemetery both antiaircraft tanks continued towards Büllingen, and we took the guys from Operation Greif with us on our tanks."

PFC Rudi Frühbeiser offers this account: "Now that Honsfeld lies in front of us in the beginning dawn, our tank stops. At a wink of our commander, the entire company dismounts. Immediately we penetrate into the houses on our right and left. Here it is swarming with Yanks. Without the company knowing, we had driven straight into the rest camp of the U.S. 99th Infantry Division and the U.S. 394th Infantry Regiment. The Yankees are disarmed straight away and their weapons rendered unusable. Then they're driven onto the street. Well, that is good booty for our commander. He is still waiting for the regimental commander, who is supposed to have been mounted up with the commander of the second battalion. Our commander finds Major Taubert, the commander of the 2nd Battalion, but our regimental commander is not with him. The regimental commander is supposed to have been picked up and sitting on the last tank. Until the regimental commander arrives, Freiherr von Schenk takes over the command of the regiment. Suddenly, when we want to mount up again, the fireworks start. From nearly all windows in the vicinity a hail of fire rains down on the paratroopers that are standing around. We open fire straightaway. American mortars are firing as well, and they're not firing badly. Already the first groups are bounding back towards the village. Our tank turns his 88-millimeter gun and fires on a machine gun. Direct hit! By now the first houses are being retaken and the Yanks are thrown out. Many Yanks fall in the fire of machine guns and machine pistols. We also suffer our first losses. Private First Class Munz of the regimental staff gets a belly shot that is hopeless. Corporal Hauprich falls, and Corporal Biehl gets a grazing shot to the head. PFC Otto Schipotini was also hit. 1st Lieutenant Later is hit by shrapnel in the leg. Corporals Schilling and Pfeifer, who are storming forward with him, are also hit."

Jim Foley of H Company, 394th Infantry Regiment, describes the situation in Honsfeld: "About 10 P.M., stuff started flying into the town. We didn't think much of it. After all, they told us, it was just a little heavy patrol action. (What a patrol!) Then a shell blew hell out of the improvised shower across

Nemesis at Honsfeld

German paratroopers at a farmyard in Honsfeld, where U.S. troops have left behind equipment including a jeep, half-tracks, and an antitank gun. U.S. ARMY

the street. We were getting pretty worried, but I wasn't going to get out of that sleeping bag until they blew me out.

"About 2 A.M., we heard vehicles in the street. What worried us was that they were going the wrong way. They were our recon cars going back to division headquarters. Still, we stayed in the sack until after 5 A.M., when we heard some heavy vehicles in the street. We didn't have any tanks in the area, so I decided to take a look. Before I had a chance, I heard a shot outside, and Wooten from G Company ran into the room. All he had on were his long johns, and he looked funny as hell. He said, 'One of those silly damn guards of ours took a shot at me when I stepped out to take a piss!' It was all very funny at the time, but what we didn't know was that the 'guard' happened to be a Jerry.

"I piled back into the sack until 6:30 A.M., when I hear Kraut voices in the street. It was confusing to say the least, so I hopped up to take a look. I stuck my head outside to see a few of our recon cars burning across the street and three Kraut tanks very much intact! Then some bastard opened up on me with a burp gun, and I got my ass back inside quick. We barricaded the door and decided to make a break out the back window. We changed our mind when we saw the fields crawling with Jerry infantry. We were stuck but good. So we sat on the floor, me with my trusty .45, which couldn't hit a B-29 at ten paces, and waited. The next thing we heard was that the staff sergeant from E Company was going to surrender the whole rest camp. After a few minutes of horrible confusion, we were all lined up

German paratroopers collect American equipment in Honsfeld. In the street are dead GIs, probably from a tank destroyer unit. U.S. ARMY

outside with a bunch of stupid Supermen screaming like crazy at us. I hated to give up like that but I guess it was the best thing to do. We didn't have so much as a BAR in the whole place. If we had started shooting we would have been slaughtered like a bunch of cattle."

Lt. Col. Joachim Peiper describes the scene: "The entrance of the village was guarded by antitank guns. In position but unarmed! The whole place was crammed with armored vehicles, obviously belonging to a reconnaissance battalion, but again deserted. We fire at everything while sweeping through the little town, in order to cause panic and to secure the rear exit. And panic did arise. It was a disturbed group. Half-clad soldiers either surrendered or tried to escape. No resistance to speak of. I ordered the commanding officer of the parachute battalion that accompanied me to stay in Honsfeld, mop up the place and to await further orders from his regiment. In all, our booty consisted of fifty reconnaissance vehicles, including half-tracks, about thirty two-and-a-half-ton trucks, and fifteen or sixteen antitank guns. My combat group then proceeded to Büllingen, receiving some small-arms fire, but this didn't make us unhappy, because although there was a slight delay, it allowed rear vehicles to close up."

Sgt. Walter Wittlinger of the 9th Regiment of the 3rd Fallschirmjäger Division remembers: "After the end of the battle in Honsfeld, both sides had

American POWs, almost all of whom were taken in Honsfeld. U.S. ARMY

taken losses. The American prisoners were brought to the hall in the inn Eifeler Hof. There they were guarded until they could be transported to the rear. Even before the end of the battle, I was in the hall of the inn. Here everything had been prepared for Christmas. One decorated Christmas tree stood in the hall. I still remember well that I drank a beer here. In the hall, as I remember it, there were over 100 prisoners. Among them there was a captain. This I know, as I was detailed to guard them while my comrades searched for, and found, something edible.

"While I was guarding the prisoners, three soldiers, partially dressed in American uniform, came up and asked me to collect various bits of American equipment from the prisoners for them. At that time the entrance to the hall was separated from the street by an entrance room. I told them, 'Anyone can come and demand this!' Now one of the three said, 'According to Führer orders, anyone who objects to us can be shot on the spot without trial!' Now I demanded their papers. Silently they showed their army pay books (identification cards). I had to conclude that they were an SS officer and two SS NCOs. After seeing this information I told them, 'Get the kit yourselves!' Even today I wonder at my courage in saying something like that to an SS officer. No one would have made a fuss if they had shot me on the spot. I can only assume that they wanted to make as little fuss as possible. I

This German propaganda photo from the vicinity of Honsfeld shows an M3 Stuart light tank in the background; the markings indicate that it is from the 18th Cavalry Reconnaissance Squadron. U.S. ARMY

went with them into the hall and saw them take rubber overshoes and steel helmets from the prisoners. Apart from this activity, I did not see anything illegal. After the three had got their equipment, they got in a jeep and drove off. I don't know where. I have to mention here that during this action nothing that was against the Geneva convention happened. For our side I know that, apart from weapons, no personal possessions were taken and no maltreatment occurred. A big booty was captured, but everything had to go to the rear."

At 0500 hours, the company commander of B Company, 612th Tank Destroyer Battalion, received a report by radio that tanks were attacking Honsfeld. He immediately decided to try to reach Honsfeld by going through Büllingen. While going down the road toward Honsfeld, he was met by elements of 801st Tank Destroyer Battalion moving on foot who told him that their positions in front of Honsfeld had been hit by hordes of German tanks, followed by infantry, and that the company had nothing left— only a few personal weapons. The company commander then decided to approach Honsfeld on foot. Since enemy planes had become very active and flares were being dropped throughout the area, he therefore had no trouble looking into the town. What he saw was a very shocking sight, even to a company commander who had been fighting since right after D-Day the previous June. The entire town was surrounded by enemy troops, and tanks could be seen milling around the area. It was immediately apparent that elements of B Company and the reconnaissance platoon had been lost. With a heavy heart, he proceeded to Büllingen, where a direct wire to the 99th Infantry Division's command post was found, and the chaotic situation was reported. He was ordered by the divisional chief of staff to gather any available troops and to block the road to Bütgenbach.

CHAPTER 11

The 254th Engineers Block the Road

In Büllingen, the 254th Engineer Combat Battalion—a unit formed out of the 107th Engineers—was in positions it had occupied since November. The 254th operated in support of the 2nd and 99th Infantry Divisions. The battalion earned its bread and butter as an engineer unit; however, it was as infantry that it experienced its finest hour during the Battle of the Bulge.

At midnight on 16 December, the battalion command post received a message from the 1121st Engineer Group. The group put the 254th on a two-hour alert for an infantry mission. They directed the battalion commander to report to the G-3 of the 99th Infantry Division in Bütgenbach. Lieutenant Colonel Jenkins left at once. The roads were jammed with traffic, mostly light tanks and antiaircraft artillery. Jenkins could not report until 1 A.M. on the seventeenth. The G-3 briefed the commander that the enemy breakthrough occurred to the southeast. The axis of advance was up to the Honsfeld-Büllingen highway. The 254th was to move immediately to form a defensive line south and east of Büllingen, Belgium, to protect U.S. tanks and tank destroyers. The vehicles were clogging the area roads.

When the commander returned, the battalion was formed into two echelons. The forward echelon set up a command post at the road junction of the St. Vith road and bivouac road in Büllingen. The line companies dug in on the south and west side of the town. The rear echelon, under the command of Capt. Reginald Fairfax of Headquarters and Service Company, moved to the rear in the vicinity of Waimes, Belgium. By 6 A.M., the forward units were in position. C Company was in the north, A in the center, and B in the south. The movement to battle forced the men to leave their comfortable "dug-in-for-the-winter" bivouac positions. As usual, the move was done in the dark of night.

As soon as the battalion established the command post at Büllingen, other units of the 254th were notified of the situation. Runners were sent to locate the tanks and tank destroyers they were supposed to protect. When

The 254th Engineers Block the Road

The center of Büllingen.

the runners returned, they reported none could be found. Regardless, the battalion's mission was to defend, and defend they would.

All around the 254th's positions swirled the confused American army as it fled from the unexpected German onslaught. B Company brought one straggler into the command post, a sergeant from a tank destroyer unit. He reported that he had escaped from the enemy after being captured near Honsfeld. The wild-eyed NCO reported that enemy armor was headed to Büllingen in full strength. He had counted twelve German tanks and could hear more. A while later, a lieutenant from a tank destroyer outfit came into the command post to get warm. When questioned, he replied he had a platoon of armored infantry with him in half-tracks. When further questioned as to where his own command post was, he replied, "I'm mobile. The Germans are coming and I'm leaving." With that comment he left.

Sgt. Otto Siegmund of the 1st SS Panzer Division recalls: "After we had captured Honsfeld, we took the lead toward Büllingen, because Preuss had already moved out. Our group was formed as follows: two or three half-tracks in front, then a Panzer IV, again another half-track, a Panther tank, another half-track, etc. When one of our half-tracks would be destroyed by a mine or shot by antitank fire, that would be 'cheaper' than losing a tank, and we could easily trace the enemy."

The first Americans to encounter the advance party of *Kampfgruppe Peiper* were members of the 924th Field Artillery of the 99th Infantry Division. The 924th's PFC Roger Foehringer remembers: "I was with the service battery, and we slept in houses in the town of Büllingen. Early in the morning on 17 December, I was on guard duty. At approximately 2 A.M., an M8

Otto Siegmund.

scout car came speeding up, and the driver said they were with a cavalry unit, and they just came from the front. He said, 'The whole German army is coming, and they are just a couple miles up the road!!' I ran over to headquarters and told Captain Cobb, our commander, and then I ran back to my post, where I was guarding the 6x6s on a little side road just on the edge of town. There were two air strips, one used by the 2nd Division which was near the farmhouse I slept in, and the other was used by the 99th, a little out of town to the right about ninety degrees.

"We were walking up the hill heading out of town with a case of grenades when a Panther tank came down on us. I jumped over a hedgerow, and my buddy Pvt. Preston Davis ran out into the field to the right. I never knew he made it until forty-five years later. He feigned death, and I ran back to the farmhouse to warn the others in the supply battery. The tanks were just up the road, and by that time they were already there. We went upstairs and started shooting out the windows at the troops in the field, but we could hear the German tanks and troops right outside, so we ran down into the basement where we were captured. When the Germans shot the cellar door open, they kicked us in the ass and took any belongings and then marched the five of us to Honsfeld to an old beer hall to interrogate us. The German who spoke to me was educated in Boston and wore GI clothes; he took my dog tags, and I assume he used my identity."

At approximately 6 A.M., four flares, blue, white, red and white appeared to the right of B Company. Five minutes later, tracked vehicles were heard approaching. Since the noise could have been from friendly units in front of the engineers' positions, firing was withheld. In spite of the dark, armored vehicles could be seen moving towards the waiting engineers. When shouts in German were heard, there was no longer any doubt. The 254th opened

The 254th Engineers Block the Road

fire with rifles, bazookas and machine guns. Immediately, German infantry leaped from the panzers and half-tracks. The vehicles withdrew, but the German infantry pressed their attack forward. Before being driven back, they stormed to within fifteen yards of the battalion's positions. Later, the Germans were identified as part of the elite 9th Parachute Division and 1st SS Panzer Division.

PFC Edward R. Ponatoski, a member of C Company, 254th Engineer Battalion, wrote home a few months later: "Remember the big breakthrough on the First Army front? Well, we just happened to be there. We were awakened at twelve o'clock on 17 December. The company commander said we had to go up as infantry. We were told there would be nothing to worry about, just a few tanks broke through the line. We were bivouacked next to a town called Büllingen. It is right on the Belgium border. It is in Belgium. So we pulled out of our area about three o'clock in the morning. There was snow on the ground, and it was very cold and wet. Well, we got to our area we were to defend and set up our line of defense. We sat there till about six in the morning. Dawn was just breaking when all of a sudden—Bang!—all hell broke loose, 88s, .50-caliber machine guns, burp guns, and what-not opened up on us. It was like the Fourth of July, only more so."

1st Lt. Werner Sternebeck, commander of the advance units (the 6th and 9th Companies of the 1st Panzer Regiment) of *Kampfgruppe Peiper*, recounts: "At 0600 hours, the lead panzer element surprised a truck column coming from the direction of Büllingen, north of Honsfeld. The column was brought to a halt by blinking a red flashlight. It was a supply column of about

Werner Sternebeck.

eight trucks. It was overpowered without firing a shot. Then we moved onward toward Büllingen; at approximately 0700 hours, we received fire from automatic weapons approximately 1,500 to 2,000 meters south of the edge of town and west of the march route. The lead panzer element veered off, returned the fire and attacked an airfield containing reconnaissance aircraft."

Also stationed in Büllingen were troops of the 2nd Infantry Division: the 2nd Quartermaster Company, the 2nd Signal Company, supply installations of the division, the Medical Supply Dump, B Company of the 2nd Engineer Battalion, the kitchens of the 3rd Battalion of the 23rd Infantry (2nd Infantry Division) and the pilots of the spotter planes of the artillery. All but one of the 99th pilots got out, but of the pilots of the 2nd Infantry Division, who were stationed at the airfield south of Büllingen, only one managed to get out. The 2nd Infantry Division's artillery air section had its field near Büllingen, and all personnel were quartered in the town itself. Word to move was received early in the morning of 17 December, and the pilots and enlisted personnel were completing packing, or making their way to the field, when the first German tanks came. Those near the field got away, either by vehicle or on foot, and eventually all rejoined the battalion. Those in town were trapped, unable to escape, and one group, including 2nd Lt. Herbert T. Weyenberg and Sgt. Eugene Taylor, fled before the tankers fired machine guns into the cellar of the house.

THE STORY OF THE 99TH INFANTRY DIVISION'S ARTILLERY AIR SECTION

There were ten L-4 observation planes in the division's air section, two for each of the field artillery battalions and two for division field artillery headquarters, which had three pilots—the commander, assistant commander, and a lieutenant—plus a ground crew. So there were eleven pilots for the division air section. Each battalion had two pilots and a ground crew plus assigned air observers. All the planes and crews were stationed at the same landing strip near Büllingen. There was also a kitchen crew for the section.

Lt. Charles E. Whitehead, an air observer with the 370th Field Artillery Battalion, tells his story: "The day [16 December] was overcast and foggy. We didn't see any prospects of being able to fly, so I went to battalion headquarters at Krinkelt to pick up mail and rations. When I checked in with the colonel, he told me division had advised that there was an armored patrol in force behind the front lines and all units were to post double guard. When I got back to Büllingen, it had cleared enough that Proctor and Sears [both pilots for the 370th] (one flying, the other as observer) had made a flight to the front. The ack-ack had been so heavy they weren't able to stay high

Charles Proctor and Charles Whithead (right), February 1945.
CHARLES WHITEHEAD

enough to fire on a target. Sears and I then tried to get to the front, but fog had moved in over the front and we couldn't see any targets.

"About 4:30 A.M. on 17 December, we were awakened and told there were tanks in a little town, we couldn't find on the map [probably Honsfeld]. It was suggested we pack and be ready to move. About 7 A.M., Proctor told me to see if the cooks could fix us something, and as soon as it was light we would take off for the front. I went downstairs and was startled to find the kitchen gone. I found Caldwell [the cook] and was told everyone was loaded and leaving. I ran outside, found Staff Sergeant Watts in column, told him to wait until the pilots and I could get our gear. We got bed-rolls, etc. and tossed them in his jeep and he took off after the tail of the column. All the other pilots had taken off when Proctor, Sears and I got out to the strip. Sears's plane was parked on top of the ridge. I helped him start, then went to Proctor's who was parked down the hill near the little house we used as a command post. I got Proctor's plane started and got in; he taxied about thirty feet and got stuck in the mud. I got out and pushed the plane till it would roll on its own, then hopped in on the move. As we were taking off, we were fired on by machine guns from tanks on the 2nd Division air strip, which was on the next ridge south. There was a tank on the far end of our air strip.

"When we got airborne, we found Sears and Tadlock [pilot, 371st]. The three planes flew to an air strip at Spa. We bummed a ride to 1st Army HQ, went to the air section and told our story to a Captain Stevenson. (I'll never forget his name.) He told us we were just 'new to combat and got spooked.' Then, he told us that '2nd Division was an old experienced outfit and they hadn't reported anything' and to 'go to mess hall and get something to eat and go back to Büllingen.' (By that time, the Germans had burned the 2nd Division's planes and the air crews were holed up in a basement). The three pilots thought everyone was supposed to go back to Spa. After some discussion it was decided the rest of the air section might be at the auxiliary field near Malmédy. We then flew from Spa to Malmédy and found the rest of the 99th air section. We got nine of our ten planes out. One was left, because the pilot [Weckerle] had been grounded after a motor accident in England and was not on flying status.

"About 4 P.M., since we hadn't seen and didn't know where the air section commander was, Proctor, Sears and I decided we couldn't spend the night on this exposed ridge. I took our jeep and three-quarter-ton with our ground crew along with Birkhead Jackson (observer for the 372nd Field Artillery) and his ground crew and took off for Spa. All the planes were there at MR&R by the time we got there, and we spent the night of the seventeenth there.

"Monday, 18 December, the First Army began to leave Spa. At MR&R, there were two planes that had been left for repairs. Therefore, no one was available to fly them. Sergeant Watts and Sergeant Perrick (mechanics for the air section) volunteered to fly them out (they had soloed in the States). The commander refused because they were not on flying status (the same reason Joe Weckerle didn't fly the plane we left at Büllingen). The commander was asked what would happen if they took off when he wasn't looking. He told them, 'Nothing.' The following makes a good story, but I can't vouch for it: Supposedly, they suggested he might have a terrible case of cramps and should make a quick trip to the latrine. Which he did. To the best of my knowledge, Kean, Proctor, Sears, Hilson, Tadlock, Lehman, Little, Gaston, and Ramsey flew the planes from Büllingen to the field at Malmédy, then later to the MR&R at Spa. Joe Weckerle led the trucks out, and I don't know where the commander was.

"After leaving Spa on 18 December, in convoy, the ground crew and I spent the night in either Liege or Verviers. I can't remember which. It was in an old theater building. The next day we went to Eupen. I don't remember for sure, but think the planes flew directly from Spa to Eupen. When we all finally got to Eupen, we had no idea where our units were. Several of the pilots took the jeeps and drivers and scouted around until they found divisional headquarters. The weather in Eupen was so foggy, we couldn't fly. In order to find a spot clear enough to take off, we had our mechanics (Watts and Zehner) take the wings and prop off of one of our planes. We put the wings and prop on our 3/4 ton truck and hung the tail over the back of the jeep. Then Proctor and I with the mechanics, went south to near Ovifat, Belgium. We found a clear spot, put the plane back together and flew a mission. Toward evening the fog lifted and the other eight planes joined us.

"All nine pilots, who flew out of Bülligen received the Distinguished Flying Cross. The air force was reluctant at first, but when it was pointed out they had been trained by the air force and were drawing flight pay, they OK'd it. The 99th air section was the only section to ever receive the Distinguished Flying Cross. I have a picture of the presentation. By the twentieth, we had found an air strip just west of Elsenborn Ridge and were again flying missions for the division.

"Lt. Joe Weckerle was the assistant division air section commander, and Major Cunningham was the commander. On the morning of the seventeenth, Major Cunningham went to divisional headquarters at Bütgenbach. Lt. Joe Weckerle had been in a truck wreck while we were in England. Since he couldn't fly, he led the column of trucks and the enlisted men out of Büllingen. Therefore, we had ten planes and only nine pilots—eight from the four battalions and Lieutenant Keen from divisional artillery."

1st Lt. Werner Sternebeck continues: "Peiper 'whistled' us on and urged us to hasten the advance to capture Büllingen. Captain Preuss's lead company took over the elimination of the airfield with their heavy platoon under 2nd Lieutenant Aschendorff. Six American spotter planes, Pipers, were surprised with their motors running, taken under fire and destroyed. The point company pushed into Büllingen and, during their passage through the village, took heavy fire from the houses on both sides of the streets. In the course of this action, the company commander Captain Preuss was separated from his company."

Captain Preuss takes up the story: "2nd Lieutenant Aschendorff had strict orders from me to take care that all of my company's schützenpanzerwagens stayed closed up. This was his most important mission at the end of the company. I suffered losses in Büllingen, including my two platoon leaders. The 'Amis' fired down out of the houses into our open SPWs, and I had to get us out of the city as quickly as possible. As I myself took the lead, there was no one else behind me. Wedged into a fleeing American column, I was carried into the enemy rear area. Dropping out in open land was impossible, since my five men with three rifles and two pistols—I must have shoved my machine gun into the hands of 2nd Lieutenant Behrend back in Losheim—were not up to the pressure of the horde that would be upon us. Only in a big patch of woods was I successful in breaking free, but even here I had to change posi-

Captain Preuss.

tions twice as brief firefights developed with withdrawing American infantry groups. Then, however, we fought our way back to the troop and, on 18 December were already back in action again. On this day 2nd Lieutenant Aschendorff was killed."

Twenty minutes later, the German infantry again charged forward. They now had the close support of their tanks. Large-caliber shells exploded on the hastily dug-in engineers; 20-millimeter rounds and machine-gun fire swept their positions. Despite the heavy fire, the battalion again repulsed the surging German infantry. In both attacks, the Germans suffered heavy losses due to the sustained and accurate fire of the men of the 254th.

There was a brief delay of ten minutes before the Germans renewed their attack. It was just enough time for the battalion to evacuate its wounded. As the dawn was breaking, the third German assault surged forward like a firestorm. A dozen heavy panzers and Tiger tanks led this assault. Since the 254th had no antitank weapons, the tanks swept on and overran B Company's positions. They crushed two machine guns along with B Company's fine platoon sergeant, Charles "Snake" Senical. But the men stayed in their foxholes and waited for the fearsome tanks to pass through. The men then delivered deadly fire on the approaching infantry. Their fire was so intense that the German infantry withdrew. The enemy then maneuvered around the company's flank. In the desperate fighting, one panzer was

The 254th Engineers Block the Road 159

knocked out by bazooka fire and two more damaged. The area forward of the position was littered with dead and wounded infantry. Simultaneously, Mark IV enemy tanks drove battalion headquarters out of Büllingen.

Sternebeck resumes his account: "Back on the road to Büllingen, at a blind spot several hundred meters from the entrance to the town, the Panzer IV in front of me was destroyed by cole-combat weapons. The crew was shot while dismounting; no one survived! Driving wildly and firing with all weapons, the rest of the lead panzer element entered Büllingen. The enemy was in total confusion. We had achieved surprise. There was no organized enemy resistance apparent. The confusion also affected us. We became completely muddled in the town and drove to the north in the direction of Wirtzfeld instead of to the west."

During this action, there were two incidents regarding firing at a tank with a bazooka. The first was when Grant Yager of the 924th Field Artillery Service Battery, along with another GI, fired at and hit a Panther tank near the fork in the road just at the entrance of the town. In this Panther, SS Obersturmführer Horst Rempel, commander of this tank, was killed. Shortly afterward, Grant Yager was taken prisoner. The other incident was when PFC Roger Foehringer of the 924th Field Artillery and Al Weiss fired at a tank at twenty-five yards and missed twice. According to Foehringer, "He was aiming, and after the second shot, I looked at him and noticed he had lost his glasses in all the confusion, and they were as thick as coke bottle bottoms. Thank God we missed, because instead of capturing us they probably would have killed us for knocking out their tank right in the middle of the road in town. It was right next to the house we slept in, probably the third house on the right going into town from the direction the Germans were coming from."

In the vicinity of Krinkelt, defensive positions were taken by the men of the 2nd Infantry Division. Before daylight on 17 December, the 2nd Battalion of the 23rd Infantry Regiment, which had positions in and around Krinkelt, was alerted to expect American tanks coming into the assembly area from the northeast (tank destroyer of the 644th Tank Destroyer Battalion and tanks from the 741st Tank Battalion). At 0845 hours, four tanks and three tank destroyers arrived in the battalion assembly area. E Company men were placed on the tanks and tank destroyers, which then started for Krinkelt, followed by the antitank platoon. All staff officers of the battalion except Major Smith, battalion executive officer, went with E Company and the tanks toward Krinkelt. Major Smith set out with the remainder of the battalion toward Wirtzfeld, where the division command post was located. When Major Smith reached Wirtzfeld, General Robertson ordered the unit to assume positions on the high ground south of the town. At this time enemy tanks were within sight of the division command post in Wirtzfeld.

Two of the knocked-out Panzer IVs of Werner Sternebeck's group, which came out of Büllingen on the road to Wirtzfeld. A tank destroyer of the 1st Platoon, C Company, 644th Tank Destroyer Battalion, knocked out the first one alone and was helped by 57-millimeter guns with the second. The tank destroyer's crew included Sgt. Tom Myers, T/5 Bill Hooper (driver), Pvt. Dennis Hebert (codriver), Pvt. George Oswald (gunner), and Pvt. George Brower (loader). U.S. ARMY

Lt. Col. Matt F. C. Konop (known as "Mad Matt"), headquarters commander in the 2nd Infantry Division, remembers: "About 0920, I notice an armored vehicle in the haze near the crest of the hill to our front (south), but can't tell if it's one of our tank destroyers or an enemy tank. I ask Captain Albright and Sergeant Brown if they see it and if they know what it is. Neither is sure as to its identity. Suddenly a burst or several bursts of machine gun bullets land in our area; some fly high over the fir trees and no doubt land in the command post. Then a shot is heard landing on our left flank near the cemetery followed by a loud report of a heavy gun. The tank destroyer is seen to turn left and fire; the German tank is hit as it swerves to the right and stops ablaze. .50-cal machine guns on our line open up pouring bullets into the disabled tank, and suddenly it explodes and bursts into flames when tank destroyer fires again. Lieutenant Juneau comes in from the gun position several minutes after this tank is hit. I direct him to go up to the southern (Büllingen) road gun position and render what assistance he can there. He proceeds. Soon another vehicle is seen coming down the hill following the path of the first one. It stops momentarily and is fired on by the tank destroyer, which misses the vehicle. The 57-millimeter gun near the church fires a round and hits a bull's-eye, and that vehicle goes up in flames. Several other guns fire at it and the .50s pour more bullets into it.

The 254th Engineers Block the Road

"Lieutenant Juneau arrives with his driver (Tech 5 Williams) and advises that there are more tanks on the way, and that he was going to the gun on our left as that one seemed to be in the best firing position. Another vehicle is seen coming down the same route as the previous two and as soon as it is sighted, .50-cal guns from the observation post area open up and ignite it; 57-millimeter gun fires a round, and the tank destroyers fire also. All three vehicles are burning with no apparent sign of enemy getting out. Firing in the background (Büllingen) becomes more intense; machine guns and heavy caliber guns are heard with enemy artillery shells heard overhead and some hitting in the area; several rounds hit near the church (Wirtzfeld). I heard later that one NCO in the divional artillery was a casualty. No more tanks appear for five or ten minutes. Lieutneant Juneau arrives and states that one enemy did get out of the last vehicle which seemed to be an armored car but that one of his men got him with an M1. An officer from the tank destroyers comes from the southern (Büllingen) tank destroyer position and reports that some enemy got out of the armored vehicles, were engaged in a firefight, and about a dozen surrendered; also was reported that three tanks were knocked out and that the rest turned back towards Büllingen."

Sternebeck continues his story: "We drove back fast through Büllingen, to the western exit. The lead panzer element now consisted of only two Panzer IVs and the engineer squad. We drove along the Büllingen-Bütgenbach road to the Domaine, where an American first-aid station was established. Although the surgeons approached us in order to surrender the first-aid station, we turned to the south along the Büllingen-Möderscheid road."

Rolf Ehrhardt, panzer driver for Captain Klingelhöfer in the 1st SS Panzer Division, recounts: "We continued in the direction of Büllingen. We had just passed an American airfield on which several high winged planes, apparently reconnaissance aircraft, were burning. Forward—an intersection in town, stop! The chief dismounted, watched the platoons catch up, spoke with the platoon leaders and attempted to orient himself. While I checked the tracks of our vehicle, the rest of the crew reconnoitered the nearby area. It had, in the meantime, become daytime and we sat back in our seats. Radio readiness was ordered. Suddenly an American ambulance sped past us, completely oblivious. I jumped out of my driver's seat and got hung up on the radio line. In my haste I forgot to take my throat-microphone off. I freed myself and ran toward the ambulance, which had, in the meantime, stopped. The driver and his escort raised their hands, and I made it clear to them that they were to drive in the direction of Honsfeld. Hardly were these

On 7 January 1945, near Sourbrodt, Belgium, a sanding device designed by Lt. Col. Loren W. Jenkins and made from a salvaged German vehicle is put to use by members of A Company, 254th Combat Engineers, U.S. First Army, on an icy road near Sourbrodt, Belgium.

Rolf Ehrhardt.

heroes gone, when a three-axle GMC came into sight, also from the direction of Büllingen. However, this one quickly comprehended the situation and immediately turned around and disappeared.

"On the right side of the curve was an apothecary shop. At the window in the upper story I saw an old man. His sleeping cap made me think of the William Busch paintings. He motioned that I should be cautious, pointing below, in the direction of the front door. There, for the first time, I saw an olive-green tent between the big firs in the front garden. That changed things in a hurry for me, as I looked down and saw three sleepy Americans trying to get untangled from their sleeping bags. Fortunately, my loader, Peter Mühlbach followed me. In the same glance I discovered a heap of gasoline cans in a small building. With hands and feet we made it clear to the three sleepy Americans that they should bring the gas cans to the roadside.

"Under the watchful eye of Peter Mühlbach, they began immediately as a work commando with the transport. I reported to the commander and drove out with my tank. We were able to tank up with a few cans of gas and and load on a few left over. The other panzers in our company did the same."

The 254th Engineers Block the Road

The 254th Engineer Battalion was overrun. The G-3 of the 99th Division ordered them to fight a delaying action. They were to fall back on Bütgenbach. C Company, the northern most unit, was ordered to fight out of town, northwest along the railroad tracks; A Company back towards Wirtzfeld; B Company and Headquarters down the Büllingen-Bütgenbach road. This all was easier said than done.

After a sharp action, C Company of the 254th Engineer Battalion managed to fight its way through the town to new positions north of Büllingen. During the fight, the unit had been cut in two. Many of those that reached the new position arrived in groups of two and three. Many others were killed or captured.

In his letter a few months after the battle, PFC Edward R. Ponatoski wrote: "We held them off for a while with our rifles, which by the way isn't very effective against a tank if you know what I mean. So we got called back to our assembly area. They told us we'd have to retreat and set up a new line of defense. Everybody and everything was all confused. In fact, every one was running around like a chicken with his head knocked off. It all happened so fast it caught everyone unaware. Well, anyway, we were told to withdraw along the highway up a big hill, which in our case was very costly. Because the tanks came right on up after us firing away. We lost quite a few boys. All around us, there were open fields. No cover whatsoever. We just had to stay in the open and fight it out. I lay there in the field with one of the boys and picked off as many as we could. It was hopeless, though. We were too outnumbered. My platoon commander, realizing this, gave the word to surrender. Until today, I still don't know how I lived through all that. All the bullets that whizzed by me. I was sure one had my name on it. Well, we were taken prisoner and thought the worst. We expected them to shoot us. But they didn't. They put us on a truck and were going to send us back to their lines, but we escaped. We holed up in a house all day on the seventeenth and eighteenth not knowing how far they had pushed the Americans back."

A Company, through a communications problem, didn't receive the order to move. Since the unit was still holding its original positions, it stayed in place. B Company, however, had a far more difficult time. When the Germans overran the battalion, the unit was cut off and consequently couldn't be withdrawn from the Büllingen-Butgenbach road. They simply disappeared in the German surge. Headquarters and Service Company was able to quickly form a new defensive line west of the town. To give the appearance of having more strength than it actually did, men were constantly shifted from position to position! The 254th Battalion headquarters used any and all available men to hold the new line. This included cooks, drivers, clerks, and a motley collection of stragglers from the 99th Division headquarters. They were also joined by two tank destroyers. The headquarters line was clearly visible from the town. When the German lead vehicles arrived around 0800 hours, they recognized the line of positions. The Germans turned south on the St. Vith road. The battalion mission of turning the enemy advance was achieved.

After working their way through the woods, two platoons of B Company reached the headquarters positions around noon. As soon as the men were placed into the new line, three mobile antitank guns from the 612th Tank Destroyer Battalion moved into the hastily prepared defensive line. The tank destroyers immediately opened fire. The Germans saw the danger of the engineers' line. They brought up artillery and swept the positions with shellfire. At 1300 hours, under the cover of several arriving light tanks, the engineers slipped out of their positions. They established a new line at the crossroads. At 1500 hours, the 26th Infantry Regiment of the 1st Infantry Division quickly moved up from a rear rest area to relieve the battalion. A Company was still holding the original forward positions. They had been bypassed by the advancing enemy. Now they were subjected to shelling and strafing by their own troops. The unit was so far forward that everyone thought they were Germans. Under his own authority, the commander withdrew his company and successfully rejoined the battalion. They were withdrawn to Camp Elsenborn to reorganize.

1st Lt. Harold L. Hoffer, commander of the Recconnaissance Company of the 644th Tank Destroyer Battalion, recalls: "At about 1500 hours on 17 December, I noticed a motorized column moving from east to west through the town of Büllingen. Our command post was located to the south edge of Krinkelt, some two miles from the column which appeared to contain U.S. Army and German vehicles. I sent a platoon led by S/Sgt. Edward Patterson

In Waimes, Belgium, in December 1944, gun crews of B Battery, 37th Field Artillery Battalion, 2nd Division, stand by their guns, ready for the order to fire into enemy territory.
U.S. ARMY

toward Büllingen to determine the make-up of the column, report the information by radio and to return to Krinkelt. Sergeant Patterson [his battle field commission had not yet been effected] led his platoon to Büllingen, and, from the basement of the Rauw Hotel, reported the column to be German. Communications with the platoon were terminated during the early-morning hours of 18 December."

On the way from the Losheimergraben Crossroads were elements of the 12th Volksgrenadier Division, which after completely overrunning the 1st Battalion of the 394th Infantry in the afternoon, moved toward Büllingen. After the occupying American forces were overrun by *Kampfgruppe Peiper*, stragglers from all units out of the area came into Büllingen on their way to the Elsenborn Ridge. After the move out of Büllingen by *Kampfgruppe Peiper*, the town was not occupied by German troops and had to be retaken with a renewed attack by *Vorausabteilung Holz* of the 12th Volksgrenadier Division.

According to Maj. Günther Holz, "Again the battalion advanced, with Büllingen as its first objective, now on an entirely open road without any cover. On the left there were open fields, on the right meadows with a small brook. Just as the point reached Neuhaus, the hamlet from which some Americans had already withdrawn, an order came from division: 'Halt!' It possibly was the unluckiest circumstance in which a halt order could reach a marching unit that had to count on being attacked from the air at any moment; no cover for miles around. Though vehicles kept distance for air attacks and the flak platoons took up positions, this could not have prevented severe losses in case of a determined aerial attack.

"Over radio we requested permission to continue the advance, in vain. Hours passed, and still we stood on the road. Finally Major Petter showed up and ordered us to take Büllingen, but not one step beyond! The flanks of the unit that had penetrated deep into the enemy area were without cover, and fighting still took place to our rear. But now there were no more second thoughts, the men could not spend a third night on the road, and noon had long since passed. The enemy had been warned a long time ago, and any element of surprise had been lost. At a quick clip we advanced, we had to take Büllingen on this day. The first houses appeared. When we reached them the first shots fell from hatches in the roofs. The flak, which only now understood its unusual task for ground operations fully, quickly reduced the resistance nests. Soon the first crossroad was reached, American jeeps and trucks were standing around, but the enemy had lost all appetite for a strong resistance when the strong armored unit appeared. But road by road, house by house, all had to be secured, and in the end we had nearly 300 prisoners, among whom were over a dozen officers. At first they were housed in a hall, and Leutnant Bieschke took guard duties with his signallers. In the beginning this was easy, the Yanks were relieved to have come out of this with their skins intact, but it became progressively more difficult as now the American leadership fully had recognized the danger.

"First with a battery, then with the full strength of several battalions, the U.S. artillery opened up on the village. More and more buildings received hits, and our prisoners became desperate in their fear. We had urgently requested a detachment to take them away from division, but that did not show up until dusk. Then we were relieved to shove off this ballast to the rear. Our own soldiers could not be spared for this; every man was needed to hold the town in case of a counterattack. Again we asked the division permission via radio to at least take the Domaine Bütgenbach, which was in front of us, in the evening. It lay on the route of our advance and with further waiting could become a resistance nest for the enemy that would be hard to take. The answer was a clear 'No!' This was a pity, for the Domaine was to cause us grief as it lay high and controlled the terrain. On the road, shortly in front of it, clearly the same mine belt, which also laid in front of Losheimergraben, could be made out. The night was relatively quiet, finally the men could sleep late."

CHAPTER 12

Withdrawal toward Elsenborn

ESTABLISHING A BACKUP FRONT LINE AT MÜRRINGEN

On the evening of 16 December, Lt. Col. John M. Hightower was informed by the regimental commander that his 1st Battalion was attached to the 394th Infantry, 99th Division. The battalion was to load on trucks and proceed to the 99th Division, where guides awaited to lead the companies into position.

According to Hightower's personal diary, "On 13 December 1944, after a month in and around the Siegfried Line, the 23rd Infantry was moved into reserve in the vicinity of Camp Elsenborn, Belgium, and was assured that we would have a few days for rest and cleanup. It was bitterly cold, and the ground was frozen, but the men had managed to make themselves reasonably comfortable and were enjoying being out of harm's way for a while.

"Little did we know! The evening of 16 December, I was informed by Col. Jay B. Lovless, the Regimental Commander, that the 1st Battalion was now attached to the 394th Infantry; 99th Division which was under heavy attack by the German Army. We were to load onto trucks without delay and proceed to the 99th Division where we would be guided into backup positions behind the 394th Infantry Regiment. A splendid battalion that had managed the cold conditions now prepared for the move and waited for the trucks which arrived in good time.

"The motor column with MP guides moved out at 2230 hours and was soon on the road to Büllingen where we were to receive our orders and meet our 394th Infantry guides. We soon began to meet personnel and cargo trucks, artillery of all sizes, tanks and tank destroyers in large numbers on the road, all going the wrong way. At least, they were not going the same direction that we were, and I had the strange feeling that they were withdrawing. THEY WERE! From time to time, we had to pull over to the side of the road and stop until certain elements cleared us. I had an almost compelling urge to turn around and join them. I rejected that urge, however, because I was sure that Jay Lovless, my good friend and regimental commander, would kill me if I did. So, what the hell, let's go for the Germans."

The motor column moved out and proceeded to Büllingen, detrucked and marched southeast to Mürringen. Guides from the 99th Division led A, B, and C Companies into position on the south and southeastern edges of the town. The battalion command post was established in Mürringen. By 0600 hours on 17 December, all companies were dug in. C Company, less one platoon, was stretched on a 1,700-yard front on the southeast edge of Mürringen. B Company, on the right, held positions south of Hünningen with a platoon of C Company attached. A Company, in a semi-reserve position, had one platoon defending Hünningen from the west, another platoon east of the town covering a gap in B Company's line and a third platoon on the southern edge of Mürringen. Harassing artillery fire constituted enemy action during the night and early morning of 17 December in the sector defended by A, B, and C Companies. Hightower was instructed by the commander of the 394th Infantry to hold his position at all costs and engage any breakthrough in the 394th Infantry lines. From the battalion command post in Mürringen, a long stream of enemy armor was observed moving northwest along a road leading into Büllingen on the morning of 17 December. Well over 200 vehicles were estimated to have passed over the road that day. Poor observation prevented accurate estimates of damage done to these vehicles by division artillery.

Hightower's diary continues: "We reached Büllingen about midnight, found our guides and learned that the 99th Division had been under heavy attack, that the 394th Infantry Regiment could no longer hold its positions, and that we were to occupy backup positions which they had prepared earlier. We detrucked and moved by foot and organic vehicles to Hünningen where the guides moved the companies into well prepared positions. I was delighted with them. At that time there was no firing by either side. There

U.S. troops on their way out to Elsenborn Ridge.
U.S. ARMY

was some confusion about the location of my command post. It was supposed to be 'somewhere' in Mürringen, a village a short way from Hünningen. I told the Headquarters Company commander, Capt. John Fornaro, and 1st Lt. William F. Kinney, intelligence officer (S-2), to find the command post and come and get me when they had done so. When asked where I might be found, I answered that they would find me right where they left me—in my jeep, hopefully asleep. Sometime later, that is just where they found me. It was then 17 December 1944.

"I first took a quick look at the command post and then went to Hünnigen and checked the companies. They were in good shape. The 394th Infantry had done a good job of preparing the positions, both personnel and weapons placements, and I considered us ready for whatever was about to happen. I then found the 394th command post and reported to the regimental commander, Col. Don Riley. I thanked him for the reception and fine positions and asked him for a briefing. During this time Colonel Riley and his staff were busily shoving maps and papers into a pot-bellied heater. He explained that his front had fallen apart and that he was planning to withdraw whatever he could to Hünningen. He told me that he planned for my battalion to counterattack and restore his lines while he tried to reorganize as much of his regiment as he could. He asked me what I thought of the plan, and I reminded him that we had just arrived and had not had time to reconnoiter or try to find whatever we could of his units to help. I asked about artillery, tanks, and tank destroyers. There were none that he knew of. The artillery had fired all of its ammunition, and when the line units started coming apart, had begun a withdrawal. No one knew anything at all about tanks or tank destroyers.

"To compound the problem of support, the 2nd Division artillery that was moving to support us had not arrived. We did, however, have a forward observer, Lt. Charles W. Stockell (twenty-nine years later, we were to become neighbors in Beaufort County, South Carolina). Not knowing just when the artillery would reach us, I questioned the wisdom of trying to do with an unsupported battalion what the regiment had been unable to do. I suggested that they stop burning their papers long enough to find their troops which could, if he agreed, take up positions with us, and maybe we could hold the bastards. I offered an alternate plan to let us hold while his units passed through us and establish positions behind us that we could fall back to if we had to. This he liked, so we set about trying to do it. It did not work because they never found enough combat strength to make it possible.

"Shortly after I left Colonel Riley to get on with my work, the Germans renewed their assault on whatever was left of the 394th Infantry lines, and they collapsed under the weight of the attack. Hundreds of stragglers and

A modern shot of the command post of Lt. Col. John M. Hightower in Mürringen. The house is now empty, but it still has the marks and scars of the battle fought there many years ago. HANS WIJERS

vehicles began streaming out. We could see in the distance an armored column loaded with infantry moving across our front on its way to Büllingen. This put them to our right rear in strength. What was left of a company of the 2nd Engineers in Büllingen (about 100 men with one lieutenant) made their way to my command post where we fed them, gave them dry clothing and established a roadblock with them on the Büllingen side of Mürringen. As always, they gave a good account of themselves and kept several armored patrols from reaching Mürringen or Hünningen."

Shortly after noon, one officer and forty men from the 2nd Engineer Battalion and eighty men from the 254th Engineer Battalion came in to the 1st Battalion, 23rd Infantry, command post, having escaped from Büllingen before enemy armor cut off routes of withdrawal. Hightower sent these men to form a road block at a junction between Büllingen and the battalion command post to prevent enemy tanks in Büllingen from turning east and attacking the 1st Battalion from the rear.

PFC Rex Whitehead of H Company, 394th Infantry, 99th Infantry Division, remembers: "The reason I was at Mürringen on 17 December 1944 was due to my 81-millimeter mortar section (H/394) becoming detached from the main body of our battalion. We had been in position supporting G Company on the extreme right of the 2nd Battalion on the seam between the 1st and 2nd Battalions, just north of Losheimergraben and east of 'California Road' (International Highway). I had missed the morning shelling on the 16th, being at Honsfeld for a shower with others from the section. We spent the night of the sixteenth with the other sections on Corduroy Road and were told that Larson and Zimmerman had been killed. (They are still listed as missin in action.) Later, we found that two of our squad that did not return to our positions with us were captured at Honsfeld. Barney Welch drove us to our positions the morning of the seventeenth, and we witnessed a dogfight of fighter planes en route. The area was covered by shell holes and tree branches. Soon after arriving at our second section positions, Sergeant Failer was notified to withdraw. A jeep arrived, took the mortars, and we were told to leave the ammo and come out with G Company.

"While waiting for them on 'California Road,' troops passed walking north, saying they were part of the 3rd Battalion (perhaps the 1st) and that 'there is no one behind us but Germans.' We soon started walking north on 'California Road' and found later that G Company had taken another route to withdraw. We could hear the sound of heavy vehicles from the Losheimergraben area, three-fourths of a mile south. Our squad jeeps with Stewart, Qualkenbusch, and Paybe approached, and we piled on for a wild ride to 'Corduroy Road' and west to the battalion command post. At times we had to push the jeeps and trailers through shell holes on the log road. We were told it had been decided our section would have to be left, but Lt. Rufus Carpenter disagreed, and the three mentioned above volunteered to try to reach us (thank you, friends!). At the battalion command post, we were were told to keep going and catch the battalion headquarters company. We drove past the rest of the battalion, including our other sections, who were handcarrying their mortars. The convoy was joined, and as we left the woods and turned right, tracers were seen on our left, coming from the Hünningen area. 'Judge' Bartel stated that one would get busted on maneuvers having vehicles in a high, exposed position as we were.

"As we approached the first houses of Mürringen, shells came in, stopping the convoy, and three of us piled into a hole. It was my first shelling; I remembered a joke might relieve the tension, so asked Judge if he wanted a bite of a D bar. He replied that he did not—in very GI terms. Our group found a house for it was getting dark and the shelling continued. At this time we felt as if we were cutting out without a fight, not knowing of the fighting the other two battalions had been having and the magnitude of the German attack underway. Perhaps the worst was feeling isolated and alone. Sergeant Failor was told we were to join the 3rd Battalion, but could not make contact with them. Hearing a rumor that our battalion was just out of town, we drove east and the sky was lighted by flares, we assumed, but now think it was German searchlights reflecting from the clouds. Returning, I was left at a house as a runner, and guessed it was the 394th's command post. I sat on the stairs and was aware of much confusion and that it was difficult to stay awake. At this point, I can endorse what others have said and written about being apart from your unit, for we did not like being 'strangers,' and our concern was to find our battalion. We would learn later that they were still in the woods east of Mürringen that night."

First contact with the enemy came in the sector of B Company, 1st Battalion, 23rd Infantry, at about 1030 hours. From the 2nd Platoon's area, twelve tanks and an unknown number of infantry were sighted at the edge of a wooded area at a range of approximately 800 yards. Two three-inch tank destroyer guns of the 801st Tank Destroyer Battalion, which escaped from the Honsfeld area (attached to the 394th Infantry), were located in the 3rd Platoon's area when the tanks were sighted. Only one of these guns opened fire, but with six rounds it scored five direct hits and knocked out four of the tanks. The remaining tanks withdrew and were not seen again until mid-afternoon at a range of about two thousand yards. They never approached the company position again. During the morning there was considerable air activity in front of the 1st Battalion positions. P-47s strafed and dive-bombed enemy installations and targets of opportunity, but results could not be observed from the 1st Battalion area. The battalion's command post was bombed by a lone German plane during the afternoon. A five hundred pound bomb landed within fifty feet of the command post, but only one casualty resulted. Three American planes were shot down by heavy anti-aircraft fire within sight of the command post during the day.

The enemy did not display much activity until 1600 hours when a tremendous artillery barrage came down on the entire battalion. Lasting six minutes, most of the barrage fell in Hünningen, but A, B, and C Companies, 23rd Infantry, were caught on the edge of it. Almost immediately after the barrage lifted, enemy infantry could be seen advancing on the 2nd Platoon position through a long neck of woods which led directly into B Company's area.

An artillery observer (of the 2nd Infantry Division) who was with C Company of 23rd Infantry, climbed to a church steeple in the town, and despite poor observation of the target area, brought artillery down on the enemy attack to within one hundred yards of B Company's position. Then a heavy machine gun on the right flank of C Company opened fire, taking a heavy toll of casualties, and forcing most of the attacking force into a sunken road which ran down the center of the wooded area leading into the 2nd Platoon position. A light machine gun in the 2nd Platoon area immediately took up the fire and caught many of the enemy in the road bed.

Lt. Col. John M. Hightower recorded in his diary: "We still had no artillery, and the sky was heavily overcast so the Air Corps could do nothing for us. Colonel Riley had moved his command post to Mürringen not far from mine. I never saw a unit from the 394th Infantry or any other unit from the 99th Division. The 1st Battalion, 23rd Infantry, 2nd Division, became a frontline battalion responsible for defending the left flank of the 99th Division, and we accepted that responsibility with confidence. From then on we fought our own war with neither support nor interference from Colonel Riley. He realized that this was the best way to go. I appreciated it and kept him informed all the way. He appreciated that. We were shelled sporadically, but casualties were light. We could hear aircraft over us but did not know whose. At last the clouds broke, and lo and behold, the airplanes were ours, and they had that armored column in their sights. Down they came out of the wild blue yonder and scattered those German tanks to hell and gone. At about 1400 hours, six of them turned our way but stopped in confusion, apparently sizing up the situation. There were a couple of abandoned antitank guns and plenty of ammunition in our area, and some of our people knew how to shoot them. A good thing because they knocked four of them out. I never did know who did it. The other two got away.

"Sometime during the action, Charles Stockell was in a church steeple trying to raise his 37th Field Artillery by radio. I was monitoring his efforts when he reached them. They had just gone into position, and it was just in the nick of time. The Germans fired an intense artillery preparation on us. Before our artillery had fired its own concentrations they (Germans) moved about a battalion out of the woods to our front into an open field and, for some strange reason, stopped and methodically began positioning their men for an attack on B Company. Stockell barely had time to adjust his guns, but follow ing proper artillery procedure, as I understood it, he put a round to the right of target, a round left, one short, one long, adjustments, and then 'Fire for effect!' Then everything fired right on target. Charles yelled for them to fire the concentration again, and then once more. He then said, 'That is perfect. The Infantry thanks you, and I thank you. Mark that concentration!' That broke the attack, and the Germans fled back into the woods with Stockell and the 37th Field Artillery all over them. Later, they came after us again with greater strength and caution. That attack was beaten off within a hundred yards of our line by artillery and brave men with small arms, machine guns, and mortars. As our guns mowed down a line of them others took their place. They withdrew leaving more than a hundred dead on the field. It was awful. I can't speak for Charles, but the infantry still thanks the 37th Field Artillery.

"Later in the afternoon, five German aircraft bombed and strafed us but did little damage. Their infantry attacked the center of our line with at least a battalion. We stopped the first assault, but finally they succeeded in penetrating B Company's line. I had kept A Company in reserve for just such a need. I was there when it came, so I took a platoon of the company to support B Company. Before long, I had to take another platoon from A Company to work for B Company, and a real donnybrook took place across the entire front. The enemy took a section of our machine guns and used it against us in support of about fifty men. One of our light machine gun sections wiped the German gunners out and then took care of the riflemen at very close range. German losses again were heavy, and ours were certainly not insignificant. The fighting went on with small attacks across the front resulting in small but violent battles."

Hubert Eggert, of the 27th Fusilier Regiment, 12th Volksgrenadier Division, recalls: "Before we reach the edge of the woods in front of the village of Hünningen, we're stopped and a radio message comes in: 'The infantry will attack at 1600 hours with an artillery preparation of twenty minutes.' We wait; nothing happens and then another message comes over the radio: 'Attack at 1600 hours without artillery preparation.' There we have it. Food is not coming up, and with that neither is our dear old good field kitchen.

"The watch shows 1600 hours and we start off, again dispersed and immediately we receive a lively machine-gun fire from the direction of the road Hünningen to Büllingen, once again it is a jeep with a mounted machine gune. Heaven watches over us, and we find good cover in a hollow sand road that leads straight to Hünningen. I get orders to stay here with the company troops, while Leutenant Kirsten immediately attacks again, always along the road. Now the first overwhelmed American soldiers behind us reach the road. I shout at the GIs, and they immediately obey my 'Hands up,' and they lay themselves between us and next to us. Again some come in, 'let's go, go on down!' It all goes like clockwork, and we meet them in a friendly manner. We've got one who tells he is a football player, another tells he's a cricketer. Yet another German listens intently and then tells me: 'Don't trouble yourself so much with English, I speak quite good German.'

"Suddenly, Lieutenant Kirsten shows up, he is wounded by one shot through the upper thigh and now has been shot through the upper right arm. He says, 'Eggert, now I can't fire anymore, I'll go.' With him go our prisoners and an escort from our company. So, since I now am the oldest sergeant left of the remaining group, I take over command of the company, which now is exactly twenty-four men. But we get into Hünningen. It is getting dark; we sit in the cellar of a house and open conserve jars to take the water with spoons. Now we penetrate the village in single file. We notice we're not alone. But how are the once proud companies looking now? Here I learn that the battalion is only about sixty soldiers strong. A very young leutenant is leading the battalion. I advance up to the crossroads in the village, have a machine gun positioned, another company is coming up. A runner dashes up, brings a report to this company, yes, senior sergeant major. Then over there, about 30 meters away, I hear, 'Many men, many men.' I shout,

'Cover!' and already a salvo from a submachine gun is fired at us. Result: one dead comrade and three wounded, among whom is me. So now we're left with twenty men. I can speak and hand over the remains of the 3rd Company to a sergeant, PFC Fritz Page."

Despite heavy casualties, the Germans continued to advance in formation hitting the 1st and 2nd Platoons almost simultaneously. Twenty-five to thirty-yard spacing of their foxholes made covering their front and flanks difficult for B Company rifleman. Some Germans did manage to overrun 1st Platoon. No German reached a point beyond the platoon command post. Four men with automatic weapons killed about fifty of the Germans who made the penetration.

The Germans hit B Company in seven distinct waves on the afternoon and evening of 17 December. The Germans overran two heavy machine-gun positions and turned the guns on an A Company platoon that was covering a gap in B Company's line. An A Company light machine gun section opened fire and wiped out the German gun crews. The A Company light machine-gun crews also cut down German infantry trying to advance through the gap. After that attack was repulsed, Captain Fugit was ordered to move the platoon covering the gap to another position to meet another threat along the B Company front. The order was later changed to move the A Company platoon south of Mürringen to cover a gap between B Company's 2nd and 3rd Platoons. Moving under fire, the A Company platoon did not reach the new position until the early-morning hours of 18 December.

Meanwhile, Lieutenant Colonel Douglas, 1st Battalion, 394th Infantry, and Captain Sandiland, having received the order to withdraw, went north through the woods towards the corduroy east-west road which ran from Mürringen to the 2nd Battalion's command post. For part of the way, they were chased by a small German patrol which fired several times, but fortunately missed. The sole means of maintaining contact was over the 300 radio carried along with them. Douglas's jeep had been destroyed by the direct hit of enemy artillery fire. Regiment could not be contacted on radio, but contact was maintained with A and C companies. At about 1630 hours, Colonel Douglas arrived at the command post of the 2nd Battalion of the 394th Infantry Regiment, at the moment they started to move toward Elsenborn. By radio, Lieutenant Colonel Douglas ordered the mortar platoon of D Company to withdraw to the command post.

Pvt. Devon A. Lewis of HQ Company, 1st Battalion, 394th Infantry, who was with Douglas's group, describes what happened: "They told us we were going to have to withdraw from our present position and try to get to Elsenborn. We had a jeep and trailer, so Sergeants Haggerty and Ferrari, a jeep driver, got the jeep started, and two of our message-center personnel got

into the jeep also. I laid flat on the trailer top. We pulled out from the woods onto the Losheimergraben and Losheim road. Our jeep driver got mixed up in his directions and turned toward Losheim, and as he did so the German soldiers were coming up this road shouting 'Heil Hitler' and shooting at us with burp guns and rifles. The jeep driver turned quickly to go in the other direction. We went down in a ditch and almost turned our jeep over, but we were lucky and got back onto the road. We drove down this road as fast as we could. We went by a side road that came into the Losheimergraben road, and I saw a German tank coming at us on this side road. We kept on driving and we came upon what was left of 1st Battalion and Headquarters Company, 394th Infantry, 99th Division. We met Colonel Douglas and other officers, and they told us to get on this high knoll and get next to a hedge row and start digging foxholes.

"It started to get dark towards evening and the visibility was poor, so the Germans started to shoot up flares to try and see if there was any troop movement below. As they did this everybody tried not to move, but I guess they saw our position and started to use mortars and shells on us. The colonel and other officers went into a nearby building or shed and talked about what they should do about what was left of our HQ Company, 1st Battalion, and the line companies. They said we were going on a long walk and what we thought was a burden to carry we could leave it where we were. We

Withdrawal toward Elsenborn

These four images came from the son of a German soldier who served with the 27th Fusilier Regiment in the Ardennes. HANS WIJERS

all took our full field packs off and left them behind. But we kept our rifles, bayonets, two bandoliers of ammunition, cartridge belts, and canteens and overcoats. We started across this field and walked quite awhile, till we came to a road. Then we moved out on the road and stayed about ten feet apart and walked on each side of the road. After we walked a few miles we ran into some machine gun fire, and we all went for the ditch and laid in ice water. When the firing subsided, we started out again on this road, and finally we got off the road and went into a field or farm yard and approached a barn that had German and American vehicles parked outside. We were so close to this barn that I could have touched it. I don't know if there were any Germans sleeping in the barn or not, but we sure walked real slow and quiet. You felt as if someone was pointing a rifle at you and you were going to be shot anytime. That's when we were really sweating blood, and our hearts were pounding like a trip hammer. We passed by this barn and still continued to walk awhile, and finally we came to a river or stream. The banks of this river were at a forty-five-degree angle and very steep. Colonel Douglas told us to walk on this slanting river bank as there were German soldiers up above in the woods. As we tried to walk on this steep river bank, we had one hell of a time as we slipped and fell.

"Colonel Douglas finally said that we should get into the river or stream and try to walk up the stream and against the current. It was rough going as we tried to walk. The bottom was slippery and full of rocks, and we made little headway as some of us slipped and fell. Colonel Douglas said we should get out and get on top of the bank so we did, and it was pitch dark, and there were some big trees in the woods; so we followed the colonel and walked through the woods a long way. All of a sudden, the colonel said, 'Halt,' and we stopped. I looked to my right in the woods and saw the outline of a building, and you could see a light coming from the building. As we stood there with our guns trained on the building, the door opened and two German soldiers came out of the door and walked toward us carrying a garbage can. They walked about fifty feet from us and put the garbage can down and turned around and went back inside the building without seeing us. Colonel Douglas said, 'Let's get the hell out of here fast!' and we sure did! As we moved fast through the woods we came upon a gully, so we went down from the high ground into the gully. As we moved through this gully, a machine gun opened up over our heads on the high ground. Everybody took off in one direction, and I dove into some brush that was near me. When the machine gun stopped shooting, I came out of the brush and there was nobody around. I sure was all alone! Then I guessed that they went in the direction that we were originally heading, so moved that way and walked about 300 feet when I came upon a road. I saw some American jeeps and some big two-and-a-half-ton American trucks. This is where I met up with my lost buddies, and was I ever glad to see them!"

The mortar platoon—all that was left from D Company—arrived at the command post about 1700 hours and joined the rear of the motorized column of the 2nd Battalion, which cut through the woods, over muddy roads, quitting the front lines.

PFC Howard I. Bowers, the ammunition bearer for the machine-gun squad of 2nd Platoon, D Company, 394th Infantry, remembers: "As evening approached, we were told that orders had been received to withdraw to regimental headquarters in Mürringen, a few miles to the west. We were ordered to destroy the machine gun and to carry only our personal weapons. I removed the buttplate from the machine gun and put it in my overcoat pocket, then removed the inside mechanism and carried it a short distance before throwing it into the snow. There were about fifty men in this group, led by a lieutenant from A Company. At dusk, we headed across country to Mürringen and arrived there after midnight on Monday, 18 December, and dug in on a hillside. During the withdrawal, I stayed close to the lieutenant and his radioman until word was passed forward for all D Company men to fall to the rear. Someone wanted to count heads. We did not make contact with any German soldiers during the withdrawal, but most of the time there were sounds of a fierce fire fight to our left. We could hear rifles and the

Howard Bowers.

rapid fire of German burp guns and the slower firing of American machine guns. We soon left the woods, and as we crossed into the middle of an open field, a flare suddenly lit the night like day. Rogers yelled, 'Freeze! and I can still see a tableau of soldiers frozen in different positions like statues. I held my breath waiting for the burp guns to open fire and wanting to hit the ground. But no one moved and no one fired on us. After an eternity the flare burned out, and we moved on across the field into the woods along a stream and up a hill to Mürringen. Even now I can close my eyes and see the flare and wait for the burp guns and feel the fear. We stopped in an open field on a hillside east of Mürringen. It was so dark that I couldn't see the men around me. The ground was frozen hard like the previous night, and after digging a shallow slit trench I tried to sleep."

The rifle companies of the 2nd Battalion were reported to be still in line to the east at this time. The fifty-man column, after going about 500 yards, was fired upon by small numbers of Germans armed with rifles. The column continued on, emerged from the woods, and started up over a bald hill. Here it was plastered by enemy artillery and lost about twelve men as casualties. The head of the column finally reached Mürringen about 1930 hours.

After Douglas reached Mürringen, he immediately posted guides along all the roads leading to the village, to bring in any elements of friendly forces which succeeded in getting through to the position. The defensive position was manned, greatly under strength. Lieutenant Colonel Douglas, who went ahead of the column with his S-3, reported to the regimental command post at about 1830 hours. He reported that he had about fifty men available, the rest were still out somewhere. He was ordered to organize an assembly position behind the 3rd Battalion, east of Mürringen, at the head of the draw. This was about 2100 hours. The men of the battalion were located about 400 yards due south of this position. Douglas ordered the men to move about 200 yards due north, and started them digging in on the forward slope, the positions there offering better defensive possibilities. He then returned to the regimental command post, where he learned that contact had been lost with the balance of the 2nd Battalion. The 3rd Battalion took up positions south of the east-west road running into Mürringen.

About 2130 hours, Douglas sent his A&P Platoon to reestablish contact between the left flank of the 3rd Battalion, 394th Infantry, and the rifle companies of the 2nd Battalion, known only to be somewhere to the east. Two plans were under consideration at the time. The first was to hold the present position at Mürringen and Hünningen, and depend on resupply by air. Ammunition was extremely low, and weather had grounded air on previous days. The other plan was to withdraw over the only open route, the road north to Krinkelt. The regimental commander, Lt. Col. Donald Riley, decided on the latter course. 2nd Battalion, 23rd Infantry, commander, Major Buck, stated that he would put his vehicles behind the regiment's vehicles, and that his infantry would proceed crosscountry to Krinkelt. Douglas volunteered to protect the right flank of the route of withdrawal.

By this time, the battalion strength—swelled by A Company, the remnants of B and C under Lieutenant Plankers—numbered about 260 officers and men. The motor column was to start north at 0215 hours. The foot column was to start at about 0230 hours (Captain Sandiland). All through this period the town of Mürringen and vicinity were subjected to heavy enemy artillery fire, which fell with clockwise regularity every five minutes and lasted for about 4 minutes each time. Exceed ingly accurate fire interdicted all the crossroads and the road leading north from Mürringen to Krinkelt.

Pvt. Josef Peters of the 12th Engineer Battalion, 12th Volksgrenadier Division, recalls: "Our division was located in the Frauenkron-Hallschlag area. I belonged to the engineer battalion and had been attached to the 89th Regiment. From the woods in the direction of Losheimergraben by mid afternoon of 16 December, we advanced toward Losheimergraben. Until then we had no contact with the enemy. There we made several prisoners in the woods. We did not see any tanks. A few German jeeps came driving up from the direction of Hollerath; in one of them the commander of the 12th Volksgrenaider Division; Engel stood up straight. I saw my first tank (knocked

Josef Peters.

out) in a row of firs a short distance in front of Mürringen. Our task was to sweep through the woods in the direction of Hünningen-Büllingen.

"Then we advanced on Mürringen in the late afternoon on 17 December. At the forestry house, at the edge of Mürringen, we ran into resistance. After the conclusion of this fight, the Yankees had six killed. I can still remember clearly that a wounded man who was still alive was lying in front of the house. I took him in my arms to give him something to drink; he spoke a few words and then he died as well. I took a letter pouch and a small wallet from him. The letter pouch contained the photo of his wife and two children, it was a colored woman. The dead then were buried at the hedge. By evening outposts were positioned. Our company command post remained in the forestry house. I formed a scouting party on my own account. Directly behind Mürringen we found an American artillery position [371st Artillery, 99th Infantry Division]. I crawled up to it and found that the position had been abandoned. Vehicles, everything had been left in place. When I searched it, I found everything we needed. With a loaded American truck, I drove to the command post through Mürringen; this was the first large haul. By the next morning, we went off toward Wirtzfeld-Krinkelt-Elsenborn. Though supported by the 12th SS Panzer Division *Hitlerjugend*, the attack was unsuccessful."

Lieutenant Colonel Lemcke, commander of the 89th Grenadier Regiment, 12th Volksgrenadier Division, offers his story: "The 89th Regiment on

A killed American soldier in his foxhole.

the day of the attack was in reserve and had a strength of 120 men in each of the six companies of both battalions. We had come from the battle for Aix-la-Chapelle and had gotten few replacements. We were supposed to get thirty-six assault guns, but had to enter battle with six 'veterans.' No Tiger tanks. By the afternoon of 16 December, I made reconnaissance trip and followed in the tracks of the 27th Regiment under Lemm along the railroad to Büllingen, which has quite deep ravines at times. There we met several wounded of the 27th, which I had transported to the rear. When I met Lemm, he asked me to cover his advance northward. With thirty men we formed a chain and advanced. We ambushed an American regimental staff with six new jeeps and stayed there overnight.

"The village of Mürringen was conquered by part of the 1st Battalion, 89th Regiment, led by Major Ripcke during 17 December. They luckily, and favored by fog, marched through the U.S. field positions and penetrated the village. A farmer of Mürringen advised Ripcke of the cellars holding the US reserves. He took about 100 of those for prisoner. Due to a lack of any messages, I followed Ripcke's force on his way to Mürringen in a captured jeep, however missed access from the southwest and entered the village from northwest. The moment I arrived at Mürringen, the fight started between Ripcke's force in the village and the U.S. forces in the field positions east of the village. Ripcke asked me to supervise the column of prisoners sent back under the custody of four of his men. The same moment the column was hit

Lieutenant Colonel Lemcke.

already by American small-arms fire which caused several dead and wounded (ten and sixteen, respectively). When about hundred men of the 2nd Battalion came for support, the American force withdrew. When I met the commander of the 27th Fusilier Regiment (Lemm) the day before, the advance party of Task Force Peiper had just set out . Riding in my jeep towards Mürringen, I was accompanied by Major Müller, an artillery officer. There was no knowledge at division headquarters of my intention to follow Ripcke. Division headquarters having missed me despite getting several messages showing my signature, temporarily put the commander of the 12th Engineer Battalion, Major Petter, in command of the 89th Grenadier Regiment. After return to my command post, I was addressed reproachfully by the commander of the division, General Engel; several packages of Camels, however, made him speechless."

MOVING OUT TO WIRTZFELD

Colonel Hightower's 1st Battalion, 23rd Infantry, was in a difficult and exposed position at Hünningen. His main strength, deployed to counter German pressure from the Buchholz-Honsfeld area, faced south and southeast, but the German columns taking the Honsfeld-Büllingen detour were moving toward the northwest and thus behind the Hünningen defenders. Whether any part of this latter enemy force would turn against the rear of the 1st Battalion was the question.

Late in the night of 17 December, Hightower received garbled radio messages from the 394th Infantry. It subsequently developed that the 394th Infantry was withdrawing to positions east of Wirtzfeld, and Hightower's 1st Battalion, 23rd Infantry, was now attached to the 9th Infantry Regiment, 2nd Infantry Division, which was in Krinkelt-Rockerath after withdrawing from a bloody engagement in the Roer River campaign. The 9th Infantry's commander instructed Hightower to withdraw, but the battalion could not withdraw as it was still in close engagement with the attacking Germans.

An eight-man patrol from the 2nd Battalion, 23rd. Infantry, under Lieutenant Starling, arrived at the 1st Battalion's command post shortly before midnight of 17 December for the purpose of guiding the 1st Battalion to the rear to positions pre-arranged by the 9th Infantry. Although some units were still under attack by German units, orders to begin preparing for withdrawal were issued to the company commanders. Roads to the rear were thought to have been cut by enemy armor, so preparations were in progress to destroy all vehicles when a 2nd Medical Battalion officer volunteered to lead the convoy over a route he thought was still open. Organic vehicles under S-2 Lieutenant Kinney departed at 0215 hours on 18 December, but were held up in Mürringen by abandoned vehicles of the 394th Infantry blocking the road. Here Lieutenant Kinney was told that German tanks controlled the town of Krinkelt. When it was discovered that the German tanks in Krinkelt had been knocked out, some men of the 1st Battalion, 23rd Infantry, became truck drivers and drove the trucks out. Some of the trucks carried wounded men. The convey moved westward until 0800 when it reached Wirtzfeld where foot troops of the 1st Battalion who had marched cross country were already in position.

At 0200 hours, Hightower ordered his companies to withdraw, although the Germans were still attacking in the B Company sector. After the withdrawal there were sixteen men from the 2nd Platoon, five men from the 1st Platoon, fifteen men from the mortar section, and twelve men from headquarters remaining in B Company. The 3rd Platoon was under attack and was unable to pull out and leave with the company. C Company had less difficulty executing its withdrawal. A covering force of nine men and one officer allowed the company to pull back in an orderly manner. A Company was last to leave the Hünningen-Mürringen area after Captain Fugit gathered his widely scattered platoons. One squad of the 2nd Platoon of A Company was taken prisoner by the Germans. That squad was a rear guard covering force for A Company's withdrawal.

Lt. Col. John M. Hightower wrote in his diary: "Shortly after going back to the command post to see what all was going on, a radio call came from Col. Chester J. Herschfelder, commanding officer of the 9th Infantry, 2nd

William Fugit.

Division. He told me that we had been relieved from being attached to the 394th Infantry and now attached to the 9th Infantry. He said that our situation was very grave and that we should withdraw and come to Wirtzfeld. I replied that we were in close combat and that it was impossible to disengage now. I told him that since I was responsible for the right flank of the 394th Infantry, I would discuss the situation with Colonel Riley. He agreed and told me to use my own judgement. Shortly after that a lieutenant and an eight man patrol from the 2nd Battalion, 23rd Infantry, attached to the 9th Infantry, arrived at the command post for the purpose of leading us to positions in the 9th Infantry's area. At about that time fighting had almost stopped, so I left word for the company commanders to meet me at the command post and went to Colonel Riley's command post. There I told him about my call from Colonel Herschfelder and found he had heard nothing from his division commander about withdrawing. I told him that I was in the process of making plans to do so and that maybe he should let his division commander know it. He agreed and asked me to include whatever was left of the 394th in my plans. He also told me that they would do whatever I wanted them to do. I was happy to agree and asked him to give me a liaison officer from his staff to help coordinate the operation. He sent a captain with us back to my command post. His name might have been Sandiland. On the way back, I met one of our doctors with a question, 'Sir, what do you think our chances are? Any?' I patted him on the shoulder and answered, 'Stay with me, and they are 100 percent. He said, 'Thank you, sir. I'll be there.' So then all I had to do was whatever I had to do.

"Colonel Herschfelder called again to tell me where the Germans were and that if we didn't come out, we would surely be surrounded. I told him that we were making plans to do so and had his patrol to guide us out. He was pleased. I must digress a little to describe Colonel Herschfeld. I am sure that he had come up through the ranks. I know that he was as tough as a boot, looked like a bulldog, and that everyone in his regiment was scared to death of him. He had the Distinguished Service Cross from World War I and another from World War II, so everyone respected him as a combat soldier. I would not have been happy serving under his command ordinarily, but I was happy to do so now, since I could not be with the 23rd and Colonel Lovless. I had full confidence in both.

"Colonel Riley called that his division commander had ordered him to withdraw and asked me to let him know what to do. I told him that his captain had done a good job and would soon be there with the plan. He thanked me and reassured me that they would follow them. We thought that the roads to Krinkelt to our north and to Wirtzfeld east of Krinkelt would be impassable, so we tried to figure out what to do about our vehicles. Fire was out of the question, so we were prepared for sugar in the gas tanks. Then, an ambulance driver who had just returned from an evacuation of wounded told me that he had come over those roads and that they were passable. Good news. That ambulance driver became the convoy guide without opposition. Here is what we planned and did: The 394th, men and vehicles out by road followed by our vehicles with a rear guard along with antitank weapons bringing up the rear. I didn't have an executive officer, so I put my S-2 Lt. Bill Kinney, a fine officer, in charge of our vehicle convoy. The 'foot soldiers' led by the guide patrol and Capt. Frank W. Luchowsky, my S-3, another fine officer, would go cross country directly to Wirtzfeld. Company B would leave a platoon commanded by Lt. William H. Crane in our positions until we had cleared. It was to answer any threat with enough firepower to keep the Germans confused as much as possible. The rest of the company would be at the tail of the column as our rear guard and to receive its platoon if it could get away. The decision to leave that platoon behind on what I knew could and probably would be a suicide mission was the toughest one that I have ever made in my life, but someone had to make it. I was that someone, and I agonized over it. Company commanders would be at the tail of their companies, and I would be at the tail of the battalion. This to prevent straggling, and would be where an attack would most likely come if one came."

Lieutenant Colonel Douglas learned that the general situation on the front of the 99th Division was very unclear. The positions to the south of the village of Hünningen, occupied on the evening of 16 December by the 1st Battalion, 23rd Infantry, 2nd Infantry Division, were pressurized most by the German attacks. In the morning, troops of Peiper's column had surrounded the village of Büllingen, to the rear of the 394th Regiment. By the evening of 17 December, the only route that still permitted an escape out of this sector ran through Krinkelt. But in this place, the situation was far from clear. In the evening, battle had raged in Krinkelt and Rocherath, which could only mean that the Germans had reached them. This situation meant that the 394th Regiment ran the risk of being cut off from its rear. The 99th Division proposed that the 394th Regiment remain in its current position and be resupplied by air if need be. Very late in the evening the regiment decided to withdraw its forces northeast, towards Elsenborn, via Krinkelt and Wirtzfeld. They were almost out of ammunition and the bad weather had grounded the allied aircraft during the preceding days.

The 1st Battalion left Mürringen at 0400 hours on 18 December and marched cross-country under harrassing artillery fire until reaching positions north and east of Wirtzfeld about 0800. Badly depleted in manpower, the battalion dug in during the day to defend Wirtzfeld. Late in the afternoon on 18 December, A and C Companies were dispatched back to Krinkelt and attached to the 38th Infantry Regiment.

PFC Howard I. Bowers, D Company, 394th Infantry, remembers: "Some time after midnight we were ordered up again and told that we were moving north a couple of miles to Krinkelt and a few miles west to Elsenborn where there was a Belgian army camp. The main body of the 394th Regiment would take vehicles, but I was in a group of men from the 1st Battalion led by Lt. Col. Robert Douglas, battalion commander, that went overland on foot. We headed north on the east side of the road running from Murringen to Krinkelt. I learned many years later that we were supposed to be the flank protection for the main group. We moved off the open hillside into the woods and up onto a ridge. I had to place a hand on the backpack of the man ahead of me so as not to become separated in the pitch black darkness. After about an hour we came down off the ridge, waded through knee deep mud, crossed a creek, and climbed up a steep bank onto a road. It was just starting to become daylight, and I could see a long line of vehicles abandoned along the road. I learned later that on approaching Krinkelt, the front of the vehicle column had been fired on and that Colonel Riley, thinking this was a German roadblock, had ordered everyone to leave their vehicles and head west across country, every man for himself. Colonel Douglas sent a patrol forward, and word was soon passed back that 2nd Infantry Division men were holding Krinkelt. We boarded the vehicles, and anyone who could drive took a driver's seat. I climbed into the back seat of a weapons

All kinds of U.S. vehicles are standing beside the road, and soldiers are moving the opposite way—a confused U.S. Army. U.S. ARMY

Dick Bowers.

carrier, an open vehicle a little larger than a jeep. Two men from D Company were in the front seat. I'm not sure who they were, but the driver might have been Paul Rosenberry. Sitting next to me was a lieutenant who might have been from D Company, but I am not sure.

"It was nearing daylight, and we soon came to an intersection where there were buildings on both sides and American soldiers with 2nd Division shoulder patches. They waved us through, and as we passed beyond the intersection, a medic beside the road asked if someone had room for a wounded man. The lieutenant said we had room, but the vehicles were moving bumper-to-bumper at a fast speed, and we didn't stop. I have often wondered if someone stopped for that wounded man. We soon came to the village of Wirtzfeld where we unloaded, and what was left of D Company assembled along a hedgerow in an open field. It was here that I first learned that D Company's 1st Platoon and B Company had been overrun and all but destroyed in the fighting at Losheimergraben and that less than half of the 1st Battalion's 850 men had escaped. Sergeant Murray, my squad leader in B Company, was killed charging into attacking German soldiers while firing a Browning automatic rifle after his squad had been wiped out. I still wonder what would have happened to me if I had not been transferred from B Company to D Company and then from the 1st Platoon to the 2nd Platoon back at Camp Maxey.

"Two columns of weary foot soldiers headed west from Wirtzfeld toward Elsenborn, one column on each side of the muddy road, while trucks loaded with 2nd Division soldiers headed east toward Krinkelt down the middle of the road. They yelled at us asking why we were headed to the rear away from the battle, some making derogatory comments about our fighting ability. Some of our men retorted in kind, but I was too tired to care what they said. We rounded a corner and started up a hill where there was a kitchen truck overturned in the ditch and several Belgian civilians taking food from it. I picked up a can of tomatoes. At the top of the hill we stopped for a break, and I opened the can with my trench knife and shared it with a buddy. It was Monday, December 18, and those few cold tomatoes and the D ration on Sunday afternoon were my only food in almost three days. I don't remember being hungry. While sitting in the snow beside the road, Bill Bray of L Company, a friend from basic training at Fort Benning and ASTP at Arkansas State, came up the hill, and we talked for a few minutes before moving on. About noon we arrived in the village of Elsenborn. There was a field kitchen in the village square, and I ate my first full meal in almost seventy-two hours. I still thought that we were being pulled out of combat and would go on to Camp Elsenborn for rest and reorganization, but this was not to be. We found a cellar for a few hours rest, and I was awakened during the afternoon by artillery shells falling on Elsenborn."

Pvt. William Bray, L Company, 394th Infantry, tells his story: "From the station we began our move back toward Mürringen, Wirtzfeld and finally Elsenborn. From then on, and after 52 years, things are a bit of a blur. Most of the platoon took off up the road that ran behind the station. The snow was at least knee deep, and the going was difficult. We had gone only a short distance when I ran through the command post tent of I Company or K Company and found their candy ration. Boxes of candy bars. I grabbed a box of Clark bars and put them in my jacket. That was all three or four of us had to eat for quite a while. At a cross roads we turned west, I believe, and headed towards Mürringen. As we trudged up that road it grew dark. I had a BAR and a full ammo belt which was quite heavy. It would come loose at the expansion buckle and fall down around my ankles. Finally, I had to stop and fix the belt. This took a few minutes.

"When I started to move on up the road, the rest of the platoon was out of sight. It was quite dark. I kept going, and in a few minutes I came to a group of men standing by an overturned truck or ambulance. I asked one of them if this was third platoon, and when he answered I knew he was no GI. I then saw the cutaway helmet against the sky. In the confusion I just pushed him aside and walked through that group of Germans and on up the road. I had gone only a few hundred yards when I ran into the end of my platoon hiking up the road. How they walked through that group of Germans, I cannot understand. I often wonder what that German soldier thought I said to him. Perhaps he was as startled as I. This incident has always highlighted to me the confusion that existed at that time. The Germans for a short period went so fast they became disorganized. The Americans were going in all directions which added to the confusion. "Just outside Mürringen we were ordered off the road and told to take positions on the side of a hill facing the enemy. We dug shallow foxholes which was no small feat with an entrenching tool in that frozen ground. No sooner had we got them dug than we were ordered to move out. Unfortunately, our company runner could not find all of the men, and several did not get the word to move. My platoon was now leading the march up the road. About midnight we were stopped by some officers, one of which was Colonel Riley, 394th regimental commander. He asked who we were, and when we identified ourselves he said, 'Men, we don't know what is happening. We can't determine where the enemy is, or where our troops are. We do know that you are in front, so I want you to take a 270-degree azimuth, due west toward where you see those howitzers firing. We believe those guns are ours, but be careful when you get there. About 2000 men will be following you; God bless you.' With that, we took off cross-country due west.

"After an hour or so we stopped at a hedgerow for a bit of a rest only to discover that after the seventh man, there were no others. In some way we had gotten away from the others, and the connection was lost. We went back a short distance but could not find anyone. We spent the rest of the night in a wooded area which in the morning we discovered was an orchard. We were lost. After what we had been through, we said, 'Let's stay lost.' We had had enough. Moving on we came to a road and an overturned supply truck [this is the location where Bill and Howard met]. We found a gallon can of powdered eggs, a gallon of peanut butter and a gallon of pineapple preserves. There was nothing we could do with the eggs, but we ate peanut butter and preserves. We went down the road and came to a small town. I never knew the name of it. As we went down the street a captain came up to us and asked us who we were. When we told him, he said, 'You are no longer in the 99th. I'm putting you in the 2nd Division. Wait right here until I get back.' We had

William Bray.

no desire to join the 2nd Division, and when he turned his back on us, we took off out of town and out of sight. We ran into some woods and wandered around for a while and came back out on a road, either the one we had been on or another. We still had some of our peanut butter and preserves. As we sat on the bank of the road eating, a Jeep came barreling over hill, and when it saw us it stopped and backed up. We recognized our battalion commander, Major Kriz. He asked who we were, and then told us to take off down the road in the same direction he was going and we would come to our outfit. We couldn't stay lost any longer. Sure enough, we came in Wirtzfeld and found most of our company."

All around the towns of Mürringen, Hünningen, and others, small groups of men were still hiding in the woods, trying to find their way to Elsenborn Ridge, or finding other groups so they could join in. But the enemy seemed to be everywhere, and they didn't know which place was still in friendly hands.

Lt. Dick Ralston, weapons platoon commander, K Company, 394th Infantry, recalls: "We headed back into the woods (away from the front lines) and ended this day (seventeenth) hiding in the forest in thick planted trees. The Jerries were all around us. We could see several camp fires, and hear singing here and there. Before dawn we headed out in the direction of Mürringen and Krinkelt, we thought (now the eighteenth). We had abandoned the jeeps and trailers when we headed into the woods. After carrying mortars and machine guns and loads of ammo for same, even with rotating the loads, it was too much. The going was rough and sometimes very dense in the trees. Some of the men hurt so much from the overpowering weight they were actually crying. We finally had to leave the majority of it, hidden here and there in the woods. We would check wire when we crossed it, putting our field telephones on it, to see if we could gain contact with someone. But never could.

"In the middle of the afternoon, we came out into a large open area. In the distance straight ahead we could see what we thought was Mürringen, and off to the right, Krinkelt. As we moved toward the former, we could see and hear that the Germans were firing into Krinkelt (and its twin town) from three sides. We felt sure they could see us, but hoped they were too busy shelling the towns to shell us. We didn't know if the Jerries were in Mürringen, but hoped not. We got a good way across a field going along a dirt road headed for Mürringen when we began to receive fire from that town. As I recall it, it must have been mortar fire for us to hear the firing sounds so as to know from whence it was coming. We kept going for awhile, and probably picked up small arms fire too, because we branched off to the right toward the rear of Krinkelt. It was very spooky being out on that wide open field with a big fight going on at the village to our right as we passed it. I believe this was the night we spent in the large tents left by an artillery unit. We zonked out, dead tired.

Dick Ralston.

"Early the next morning (the nineteenth), I was awakened by one of our sentries who said a GI was out there, and he had come down the road licketysplit, and had been accosted verbally by our guard. The GI told him (and he repeated it to me) that a column of German tanks was coming down that road, with a company or more of infantry fanned out around it attacking and taking prisoners, and that they had a column of GI prisoners following the tanks. He had rolled off the road and down into the bushes, and somehow gotten around them. We were packed into the two tents, no defense. I radioed the captain in the next tent, and he said, 'Lets get the hell out of here on the double,' and we did. Thank God for that kid. If they had sprayed those tents with bullets, we would have had it.

"I'm vague here now, but I think it was the same day that we finally began to see some American troops again, and made our way into Elsenborn (just by pure luck). Talk about another stroke of luck, we ran into our very own company kitchen truck and mess sergeant and staff. They cooked us up some biscuits and dried beef gravy!! We sat there and ate a little, but our stomachs had shriveled up so from lack of food, that we couldn't eat it all, even though we must have been still hungry. We reported in and told them what we had

Digging in at Elsenborn Ridge. U.S. troops prepare for another large-scale attack on Elsenborn. U.S. ARMY

Senior officers of the 2nd Infantry Division. Lt. Col. John M. Hightower is third from left in the front row. HIGHTOWER FAMILY

left of the company, and we found a couple houses and a barn in which to spend the night. Pooped? Oh man! The next day we headed up onto Elsenborn Ridge and started digging in."

SITUATION OF THE 2ND BATTALION, 394TH INFANTRY

All hell seemed to break loose on the 2nd Battalion's flanks, and there was no doubt that the situation was becoming worse when Capt. Boyd M. McCune, assistant regimental S-3, arrived at the battalion's command post at about 1415 hours with an order for withdrawal and an overlay showing the tentative line to which to fall back. This order called for the retrograde movement to start at 1500 hours on 17 December so that representatives were hastily summoned from the companies and given their instructions and all plans for the withdrawal. They were told that a battalion of the 2nd Division had gone into position around Honsfeld about that time and that conditions looked bad.

The shortness of time between receipt of the order and its execution was a serious problem, although McGee said this didn't give the battalion staff too much cause for worry, since the route of withdrawal led over ground with which the company commanders were familiar. However, the withdrawal did not start on time. The battalion vehicles, which had been farther back, were evacuated, with Captain Legare, the executive officer, going with them. A covering force of one-third of each platoon was ordered to remain in position until 1630; the battalion command post party was to pull back to establish a new command post in the rear, and the companies were ordered to come out via three routes over trails and fire breaks. The new temporary commandp ost and the rendezvous point was in place. The companies started to pull back and the command group was in constant radio communication with them. (They had no contact with regiment directly, because, has been pointed out in the story of Captain Legare, the battalion commander's radio was left behind in the jeep.) The companies were separated but had direct radio contact with each other.

The command group moved out in an attempt to find the battalion's rear command post when, about dusk, as they were going straight down the road on their north, McGee said they heard men talking and digging in to their right. They stopped, got under cover, and listened. The voices sounded American, so they put their hands over their heads in order not to surprise the digging men and be shot, and walked into the middle of them. After sufficiently identifying themselves, McGee said they convinced the men to take them to their command post, which turned out to be that of C Company, 393rd Infantry. They talked things over, found out that the situation had become extremely serious, and decided to go back out on the road and try again to find their rear command post. By then it was dark. They made radio contact with the companies and were notified that they were digging in for the night. The colonel, McGee, and the approximately fifty men with them, returned to the C Company command post and made arrangements to stay for the night, since they decided that it would be more dangerous to work their way back to the companies in the darkness.

They tied in with C Company's command post and made plans to help in the defense of the area should the Germans attack. But that night in that area the Germans were very quiet, save for the sound of burp guns around the whole area throughout the night. The radio they had with them, McGee said, was growing very weak, and it was difficult to keep contact with the companies. In fact, it was impossible to gain any contact with some of them. Finally, they worked out a system whereby they would to reach E Company by turning on their set every hour, have them check in and pass back any instructions for the rest of the battalion, which could be relayed by E Company. This contact was first established about 1900 and was retained throughout the night.

Just before daylight, it was decided to swing E Company around and make contact with C Company of the 393rd on their left, thus presenting a semisolid front to the enemy and closing the gap which they then knew existed between the two battalions. Some friendly artillery fell on the area during the night, but there were no casualties. Since there was no communication with any higher headquarters by either battalion, it was then decided to withdraw farther to the west in an effort to contact friendly lines. Thus, the companies of the 2nd Battalion were ordered to move into the area of the 1st Battalion, 393rd, and join forces, so that the whole group could move out together. Captain Patterson was ordered to move his company out first; the rest followed. They joined the 1st Battalion, 393rd, at about 0830 and the move to the west started. McGee said that the command group of the 2nd Bn met the companies en route. They moved into the 1st Battalion's area in the order of G, elements of H, and F, along with a C Company platoon, which had been attached the day before, at the tail.

There were no incidents as they moved to this location, although E Company spotted a few Jerries, dispersing them with fire. McGee said they decided to get out through the draw in a double column of companies, with one company on each side of the ravine. They set out on that plan about 0930 on the eighteenth and moved with E Company leading on the right and G Company leading on the left, with G, F, and the C Company platoon of the 394th. Following E Company were the companies of the 1st Battalion, 393rd. The column moved forward without serious incident, the men spread out on the high part of both sides of the draw, and reached the edge of the woods, where it halted at about 1200. McGee emphasized that they did not know what was ahead of them, they did not know the situation, and they did not know where the American positions were located. During the move through the draw, they had been hit by what they interpreted as friendly artillery fire, but suffered no casualties.

In an effort to find out what the score was, McGee said that they brought up their fast-fading radio and, after repeated tries, managed to make contact with a friendly unit. It took them some time to identify themselves and, in a veiled kind of double talk and by use of a slidex code, they told the strange voice that they were Americans and asked for information about friendly dispositions. Since the radio was very weak and in danger of going out altogether, they asked the voice to come back on in fifteen minutes, at which time they again would switch on their radio. The voice agreed and, when he came back at the specified time, told them that the nearest friendly troops were in the vicinity of Krinkelt. All this conversation was carried out in a guarded manner, McGee said, for they suspected that the Germans had captured American radios and perhaps the SOI had been compromised, so they didn't want to give away any information if it could be helped.

However, as has been pointed out, it took some time to make radio contact with anyone because of the weak radio, and therefore, when they

Withdrawal toward Elsenborn

reached the edge of the woods, McGee said they debated which way to go, finally deciding to head in the direction of Mürringen. He said they knew from the fact that they had seen at least one German tank headed up the road to Krinkelt the night before, and from the fact that they had heard a great deal of shooting from that direction and little from Mürringen, the odds were that Mürringen was in American hands.

Working on that assumption, they decided to pull out of the woods at about 1400 and move on down to Mürringen. They moved along both sides of the road in the same order they had come through the draw and were fired upon by American weapons. McGee said there was no mistaking the sound. E Company was fired on first and then G Company. The two companies and the rest of the column quickly dispersed into the hedgerows. They didn't know what to think. They had passed some knocked-out vehicles of their own regiment as they moved up the road and they could see nothing in the town except several other American vehicles.

By using one of the company radios which had a very short range and could be used here—although it could not be used to contact anyone when they came out of the woods—they raised someone they did not identify and queried about the shooting of American weapons. They said they were Americans, and the man on the other end told E Company to come on into the town with their hands raised and promised that if it was his outfit doing the shooting, they would quit. The battalion decided not to accept the offer, suspecting a Jerry trick. Finally, it was determined that the Germans did occupy Mürringen and were shooting captured American guns, for German tanks rolled up to its eastern edge and fired several times at the companies spread out along the road. Then G Company got in a fire fight, and the Jerries poured in a heavy barrage of mortar and artillery fire on them, never attempting to close, but content to stay in the buildings and fire their captured American guns as well as their own and throw in scores of mortar shells.

PFC A. J. Spinato, E Company, 2nd Battalion, 394th Infantry, picks up the story: "I started the war as a runner from the 4th Platoon and ended as Communications Sergeant of the company. I never missed a day on the line throughout. One of my jobs was to carry the situation map in combat and make it available to the company commander as he needed it. Where he went, I went with the map. Before that I was the radio operator. So you can see that I was a target most of the time, although I had my moments and was responsible on several occasions of ending the war for some enemy soldiers. We moved towards Mürringen, but finding Germans entrenched, withdrew toward Krinkelt. Incidently, we lost some people when the enemy fired a machine gun down the main street, cutting off some troops from retreat.

A. J. Spinato.

"I was one of the few of E Company in the town of Mürringen with Capt. "Pat" Paterson and his executive, Lt. Jim Holder, and a mortar squad. I had the radio. The 2nd Battalion got through that night to Krinkelt, and the next day took up positions on Elsenborn Ridge. I was with the company command group about 300 to 500 feet west of the highway. At some time I was with a group of five men, only us five, covering the left rear where we exchanged fire with the enemy seeming to 'out flank' the battalion. Had they known that they were facing such few men and attacked in strength, the battalion and possibly the regiment would have been cut of from the route we took to escape."

CHAPTER 13

The 277th Volksgrenadier Division Continues Its Attack

On the morning of 17 December all along the International Highway, units of the 3rd Battalion, 393rd Infantry, 99th Infantry Division, were trying to hold off the attacking Germans and find a way back. The battalion had even made plans to launch an attack to restore the lines. At around 0800 hours the attack began, moving slowly and carefully. I Company, 394th, had just about reached its line on the left and abreast of the other companies. I Company, 393rd, was almost at its reserve position when the Germans struck the M Company front at about 0930 hours. This cracked the perimeter defense and quickly forced the battalion commander to call off his own counterattack. He shifted his forces swiftly towards the threat. Contacting his companies by radio, he ordered I Company, 394th Infantry, to turn and come south, cutting between M Company's rear and the battalion command post to act as a block there. He then ordered I Company, 393rd Infantry, to send back two platoons to go into position immediately behind I Company, 394th, to act as a cushion there as well as to serve as a mobile reserve.

The Germans pressed their attack and were successful in forcing M Company to yield about 100 yards, stubbornly and unwillingly. This was regained when the two I Company, 393rd, platoons joined with M Company to push the Germans back, but the German pressure continued. They hit first with infantry, but then, about a half hour after the start of the attack, the first German tank appeared, coming along the former MSR, where it was stopped and, for about fifteen to twenty minutes, fired its machine guns but not its heavier cannon. There were some casualties from this fire, and the battalion tried to put artillery fire on it. This was difficult because of the poor observation and communication. An M Company mortar observer acted as a forward observer, called back his range readings to battalion headquarterse, where the artillery liaison officer relayed it back to the firing positions.

Friendly artillery fire was poured in, but had no effect on the German tank. It did help to dissipate the German infantry accompanying the tank. They were scattered and disorganized, allowing the battalion to bring up four bazooka teams to try to knock out the tank. However, after the artillery fire came down upon it, the German tank moved on down the road—actually, a dirt trail—almost into M Company's command post and continued to stir up trouble. The bazooka men poured desperate shots at it and finally succeeded in hitting one of its tracks, immobilizing the vehicle. Otherwise it suffered no casualties because the crew continued to fire their machine guns. About this time two more German tanks appeared, coming down the main road from the east, probably from Hollerath. They, too, were accompanied by infantry and, when American artillery fire was brought to bear, they scattered. The bazooka men turned their attention to these tanks and knocked one out. The other stopped behind it and continued to fire its machine guns while standing in the main road. Then two more enemy tanks appeared—making five in all—and these worked into the network of confused trails in the command post area. One of these was knocked out.

PFC Jack Pricket, L Company, 3rd Battalion, 393rd Infantry, recalls: "This was the longest night of our lives. We normally had a routine where one guy would stay awake for four hours and the other would sleep. We had only managed about thirty minutes the night before. German patrols, some as many as fifty men, roamed the woods firing from time to time, trying to draw fire so they could locate our positions. They had cut the trail back to Krinkelt so that we could not evacuate our wounded. We heard talk that some of our officers thought we might have to surrender. Miller and I talked about it, and we were going to take off through the woods if the idiots tried to do something like that. At last, it got light enough to see—it was a cold foggy morning, we could hear fighting some where not too far away. No one told us anything. We tried digging deeper; that was the only hope for us doggies. I felt as lonely as I had ever felt in my life. After maybe an hour, mortar and artillery shells began to hit in our general area. We heard what was probably heavy German machine guns, going in spurts, then high velocity guns, maybe 88s. Our people were answering with the pop of 81-millimeter mortars. A few American shells came over us, but not many.

"This battle seemed to be increasing, but it was like we were just hearing it but not taking part. Some mothers very close, too close, hit with mud and crap. Several officers come running from our rear with two bazookas. They ask us if we want to cover them while they try to knock out some tanks or armored cars. We say no thanks, we will wait, our sergeants say no also. A big shell hits right next to Miller, about two feet from the edge of our three-foot-deep foxhole; we both get covered with mud. Lucky to be alive, but how long will our luck last. Mortars are going like crazy; also small-arms fire is really building up to our left, probably on the road to Krinkelt. Little did we know of the battle taking place on the road.

Dragon's teeth.

"T/Sgt. Vernon McGarity had his squad dug in along the Krinkelt road, starting at the trail that led south to the 3rd Battalion command post, east where the foxhole line turned nearly due south with another squad. The 3rd Squad in reserve tied in to the ends of each squad on line. McGarity, painfully wounded the day before, refused to be evacuated, and returned to his squad. McGarity performed a number of feats of valor including knocking out an armored car, a machine gun and efforts to re-man it, and kept his squad fighting until they were out of ammunition. He spent the rest of the war as a POW. In 1945, he received the Medal of Honor, the highest medal awarded for valor. Edward W. Schuhardt, just across the trail from McGarity, was awarded the Silver Star for his actions on 17 December 1944. PFC Robert J. Smith won the Distinguished Service Cross for his actions on the sixteenth and seventeenth. The DSC is the second highest medal awarded for valor. One of the guys with the bazooka teams, we had four or five that tried, had his leg blown off. A GI used his belt to stop the blood and saved his life. The guy returned the belt about fifty years later."

Lt. Wingolf Scherer of the 990th Grenadier Regiment, 277th Volksgrenadier Division, remembers: "The situation brought the division command of the 277th Volksgrenadier Division to the obvious conclusion that it should concentrate its units there where the deepest penetration had been achieved, in the area of advance axis A and therefore to reinforce the 989th Grenadier Regiment, with the 990th Grenadier Regiment to continue the attack in the right-most sector with emphasis. For this purpose the corps command attached the reinforced 25th Panzergrenadier Regiment of the 12th SS Panzer Division *Hitlerjugend* to the 277th Volksgrenadier Division. What role the better progress of attack of their leftmost neighbor, the 12th Volksgrenadier Division, along advance axis C had played in reaching this decision cannot be determined for sure. As the remains of the 991st Grenadier Regiment had to cover the left flank after the change of focus to the right, and with Lt. Col. O. Jaquet dropping out due to an arm wound and Colonel Fieger collapsing in his command post, the division was reorganized into two combat groups, the command of which was taken up by Major Johe (989th) and Lieutenatn Colonel Bremm (990th).

"Group Bremm was to take up position next to Group Johe, and when they quit the forest east of Rocherath, advance as the right wing in a northwesterly direction. This reorganization and the mission suited the road conditions in that the forest track on the other side of the Jansbach split itself into a northern branch that ran via Lausdell towards Rocherath and a southern branch that ran to Krinkelt via Ruppenvenn.

"While the Group Bremm tried to go forward on the left of advance axis A—the road itself was hopelessly jammed with vehicles and heavy units—the commander of the reinforced 25th Regiment of the 12th SS Panzer Division, Maj. Siegfried Müller, sent his 2nd Battalion in on the right side of the road (commander Lt. Col. Richard Schulze). The battalion overran the command post of the 3rd Battalion of the 393rd Infantry and forced a passage across the Jansbach. The tank hunter company of the regiment (12th Tank Destroyer Battalion), which was suffering less from enemy snipers in trees than the panzer grenadiers, continued the attack on Rocherath, and its first units reached the edge of Rocherath village after dark. The mass of the regiment east of Rocherath ran into a superior opponent, whose artillery stopped the advance."

This engagement had taken about an hour. All the time the enemy infantry had continued to press its attack along the M Company front, with the result that this position was becoming more and more endangered, while the rest of the battalion area was being swept more and more intensely with small-arms fire. The situation was becoming desperate. Frequent reports to regiment were made to this effect. The battalion was running out of ammunition; the Germans were working through its positions in increasingly strong numbers; the men were becoming increasingly tired and hungry; casualties were piling up and there was no way to get them out. Altogether it was an unhappy situation.

Finally, at about 1030 hours on this critical morning, regiment gave permission to the battalion to withdraw to the old regimental reserve sector located approximately 2,400 yards from Rocherath. Regiment also said that a unit of the 23rd Infantry, 2nd Division (the 3rd Battalion) had gone into positions about 1,600 yards to the west of the battalion's present location and ordered them to withdraw to the assigned sector through this 23rd Infantry group. Immediately, McElroy said, they got busy organizing for the

After the battle in 1945, equipment of both armies could be found everywhere. Here is shown a *zugmaschine* for heavy artillery, which was left behind in Honsfeld opposite the inn. K. H. HECK/HANS WIJERS

withdrawal. Because of the large number of wounded, they were given first priority in the evacuation. All available transportation was used to load as many as possible aboard. When all the vehicles were filled, there still remained about twelve to fifteen wounded for whom there was no room and who could not be carried. These were left behind, and Capt. Fredrick J. McIntyre, the battalion surgeon, and some of the aid station personnel remained behind with them. They were not heard from later and were presumed to have been captured.

PFC Allan Nelson, bazooka man in the 3rd Squad, 2nd Platoon, I Company, 393rd Infantry, describes his experience: "The next morning [17 December], our company was ordered to withdraw to the area around the battalion command post where we dug in on a defensive perimeter. Colonel Allen, the battalion commander, gave orders for all to withdraw to a position behind the line of defense that the 2nd Division was setting up. Captain McIntyre, the battalion doctor, stayed behind with the wounded. It was later reported that the Germans captured the medics, taking the ones not injured and leaving the wounded for three days unattended in the woods. When we got the command to pull out of the 3rd Battalion headquarters area, I took off on my own, figuring that one person by himself did not present as big a target as a group of guys together. I had not gone far and was still in the woods when a tremendous artillery barrage started landing nearby. I hit the ground and remember the loud explosions and big flashes of white light, and I thought the world was coming to an end.

"When the barrage stopped, I broke out of the woods and headed across an open field. It was bright and sunny and there were a few small groups of other Americans plodding through a couple feet of snow up to the knees. When I got to the far side of the open field I reached a dirt road which I think must have gone into Krinkelt. I caught up with some other GIs, and we shortly passed through the line being set up by the 2nd Division. I felt really sorry for them because they were going to have to face the Germans shortly and make their stand. By this time I was back with I Company, and we were directed to leave the road and move into a forest for the night. During the night, we heard a terrific fire fight going, and as we looked out, we could see tracers from German tanks moving in toward Krinkelt. My next clear memory is our company pulling back up the hill to Elsenborn Ridge and digging in."

The move out was to be made with as few impediments as possible. All radios, switchboards, and other non-portable equipment were destroyed and all the battalion documents burned about an hour before the retreat began. The remaining kitchen equipment was abandoned. At about noon they started, sending the vehicles with the wounded first, following with the companies in column in the order of I, 394th, HQ, K, M, I, 393rd, and L, which was to remain in position to act as a rear guard while the rest of the battalion moved back a short distance for reorganization before making the actual move to the new positions designated by regiment.

As the withdrawal started, the enemy continued his pressure and inflicted several more casualties on L Company, which withdrew by stages, fighting and disengaging by degrees. Just to the rear of the command post area, L Company received a fairly intense mortar shelling, but kept going back. Then they were raked by machine-gun fire, but this did not interfere with the withdrawal. The three or four wounded that L Company suffered remained with the company throughout its rearward move.

PFC Jack Pricket of L Company, 3rd Battalion, 393rd Infantry, recounts: "It seemed like the fighting was almost stopped when we got word to pull back. We went back to the 3rd Battalion command post, which was loaded with wounded who could not be moved. All vehicles had been used to take wounded out. Several medics and a doctor stayed with the wounded. About fifty yards behind the command post, the rest of L Company broke into two groups, one by the road and one across the woods. Les Miller and I went with the woods bunch. At this point I did not see any officers, at least anyone

The 277th Volksgrenadier Division Continues Its Attack

that I knew. We cross the little creek, spread out in several columns and began to receive mortar fire. It didn't worry us too much because we were going back where we could get ammo and food, hopefully something hot. There was almost no talking.

"We walked up a snow covered field; trees which we didn't like because when shells hit the limbs, they spread hot metal all over. Almost no talking when suddenly my right leg was in the air in front of me, and I seemed to be flying through it. My leg felt like some one had hit me with a baseball bat right at the joint. I landed on my light field pack in the snow next to a tree. I was too stunned to talk for a minute. Miller asked if I was okay and where was I hit. The mortar shell hit some where behind me, among our spread out group. Some were knocked down by the explosion but not hurt. My ears hurt a little, and I had trouble hearing. I didn't want to feel where I was hit so Miller checked it for me. We always talked about the million dollar wound. I had one, but it didn't seem like it to me. Until you actually get hit, I think most soldiers think it will always be the other guy. I set up by the tree and was afraid to stand up and try to walk. I looked across an open field, toward the road and saw soldiers, Les said they looked like Germans, man I got up real quick. I could walk but knew it would get sore and hurt after the numbness wore off. Some one took my twenty-pound BAR and that helped. Miller kept saying, 'You lucky SOB,' he knew this would send me back at least for a few days. We ran into another group of trees or forest. As we crossed a fire break we saw a bunch of GIs digging in. They yelled at us as we walked through that they would show us how to stop the Germans. (This was the company commanded by Capt. Charles MacDonald, who wrote several books about the war and this battle.)

"We exited the forest where two trails or roads merged. A Sherman tank was behind the branches of trees on the north side of the road. This tank was knocked out about two hours later and the crew killed. The sight that greeted us when we could see up the slope toward Krinkelt-Rotherath was numbing. In all directions we could see burning installations, artillery, antiaircraft guns, trucks, and houses. We crossed to the right into another wooded area, and I was put in a covered foxhole with several wounded GIs. Shells were hitting the area in a random fashion. A man came walking out of the heavy woods with blood coming from his ears, nose, mouth and parts of his body. Medics ran to treat him. As it started to get dark several jeeps showed up to take the wounded into Krinkelt. Guys ended up on the hood, hanging on the sides, any way to get as many back as possible. In Krinkelt I could see a line of trucks winding out of sight. They took me to a truck and helped me into it. I looked down and there was Captain Fogleman. He seemed happy to see me and said that Les and I had been made squad leaders. We talked for several minutes and the scream of dive bombers sounded, and the captain, after going through the rocket attack, wanted to jump out and get some shelter. I talked him into staying, maybe I thought this was our only chance out. We stayed in the large truck in Krinkelt-Rotherath as a truck convoy assembled to take out the wounded back to hospitals. Shells were still coming in but none real close to us. Infantry groups came through and it was obvious that they were getting ready for battle. Finally, just at dusk, we started moving slowly out, up a winding road. Some of the drivers said we had some Sherman tanks leading us since German tanks were west of us. The truck column was as far as I could see back to Krinkelt."

1st Lt John S. Schwab, commander of the 4th Platoon, I Company, 393rd Infantry, recalls: "The next morning, the Germans renewed their attack. Fighting was heavy along the front when Colonel Allen directed me and my weapons platoon to fight a rearguard action covering the withdrawal of our infantrymen. This we did, and as the last I Company rifleman came through, I directed our withdrawal. Mortar shells were dropping all around us, so I sent the platoon over the ridge in three groups. Once they were over, I decided to leave when I was momentarily held up by fire from what I thought were German scouts. Instead it was apparently a platoon. I exhausted my

A German Panther tank, possibly from the 12th SS Panzer Division, somewhere between Losheimergraben and Büllingen, probably lost during the retreat in January 1945. K. H. HECK/HANS WIJERS

ammo and made a run for the ridge just as the mortar shelling began again. I hit the ground and a shell hit close by. My helmet went flying one way and my carbine was broken in half. I felt no pain until I tried to get up. At that moment I knew that my left side had been hit. I tried to crawl to the ridge but could not make too much headway.

"Then from nowhere came a soldier from the 394th. He spotted me and crawled to me and carried me over the ridge; and he said that he would go for help. He told me that he was the last one out and also that I had given him basic training at Camp Walters, Texas. Small world, I thought. With that comment he ran across an open field to an area occupied by a battalion from the 2nd Division. Shortly thereafter, Sergeants Sell, Hill, and Suitt arrived with an aid man from the 2nd Division who cut my pants leg off, bandaged my leg, arm and hip, and they carried me to what they thought was a safe haven with the 2nd Division, as they were promised that a jeep would take me to the rear. The local 2nd Division platoon leader boldly came over to me and said, 'We are going to show you guys how to fight.' I said, 'Bullshit! I'll give you guys another half hour on this forward slope.' About ten minutes later he was cut down, and the aid man who had assisted me went to help him and was also killed. At that moment, a fellow Kentuckian, Baylor Elder, and our other cooks spotted me lying behind some logs. Just then, mortars started dropping, so I told them to get out of the area and that a jeep (which never came) was on its way to evacuate me. At this point the German infantry began their attack on the hill. The 2nd Division platoon sergeant ran over to me and asked, 'Can you walk?' and I answered, 'Not too well.' Without hesitation he carried me to a foxhole and continued shouting orders and directing his platoon's fire on the onrushing Germans until his men had depleted their ammo. He then ordered his men to withdraw over the hill. He was truly a brave soldier and superb leader directing his platoon's withdrawal in an orderly fashion despite heavy incoming fire.

"Once all his platoon had left, he said, 'Let's go!' With him as a crutch we climbed half way up the edge of the forest fire-lane when he took a shot in the back. I told him to go ahead and I would be OK. As he reluctantly left, I rolled under some small pine trees where fortunately a soldier's pack had been left behind. Since I could not use my left hand, I had to gnaw through the damned thing to get the bedroll out which was sufficient to cover my bare leg. I put the pack over my face to smother my breath. As darkness came, the Germans occupied the area; but none paid any attention to me. What a blessing! Before they could dig in, our artillery peppered the area. It was accurate, because when it lifted I heard the Germans moaning and shouting, 'Sany! Sany!' It dawned on me that was a cry for aid men. The next morning the Germans stayed put. I thought I was surrounded by a heavy mortar crew, because when I would hear someone walking, I would hold my breath and take a peek to see the passersby carrying what seemed to be heavy mortar shells. Oh, how I prayed the 99th would counterattack.

"The second morning, I was hungry and damned near frozen when our artillery opened up. Again our fire was accurate; but too accurate for me as the shells exploded close by. But as fate has a way, these explosives saved my life. Three Germans in the fire lane spotted me and started running toward my position with rifles aimed, when 'Bang!' a round landed in their midst killing all three. Suddenly I heard Americans talking; so I rolled down the hill by the road where I could see German tanks moving toward the rear. Also, many troops were being headed to the rear. My heart sank. They were American prisoners. Just then a German lieutenant came down the hill and caught me by surprise. 'Ach!' he said, 'You are wounded.' Then he said, 'You are a lieutenant and, I see, a Catholic.' I had my rosary around my wrist praying to beat the band. 'Can you walk?' I said, 'No.' So he gathered four of our American POWs and had them carry me and place me on a tank going to the rear. The tank took me to an unfamiliar area. I believe it must have been the 394th command post. Here there were about ten to twenty German tanks refueling and rearming. German aid men carried me on a stretcher to a large underground bunker converted to an aid station. There were three badly wounded Americans and four critically wounded Germans. The doctor spoke broken English. He took my overshoes and asked for my watch. I told him I didn't have a watch. The German medics were in and out of the bunker and appeared nervous and scared."

When the battalion reached its predesignated assembly area, it reorganized; L Company fell back to it, broke off contact with the enemy, and the whole column started for the rear in the same order that it had moved out of its first positions. Company L again brought up the rear. They passed on through the 3rd Battalion, 23rd Infantry, 2nd Infantry Division, and went to their assigned position, reaching it by about 1400 hours. By this time, the battalion had about 475 enlisted men and had lost a couple of other officers wounded, including 2nd Lt. Richard A. Barr, a mortar section leader who had been acting as an observer with Company L; 1st Lt. John S. Schwab, 4th Platoon leader of I Company; and 2nd Lt. Melvin Addis of I Company. The outfit was in bad shape. It had lost all of its mortars, had rescued only two heavy machine guns from M Company, had three or four mortars left, was low on all kinds of ammunition and the men were all worn out. The crowning blow, after they had passed through the 23rd Infantry and thought that they were relatively safe in the rest area, came when the Germans threw in an artillery barrage—most of the shells being tree bursts—causing six more casualties who had to be evacuated from the regimental rest area. But the

The 277th Volksgrenadier Division Continues Its Attack

rest was to last for only a short time. The Germans had wasted no time in pursuing the retreating battalion. Within an hour and a half, they had pressed on, hit the 3rd Battalion of the 23rd Infantry hard, and had forced its left flank, causing the whole battalion to fall back towards Rocherath.

PFC J. Fanala of K Company headquarters, 393rd Infantry, remembers: "I thank God every day of my life; fortunately, I was not a prisoner of war. I was part of K Company's kitchen, but not for long. As the enemy approached with Tiger tanks, infantry, paratroopers, SS, and all they could muster for their major assault, we were ordered to prepare for battle. 'Every soldier available get your arms and defend and replace those lost in the line;' many where killed and taken prisoner. Every available man was now a frontline troop. We were quickly organized by officers and deployed into defensive positions, held the enemy off for a time. At last the enemy surrounded us, a small group from K and L Company. But we decided not to become POWs. We had an officer in charge who was a member of L Company, I think he was a captain, that I'm sure of. I do believe his name was MacElory [Captain McIlroy] or something, I'm not sure. But he saved this group, a great leader. He had maps of the area and a walkie radio. There are enemy troops all around us, but he managed to guide us through this wooded area.

"The 2nd Division had a defensive line; it would engage the enemy while we made a dash of about three hundred yards or so across an open field; no cover, just get up and go, one by one, as the enemy raked this area with machine gun and small arms fire. It was a very frightening time—do or die—my turn to go. Ahead of me was a young Jewish boy named Isadore Perrel; he got about half way, got hit in the legs with machine-gun fire, and fell there. When I got there he pleaded to me not to let him stay there. Well, I would not let him lie there to die, so I told him, 'Izzy, I'm a Catholic, you are Jewish, it's time for us to pray, you do your way, and I'll do mine.' We prayed together lying flat on our stomachs; then I told him, 'Get on my back.' He couldn't walk or run, so I got up with him on my back and ran zig-zag, all the way; we made it to the American lines.

"However, when we got there he lay on the ground, and I took his first aid packet, opened his trousers leg and applied bandage. Also took my aid package and pushed it. Bandaged his leg as best I could. Shortly thereafter a medic jeep came, put him on a stretcher and took him to a hospital or aid station. That's the last I saw of him. I have tried to locate him since the end of the war, to no avail. His home was in the Bronx, New York; I met him in Texas before we went overseas. He was a rifleman in K Company, 393rd, a former ASTP student; well, so much for that. I was not a hero, just another GI doing what had to be done. As it was, we regrouped and formed a segment or number of men who were marched to a place called Elsenborn Ridge."

PFC Jack Pricket of L Company, 3rd Battalion, 393rd Infantry, resumes his story: "Coming in to Krinkelt was another column of trucks loaded with American Infantry. I later learned that this was the 1st Infantry Division, along with the 2nd Infantry Division, two of the toughest combat divisions in the U.S. Army. We stopped at times, I guess, for traffic jams. Suddenly guns started firing all around us and increased louder and became almost a roar. At first we were afraid that we were under attack, but looking back toward Krinkelt, one area was a mass of explosions. This was the American artillery using what they called TOT (time on target). German tanks and infantry had started to pour out of the woods road against a small U.S. battalion. An artillery forward observer had called for help to keep the infantry from being overrun. I have heard that guns were massed on Elsenborn almost hub to hub in places and the number at 200 plus to over 350. This included most artillery from the 99th, 2nd, and 1st Divisions, plus corps and army battalions up to 8-inch guns. American artillery was the saving item for the poor infantry trying to hold off German tanks and armored cars. The infantry battalion in front of Krinkelt went on line with over 800, and a day later was pulled back with 200. In a few cases, American companies being overrun called for U.S. fire on their own positions."

CHAPTER 14

Conclusion to Book One

In the afternoon of the seventeenth, having sent in the 25th Panzer Grenadier Regiment and the tank hunter battalion of the 12th SS Panzer Division, the Germans managed to push as far as the edge of the woods east of Krinkelt and Rocherath. At dawn isolated elements infiltrated into the two villages but were unable to hold there. Farther south, at the Losheimergraben Crossroads on 17 December, the 12th Volksgrenadier Division was severely delayed from its time schedule by the tenacious resistance of American soldiers. Until rather late in the afternoon, the Americans disputed with the Volksgrenadiers for possession of the crossroads. There, as well, I SS Panzer Corps authorized the use of armor to break the resistance at the junction.

The 12th SS Panzer Division's mission was to seize Krinkelt and Rocherath, from which they were to continue towards Büllingen to make the advance route assigned to them in the plan, the Panzer Rollbahn C. On 18 December, shortly before dawn, a tank regiment of the 12th SS Panzer Division launched an attack on the twin villages of Rocherath and Krinkelt. Despite fierce resistance, the panzers penetrated between the roads, between the gardens and between the houses, but were repulsed after violent fighting and a deluge of shells. Though the general attack failed with serious losses, most notably in vehicles, it allowed a partial occupation of the villages by taking several buildings at the edge of the towns.

At the same time, south of the railway running from Losheim to Büllingen, the other tank formation in the I SS Panzer Corps, the 1st SS Panzer Division *Leibstandarte*, under the command of Lt. Gen. Hermann Priess, advanced west through the gap between Losheim and Lanzerath, with the combat group of Joachim Peiper as its spearhead. By late afternoon of 17 December, the 12th Volksgrenadier Division finally took the Losheimergraben Crossroads and advanced as far as Büllingen. The I SS Panzer Corps therefore modified its plan to use the 12th SS Panzer Division on the left flank of its sector. Those elements of the panzer division not yet engaged—the 26th Panzer Grenadier Regiment, the Armored Reconnaissance Battalion and the Armored Pioneer Battalion—were directed toward Losheimergraben. Later, in the afternoon of

18 December, the other elements of the division received orders to disengage, but the relief by units of the 12th Volksgrenadier Division was exceedingly slow and lasted until 19 December, because of the proximity of the enemy lines and the poor conditions of the road net.

On 18 December, Wirtzfeld also fell into German hands, but then the advance of the German divisions slowed. The German attack came to a halt in the sector of the 99th Infantry Division. From Höfen on the north flank to as far as Lanzerath on the south, the whole sector had been under extreme attack since 16 December. The ferocious and heroic resistance of the defenders of Losheimergraben would have long-term consequences. For two days, the regiments of the 12th Volksgrenadier Division found their passage blocked. The German plan of attack, which was based on breaking the American line quickly by surprise and opening the road for the vehicles of the 12th SS Panzer Division, failed completely. Very much weakened by the preceding combat and obliged to move a regiment to the right flank at Wirtzfeld, where the gains of adjacent units had remained minimal, the 12th Volksgrenadier Division lacked the strength to drive the attack farther to the west. At this stage of the battle, all the division could do was consolidate the positions reached and to wait for the tanks of the 12th SS Panzer Division. But, on that day the tanks were already engaged in a fierce battle for the twin villages of Krinkelt and Rocherath.

After two days of fierce fighting all along the 99th Division front, during which the main thrust of the German onslaught was blunted, units of all sizes and configurations withdrew piecemeal to positions on Elsenborn Ridge, about five miles to the west. By the nineteenth, a collection of stragglers from various units manned a defensive line from Höfen on the north to Bütgenbach on the south. Gradually, identification of men with units was sorted out, replacements were brought in and promotions to leadership positions accomplished. Units were still severely short of manpower, however. The situation on the twentieth had part of the 9th Infantry Division at the north on the left flank of the 99th. Next to the 99th on the south was the 2nd Infantry Division, also seriously short of men. To the south of the 2nd was the 1st Infantry Division in the Bütgenbach area. Attacks by the Germans continued with ferocity all along the line until the 23rd, when, after heavy losses, the attacks began to weaken. Eventually, the battle at the north shoulder became a stalemate until the latter part of January 1945, when the Americans attacked and restored the original 16 December line.

The German plan to pierce the 99th by the first day and to reach the Meuse River by the second day was a failure. Young, inexperienced troops—later bolstered by units with more combat experience—accomplished a remarkable feat in the face of overwhelming odds, but at a terrible loss of life.

BOOK TWO

Holding the Line

Foreword to Book Two

In June 1974, thirty years after the battle, in an interview with a British writer, Gen. of Panzer Troops Hasso von Manteuffel, commander of the 5th Panzer Army, which was south of the main 6th Panzer Army thrust in December 1944, stated, "The Battle of the Bulge was not fought solely in Bastogne. Here in the northern sector of the Ardennes, elements of tragedy, heroism and self-sacrifice exerted great influence upon the result of German intentions. Battles are won in the hearts of men, not only by the combination of fire and movement, but by working together. Teamwork is decisive, as was shown in the northern part of the Ardennes."

None of us who were there would for a moment in any way detract from the superb defensive actions of our brothers-in-arms in such places as St. Vith and Bastogne, both of which were in Manteuffel's zone of attack. Their consummate soldiery has been well recorded. Not that historians have neglected the north shoulder: *A Time For Trumpets: The Untold Story of the Battle of the Bulge*, written by the late Charles B. MacDonald, himself a rifle company commander in the 23rd Infantry Regiment of the 2nd Infantry Division, is probably the best one-volume account of the whole battle, with appropriate emphasis where it belongs. And there are others, of course.

The lack of knowledge about the northern shoulder on the part of many is being remedied by writers such as Hans Wijers, a resident of The Netherlands who lives within weekend distance of the north shoulder. The first book in this volume, *The Losheim Gap*, skillfully weaves together essential, authentic history with personal recollections of those who took part and strikes a good balance between the two.

Hans does well in describing combat in the miserable weather in the dense woods of the Krinkelter Woods and on the more open terrain around Losheimergraben and Buchholz Station. He describes the passage through the 99th Infantry Division lines by the 2nd Infantry Division in its attack toward the Roer River Dams on 13 December. This initial success was foiled by the start of the German counteroffensive, Operation Entwerp, three days later. The overwhelming combat power of the German attack forced these two divisions to break off their attack and to fight a delaying action by countless small-unit actions for two days. This successfully prevented the leading enemy troops from clearing the woods and preparing to assault the twin villages until late 17 December.

This is where this book, *Holding the Line*, begins. During the period covered by this book, 13–19 December, hardly anyone, except for a possible few at army group or higher level, had a clue about the strategic picture. For everyone down at the shooting level, it was a matter of not letting your fellow squad members down and supporting the company on your left or right. We knew we were in a helluva fight with an enemy that outnumbered us, at our particular level, by two, three, or even ten to one. It was not until years later that we got the big picture and learned how our small parts fit into the whole drama.

We now know that Hitler announced his plan to take Antwerp in mid-September 1944. In spite of the advice of his military advisers to adopt a less ambitious offensive, he insisted on Antwerp as the objective to be taken in about seven days. Such a grandiose plan would depend on three elements: surprise, sheer weight of numbers, and minimum hard fighting. The first of these, surprise, was almost complete. Dense fog, bad weather and security measures by both sides permitted major units to be concentrated largely undetected. The second element, numbers, was only partial. Much of his armies' damage and casualties from the campaign across France and Belgium had been repaired or replaced. However, many units had not had received adequate retraining. Only two divisions, the 1st and 12th SS Panzer Divisions were at full strength. Third, minimum hard fighting, was probably based on Hitler's pleasant memories of the German attack through roughly the same area in the late spring and summer of 1940. He remembered the dry roads and farmland across which his attack enjoyed easy going. Now, with the soft ground not yet frozen during the first week of his offensive, his tanks and other vehicles were road-bound, moving no faster than his infantry. If we were surprised, so was he. For example, the sector through the Krinkelter Woods and Losheim Gap was, and had been, occupied by the newly arrived 99th Infantry Division for just over a month. The going in that area should have permitted "minimum hard fighting." What he did not know was that on 10 December, the veteran 2nd Infantry Division had moved north from St. Vith and the Schnee Eifel and was preparing for its own attack.

The area of Krinkelt–Rocherath–Büllingen–Wirtzfeld–Domaine Bütgenbach was athwart the axis of his main effort, the strongpoint, that is, the 6th Panzer Army, commanded by SS Col. Gen. Josef ("Sepp") Dietrich. This area was the key to three of Dietrich's five battle routes. His army was comprised of all four of the Waffen-SS panzer divisions, five infantry (Volksgrenadier) divisions, one mechanized panzergrenadier division, one parachute division,

Skorzeny's brigade, 800 tanks and assault guns, and more artillery than the other two armies (the 5th and 7th) combined. Since his ultimate objective, Antwerp, was some 80 to 100 miles away, Dietrich would have had to cross the Meuse at Liege, thirty-five miles away, by the third day in order to reach Antwerp on the seventh day. Further, the staff of the 6th Panzer Army estimated that its infantry could cover the three to five miles from the line of departure to the Elsenborn Ridge by noon of the first day.

How badly did we upset Sepp's timetable? By the end of the third day, elements of his 1st SS and 12th SS Panzer Divisions and his 277th Volksgrenadier Division were barely out of the woods and getting a toehold in Krinkelt-Rocherath and Domaine Bütgenbach. The 12th SS Panzer Division started the battle with 105 tanks and tank destroyers, plus 12 heavy tank destroyers. By 21 December, the division had lost 67 tanks and tank destroyers in Krinkelt-Rocherath and 47 in Domaine Bütgenbach. It was no longer a viable force. Dietrich never got to the Elsenborn Ridge. We thus deflected his attack to the south and west of the shoulder where, by Christmas Eve, it eventually ran out fuel, ammunition, tanks, food, and the will to fight. This book tells the story of many of the countless small-unit actions which, together, gave the lie to Hitler's belief that the American soldier was a product of a decadent society that could not produce real fighting men.

After the Battle of the Bulge was over, on 18 January 1945, Winston Churchill told the House of Commons: "The Americans have engaged thirty to forty men for one of us. It was the greatest American battle of the war and will, I believe, be regarded as an ever famous American victory."

James W. Love
Commander, Antitank Company, 38th Infantry Regiment, 2nd Infantry Division
Williamsburg, Virginia

Introduction to Book Two

After finishing the first book in this volume—on the 99th Infantry Division sector of the Battle of the Bulge—it was obvious that it could not be the only book written on the battle fought in this area. This book covers the sector strongly defended by the 2nd Infantry Division and the 395th Regimental Combat Team of the 99th Infantry Division.

This work describes combat in the V Corps sector; this is the area—at locations with names such as Wahlerscheid, Höfen, Krinkelt, Rocherath, and Elsenborn—where the 2nd Infantry Division and the 395th Regimental Combat Team defended themselves from 16 December 1944 to the withdrawal back to Elsenborn Ridge. It is based on official U.S. Army documents and after-action reports and is supplemented with testimonies by several members of the 2nd Infantry Division, the 395th Regimental Combat Team, other troops of the 99th Infantry Division, and its supporting troops. Documents and testimonies from the German side also grace this story.

CHAPTER 1

The German Plan of Attack

THE REORGANIZATION OF THE 6TH PANZER ARMY
The refitting and reorganization of the armored divisions was another difficult task faced by the 6th Panzer Army. A report of Dietrich's meeting with General Thomale at the end of September shows that the German Army at this stage of the war was no longer capable of bringing back into the field large armored formations. Although all efforts were being made and highest priority would be given to the reequipment of the armored divisions of the 6th Panzer Army, Thomale told Dietrich that his divisions were to be reequipped to a much reduced strength. The armored regiments of the divisions would contain only one tank battalion consisting of a mixed composition of Panzer IV medium tanks and the heavier Panzer V Panther tanks. The armored regiments of the divisions would number some sixty tanks. The armored divisions of the Waffen-SS originally had an authorized establishment of nearly 200 tanks, and this constituted a sharp reduction of armored power. To compensate for this loss, each division would be given one independent heavy tank battalion of the regular army, equipped with a number of heavy tanks or tank destoyers.

Each armored division also contained an organic tank destroyer battalion equipped with some twenty tank destroyers or assault guns. With these additions, the grand total of the armored strengths of the divisions would finally reach some 125 tanks. Yet tank destroyers and assault guns, with their mounted and inflexible guns, constituted no real substitute for tanks. The offensive power of the divisions remained seriously affected.

According to General Thomale, most of the new tanks were scheduled to arrive at the start of October in the army depots from which they would be distributed. By mid-October, they were expected to arrive at the armored divisions. But the scant resources, the rate of production of new tanks, losses at the front and during the transport to the front, and the shifting of units from one place to another all contributed to the fact the early plans had to be revised frequently. Moreover, on 27 October 1944, Hitler ordered the doubling of the authorized armored establishment of the SS panzer divi-

The German Plan of Attack

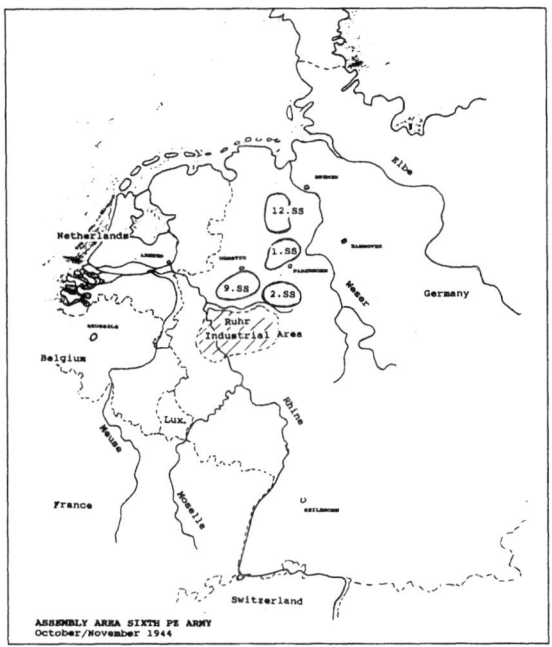

sions. As a result of this order, the resulting strength of the armored complement of the panzer divisions and heavy tank battalions of the 6th Panzer Army can only be estimated. The fragmentary documents give the following approximate authorized numbers:

1ST AND 12TH SS PANZER DIVISIONS
(1ST AND 12TH ARMORED REGIMENTS)

Regimental staff:	2 Panthers
1st Panzer Battalion staff:	2 Panthers
	2 companies of 17 Panzer IVs each
	2 companies of 17 Panthers each
1 antiaircraft platoon:	4 2-centimeter Flakpanzer IVs
	4 5.7cm Flakpanzer IVs
Tank Destroyer Battalion:	2 L70 Panzerjäger IVs
	2 companies of 10 L70 Panzerjäger IVs each

The deficiencies in late 1944 were not merely restricted to the armored complement of the panzer divisions. The severe losses in armored fighting vehicles and motor transport during the battles in France had severely affected mobility. These, however, were only to be replaced to a maximum of 75 percent. According to Dietrich, few new vehicles were received and he had to rely primarily on old and mostly obsolete vehicles, and these could only be kept in good running condition by numerous repairs. Because of the many different types of vehicles, there existed a chronic shortage of spare parts, tires and accessories, especially for captured vehicles. Because of the shortage in motor transport, some units within the armored divisions were even mounted on bicycles. Each armored division was to receive a complement of only 135 half-tracks representing 40 percent of the authorized number. The armored divisions had abandoned most of their half-tracks to other divisions in the lines when they were relieved. This also applied to other heavy weapons, also to be fully replaced at a later date.

It comes as no surprise, therefore, that the divisions, despite all feverish attempts, only slowly managed to rebuild their combat readiness. At the start of November, the commander of the 1st SS estimated that his division, after a resting period of five to eight weeks, had only a "limited capability for defensive action." The commander of the 12th SS reached a similar conclusion. The I SS Panzer Corps endorsed the judgements of its subordinate commands. It added that only a reinforced battalion of infantry with tanks

By the end of September 1944, General Thomale (center) visited the commanders on the Western Front to discuss the reorganization and refitting of the panzer divisions scheduled to participate in the German offensive. Here he is shown with Gen. Hasso von Manteuffel (left), the commander of the 5th Panzer Army, and Field Marshal Walter Model (right). J. WIJERS

and some artillery of each division were ready for offensive as well as defensive tasks. Furthermore, even after the missing vehicles and heavy weapons became available, the divisions would be in a limited capacity for offensive action. The commander of the 2nd SS Panzer Division, last to arrive in the 6th SS Panzer Army's assembly area, did not expect his division to be ready for offensive action until 10 December.

Despite all this, the 6th Panzer Army was not to be left much breathing space. By mid-October 1944, Alfred Jodl had announced the arrival of reinforcements on the western bank of the Rhine, so as to back up the most threatened sectors of the front and ordered OB West to arrange billeting areas. This order was followed at the beginning of November, after the commanders in the west had been informed of the offensive plan, by an OKW order, specifying the secrecy and deceptive measures for the concentration of the assault forces west of the Rhine in more detail. The order decreed that the assembly of the forces west of the Rhine were to be masked as a defensive move against the threat of an all-out Allied offensive aimed at the line Cologne-Bonn. In order to repel such an attack by taking it from both sides, a strong force was to be positioned to the northwest of Cologne and another further to the south in the Eifel. While the build up of a reserve in the rugged and wooded Eifel had to be kept secret from the enemy, northwest of Cologne was to be conducted fairly open in order to attract enemy attention. In the area of Rheydt-Jülich-Cologne, reinforcements were to be deliberately detrained during daylight hours.

On 2 November 1944, OKW summoned the 6th Panzer Army to move under the code-name of the 16th Training Staff to the west bank of the Rhine and assemble near Cologne. Here the army would be in a position to block any Allied thrust in the direction of Cologne and the Rhine River. The move had to be accomplished by 24 November 1944. Not yet apprised of the offensive plan, Dietrich received the order with disbelief. He strongly protested against this premature interruption of the refitting program and pleaded for a postponement of the move. Dietrich pointed out that his panzer army was not yet ready, since most of his materiel had not arrived. But OKW was not to be persuaded by Dietrich's pleas. It advised that most of the still missing materiel had just arrived, or was in transit to 6th Panzer Army. When Dietrich transmitted the order to his subordinate commands and divisions, they in turn pleaded for a delay of the move, requesting at least two to three more weeks to finish their training programs. Dietrich, his hands tied by the OKW directive, had no choice but to order his panzer divisions to entrain and move to the west bank of the Rhine, where they were to take up Operation *Wacht am Rhein* ("Guard on the Rhine").

It took two to three weeks to move the panzer army's staff, the panzer divisions, and the other army units by train to the new concentration area west of the Rhine. The fuel shortage again caused delays in the arrival of units at their entraining points. As a result of this, the inspector general of transport on 10 November demanded that the 6th Panzer Army tell all its formations to ensure strict punctuality, as otherwise the prescribed timetable—already provided for the maximum number of trains per day—could not be observed nor delays made good. Despite the Allied air supremacy the transportation, with deteriorating weather, was accomplished almost without loss. The panzer army's units were billeted in the following areas: Headquarters at Quadrath west of Cologne and Brühl; I SS Panzer Corps at Frechen west of Cologne; 1st SS Panzer Division *Leibstandarte Adolf Hitler* at the southwest of Cologne in the area of Jülich-Weilerwist-Mechernich-Zülpich-Düren; 12th SS Panzer Division *Hitlerjugend* at the northwest of Cologne in the region of Frechen-Bulheim-Grevenbroich-Bergheim; and panzer army supply units on the west bank of the Rhine between Cologne and Bonn.

During the second week of November 1944, the 6th Panzer Army was advised of the offensive plan. At first, only Dietrich; his chief of staff, General Gause (to be replaced on 16 November by Krämer); and a limited number of officers within the army staff—including the operations, logistical, and the artillery sections—were informed of the plan. The rank and file were to be let in on the offensive plans only at the last possible moment in order to secure secrecy. Every effort was made to give the troops the impression that the 6th Panzer Army's role was to back up the units involved in a defensive battle at the Aachen front.

Fighting flared up on the Aachen front on 16 November to help persuade the troops in accepting this impression. On this date, the U.S. First and Ninth Armies, after a period of relative quiet following the capture of the city of Aachen, launched a main effort in the direction of the Rhine. OB West was hard put to maintain its lines without the actual employment of reserves earmarked for the coming offensive; some were eventually thrown into the battle. These reinforcements, bad weather, heavily fortified defensive lines and a terrain favored for the defender took the bolt out of the American offensive. Instead of a swift advance to the Rhine, as the Americans had envisaged, the attack turned into a grim and slogging battle of attrition, where every yard of terrain was bitterly contested. After two weeks of almost incessant fighting, the American offensive had fallen short of even its intermediate goal, a crossing of the modest Roer River.

However small, the river constituted a formidable obstacle, of which the Americans belatedly became aware. Big dams in the headwaters of the Roer could be regulated to flood the river for several weeks. As long as the dams were in German hands, no commander in his right mind would dare to

The German Plan of Attack

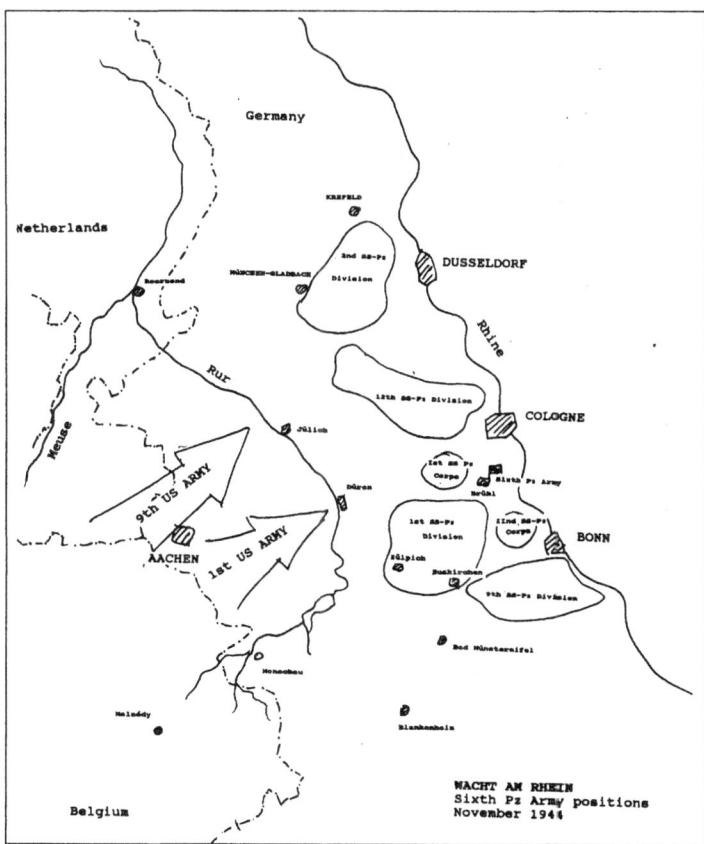

cross the river, since the rising water would cut him off and expose his troops to destruction. At the beginning of December, the American offensive petered out.

Immediately after the 6th Panzer Army had settled into its new concentration area west of the Rhine, it resumed the training program as best as it could. Although the 6th Panzer Army was not directly involved in the battle west of the Roer, it was ordered to prepare defensive positions along the River Erft, midway between the Roer and the Rhine, and hold a combat reserve at standby for a possible counterattack against any American penetration across the Roer. Unfortunately, with these additional defensive tasks, the army could not be kept intact for training purposes. Moreover, troops and materiel were still being assembled. Both panzer corps were ordered to pay special attention to night combat and also to stand by to oppose airborne assaults. Because of the proximity of the front, vehicles had to be camouflaged and movements were restricted primarily to the hours of darkness. For this reason, tactical training by large units was not feasible.

Hugo Kraas.
BURDACK

The transfer of the panzer army to the west bank of the Rhine also interrupted the training schedules of officers and noncommissioned officers. Some map exercises were conducted under the ruse of a counterattack into the flanks of an enemy penetration. To explain why the rugged Eifel was the constant scene of these exercises, the intelligence reports mentioned the possibility of an American assault in the area north of Trier; this attack was to be taken in the flank by the panzer army. This also covered up the intensive reconnaissance of the road network leading to the south, preparatory to the move to the final concentration area in the Eifel.

In early December 1944, the armored divisions of the 6th Panzer Army once again were up to the authorized strength levels for their combat establishments. Their reports reveal the armored divisions of the 6th Panzer Army, although replenished almost to full authorized strength, were still short of experienced men, especially officers and non-commissioned officers and were also desperately short of motor transport. These deficiencies severely affected combat readiness.

After the war, the commander of the 12th SS *Hitlerjugend,* SS Maj. Gen. Hugo Kraas, stated that his division had "only limited capability for offensive action." According to a report on the armored units in the west, prepared by OB West on 10 December 1944, the 12th SS was at full tank authorization, numbering thirty-eight Panthers and thirty-nine Panzer IVs in its armored regiment and twenty-two Panzerjäger IVs in its tank destroyer battalion.

The German Plan of Attack

THE OPERATIONAL PLANNING

The Commanders in the West Are Informed
When the chiefs of staff brought back the news of the offensive to their respective headquarters, both Gerd von Rundstedt and Walter Model received it with grave doubts. In his headquarters at Ziegenberg Castle near Giessen, Rundstedt considered an operation of this magnitude unrealistic. At his command post in Fichtenhain near the town of Krefeld, Model came to a similar conclusion. "The whole affair seems damned moldy," he remarked to Krebs. In the next weeks, both headquarters were occupied with profound discussions and calculations. These only confirmed their initial misgivings. An operation with Antwerp as the final goal was disproportionate to the available resources. According to Rundstedt, an advance beyond the Meuse would unnecessarily expose the flanks of the German thrust to an Allied counterattack. He therefore considered an operation beyond the Meuse in the direction of Antwerp too great a risk to be undertaken. Despite all doubts, preparations were started. In the ensuing period the Army commanders held a conference almost weekly to discuss the plans of attack and the progress of the preparations. There was a meeting on 16 November at the headquarters of Fifteenth Army, which was tasked to conduct a subsidiary attack from northwest of Aachen.

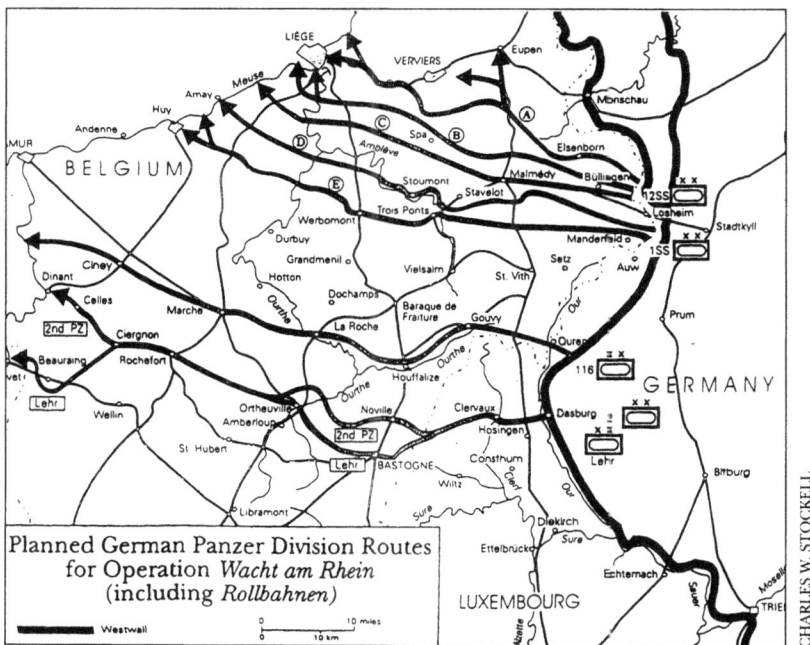

Planned German Panzer Division Routes for Operation *Wacht am Rhein* (including *Rollbahnen*)

A subsequent meeting was held on 22 November at the headquarters of the 6th Panzer Army, and finally, the army commanders conferred on 5 December at the headquarters of the 7th Army. In the meantime, Model conducted several map rehearsals with each of the army commands. Because of the shortage of time and probably to maintain secrecy, hardly any notes were taken from these conferences, and orders for the main effort were issued verbally.

As the early OKW order reveals, the 6th Panzer Army was charged with a threefold mission: (1) a quick breakthrough of the enemy lines north of the Schnee Eifel, (2) a swift exploitation by the armored forces in the direction of the Meuse and Antwerp, and (3) the build up of a strong northern shoulder to protect the German wedge against counterattacks.

Within the 6th Panzer Army's zone of attack lay part of the high plateau of the High Moors. This desolate and boggy plateau, with an altitude of almost 2,300 feet, is the highest point of the Ardennes and actually forms the roof of Belgium. The panzer army's zone of attack was a rugged area, broken by numerous small streams and rivers, covered by thick forests and supported only by a limited road network. It was highly unsuitable for the deployment of armored formations, especially in the winter season. Movements would be confined to the few narrow roads to emerge from this area. Because the area left no room to deploy both of Dietrich's panzer corps abreast, OKW had echeloned them in depth on a small frontage near the border village of Losheim, from which the only good roads in this area emptied in the direction of the Meuse. According to the OKW map, the II SS Panzer Corps—containing the 2nd and 9th SS Panzser Divisions—was put in the lead. Both divisions would have to smash through the enemy lines, thrust to the Meuse, and cross the river between Liege and Huy, followed in their wake by the panzer divisions of the I SS Panzer Corps, to be employed after the crossing of the Meuse. Infantry divisions of the LXXIV Army Corps were to protect the right flank of the armored advance against counterattacks from the north, by securing the High Moors plateau and establishing a strong defensive shoulder along its northern edge; a line to extend from Rötgen, through Eupen and Verviers toward Liege.

The Breakthrough of the Enemy Lines
Model's final operation order contained no fundamental changes in the disposition of the 6th Panzer Army. In compliance with the directives of Hitler, both corps in the first assault wave were reinforced. On the right flank, the LXVII Army Corps, commanded by Gen. Otto Hitzfeld, replaced the LXXIV Army Corps, which was entirely engaged in the November defensive battles. Hitzfeld's corps was to mount a two-division attack on both sides of Mon-

schau. While the 272nd Volksgrenadier Division was to attack north of the town, the 326th Volksgrenadier Division was to take out the American positions on the high ground to the south. The army corps then was to bypass Monschau, push on through the thick forests, and establish a defensive line running from Roetgen to Eupen. The possession of the main road intersecting Monschau and Eupen was an important prerequisite to a quick buildup of this defensive shoulder.

Between Hollerath and Ormont, the I SS Panzer Corps would strike at the enemy lines with three infantry divisions with the goal of clearing a path for the panzer divisions. Lined up from north to south were the 3rd Fallschirmjäger Division and the 12th and 277th Volksgrenadier Divisions. From within the fortified belt of the Siegfried Line, the infantry of the I SS Panzer Corps were to charge up a stretch of high ground occupied by the Americans. This feature, crowned by a dense belt of almost impenetrable forests, ran practically along the whole corps' frontage and was known as White Stone. Only at its southern reaches, opposite Losheim, did the woods disappear to make room for relatively open, broken ground. Here near the village of Lanzerath the terrain gradually descends toward Manderfeld, where it finally drops down to the Our River, only to ascend steeply on the other side to the Schnee-Eifel Ridge.

Otto Hitzfeld.
F. RIESER

Beyond the wooded belt of the White Stone, the zone of attack was dominated by the high ground of Elsenborn Ridge. This ridge, actually the first stretch of high ground behind the American lines, constitutes a kind of southern bastion or outpost of the High Moors plateau. Reaching an altitude of nearly 2,000 feet, it extends from north of Elsenborn down to the village of Bütgenbach. An early seizure of this commanding ground was vital to the German plans, since it controlled three of the five roads selected for the advance of the 6th Panzer Army. It therefore was assigned to the infantry of the I SS Panzer Corps as a first objective. On the right, the 3rd Fallschirmjäger Division was to break through the enemy lines west of Hollerath, capture the farming villages of Krinkelt-Rocherath and secure the northern part of Elsenborn Ridge. In the center the 12th Volksgrenadier Division was to seize the road junction of Losheimergraben, open the main road to Bütgenbach and secure the southern half of the Elsenborn Ridge to the northwest of the village. In the south, the 277th Volksgrenadier Division was to capture the villages of Manderfeld and Lanzerath and protect the southern flank of the I SS Panzer Corps by advancing toward the villages of Schoppen and Eibertingen.

The infantry in the first assault wave was to employ infiltration tactics. After a preparatory artillery fire had softened up the American resistance, special assault companies, a mixture of specially equipped infantry and pioneers, were to act as shock troops. These units were to avoid becoming embroiled in heavy fighting. Their task was to seek out weak spots in the enemy lines, slip through and penetrate as deep as possible into the rear. In the process they would isolate enemy strongpoints by cutting their supply and communication lines. The enemy pockets were to be mopped up by the following infantry regiments. They were strongly supported by assault guns for this purpose; a brigade of assault guns was to be attached to each infantry division.

After the infantry divisions had reached and secured the Elsenborn Ridge, the armor would be unleashed for its headlong dash to the Meuse. The 6th Panzer Army's staff estimated the infantry would cover the three to five miles to the Elsenborn Ridge before the end of the morning. If all went well, the SS panzer divisions would be launched around noon. After a short regrouping, the infantry was to pivot to the northwest to the High Moors, where it was to extend the defensive line of the LXVII Army Corps by blocking all approaches from the direction of Verviers. Since the divisions moved primarily by foot and would be slow in reaching their ultimate goal, each was to form a a composite force of battalion size, consisting of a mixture of infantry and pioneers, mobilized to advance in lorries, and reinforced by assault guns and some horse-drawn light artillery. Acting as a vanguard, these

The German Plan of Attack

forces were to move forward as fast as possible on to the High Moors plateau and block the roads around Verviers.

The opening hour of the attack and the duration of the artillery bombardment still had to be determined. The 6th Panzer Army staff eventually was of the opinion the infantry lacked the experience to conduct a night attack. It feared the infantry might get disoriented in the darkness and the attack loses momentum. Some exercises in night attacks were held using searchlights, these lit up the scenery with a kind of artificial moonlight by pointing their strong beams into the low overcast. But the results of the exercises were unsatisfactory. Since the huge searchlights lacked the mobility to follow the advancing infantry, they were only useful in the first phase of the attack. The panzer army preferred to attack at dawn. The morning darkness and fog would enable the infantry to infiltrate the forward enemy positions. The searchlights would assist this initial assault. After reaching the enemy rear positions the assault groups would be able to further orient themselves in the growing daylight, while their advance was still covered by the morning fog, which at this time of the year, clung to the valleys until well into the morning. The commander of the 7th Army, General Brandenberger, reached a similar conclusion and also advised to launch the attack at dawn. Only the commander of the 5th Panzer Army, Gen. Hasso von Manteuffel, wanted to launch the attack at night. Because all assault Armies were to start the offensive simultaneously, Model decided to set the opening hour of the attack for dawn. At 0730 hours, the artillery had to open up with a half-hour opening barrage. At 0800 hours, the infantry was to go in.

The Armored Thrust

Two SS panzer divisions of the I SS Panzer Corps were lined up for the initial armored thrust: on the right the 12th SS Panzer Division *Hitlerjugend* and on the left the 1st SS Panzer Division *Leibstandarte Adolf Hitler*. Since the ground in the northern part of the panzer corps' zone was particularly poor, both armored divisions were concentrated in the southern half. The 6th Panzer Army's staff faced the difficult task of finding enough room in the narrow zone for the employment of the forces and selecting routes of advance from the limited number of east-west roads in this area. After a careful and extensive study of the road net, the panzer army staff selected five routes, labelled A to E, from north to south. Since the ground in the northern part of the panzer corps' zone was particularly poor, the corps' main weight was concentrated in the southern part. The northernmost (route A), was to function as the line of communications for the infantry operating around Verviers. The other routes, B to E, were to act as armored routes of advance (*Panzerrollbahnen*), earmarked exclusively for the advance of the armored

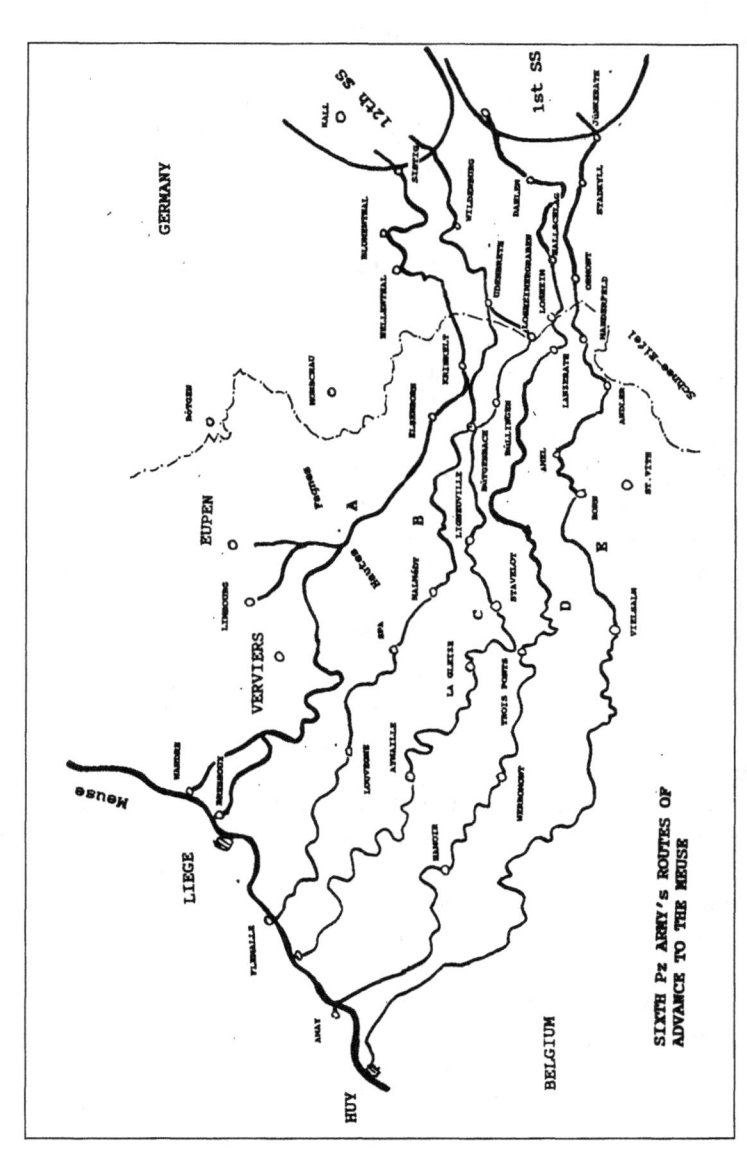

The German Plan of Attack

spearheads and their supply trains. None of them were ideal for a swift employment of armored units. Because of the restrictions imposed by the limited road net and the narrow zone, each of the panzer divisions, for longer or shorter distances, were to negotiate stretches of unpaved forest trails or boggy country lanes.

The tactical employment of the armored divisions on the armored routes was as follows: Route A—one panzer grenadier battalion of the 12th SS Panzer Division, reinforced by the Pz-12th Tank Destroyer Battalion (*Kampfgruppe Brockschmidt*); Route B—one reinforced panzer grenadier regiment (minus one battalion) of the 12th SS Panzer Division (*Kampfgruppe Müller*); Route C—the bulk of the 12th SS Panzer Division, composed of *Kampfgruppe Kuhlmann* (one panzer regiment), *Kampfgruppe Bremer* (one armored reconnaissance battalion), and *Kampfgruppe Krause* (one reinforced panzer grenadier regiment); Route D—the bulk of the 1st SS Panzer Division, composed of *Kampfgruppe Peiper* (one panzer regiment), *Kampfgruppe Knittel* (one reinforced armored reconnaissance battalion), and *Kampfgruppe Sandig* (one reinforced panzer grenadier regiment) plus the operations section of the I SS Panzer Corps; and Route E—*Kampfgruppe Hansen* (one reinforced panzer grenadier regiment of the 1st SS Panzer Division, supported by the 1st Tank Destroyer Battalion).

The main weight of the armored divisions of the I SS Panzer Corps therefore advanced shoulder-to-shoulder on the inner axis, routes C and D, protected by flanking detachments of motorized infantry regiments marching on routes B and E. Although each *kampfgruppe* was allotted a specific armored route, they were not strictly bound to it. According to Krämer, the status of the routes was "directional only. If the division commanders wanted to take others, they were free to do so." Krämer also stated: "The routes led to the general line Verviers-Spa-Stavelot, and from that line new orders were to be given according to the situation at the time."

Another special operation was to take place within the zone of attack for the 6th Panzer Army. At the beginning of December, Hitler personally inserted a parachute drop into the 6th Panzer Army's plan of attack to support the buildup of the protective northern front. A battalion of 600 to 800 paratroops under the command of 1st Lt. Friedrich August von der Heydte, an experienced parachute commander, was to be dropped at the High Moors on the night before the attack. Von der Heydte's force was to block the only main road across the Hautes Fagnes from the direction of Eupen, at the intersection of Mont Rigi, as it was the likely route to be used by American reinforcements coming down from the Aachen salient. There he was to await a link-up with elements of the 12th SS Panzer Division on the morning of the offensive. Von der Heydte's force would also drop parachutist-dummies to spread confusion in the American rear and conceal the real extent of the airborne operation.

The Move into the Eifel

An early cold had set in at the end of 1944. In the second week of November the higher regions of the Eifel and Ardennes had been covered by a blanket of snow, adding another hardship to the live of soldiers on both sides of the frontlines, but by December a sudden thaw turned the frozen ground into slush. At the start of the offensive a layer of slush and melting snow still covered the ground. This made the narrow winding roads through out the Eifel Mountains tricky to negotiate in the freezing darkness. The daily report of OB West on road conditions in the Eifel revealed on 10 December, just prior to the final concentration, there still remained up to six inches of snow in the vicinity of Prüm. The main road between Blankenheim and Stadkyll was reported frozen and partially covered by snowdrifts. The valleys and draws were filled with slush. These road-conditions did not simplify the task of the 6th Panzer Army's staff. The concentration of a large military unit is a major undertaking in itself. The involved complex movements require careful planning if they are to be carried out smoothly and without congestion of traffic. Specialized and experienced staff officers are required for the task of working out the intricate and complex schedules of such a movement.

An armored division of the Waffen-SS, for example, with all vehicles on the move needs over sixty miles of road space. Beside the armored divisions many other units also moved into the Eifel. Just how extensive the movement of the panzer army was is best illustrated by looking at the I SS Panzer Corps. Apart from both the corps' armored divisions, the following units were involved: 277th Volksgreandier Division (already in position); 12th Volksgrenadier Division (moving in from the region of Kall-Gemünd); 3rd Fallschirmjäger Division (moving in from vicinity of Düren); HARKO 6 of the II Volksartillery Corps (moving in from vicinity of Cologne); two rocket launcher brigades (from vicinity of Trier); army artillery (heavy calibers) (moving in from the railroad station at Jülich); an engineer regiment staff; a bridge commando J; two bridge commandos B; a motorized army engineer battalion (moving in from Coblenz); and the 1st Flak Division (antiaircraft artillery) (moving in from Bonn).

Prior to the movement of the armored divisions, the headquarters and supply units of 6th Panzer Army were transferred into the Eifel. On 8 December, the panzer army assumed control over all supply units within the future zone of operations, under the pretext the units of the 7th Army had not risen to the occasion because of an overstretched front, and therefore needed the assistance of the 6th Panzer Army's logistic services. This would also give the units of the 6th Panzer Army the opportunity to acquire some experience. On 10 December, the headquarters of the 6th Panzer Army moved to the

The German Plan of Attack

neighborhood of the little medieval town of Bad Münstereifel and the next day assumed command of the zone of operations.

The final warning order for the move of the panzer divisions into the Eifel was issued on Tuesday, 12 December; the next day, the move into the Eifel was to start. As soon as light had faded on the thirteenth, the air in the 6th PanzerArmy's assembly areas east of the Roer vibrated as hundreds of engines roared to life. Disarray seemed to reign as orders were shouted and men hastened to gather together some last equipment. Vehicles lumbered out of their hide-outs in villages and woods and moved on to the forming up points, mostly jammed sideroads. Finally as columns had formed up, the unit commanders motioned their men by pulling their fist twice in the air: "Marsch, Marsch!" Engines roared up, tracks rattled and screeched, as one after the other the vehicles and tanks moved up the dark crowded main roads. Drivers peered intently through the pitch-black night to trace the course of the road or catch a glimpse of the dark vehicle in front. Maintaining strict radio silence, the armored divisions of the 6th Panzer Army had started their furtive move into the Eifel. The final phase of the preparations for the German offensive was on.

On Thursday the fourteenth, the chief of staff of Army Group B, General Krebs, reported some trouble had been experienced with frozen roads in the higher regions of the Eifel, causing vehicles to skid off icy roads or collide with each other, but "no great traffic congestions had formed up," and "traffic control and discipline were properly conducted." Krebs reported the armored divisions of the 6th Panzer Army had moved to the following positions:

> 1st SS Panzer Division: reached its final concentration zone in the wooded area in the vicinity of Blankenheim (Blankenheimer Forst).
>
> 12th SS Panzer Division: reached the intermediate concentration area of Norvenich-Vettweiss-Zülpich-Schwerfen-Satzwey-Wisskirchen-Euskirchen-Esch-Heinerzheim-Badorf-Liblar-Pingsheim (the area formerly occupied by the 1st SS).
>
> 2nd SS Panzer Division: reached the intermediate area of Allrath-Frinnersdorf-Bedburg-Bergheim-Ober-Aussen-Quadrath-Horrem-Glemel-Cologne-Merkenich-Worringen-Dormagen-Butzheim (the area formerly occupied by the 12th SS).
>
> 9th SS Panzer Division: remained in place until the start of the offensive.

Though the night march of the panzer divisions generally had been carried out without great difficulties, it is known they encountered some friction. The last units of the 1st SS Panzer Division, for example, did not reach the assigned assembly area until 1000 hours. The commander of the 1st SS

Panzer Regiment, Lt. Col. Joachim Peiper, stated after the war: "On 13 December 44, we were given a detailed march order issued by I SS Panzer Corps. No mention of the impending offensive was contained; nothing was mentioned except the route of march and assembly area, which was the area of Marmagen-Blankenheimerdorf-Schmidtheim. Advance elements of the division were in Dahlem. The whole thing was to be announced to the troops only when they fell in immediately prior to departure. There was complete blackout during the night and radio silence. No signs marked the road other than simple yellow arrows without division designation. We moved out at 1900 hours on the thirteenth and had disappeared into the woods in our new assembly area by 1000 hours on the fourteenth. The weather was too foggy for any air activity, and it still was very foggy at 1000 hours when we completed our move."

The next night, 14–15 December, only two of the four armored divisions of the 6th Panzer Army were on the move—the 2nd and 12th SS. During the night, the marching columns of both divisions were hindered by extremely poor weather. A mixture of sleet and snow flurries limited visibility considerably and slowed down all traffic. As Friday, 15 December, finally dawned, grey with a low overcast, many of the columns had not yet reached their destination and were still out in the open on the roads. Fortunately for the Germans the low overcast and bad weather concealed all movements and the columns were able to accomplish their moves without being detected. On the morning of the fifteenth, Krebs reported despite the bad weather all movements had been accomplished and all units had reached the assigned areas. Discipline was properly maintained, except for the 2nd and 12th SS Panzer Divisions, many vehicles of which drove with headlights blazing.

As the target date of the German offensive approached, the woods and villages behind the German frontlines in the Eifel were packed with thousands of men and vast quantities of equipment and supplies. Even so, the Allies failed to detect this vast German concentration opposite their thinly held Ardennes line. The rugged and wooded Eifel was ideal for hiding large bodies of troops. In combination with the poor weather it provided the Germans with an assembly area almost impenetrable to Allied air reconnaissance. The weather permitted some air reconnaissance during the critical days of 14 and 15 December, and Allied reconnaissance missions flown on these dates reported an increased enemy activity East and West of the Rhine, but they did not clearly reveal an enemy build up in the Eifel area. The Germans therefore preserved secrecy and gained complete surprise—the key element to the success of their operation.

CHAPTER 2

American Defensive Positions

From 8 December, the 99th Division had been preparing for its first commitment in a large-scale operation, repairing roads, laying additional telephone wire, and shifting its guns for the V Corps attack toward the Roer dams. In addition, a new supply road was constructed from the Krinkelt area to the sector held by the 395th Infantry. The dispositions of the 99th Division were these: On the north flank the 3rd Battalion, 395th Infantry, occupied the Höfen area; the ground here was open and rolling, and had good fields of fire. On the right (south) flank of the 99th was the 18th Cavalry Squadron of the 14th Cavalry Group, with the 38th Cavalry Squadron screening the right flank and maintaining contact with the division to the south. North of the cavalry were the 394th and 393rd Infantry Regiments, forming the right and center, respectively, of the 99th Division's front.

On 12 December, the relief of the 2nd Division (in the VIII Corps sector just south of the cavalry) by the 106th Division was completed. By the end of 12 December, the 2nd Division was assembled in the vicinity of Camp Elsenborn, Belgium.

The Roer River dams were impeding the First and Ninth Armies, both by the flooded condition of the river and by the possibility that the enemy might decide to blow the dams near Schmidt. This would suddenly flood the countryside inhibiting the progress of the 2nd Infantry Division infantry and armor attacking from the south and southeast to secure this chain of dams and lakes. The 2nd Division was attacking along a line running northeast, its supply route following the section of the Höfen road, which ran through the forest to the fork. The 2nd Division was to pass through the 99th, and a regimental combat team of the 99th would attack covering the southern flank of the 2nd Division advance.

THE SITUATION OF THE GERMAN 277TH VOLKSGRENADIER DIVISION

In December 1944, the German LXVII Army Corps under Lt. Gen. Otto Hitzfeld was lined up on the first line of the Siegfried Line or in the bunkers of the Siegfried Line in the area south of Vossenack to the south of

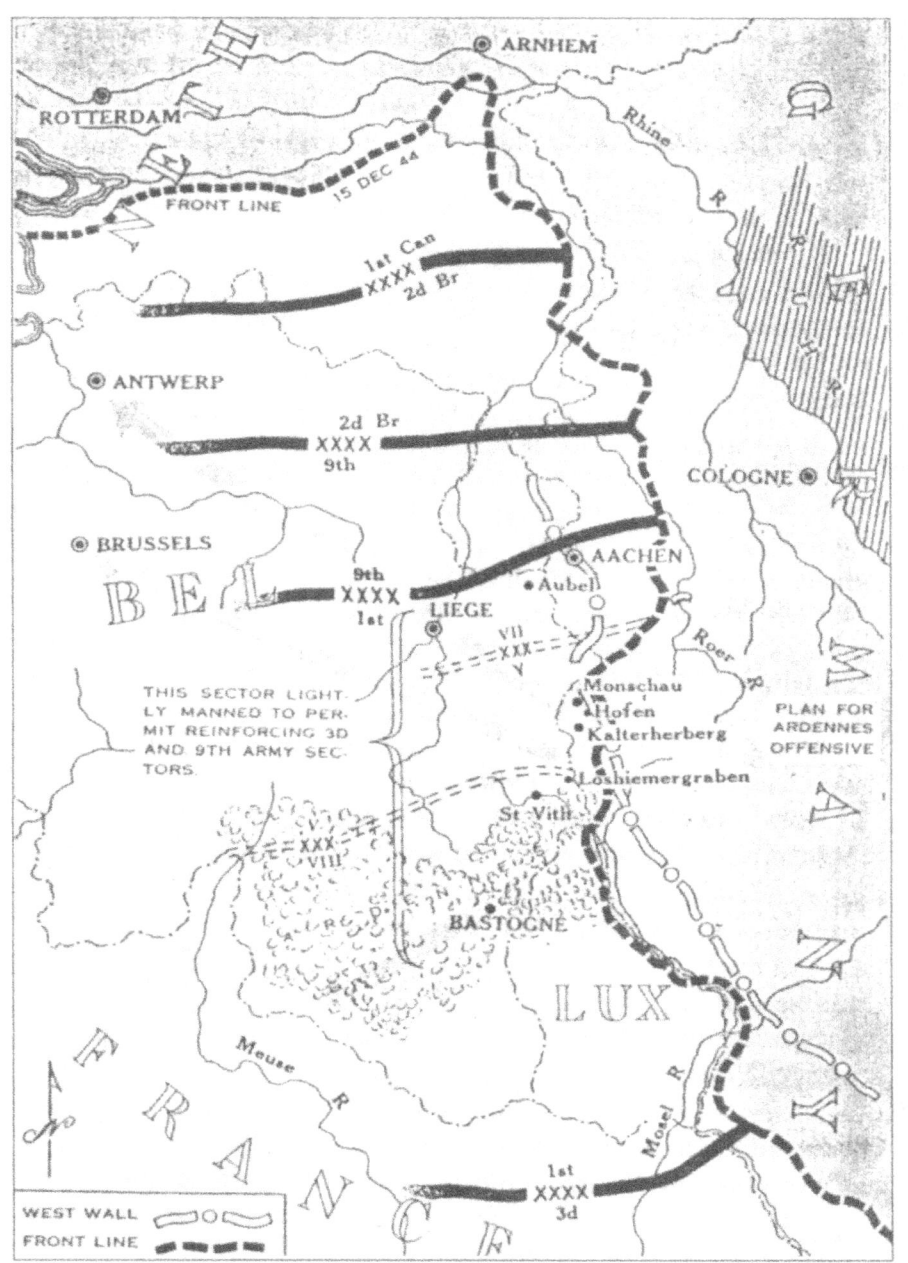

U.S. Army positions on the eve of the battle.

PFC Calvin Fisher of the 2nd Division reads a Christmas card in a mess hall on the front line in German, 30 November 1944.

Udenbreth. The northern sector of the so-called Corps Monschau was taken over by the 272nd Volksgrenadier Division under Maj. Gen. Eugen König, the southernmost sector by the 277th Volksgrenadier under Colonel Viebig. The common division boundary ran four kilometers northeast of Monschau. The regiments of the 277th Volksgrenadier Division had been positioned from north to south, so from right to left, in the sectors Höfen, Alzen, Monschau Forest (Wahlerscheid) and Udenbreth as follows: 989th Grenadier Regiment, 990th Grenadier Regiment, and 991st Grenadier Regiment.

The regimental sectors had to be expanded towards the north in order to make a larger concentration of German forces in the Hürtgen Forest possible. However, the 277th Volksgrenadier Division had not taken part in the fighting of November 1944. In the Wahlerscheid area, the 991st Grenadier Regiment of the 277th Volksgrenadier Division had its troops spread out in the pillboxes and strongholds, preparing themselves for the attack on 16 December.

According to PFC Georg Schell of the 277th Volksgrenadier Division: "After we were pulled out of the fightings in Hungary, on 8 November, our unit was sent to the West of Germany preparing for a new offensive. With our unit the next day we arrived in Vienna. Due to the many daylight air attacks of the enemy we arrived on 15 November in the Eifel (Kall). We were already informed that US troops had reached by now our Westwall. In the late afternoon that day we marched by foot to Wintzen, where we stayed overnight and then moved on to Olefe and finally reached on 22 November Schleiden. Snow was falling, and it was foggy, and due to the weather no enemy planes were in the air. On the streets, I saw many Wehrmacht vehicles

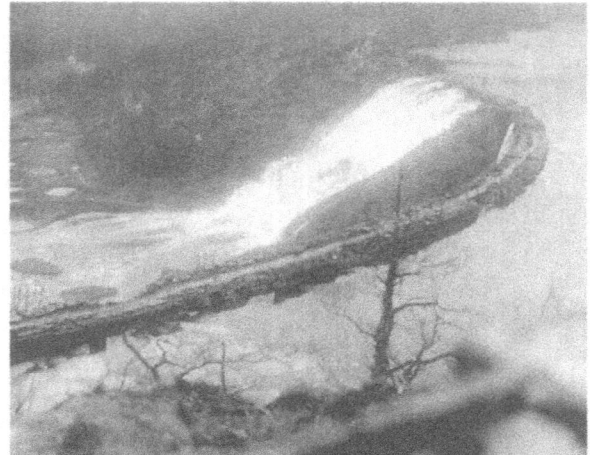

A view of dam #5 across the Roer River near Wollssifen, German. The dam was captured by troops of the 9th Infantry Division in February 1945.

A nice shot of another one of the dams, this one at Berg. DAN STYLE

and all kinds of different units, like pioneers, Luftwaffe units and all kinds of soldiers. We finally moved to our designated areas. In the pillboxes and strongholds at Wahlerscheid we settled down and took up our positions, not knowing yet what was ahead of us. I still remember that on 13 and 14 December, the enemy shelled our positions with all kinds of artillery. Many of us were already wounded before they ever saw action and were brought to Schleiden."

THE V CORPS PLANS THE ATTACK ON THE ROER RIVER DAMS

As scheduled, the 2nd Division passed through the 99th Division on 13 December, beginning its attack on a narrow front just north of the 393rd Infantry toward Dreiborn, located on the northern fork of the Höfen road beyond the Monschau Forest. The 1st and 2nd Battalions of the 395th Infantry plus the 2nd Battalion, 393rd Infantry, formed the combat team attacking on the right of the 2nd Division.

American Defensive Positions

According to Charles D. Curley Jr., 1st Platoon leader, E Company, 38th Infantry, 2nd Infantry Division, "The 38th Infantry was moved by truck from the St. Vith area into the Belgium Army camp at Elsenborn on 11–12 December. The move went into darkness, and somewhere along the way we received some long-range artillery fire. The trucks had almost stopped, and I almost lost my driver. He was ready to abandon the truck while it was still rolling. We settled into Camp Elsenborn and were re-equipped. The attack order was issued, and we moved out on the appointed day towards the border through the villages of Krinkelt and Rocherath. We were following behind the 9th Regiment as they moved towards Wahlerscheid."

T/Sgt. Edwin Norris of K Company, 9th Regiment, recalls: "I was wounded by a mortar round and sent back to England. After recuperating, I was sent back to my unit, which was located near St. Vith on the German border, holding a twenty-five-mile front. I was glad to be back. It was disappointing because a lot of my old buddies were not there. Some of the units were in pillboxes. The men of my platoon had cut trees and built flat roofed cover over dugouts, very much like log cabins. We ran combat patrols and stood guard for attacks. It started snowing and that helped camouflage our positions. Our platoon sergeant split his foot very bad cutting wood and went to the hospital and back to the United States. Later, the platoon leader, 2nd Lieutenant Brooks, sent for me and told me that I was the senior NCO and wanted me to take over the platoon as platoon sergeant and that I would be promoted to technical sergeant. It was a bad time to take over as platoon sergeant since I had only been back a short time and had not met all of the men. The squads were spread out. Quite a few of them were new men without much training and did not seem to know what it was all about, but things were going OK. Lieutenant Brooks had also just taken over as platoon leader, he was a quiet sort of person who had not seen combat before.

"In a few days, orders came down that we were moving out the next day. We would leave the platoon guide, and a staff sergeant to help the new outfit locate in our place. We found out right away that the 106th Division was a new outfit to the front line with no combat experience and very little ammunition. Some of our men handed over some of their extra ammo. We loaded on the trucks that the 106th Division came up on and got orders to roll the tarpaulins, or covers, up and to place them behind the cab of the truck. This left us open to the night air. It was about dark when we started out and road all night long, at a slow speed of stopping and starting. It was still dark when we arrived at our destination. It was also very foggy and cold. After the ride, everyone was shaking from the cold. We were issued a sleeping bag each and told to sleep in 'squad rows' after the trucks moved out. It started snowing while we were asleep, and it covered us over. They woke us up shortly after noon and we started walking. The road was very muddy. The new men had problems keeping up, they were exhausted. About dark, we came into a bivouac area and pitched our tents and had a meal."

As a part of this attack, the 2nd Infantry Division struck through the Monschau Forest northeast of Rocherath. Their mission was to surprise the Germans by attacking through positions held by the 2nd Recon Troop and the 99th Infantry Division to pierce the Siegfried Line and overrunning a stronghold of many pillboxes guarding a road net at Wahlerscheid north of where the International Highway turns east to Hollerath. It was planned for the 2nd Infantry Division ultimately to seize the roads behind the pillbox line for further exploration by armored units. The 9th Infantry's mission was to swing left, capture the town of Rohren and to trap the German troops holding the sector of the line farther north.

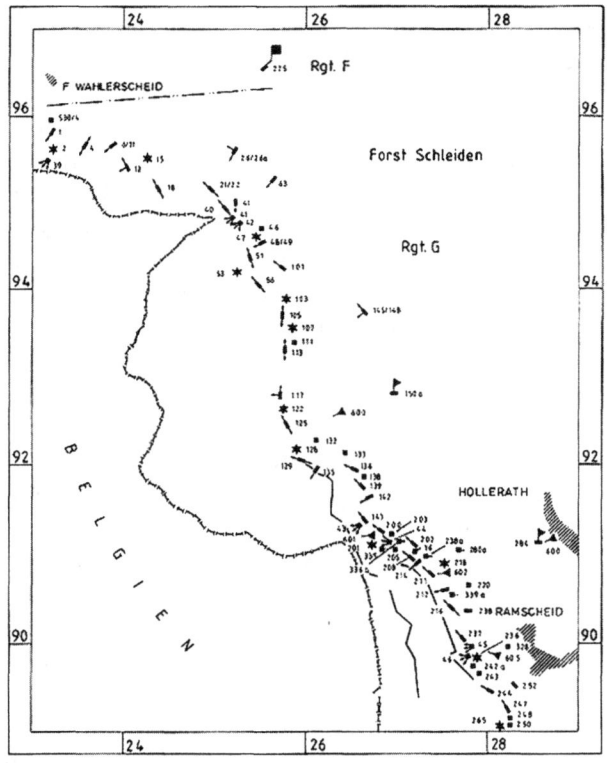

"Pillbox Alley": all the German pillboxes in the line between the Wahlerscheid and Hollerath areas.

American Defensive Positions

Infantrymen of the 3rd Battalion, 9th Regiment, 2nd Infantry Division, move silently through the snow-covered Krinkelter Woods in Belgium. U.S. ARMY

At 0830 hours on 13 December, the 9th Infantry passed its line of departure fifty yards beyond the farthest outpost of the 99th Infantry Division and attacked, striking in a northeasterly direction from the Rocherath-Krinkelt vicinity along the axis of the Rocherath-Wahlerscheid road with the seizure of the road junction at Wahlerscheid as its initial objective. The 1st Battalion moved through woods to the west of the road. The 2nd Battalion moved through woods to the east of the road. The 3rd Battalion at the outset was in reserve, following the 2nd Battalion.

THE ATTACK ON THE WAHLERSCHEID CROSSROAD, 13 DECEMBER
By dark on the evening of 12 December 1944, the 1st Battalion was in a forward assembly area about 2000 yards north of Rocherath and had completed plans for a daylight attack to be made as part of the 9th Infantry Regiment at 0830 on 13 December. The mission of the 1st Battalion was to move cross-country west of the main road leading from Rocherath to the road junction in the vicinity of Wahlerscheid and to seize and secure the road leading northwest from there, 400 yards to the northwest. That this main road paralleling the advance of the battalion was known to be heavily mined and roadblocked in numerous places, the plan was to stay off the road, to avoid all mined areas, and for individuals to carry necessary ammunition and antitank mines to secure the battalion for a twenty-four-hour period without resupply. Consequently, details were completed in the assembly area for the additional mortar ammunition, antitank mines, demolitions and extra supply of signal means necessary to the attack

At 0730 on 13 December, the battalion moved out cross-country with the battalion in closed formation, two rifle companies up. After a most taxing

German pillbox crew on the West Wall. HANS WIJERS

march, made doubly difficult on the men because of the passage through dense forests and knee-deep marshes, the battalion successfully arrived about 600 yards cross-country southwest of the objective.

Up until this time, about 1330 hours, the movement of the battalion had been made with surprise. Though small arms fire and heavy mortar fires had from time to time been received on the route of march, it is believed that the dense woods concealed the size of the movement involved, and that the enemy fired only on what he believed to be the usual heavy patrols in the area. However, upon arrival at this point, observation across the large clearing west and south of Wahlerscheid gave away the element of surprise that hitherto favored the Americans. Heavy mortar fire and direct-fire weapons came into the battalion's leading elements in great volume, and though the position because of its exposed nature became almost untenable, plans were continued in this area for a continuation of the move.

The road leading just south and west from Wahlerscheid, along which leading elements were moving, was discovered to be heavily mined. Probing across the road resulted in ten casualties in C Company from shoe and S-mines. However, mine sweepers and personnel from the Ammunition and Pioneer Platoon were moved forward and, still under fire, moved across the road and cut lanes in the mine fields as far as 400 yards north of the road.

While this work was in progress, and though the position was almost untenable, the battalion closed in, prepared for counterattack and covered the action of the mine-clearing detail north. Through the battalion artillery liaison, heavy fire was massed in the Wahlerscheid area and in and around the mine-clearing detail. Although the impact of this firing was unobserved because of the nature of the terrain and poor visibility, the volume of it definitely curtailed enemy fire and allowed the battalion to continue its operation.

By 1530, the mine-clearing detail had cleared lanes well along the route of march, but because it was getting dark, the regimental commander directed that the battalion tuck in, give no ground, and prepare to continue operation on the following day. At 1630, a few enemy riflemen endeavored to counterattack the right flank from the east under cover of intense mortar fire, but this attack was repulsed by 1715 hours.

S/Sgt. Hanford Maurice Rice of C Company, 9th Infantry, 2nd Infantry Division, writes in his war diary: "December 12, 1944 (Tuesday): Moved on trucks to the front lines. (We) attack in the morning. The snow is 3 inches deep. We are in the woods. December 13, 1944 (Wednesday): Attacked all day through the woods. I got hit in the side, and a tree fell on me. I walked (back) 5 miles to an aid station. There are only 18 men left in C Company."

The night of 13–14 December proved a perfect hell for the men, having for protection against the wintry cold only that which they had carried with them. Subjected to continuous mortar and direct artillery fire during the night, the battalion held its ground and completed plans to resume the attack at 0830 hours on 14 December. The combination of heavy loads and a cross-country march through unavoidable marsh ground had taken its toll. By daylight on the fourteenth, the battalion additionally had lost four killed and 97 wounded because of the heavy fire and antipersonnel mines.

14 and 15 December passed with the 9th Infantry continuing to attempt penetrations in the Wahlerscheid area and with the 23rd and 38th Regiments still in assembly areas in Camp Elsenborn and Wirtzfeld respectively. Combat Command B of the 9th Armored Division, assembled in Faymonville, Belgium, was attached to the 2nd Infantry Division in anticipation of being used to exploit any breakthrough achieved by the 2nd Division. This situation prevailed during the night of 15 December.

Plans for the continuation of the attack at 0830 on 14 December encompassed the movement of a rifle company north of the road with attachments of the A&P Platoon sufficient to clear further mine fields and cut the discovered concertina wire under the protection of the rifle company. Subsequent movement of the rest of the battalion in column of companies was made through these approaches. The movement was carried out slowly but according to plan, with B Company covering the breaching made by its own teams and those furnished by the A&P Platoon.

By 1200, it was felt that the necessary breaches had been made, and a careful preparatory fire plan was put into effect to cover the movement of the rest of the battalion. Heavy supporting artillery and mortar fire was placed on pillboxes in the Wahlerscheid area, and the area was continuously smoked to cover the battalion as it came up for the attack. Under the cover of this preparatory fire, A Company moved through B Company into position to jump off. However, A Company's movement north of the road and into position was subjected to the most intense mortar and automatic weapons fire. Regardless, the battalion moved across its line of departure and moved about 150 yards towards its objective. Here, however, undiscovered concertina, combined with heavy fire, interrupted the progress of the attack. Planned shelling for the attack came in magnificently and was effective to such an extent that without it, leading elements would have been blasted to pieces. Under cover of this fire, wire cutter teams from A Company began to neutralize the newly found wire.

However, at this time the regimental commander ordered the battalion commander to move back to his positions as of daylight and await further orders. The same artillery, which had been ordered to cover the battalion moving forward, was again called on to cover the battalion as it withdrew. The effectiveness of the shelling saved the battalion from disaster, and under it, the battalion returned to its position and regrouped slightly to the southwest. At this place orders were received from the regimental commander to dig in, hold the ground and to plan careful patrolling for the following day, while air support softened up the objective.

The day of the fourteenth proved even harder than the previous twenty-four-hour period, and the end of the day found the men battered, weary and cold. However, during the day, a supply road had been constructed up to the battalion, and thanks to the superior regimental supply organization, the night was eased by hot meals and blankets.

The day of the fifteenth was spent in patrolling and further probing while awaiting air support, which did not materialize, because of the very bitter weather and poor visibility. Just before midnight on the fifteenth the battalion commander was ordered to be prepared to make a reconnaissance in force (not to exceed one rifle company) over the same ground the attack previously covered. The orders were amended after midnight, and the battalion was ordered to be prepared to exploit a well-conceived and daring infiltration into the enemy position, which was then being conducted by the 2nd Battalion on the 9th Infantry's right.

The 2nd Battalion, having found its assigned assembly area occupied by other troops when it arrived on 13 December, had moved to another area within 500 yards of the line of departure. Although assurances were given to

American Defensive Positions

the contrary, this area had not been entirely cleared and the battalion had suffered two casualties from antipersonnel mines.

After a hot meal, the battalion crossed the line of departure, with E and G Companies in the lead. The men carried their overccoats and rolls. At first there was no opposition, but the advance was difficult because of the mud and snow and the thick pine forest. The weather was cold and damp. A thaw caused the snow to drop from the branches soaking the men's clothing.

As the columns moved forward, H Company captured a German who had deserted before the attack began. A fellow deserter, seeing the Americans approaching and thinking they were Germans who would shoot him for desertion, blew his head off with a hand grenade. By noon the battalion had reached the approaches to the German pillbox line. Scouts reported smoke from enemy fires and the assault companies dropped their rolls and overcoats and prepared to attack.

In front of the pillboxes the enemy had cleared a large area, filled it with massive wire obstacles, mines attached to criss-crosses, and trip wires covered well, making a well-planned final protective line. When the battalion came to the edges of the clearing, it was halted by intense fire, not only from machine guns and rifles, but from artillery and mortars. Casualties were heavy. The battalion commander's radio operator and orderly were hit. Casualties among the command group included the Battalion S-3, the company commander of G Company, the executive officer of E Company and the forward artillery observer of G Company.

Wires and other obstacles on the West Wall. HANS WIJERS

In the attack E Company was on the left and G Company on the right. One platoon of E Company tried to cross the clearing, and had actually advanced through five aprons of barbed wire when it was pinned down by enemy fire. On the right flank an attempt was made to breach the wire with bangalore torpedoes, but the fuses were wet and would not ignite. Meanwhile, one squad from G Company succeeded in crawling though and under the wire to the enemy lines. Part of a second squad in support of the first followed, cutting a four-yard gap in the barbed wire as it went. These patrols were not in communication with their company. Moreover, the commander of G Company had been wounded and evacuated, so that word of this significant penetration did not immediately reach the battalion commander. At dark the battalion was ordered to break off the attack, reorganize and prepare to renew the assault the next day.

That night the weather turned bitterly cold, causing intense suffering among the troops, whose clothing had been soaked by dripping snow during the day. A hot meal was brought up, but because of the heavy enemy shelling and the danger of mines, it was not served. The battalion command post was set up in a ditch less than 500 yards from the German pillboxes. Committing a platoon from F Company between two G Company platoons strengthened the battalion's front line.

Glynn Raby of H Company, 9th Infantry, recalls: "I have forgotten a lot of events, but vividly remember the attack we made on the Wahlerscheid Crossroads, beginning December 13, 1944. A 'surprise' attack, in daylight with no artillery preparation, was no surprise at all. Sunshine melted snow on trees, and we were soaked. Pinned down that afternoon, it turned very cold that night. We had a lot of frostbite and frozen feet. Probably as many casualties from weather as from enemy action!"

On 14 December, preparation by artillery fire began at daylight for the battalion's attack. Elements of E Company, however, were exposed to this fire, and suffered casualties. Consequently, the company did not advance. Meanwhile, Lt. Col. Walter M. Higgins Jr., battalion commander, ordered G Company to attempt a penetration through a shallow wooded draw on the right flank. F Company was in reserve behind it.

The massive wire obstacles in the draw were blasted by bangalore torpedoes, but as a squad started through the gap, four men were wounded by machine gun fire and a fifth was killed by a mine. It was realized that our artillery had not been registering properly. A further preparation was called for at 1300 hours; the attack, however, never materialized. Because of terrain peculiarities, the battalion's supporting artillery was unable to register effectively on the designated targets. Repeated attempts were made until 1400 hours when orders came from regiment for the battalion to withdraw, pending the employment of heavier artillery and an air attack to soften up the German positions. While fifty men from E Company remained in forward positions as outposts, the battalion was withdrawn to the rear of the command post.

On 15 December, the weather was too hazy for tactical bombing, nor was any assault launched by the regiment during daylight hours. That night, however, Higgins decided to try to exploit the gap in the wire made by the G Company patrol on the previous day.

Soon after dark, an eleven-man patrol was sent out with a soundpowered telephone to cross to the German lines and report on enemy strength and alertness. In the darkness the patrol kept getting lost, so one of the men who had cut the wire the day before went out and located the patrol by following the telephone line, and then led it through the wire. The patrol reached the German line at 2100 hours without being fired on. At 2130, it send word back that it had surrounded a pillbox and that the enemy seemed to be unaware of what was happening. The battalion commander thereupon ordered a thrust into the German position in strength. First, F Company was sent through the gap after the patrol to mark the path with engineer tape. There was snow on the ground, the air was cold, and the weather was typical of mid-December. In the early hours of 16 December, the 9th Infantry moved its 2nd Battalion through gaps forced between the wire and pillboxes at Wahlerscheid.

The 2nd Battalion, having started just after dark on the fifteenth, was making headway into the enemy position at such places that it was expected to relieve pressure on other parts of the attack. Their infiltration met with well-deserved success, and under their cover, the 3rd Battalion passed through.

The 3rd Battalion had been in action on the right flank of the 2nd Battalion in an effort to envelope the German stronghold from the right. On the thirteenth, with K Company on the left and L Company on the right, the battalion moved into the woods to the right of the clearing. It was seventy-five yards from the German line, but could not make further progress because of effective fire from the pillboxes. On 14 December, K and L Companies renewed their attack, but were unable to crack the German defenses. A wider envelopment was attempted by L Company, which tried to flank the German position by going around to the right through the 99th Infantry Division sector. The attempt did not succeed.

T/Sgt. Edwin Norris of K Company, 9th Regiment, describes what happened: "The NCOs were given very little information about what our unit would be doing. At best we were told to be ready to move out at 3:30 A.M. the next morning. The 9th Regiment would spearhead the attack with the 1st and 2nd Battalions attacking and the 3rd Battalion in reserve. There would be no artillery or air support strikes before the attack. We marched on a main road for a while, then took a small trail into the forest; this is when our troubles started. The trees, which were planted in rows and about thirty-five to forty feet tall, were with branches sagging with snow and intertwined with other trees. We had to force our way through them, and in doing so, became soaked with melted snow. Some of the men became exhausted and started falling out. We came up to a clearing and an antitank ditch. The platoon took cover in the ditch. Two scouts moved out and were killed by direct cannon fire. When they got to the tree line, the trees here were 75 to 100 feet tall at this point. All hell broke loose with heavy artillery and mortar fire. It was hitting in the treetops, and the treetops and shrapnel was flying down on the troops. Later, I found a piece in my pack that had cut part of the handle out of my little shovel. Our artillery started firing, but, because of the high tree line, they could not register on the German positions. Our assault troops were held up because of the mine fields under the snow and concertina wire.

"Behind that, it started getting dark and much colder. We started suffering real bad because our shoes and clothes were wet. At this time, one of my 1st Platoon men started screaming and praying, and calling for our company commander. He had worked his way fifty yards out into no-man's-land, as we call it. I could not see him because of the tree growth, but I could see up into a man-made draw. In a short time, I saw a man from our 1st Battalion on the right flank start out in the direction of the man doing all of the hollering. He was a first-aid man with a large red cross on his chest, helmet and back. I could see this very plain and I was about one hundred yards away. He got out in the open clearing about twenty five yards and a rifle shot rang out, the medic went down and did not get back up. In a few minutes, another medic started out and the same thing happened to him. I do not know what happened after that, my man quit hollering, and it got so dark, I could not see a white paper held in front of my face. We got so cold; we could not control our shaking. The pain was so very bad. For some unknown reason to me, a .50-caliber machine gun started firing tracer rounds. They were hitting the big tree trunks and ricocheting all around. One round hit just above my head where I was sitting behind a tree and fell in my lap. It melted a hole in my raincoat that I had spread over me. It was very hot, I still have the bullet today."

At the end of this, day the entire battalion reverted to reserve in its previous position behind K Company. The battalion remained in reserve until the night of 15 December when the 2nd Battalion broke into the German pillbox line through the gap in the barbed wire, and the 3rd was called upon to join in the assault. The companies passed through the gap in the

American Defensive Positions 249

order of K, L, and I. Once inside the German line, the 3rd Battalion crossed an east-west road behind the row of pillboxes being attacked by the 2nd Battalion and moved to the left toward another group of pillboxes and the Wahlerscheid road net, which was one of the regimental objectives. K Company by-passed the first five of the second group of pillboxes, as well as a customs house converted into a strongpoint, and moved on to seize the easternmost of two road junctions in Wahlerscheid. A pillbox guarding this road junction was reduced. The company's operation was completed at 0645 hours on 16 December.

Edwin Norris continues: "After a very bad night on myself and platoon, it was very cold, and as if we were in a stupor, hard to talk and give orders, just stutter. The assault troops had made very little headway trying to get through the German defense line. Artillery preparations began about daybreak, but did very little good. The air force could not support us because of the weather and fog. One company tried to work its way up a draw, which is a cut in the hillside. They used bangalore torpedoes to blow the mines and wire. Four men were wounded and one was killed. This drew heavy machine gun and mortar fire. The unit withdrew on 15 December; it was still too foggy for aircraft to bomb.

"That night a patrol was sent through the hole that was blown the day before. They strung a telephone wire and the patrol sent back word that they had surrounded a pillbox and the Germans were unaware of their presence. The gap was marked with tape and the battalion moved through. The 2nd Battalion took out a bunch of pillboxes and secured the line. The 3rd Battalion, during the night, and K Company took out five pillboxes and the customs house at the crossroads, and seized the pillbox guarding the two junction roads. K Company started setting up defense positions around the road junction. One K Company man was shot by a German who raised up from behind a fallen tree. What happened to that German is not easy for me to talk about, so I wont go into any details. L Company had taken up positions on our right flank. We heard a noise from their positions like men marching, in fact, on taking a close look in the fog, I could see a group of men marching along and they were Germans. About this time a lot of hollering and screaming started, and we found our later the Germans were trying to slip out in formation through the fog. L Company took seventy-seven prisoners without firing a shot. I took count of my platoon and could find only six men and they were NCOs. The platoon leadership was not among them, and I never did find out what happened to him. The 38th Infantry Regiment passed through our lines and continued the attack. Our objective, the Wahlerscheid crossroads and twenty four pill boxes had been taken and a line of defense set up around them."

L Company, following K, reduced two of the five by-passed pillboxes and moved up to assault the customs house, which guarded the road net. Before dawn the 2nd and 3rd Platoons were placed on a firing line encircling part of the house. With this support the 1st Platoon attacked at daylight. Seventy-seven Germans surrendered without inflicting a single casualty on the attackers. Total number of prisoners captured by the 3rd Battalion in this sector was 125. From the customs house K Company continued to its objective, the second road junction in Wahlerscheid, which it seized at 0800 hours.

Meanwhile, I Company reduced the last three of the pillboxes bypassed by K and L Company and two more pillboxes farther north. This task was completed at 0930. The battalion then formed a defensive line around the captured road junctions and remained there. As a consequence, the 1st Battalion moved at first light by the most direct route to its objective and took up positions facing north and northwest around Wahlerscheid.

Glynn Raby of H Company, 9th Infantry, describes the effect of the strongholds and pillboxes on the men of the 2nd Infantry Division during their attack on Wahlerscheid: "I have read that the crossroads was defended by twenty-four pillboxes, but I was only able to see two of them, one close up on the morning of 16 December. It was typically constructed mostly underground, with massive concrete walls and top, covered with earth and vegetation. There were two firing ports, barely above ground, and, in the rear, an entrance door. This pillbox had machine guns, but no cannon. In front of the pillboxes, an area about 150 to 200 yards had been cleared, and the fire from machine guns in the pillboxes overlapped. There were antitank ditches, communications trenches, mines and barbed wire. Their mortar and artillery fire came from farther back and, like the machine-gun fire, was intense."

The regiment continued its advance to the north and east against heavy enemy opposition and secured and held positions in a semicircle to the north of the crossroad at Wahlerscheid. At about 1030 hours on the sixteenth, the 38th Infantry passed its 1st and 2nd Battalion through the lines of the 9th Infantry, and in the order of 2nd Battalion on the right and 1st Battalion on the left, attacked positions on the left of the 38th to protect the flank of the division.

Raby continues his story: "After the objective was taken and the 38th Infantry passed through, on the morning of the sixteenth, I stopped to inspect my feet. My overshoes leaked and my boots and socks were wet. A medic said to get dry socks and boots and good overshoes—that I was almost too late. A GI that had been KIA was nearby and I took his."

When the 9th Infantry had infiltrated through the pillboxes and cleaned up the area on the morning of the sixteenth, 2nd Battalion, 38th Infantry,

American Defensive Positions 251

Pillbox in the area of the 38th Infantry. JAMES BRANCH

This modern shot shows the view from a pillbox. HANS WIJERS

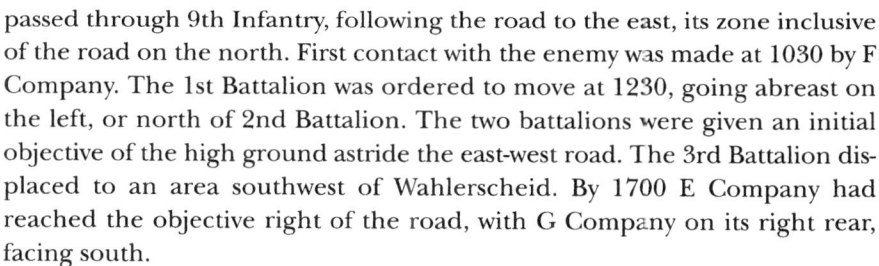

passed through 9th Infantry, following the road to the east, its zone inclusive of the road on the north. First contact with the enemy was made at 1030 by F Company. The 1st Battalion was ordered to move at 1230, going abreast on the left, or north of 2nd Battalion. The two battalions were given an initial objective of the high ground astride the east-west road. The 3rd Battalion displaced to an area southwest of Wahlerscheid. By 1700 E Company had reached the objective right of the road, with G Company on its right rear, facing south.

Joseph Jan Kiss Jr. of C Company, 38th Infantry Regiment, recounts his experience: "On the night of 15 December, we stopped and dug in by a firebreak with my squad as sort of an outpost. I dug in with Pvt. Bill Horn. At dawn I saw a small pillbox 100 feet to the right, and I went to check it out. Going down the stairs I heard a noise and I peeked around a wall with a grenade in hand, and saw Platoon Sergeant Vaughn peeking at me; he was checking also! I talked to Vaughn and returned to the foxhole. Pvt. Stanley Gawronski yelled to me, 'Sergeant, I just saw some Germans run across the firebreak about forty yards ahead.' I said, 'Why didn't you shoot?' He said,

'Well, really I couldn't see too good and besides I didn't want them to know we were here.' I said, 'That sounds O.K.'

"By now, it was daylight. Bill Horn, next to me in the hole, a good looking young man with a thin mustache said, 'Want a cracker, Joe?' (He had a K-ration open.) I said, 'Yeah, I'll pay you back.' I took it and heard a bullet hit Bill in the head. His head fell on my shoulder, blood ran onto my shoulder. He was staring at me and his mouth was opening and closing fast like a fish out of water with a slight gurgle. I felt his pulse, it was quivering and then stopped. I yelled to the other guys, 'Bill just got shot. He's dead. Keep your heads down!' (The sniper shot Bill instead of me because he was a little taller and the sniper saw him better, I believe). Then someone yelled, 'Pull back. We're pulling out.' (I reported where Bill was to the first sergeant and swore he was dead on a death form that he had me fill out and sign.)"

PFC Harold G. Barkley, first scout in G Company, 38th Infantry, remembers: "I was nineteen years old by the time we made the attack through the Monschau Forest in December 1944. After service on the Siegfried Line near St. Vith, we were moved north to attack through the Monschau Forest to capture the Roer River dams in Germany. The attack commenced on 13 December, advancing through fairly deep snow and it was cold. The 9th Infantry Regiment led the way with the 38th following close behind. The 9th ran into extremely stiff resistance at a crossroads called Wahlerscheid, which was defended by numerous concrete pillboxes, apron-up-apron of barbed wire, antitank ditches and vast open fields of fire. The 9th fought for three days in freezing weather to no avail. The 38th stayed in reserve and only received light shelling, but was sent up just as the 9th achieved success. During the battle I witnessed an entire squad wiped out as a lieutenant sent them, one by one, to cut the barbed wire before three pillboxes. Machine guns and snow-covered mines got all of them. Only one man remained in that squad and I was next in line. I knew that the other squad was not from our company but still thought that the lieutenant would have the authority to send me out there, too. I thought for sure this was my last day on earth. Fortunately, a runner came up to the lieutenant and told him something, probably that others had breached the defenses and were now behind the fortifications. The surviving fellow from the wiped out squad and I exchanged looks that I'll never forget. We had just escaped certain death."

C Company, on the north side of the road, extended northwest about 500 yards, with Company B extending west from there to the 9th Infantry. 3rd Battalion was placed on the south side of the road, leading west from Wahlerscheid to guard against penetration from enemy-held pillboxes. During the day, the operational command post displaced to previously prepared positions. B Company, 741st Tank Battalion, was detached, and A Company,

American Defensive Positions

741st Tank Battalion attached, with two platoons placed immediately behind front line positions to prevent a breakthrough as enemy action mounted along the corps front. Orders were received and transmitted to organize Antitank and Cannon Companies as rifle companies, ready to move on order by 0800. Orders from division also were relayed to all battalions to maintain present positions and have all-around command post defense against penetration, and have all men on standing alert at first light 17 December.

The only planning necessary to complete the operation was the clearing of further lanes through mine fields, and the blowing up of a single pillbox. B Company led the way on this move, and since it was over exposed ground that had been violently contested up until this time, it was made with trepidation but with great gallantry. Four casualties were incurred in the move—one by small-arms fire and three by antipersonnel mines. However, the battalion closed into position successfully by 1015 hours, consolidated and prepared for counterattack. It was later learned from captured prisoners that the heavily defended position seized by the regiment was possible due to the disorganization in relieving units in position. However enemy reaction came swiftly, and just at dark on the evening of the sixteenth, very violent attempts at infiltration into the position were made all along the line. Thanks to carefully planned artillery fire, the counterattack estimated in strength at 100 (and later confirmed by a captured prisoner) was repulsed about 2245 on 16 December.

Barkley continues: "After the pillboxes were taken, the fighting wasn't as severe, and the 38th advanced through the forest. Artillery tree bursts were still a big problem. On the night of 16 December, G Company dug in for the

Men of the 741st Tank Battalion during a "break" in the fight.

night in the snow, but I had to go out on night patrol to try to get a prisoner. We didn't get one but got lost on our return and ran into an outpost of some other company. When challenged, we had forgotten the password. Next came question on American sports, of which none of us were too keen and the outpost was ready to open fire when I called out, 'American patrol, American patrol! Don't shoot, we're coming in,' and I raised my rifle high overhead and slowly went forward. Disaster was averted.

"We only got a little sleep, curled up in our blankets in the snow. I had never received overshoes and my socks were wet. My clothing was wet, too, and it froze."

All during the night, the battalion sector was subjected to heavy mortar fire and direct fire from unobserved guns. However, the battalion was well dug in, having utilized the enemy fortification and trenches, and only eighteen casualties resulted in the occupation of the position. Forty-nine men were evacuated because of bad feet brought on by the ordeals of the operations to date. On the morning of the seventeenth, the fighting strength of the battalion was approximately 22 officers and 387 enlisted men, having dwindled from a jumping-off strength on the thirteenth of 35 officers and 678 enlisted men. By this time, the battalion was tired and had been continuously under fire for ninety-six hours. By this time, too, the chain of command had been greatly weakened, the battalion having lost two company commanders in A Company, one each in B and C Companies, and numerous platoon leaders, platoon sergeants and key men.

CHAPTER 3

Situation on the Southern Flank of the 2nd Infantry Division

THE ATTACK OF THE 395TH REGIMENTAL COMBAT TEAM
During a snowstorm on 12 December, the 395th Infantry Regiment—minus the 3rd Battalion, which was holding down a defensive position in the town of Höfen, and F Company, which was attached to the 38th Cavalry Reconnaissance Squadron north of Monschau—moved from the vicinity of Kalterherberg to a location north of Rocherath. Plans were prepared to launch an attack at 0930 on the thirteenth in conjunction with the 2nd Infantry Division.

Harold Helfrich of the 4th Platoon, C Company, 395th Infantry, recalls: "On 11 December, a call came from the company command post to the machine-gun section. They said the 1st Battalion was going to lead an attack on the Siegfried Line and capture and occupy the nearest town. We were to expect much street fighting. The 2nd Platoon, lead by Lt. Ralph Shivone, was to spearhead the attack. The two machine-gun squads were to be attached to the second platoon for reinforcements."

The area through which this attack was to be made was heavily wooded and pitted with rocky gorges. The mission of the regiment was to advance abreast of the 2nd Infantry Division and protect its right flank. As the regiment's 3rd Battalion was holding Höfen at the division's north boundary, the 2nd Battalion of the 393rd Infantry Regiment was attached to protect the right flank of the 395th. On the morning of the thirteenth, the regiment moved out in column of battalions; 1st Battalion leading, 2nd Battalion echeloned to the right rear, and the 2nd Battalion 393rd Infantry abreast and on the right of the 2nd Battalion 395th. The morning was foggy with visibility limited to about 150 yards, favorable for an attack situation. The 1st Battalion moved approximately 3,000 yards before encountering any resistance.

The 1st Battalion, which earlier had been holding a 7,600-meter defensive front, was the assault battalion of the regiment in this drive. In the line continuously since 9 November, when it went into action for the first time,

Dragon's teeth along the Siegfried Line.

the battalion was still almost full strength with more than 800 officers and men and with all of its equipment.

Helfrich continues: "On 13 December, we assembled and took off. We had gotten about half a mile and heard tremendous small arms firing about 500 yards to our left. It was burp guns, rifles, BARs, and machine guns. We wanted to go over to help but were told to keep on moving. Later, we heard that a platoon of ours was crossing an open meadow, and a German ambush pinned them down. Many were killed, wounded, and froze to death.

"Late that evening, we stopped near a ridge, and about 100 yards away was a heavy paved road. All night long we heard heavy guns, tanks, and armored carriers traveling down the road. We figured this was going to be a large attack. We had plenty of good backup. Hell, these weren't our troops. These were Germans!"

In the attack, the 395th Regimental Combat Team included D Company of the 751st Tank Battalion, C Company of the 324th Engineer Battalion, and one company of the 801st Tank Destroyer Battalion. They also had direct support from the 924th Field Artillery Battalion with other division artillery support available when needed. Along its front before he attack, the 1st Battalion was opposed by elements of the 990th Regiment of the 277th Volksgrenadier Division.

Situation on the Southern Flank of the 2nd Infantry Division

Prisoners of war captured on 12 December indicated that there were some Waffen-SS troops in the vicinity. It was assumed, however, that these troops were being brought in to block the American attack. "At no time prior to 16 December," said Hendricks, "was there any indication from interrogation of prisoners or from higher echelon reports that the Germans were preparing a build-up for a breakthrough."

The attack began at 0830 hours without artillery preparation. B and C Companies attacked abreast along the narrow road leading towards Schleiden. The terrain was rough, "straight up and down," according to Hendricks. The companies were deployed on both sides of the road in snow six to eight inches deep. It was impossible to use vehicles, so all of the heavy weapons had to be hand carried.

Despite the snow, the battalion advanced 5,000 yards without great opposition. Then it approached pillboxes, which made up the first of the Siegfried Line defenses in this sector. German mortars were targeting every draw to the east, while artillery, which appeared to be located near Hellenthal, began to fall on the battalion. The artillery was very accurate, but it was not as heavy as the mortar fire, which was the heaviest received by the battalion during the attack. In addition to the attack by artillery and mortars, the unit drew machine gun and small arms fire from three pillboxes to the east. The roads were blocked by both antitank and antipersonnel mines, and wire and boobytraps were used to establish roadblocks. These were by-passed without difficulty, however. Approximately a company of enemy troops was in front of the battalion position, deployed across the hill and in the draw. The pillboxes were thicker in the 2nd Division sector on the left. This flank was also subject to direct observation and fire from the hill on the left.

Harold Helfrich resumes his story: "On the morning of the fourteenth, we were atop a ridge, and I began to dig a larger trench for my machine gun canister. Of all things, the end of my shovel hit the trigger and off went two rounds. An officer yelled, 'Who fired those shots?' I weakly raised my hand, thinking this was the end. He said, 'Forget it. I'll call for artillery and begin the attack.' I looked over at Beuchler of the second machine-gun squad. He winked at me with a Hollywood John Wayne smile and said, 'Helfrich, this is it.' I laughed and we took off.

"Harry Duncan picked up the gun, and I carried the tripod and a can of ammo. Down the hill we went and up the other side. We received tremendous German machine-gun and burp-gun fire, and we were pinned down. We asked for smoke to cover our approach and we received it. The first round fell short, and where did it land, but right on top of the company medic. He was screaming and rolling in front of me. I wanted to go over and help, but an officer behind me yelled, 'Leave him alone. Keep moving!' I picked up the gun, and up the hill we moved amid all the returning fire and artillery shells coming in.

"We reached the top of the hill and had to stop. There were barbed wire, mines and a German pillbox in front of us. Sergeant Rickstrew and Cranny were about five yards ahead of me. A German potato-masher grenade came flying through the air. It exploded, and Rickstrew and Cranny were hit. I slammed down the machine gun beyond the tree line, but an officer came over and said, 'Helfrich, you're too far in the open.' I had good vision of the pillbox, and I could see the Germans across the firebreak mingling around. He said, 'Move back about 10 yards in the tree line.' I pulled back, and sure enough, an 88 shell hit exactly where I was digging.

"Shell fragments hit my gun belt canister and went right through it. I took off the belt and threw it away. I replaced the belt and dug down about eighteen inches then stopped. We were under heavy machine-gun, mortar and 88 artillery fire. One shell came down about thirty yards from me, and I heard someone yell for a medic. The voice said, 'Beckwith has lost his leg. He's hit.' I heard Beckwith call for his mother and then silence. The voice called for a medic again, then said, 'Forget it, he's dead.' I heard Vern Swanson was in a foxhole next to Beckwith and was knocked dizzy by the concussion. He survived."

Reaching Purple Heart Hill around 1400, the 1st Battalion suffered its heaviest casualties of the attack before having time to dig in. B Company lost its company commander, two officers and its first sergeant within fifteen minutes after reaching the hill. All the casualties of the day were suffered by B Company, which had five killed, twenty-three wounded, and six missing. The force dug in as quickly as possible, with C Company on the left flank and B Company along a bank to the right.

On the morning of 14 December, A and C Companies were ordered to assault and clear out pillboxes. The two companies jumped off at 1100, A Company on the right. They attacked over rough terrain, with little cover except for some clumps of short pine, which gave some concealment. The companies met with little fire during the advance.

The pillbox, which C Company attacked, was heavily booby-trapped and surrounded by double-apron wire. An assault squad, supported both on its right and left, surrounded the pillbox and hit it with bazookas, antitank guns, BARs and grenades. The position was soon taken, and by 1600, A and C Companies were in the woods to the east. Here A Company had one mortar squad hit by a shell and lost five men. The two companies, together, sustained about thirty casualties during the course of the day.

Situation on the Southern Flank of the 2nd Infantry Division

Helfrich continues his account: "Around 14 December, we were going to take the pillbox. My machine gun was to protect the left flank, and the second machine gun squad was to open fire on the embrasures of the pillbox. Riflemen were to crawl up under cover of smoke and, with bangalore torpedoes, blow up the barbed wire. We were already ready to attack and Lieutenant Murphy of our platoon ran by me. I yelled, 'Murphy, where are you going?' He said, 'Back, I have trench foot.' Just then Beuchler opened up with his machine gun firing at the embrasures. He was finally pinned down by returning fire from the pillbox and a German rifleman beyond the barbed wire.

"A platoon sergeant fired and hit the German in the face, killing him. Beuchler was firing with his face in the dirt and the gun over his head. The rifleman had crawled up, put the torpedo in the barbed wire and blew it up. They then crawled forward and went into the pillbox. Just then I heard a voice say, 'Helfrich, in the pillbox!' I took off my helmet, went to the barbed wire, and began to crawl through. Someone yelled, 'Stay in the tracks, watch for mines.' I took out my trusty .45 and reached the German trench works. I peered around the first L in the trench works. I stopped, aimed, and looked for Germans. I didn't want to be cut in half by a German burp gun. I reached the end of the trench works; a large mound was at the end. I went back about five yards, took a running leap, and went rolling down a steep embankment. I rolled down and ended up near the entrance to the pillbox. I started to go in and a sergeant was dragging a dead German out by his leg. I stepped over the dead German, and as I was nearly over him, the sergeant handed me a Russian flag and said the German must have been on the Eastern front. I went inside the pillbox and the phone was ringing. I answered it in German and had a conversation with a German on the other end. He asked me what was wrong. What was going on. Then he asked me some specific questions that I couldn't answer correctly. He hung up on me.

"I asked Miller where the rest of the men were. He said upstairs. I went up a steel ladder to the cupola and there were two riflemen there with the most beautiful machine gun I had ever seen. The barrel was about four feet long and it was on gears so it could be traversed. I read the label on top of the gun: 'Skoda, Czechoslovakia.' The best gun made. It was aimed toward our lines and I said let's turn it around. We opened another embrasure that was facing the other German pillbox and traversed the machine gun to face them. Someone yelled, 'Helfrich, back to the lines.' We had captured some Germans and I was to interrogate them."

Since the 2nd Division had been held up at Wahlerscheid, the 1st Battalion, 395th, was ordered to hold up its advance during the following day, except for a 300-yard push by C Company, which resulted in the capture of a pillbox around 1100, which contained five Germans armed with a machine gun, machine pistols and grenades. During the night some movement was heard in the German lines, and the German artillery was active. C Company suffered casualties of five killed and ten wounded during the day and night.

The 2nd Battalion had moved into another assembly area on 13 December, a half mile north of its current position. Here they received attacking orders for the next day. On 14 December, the battalion commander, Major Stevens, and the company commanders went forward to reconnoiter the area to which the companies were to move for the attack. F Company, at the time was still with the 38th Cavalry. As a result, the attack plan envisaged the use of E and G abreast, E on the right.

At 0700, Major Boyden led the companies up the road, turned west into the woods and led the companies into the assembly area where they met the company commanders. The companies quickly moved ahead in the attack. The terrain through which they had to pass before reaching the draw, the line of departure, was difficult to traverse. Steep slopes and some open ground, which had to be crossed on the double, exhausted many of the men before they reached the line of departure. As the men crossed the lines of departure around 1000 hours, they came under heavy artillery fire including some 88 fire. Forward movement was slowed down.

By the sixteenth, when the battalion had taken some eight more pillboxes, the situation was thus: the 2nd Battalion was on the left of the regimental front tied in with the 9th Infantry. Its attack was waiting for the 9th Inf to clear out the rest of its area before continuing the attack on 17 December in a more easterly direction. The 1st Battalion was on the right.

The first evidences of the German counterattack on 16 December were not apparent to the 1st Battalion, which was still waiting for elements on the right and left flanks to advance before taking further action. No German movement was made against the 395th sector, so that it was not until afternoon that the battalion was aware of the attack, and not until noon of the following day that it got word of the all-out counterattack in progress.

The chief problems of the 1st Battalion during the period from 13 to 16 December consisted not so much of enemy action as of supply and communications. Every pound of supply and ammunition used had to be hand carried over two hills, a distance of some 4,000 yards. The battalion and regimental antitank platoons and the A&P Platoon were used for this purpose. The men were sniped at and were hit by mortar and 88 fire. Because of the difficulties of the job, one man could make only one trip a day. However, they were able to bring up enough food for subsistence and, after the first night, to bring bedrolls for the men. Wires went out a couple of times every night and day, but the wire teams were always able to get them back in. For three days the 1st Battalion was out ahead of other units to the right and left, but the enemy made no effort to surround them after the first night.

SITUATION AT THE 2ND BATTALION, 393RD INFANTRY, 99TH INFANTRY DIVISION

The 2nd Battalion was put under division control for the attack on 13 December with the mission of protecting the 395th Infantry's right flank. The 395th was on the right of the 9th Infantry, 2nd Infantry Division, which was making the main effort at the start to take the pillbox defenses at the crossroads of Wahlerscheid. The 2nd Battalion was not holding a place in the 393rd's defensive line and had a 1200- yard gap between it and the unit on its right flank.

The 2nd Battalion moved to a forward assembly area, which served as the battalion command post, on the afternoon of 12 December. Their orders were to attack at 0830 on the morning of the thirteenth with two contact objectives. There were no supply roads, so everything was hand-carried. This was because the single main road in the area had been turned over to the 9th Inf exclusively, so that there would be no confusion.

George Lehr of F Company, 393rd Infantry Regiment, remembers: "I was nineteen years old at the time we left the U.S. in October of 1944. There were a large number of young men my age in the 99th. We were probably the best-trained division that arrived in Europe at that time. Historians later

The assembly area of the 2nd Battalion, which served as the battalion command post, on the afternoon of 12 December.

described us as poorly trained. This was incorrect. We arrived in the vicinity of Krinkelt in early November of 1944, relieving the 9th Infantry Division. There was no activity at that time. Occasionally the Germans would fire a round of artillery or mortar into our positions. Shortly before the Ardennes Offensive started, about 13 December, we were pulled out of line and sent north toward the Roer River dams. As a result we missed being in the eye of the storm."

On the morning of the thirteenth, the battalion moved out as scheduled in an inverted-V formation, with E Company in the lead, G Company to the right rear, and F Company to the left rear. One section of heavy machine guns was attached to each of the rifle companies and the fourth section was kept as a "floating section," moving with the battalion command post. They arrived at Objective A at 1100 without any opposition, the sole difficulty being the difficult terrain, which tired the men who were heavily burdened. Here they checked and then received the order to move on to Objective B.

En route to this objective, Capt. Carl S. Swisher said that F Company received some fire from 88s but suffered no casualties. They then moved forward until they came to the clearing just before Objective B—which was a crossroad for a network of secondary roads—when the leading scouts spotted several pillboxes guarding the crossroads. They notified 2nd Lt Edward P. Mann, platoon leader of the 2nd Platoon of E Company, which was out in front, and he cautiously went up to check their findings. He saw the pillboxes and notified the company commander, Capt. Donald G. Driscoll, who also came up to have a look. He ordered the scouts to pull back and had the platoon remain several hundred yards inside the woods, while he notified the battalion commander.

Lt. Col. Ernest C. Peters, the battalion commander, came up and joined Driscoll at about 1600, shortly after they had arrived at this point. They had just started to confer to decide what to do, when some of the men made a noise. The Germans heard it, and immediately opened up with MGs and mortar fire, causing five casualties in E Company, all from mortar fire. The alarm had been given, so the forward movement of the battalion stopped and was pulled back slightly. They dug in and formed a perimeter defense in the area.

Since they were then about 1,100 yards out in front of the 395th, whose flank they were supposed to be protecting, at about 0230 or 0300 on the fourteenth, they received orders to remain where there were, presumably until the 395th could catch up. Then, later that night, they got orders to move forward right away and they did so, moving about 800 yards, until they came in front of the pillboxes. Plans had been made to assault the three pillboxes (that many had been counted before dark) on the fourteenth at 0900,

Situation on the Southern Flank of the 2nd Infantry Division

The open area in front of the German pillboxes. This was where the soldiers had to cross before they could even approach the pillboxes. HANS WIJERS

but the attack was not made because the flamethrowers to be used in the operation would not work.

The night was a miserable one for the men. They spent it without blankets or bedrolls, had to dig in, try to catch a few winks of sleep, and, "at the same time, try to keep alert," Capt. Carl S. Swisher said. The HQ Company section had spent the latter part of the previous afternoon and night in carrying up rations and ammunition. The battalion remained in that position for the rest of the fourteenth, with the Germans at the pillboxes harrying them with small arms and mortar fire and in general making life as unpleasant as they could.

The day was used to consolidate positions and to get things ready for an attack on the pillboxes and to bring up supplies. There was a gap with the 395th, but a five-man patrol headed by S/Sgt. Joseph Pollock, the battalion communications sergeant, was sent out in the morning and reported making contact at 1100. The patrol reported receiving some harassing small arms fire, but suffered no casualties. They planned an attack against the two pillboxes which had been discovered around Jagdhütte and the one farther to the south at Daubenscheid. These pillboxes were guarding the approaches from the west up the few roads through the area. They were the boxes that stopped them the first day. The attack was planned for 0830, but again, because of the trouble with the flamethrowers, the attack was delayed until 1000. The plan was to send a combat patrol around to the left at Jagdhütte and then to cut through the barbed wire under cover of smoke with another force and assault the boxes directly. The attack finally did jump off at 1000. The combat patrol was made up of twenty men from F Company, led by 2nd Lt. Joseph Kagan, platoon leader of that company's 2nd Platoon. It moved out to the left and made enough demonstration to draw fire upon itself and got pinned down almost from the start.

John F. McCoy, who was on the same patrol, wrote the following about that attack: "On 13 December, our battalion went on the offensive and attacked several pillboxes. During the attack on one of the pillboxes I was laying behind a big tree firing at the pillbox observation ports so that those inside would not see one of our soldiers, creeping up to the pillbox with a flamethrower. When he pulled the trigger, of his flamethrower, only a stream of liquid came out and not the usual huge rolling ball of flame. A second man came with another flamethrower and it worked perfectly, covering the entire pillbox with flame. It had to be very toasty for those inside, they hurriedly came out and surrendered to us. Some German mortar shells fell intermittently on our positions. Most of our platoon now lay in the snow watching the proceedings. As I lay behind my thick tree, I felt a sharp knock on the side of my helmet. I looked around and tried to see who had thrown a snowball or a piece of ice at me, I saw no guilty looking person. Later I would discover that I had been hit, not by a snowball or a piece of ice, but by a piece of shrapnel from an exploding mortar shell. The sharp metal piece of shrapnel had hit my helmet just above the left ear and cut through the metal but stopped as it entered the composition liner. Lucky for me that it was not a little lower."

Another force of about the same size, under command of Lieutenant Mann, at the same time hit the wire in front of the box under cover of smoke from the 370th Field Artillery Battalion, but there the trouble started. The bangalore torpedo with which they had hoped to blow this obstacle would not ignite. The Germans laid down heavy mortar and artillery fire on them causing about thirteen casualties. The assaulting groups pressed their attack for about forty-five minutes, but finally gave up; the attempt was a failure. But, as a result of the hornet's nest, which was stirred up from this attack, the Germans continued to throw in more mortar fire on the rear area and more casualties were inflicted, especially on E Company. The day's casualties finally were one officer and sixteen enlisted men wounded and one enlisted man killed.

Radford M. Carroll of E Company, 393rd Regiment, recounts his experience: "On 13 December, we set out for our first attack on the Germans. I was carrying about 120 pounds of equipment including two days rations. There was about a foot of snow on the ground, and a light snow of big flakes

Situation on the Southern Flank of the 2nd Infantry Division

A modern-day photo of one of the few remaining German pillboxes. This one is at Daubenscheid below the old dirt road leading to the dragon's teeth of the Siegfried Line. HANS WIJERS

was falling when we set off through the woods. I slipped going down a slope and my right leg was doubled back in a painful position. Some of the people around gave sympathetic grins when I complained because it wasn't broken.

"We crossed a small wooded valley without opposition, crossing a clear mountain stream on wooden ladders thrown across. We crossed a small dirt road at the bottom of a bluff where everyone began piling up. More as a challenge than anything else, I began to climb the bluff by digging my boots in and holding to bushes. To my surprise the entire group began climbing after me. I suppose they thought that if anyone as loaded as I could climb, then they could also climb. At the top of the bluff (which we called Rat Hill), we encountered few rifle shots as the German outposts were abandoned. We were again in a planned fir forest with some very tall trees and some sections of maybe ten feet high growths. I was somewhat fatigued from the allday movement, but I felt that as long as we were at last advancing, I could go on forever.

"We moved into a region of tall trees next to the Jagdhütte bunkers of the Siegfried Line just as dusk fell. Then there started the most horrendous artillery barrage that I had yet encountered. Without any orders, everyone began to dig a sheltering hole in the ground wherever they were. This digging was done while lying flat on the ground and hacking and scraping with anything available. First a hole big enough for the head, then enlarged and deepened for the shoulders, the hole going down like a ramp with the digger sliding into the hole as it was dug. There was no organization, no disposition of troops; every one dug in where they lay. The officers did not try to assign anyone to dig their holes, because if they wanted below the surface of the earth they had to get there themselves. There was nothing like the power of those descending shells to encourage digging energy. When the shelling slacked off at about daybreak, everyone still alive was in a grave-like hole.

"There was a lull in the shelling, and we began to organize for the attack on the first pillboxes. Some of our people were to go out with explosives to blow holes in the barbed wire entanglements, and others were to test flame throwers so the Germans could see the test; this demonstration was to encourage the 'tired old men' in the pillboxes to surrender. By the way, one of the men with the flamethrower found that the ignition system wouldn't work; he was given a box of matches and told to hold a lighted match in the stream of napalm as he was using the weapon.

"I was in the group that was to give covering fire to the ones with the explosives and flame throwers. It was just like kicking a hornet nest. A terrific volume of return fire came back, both machine-gun and artillery fire. Our people could not get anywhere and were lucky to make it back to the shallow ditch at the edge of the woods. The machine-gun fire raking our positions was so intense that all the people in the group giving covering fire also crawled into the ditch, which offered the only shelter. I was uneasy about the ditch because any type of enfilading fire would be a slaughter.

"The machine-gun fire was cutting the branches from the bushes just above my head, and I was tempted to put my hand up and get a 'million dollar wound' (that is, a wound that would get you back into a hospital but not be permanently disabling). After tentatively putting my arm up, I involuntarily jerked it back as soon as the machine gun started again. I soon realized that the deliberate wound was not for me, and I never again tried that.

"When the machine-gun fire and the artillery let up, we withdrew to our foxholes dug the previous night. I had dug in at the base of a fir tree about two feet in diameter, hoping the big tree would keep off some of the bullets. While I was up in the ditch, an artillery shell had struck the tree trunk about twenty feet above the ground, blowing the trunk in two and dropping the upper segment upright just by my foxhole. My foxhole was littered with wood splinters and when I picked my sleeping bag and pack out of the foxhole, they were riddled with tiny holes from the shell fragments. Again I was in the right place at the right time.

Situation on the Southern Flank of the 2nd Infantry Division   267

"At that time someone mentioned that my friend, Atkins (the fellow that had done the church ploy with me in Paris, Texas) had been wounded. Atkins was in another platoon and I couldn't go over to find out how badly he had been wounded. This was very depressing. Later, I found that he had been wounded in the hand, a lucky wound that removed him from the infantry. One of the fixed rules in the infantry is that during attacks the soldiers do not go to help the wounded. The dramatic portions of movies and books, where the soldiers stop their action and gather around their fallen comrade, just does not actually happen. The medics are to care for the wounded, the soldiers are to keep on fighting. This is necessary because otherwise several soldiers would be removed from fighting every time one is hit. Moreover, people bunching around wounded make a wonderful target for the enemy. This is why I have remarked that I didn't know how bad someone was hurt or what happened to them. We couldn't stop or go back to attend to anyone hurt.

"This might be a good place to tell about the medics. Each infantry platoon had a medic attached to it. Instead of weapons, the medic carried first aid equipment and was trained in the preliminary treating of wounds. We all had a small first aid kit, and all had training in first aid, but the medic had much more equipment and much better training. The medic lived in the field and was with the platoon at all times. His helmet was painted with a red cross and (in theory) the combatants were not supposed to shoot at him. In fact, the medic had one of the most dangerous jobs in the infantry, which is saying a lot. When heavy fire was making us all burrow into the ground like worms, the medic had to move around to try to care for the wounded. Many of the medics had strong religious or moral convictions about killing people. The army didn't mind this in the least; the protesters were just asked if they would serve as combat medics caring for the wounded. Their reply quickly separated those with moral conviction from the coward. In World War II, the moral convictions that would not allow people to go into danger got them into prison.

"There was no shortage of openings in the ranks of the combat medics, since casualties kept their ranks thinned. All the soldiers in my platoon had a high respect for our medic. I didn't know, or care, if he was morally opposed to fighting. I did know that he was courageous and did his job in an efficient manner.

"We had a number of wounded and dead after the abortive attack on the Siegfried line, the litter bearers from the forward medical units were swamped, especially since they had to carry the wounded down the steep Rat Hill. One wounded fellow who sobbed until he was taken off embarrassed me. I was angry with one man who was shot through the foot; the rumor was that he had carefully loaded armor-piercing ammunition in his rifle before deliberately shooting himself in the foot. Anyone should have been more considerate of the litter bearers than to make them carry him down the hill.

"I was able to replace my riddled pack and sleeping bag with the equipment of one of the casualties. A welcome casualty was my bazooka, which had sustained several holes, rendering it useless. I at once discarded the bazooka rockets since I had no way to launch them. I carefully did not ask about the rockets, since I was sure that someone would want me to carry them, useless or not.

"We spent another day in the same location, trying to decide what to do. The intensity of the German defense proved that G-2 had no idea what they were talking about. There was a rumor that we were going to attack again after an intense artillery barrage to knock out some of the defense. We had not been resupplied with rations, but since I had been too busy the day before to eat but half of my rations, I still had half rations for one more day. Early in the morning darkness of 16 December, I heard a terrific artillery barrage in the distance. The explosions were so frequent they sounded like a continuous rumble; I had never heard a barrage of that intensity before. I felt that our artillery was really giving the Germans the business. What I didn't know was that it was German artillery, opening the Battle of the Bulge, and the other sections of the 99th Division, resting in a nice holding position, were the victims of the artillery."

The battalion pulled back into its positions and remained there for the rest of the day, not making any further attempts to push on. Then on the morning of the sixteenth, they received some artillery fire—but not much—and some small-arms and mortar fire from the right. They had been alerted during the night of 15–16 December when they received word that tanks were seen approaching in the east. On the morning of the sixteenth, Capt. Carl S. Swisher said he called regiment and asked what was up, and all he got in reply was that the situation was "terrible." This was the only word they received that whole day and until the afternoon of the seventeenth. They could hear sounds of fighting and firing to their south and farther to the north, but there were no attempts made against their positions and no unusual amount of artillery thrown in against them.

CHAPTER 4

The Germans Attack

THE 2ND DIVISION ENDS THE WAHLERSCHEID ATTACK
The initial dispositions of the 2nd Infantry Division are important in considering the subsequent actions. The division had begun attacking northeast through the Wahlerscheid area on 13 December, and on 16 December, General Robertson started passing the 38th Infantry through the 9th Infantry for exploitation of the breakthrough. On the night of 16 December the division had a bridgehead around the Wahlerscheid hedgehog, and all three battalions of the 9th Infantry and two battalions of the 38th Infantry were in contact with the enemy, thus making five battalions committed in that sector. The last battalion of the 38th Infantry was about a mile south of Wahlerscheid preparing to pass through the 9th to reinforce the 38th.

When the initial operation had been projected, Robertson had at his disposal and under his command the 2nd Infantry Division (including the 395th Regimental Combat Team of the 99th Infantry Division) plus Combat Command B (CCB) of the 9th Armored Division. Realizing that the 99th Division was spread very thin on the east, the general had planned to use CCB to cover the north flank of the 2nd Division, where the main supply route lay, until such time as the area between Wahlerscheid and Höfen was cleared and opened as a main supply route.

On the afternoon of 16 December, CCB was detached from the 2nd Division. The 23rd Infantry was in division reserve, but had begun its move forward from the vicinity of Camp Elsenborn to aid in the taking of Wahlerscheid.

The leading battalion, the 1st, of the 23rd Infantry was in an assembly area about a mile and half north of Rocherath on the night of 15 December. On the afternoon of 16 December, General Robertson received orders not to commit the 23rd Infantry until further orders were received. Late in the afternoon of 16 December, the 3rd Battalion of the 23rd Infantry was detached from the 2nd Division and attached to the 99th Division to plug a gap in their lines. Shortly thereafter, the 2nd Battalion of the 23rd was also attached to the 99th Division. Thus instead of having CCB of the 9th Armored Division and one regimental combat team in division reserve, there remained only one battalion of the 23rd Infantry.

THE KRINKELTER WOODS

On 16 December, the 99th Division was on the right of the 2nd Division sector, with the 3rd Battalion, 393rd Infantry, in defensive positions in the Krinkelter Wald about four thousand yards east-northeast of Krinkelt and the 1st Battalion, 393rd Infantry, in defensive positions in the Mürringer Wald about five thousand 200 yards east of Krinkelt, and just south of the 3rd Battalion.

After assembling in the Westwall bunkers around Udenbreth, the 990th Grenadier Regiment of the 277th Volksgrenadier Division, reinforced with a company of fusiliers and a company of engineers, attacked. On the left, the fusilier company mounted the attack from the southern part of the village (Neuhof) on both sides of the road that ran to the Reichsstrasse, and from there down the forest track that ran to Krinkelt. Here the company presumably ran into C Company of the 1st Battalion, 393rd Infantry Regiment, which formed the rightmost wing of the regiment on the border of the sector of the 394th Regiment. Early in the morning of 16 December, it appeared that the 3rd Battalion, 393rd Infantry, might be cut off by an enemy attack around its left flank. The story seemed to be that the Germans had hit between the two battalions and had surrounded K Company on the 3rd Bat-

German soldiers.

The Germans Attack

talion's right flank and driven back B Company on the 1st Battalion's left flank. Two of C Company's platoons of the 393rd Infantry Regiment on the right wing were overrun, the leftmost could only hold with difficulty.

By now it was ten o'clock. On the right flank of the fusilier company the 990th Grenadier Regiment was attacking from the western part of Udenbreth, with its assault company out in front. It was able to break into the positions of B Company on the left of the 1st Battalion sector, overrun two platoons and encircle the third. The battalion commander ordered his reserve, A Company, to reestablish the situation with the leftmost company (B) and asked the regimental commander for help for C Company on the right. Meanwhile, the leftmost had been encircled, but was still fighting. Here the reserve company, which attacked determinedly, almost managed to re-establish the situation. It had to yield about 300 meters for a counterattack—probably by the reserve of the 990th Grenadier Regiment, but there it managed to establish itself and stop the attack of the 990th, which had suffered severe losses. The 393rd regimental commander had no more rifle units available to reinforce C Company, as his 2nd Battalion had been included in the 395th Regimental Combat Team. He improvised by sending the minelayer platoon of the Anti-Tank Company to the severely pressured C Company. By 1030 hours, it arrived at the 1st Battalion and together with the engineer platoon and individual members of the staff it attacked to free C Company, which meanwhile had been encircled. They managed to retake the company headquarters and re-establish communications with the platoon that had remained in its positions.

Capt. Lawrence H. Duffin, S-3 of the 1st Battalion, 393rd Infantry, 99th Division, remembers: "Shortly after the barrage, enemy riflemen supported by automatic weapons attacked both flanks of the battalion front. This initial attack was repulsed with only a few casualties reported among the battalion troops. At approximately 0800, the enemy again attacked in force, this time using successive waves of infantry. The artillery forward observers estimated an almost continuous artillery barrage in front of our lines. Our own mortars and machine guns fired their final protective lines. Both front line companies reported numerous dead piled up immediately in front of their positions, but at approximately 0830 hours, C Company reported an enemy breakthrough on their right flank."

PFC Don W. Rader, a bazooka man in the 1st Platoon, K Company, 393rd Infantry, tells his story: "We were awakened by an artillery barrage that lasted nearly two hours. When it first started, I thought it was our own artillery dropping short rounds; but when the barrage stopped, German soldiers in great numbers crossed the International Highway to the right of our

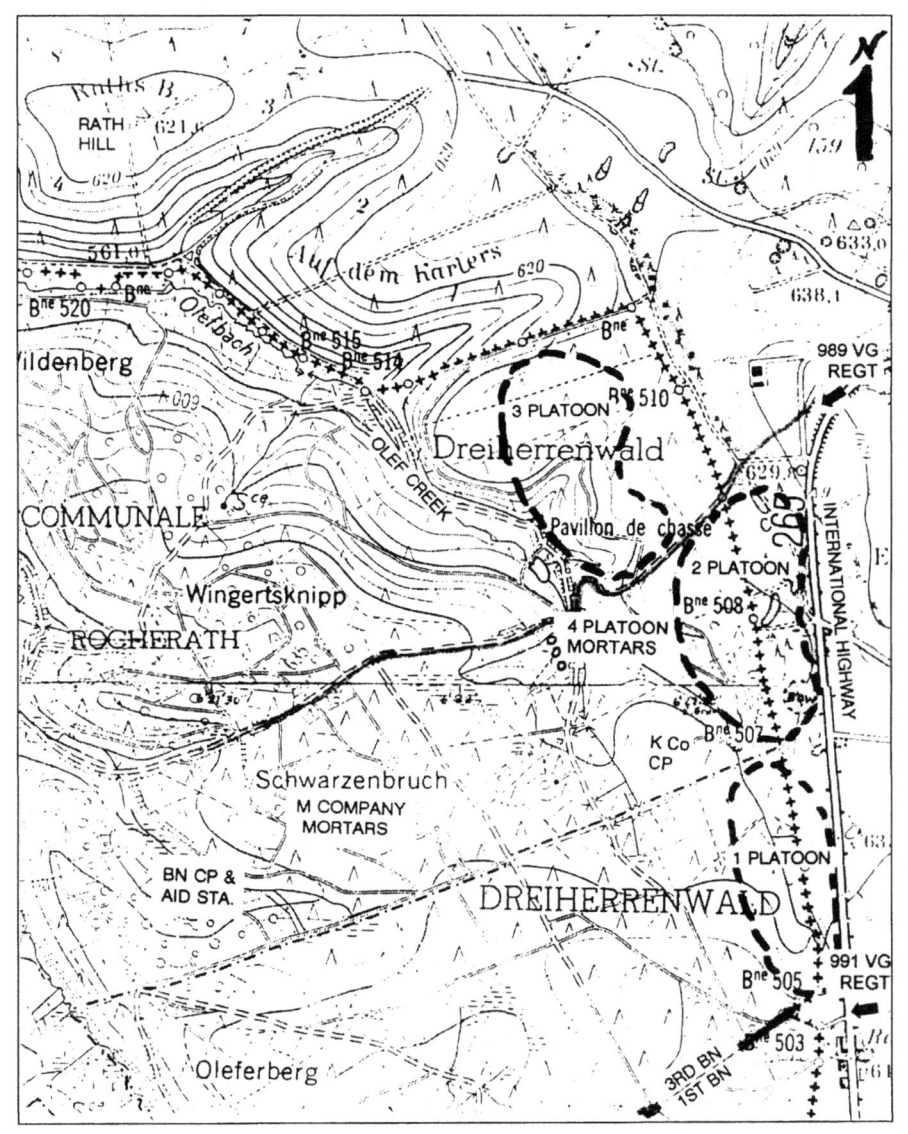

Positions of the 393rd Infantry Regiment in the Krinkelter Woods. B. O. WILKINS

outpost position into other squads of our own K Company. We didn't fire initially, and were not attacked in the initial onslaught; however, Sergeant Langford thought Germans were in the forest behind us, and ordered us to be quiet till he could go to the company command post as the artillery had already knocked out all communications. [He] returned in a few minutes and led us to the company command post, which had once been a woodcutter's cabin.

"We were greeted by Captain Plume and radio operator Sergeant Warrick. My first observation of Captain Plume was the way he was dressed. He apparently had been in his sleeping bag during the artillery barrage and ensuing infantry attack, and had just slipped on his combat boots and leather jacket over his silk pajamas. He addressed Sergeant Langford, 'Sergeant, we're surrounded; you'd just as well surrender.' And to that, Sergeant Langford said, 'Captain Plume, you can go straight to hell; we're getting out of here.' So with that, Langford led us west leaving both men standing at the command post."

"Don said they moved west through the snow until they reached the K Company mortar positions, where Lieutenant Holloway told them to take up positions to the left of his mortars. "The man next to me was a young man named Green; I believe he was killed later. Within a short time . . . I could see soldiers coming from the command post area in the front. As they came closer, I could see only their legs as they came down the hill, and then their whole body. The were speaking German! I fired. I grew up in a German community that spoke German, and I could recognize it immediately and fired. As soon as I fired, a voice came from the mortar positions saying not to fire anymore, as they were our own men. This scared me, but in a short time, whoever called out could see that they were Germans wearing GI overcoats, probably taken from prisoners. A battle ensued during which time Lieutenant Holloway was killed, probably a blast from a burp gun in his throat.

"The mortar men did a fantastic job of firing at close range. I heard later that they took their barrels out of their base plate and held the barrels more straight up in order to do damage at close range. With our few rifles and two mortars, we dispersed the Germans and they retreated back up the hill."

Both battalion commanders reported that they believed they could hang on, and Maj. Matthew Legler, commander of the 1st Battalion, 393rd Infantry, said he was going to counterattack with A Company in rear of the B Company sector to restore B's positions. To give the 3rd Battalion some help, I Company of the 394th Infantry later in the day was obtained and shoved in behind the battalion sector, and the company commander ordered to attack to relieve the battalion.

The Germans were pushing very aggressively against this part of the front, and it wasn't long before they had worked in as far as the area in front of the M Company command post, which was about 200 yards to the east of the battalion command post, just across a dirt trail which ran in a general northwest-southeast direction between the two command posts. The Germans had hit and folded back K Company and were on the command post front by about 0915 or 0930. By this time, the relieving platoon from L Company had been hit, too, and had retreated to the west side of this dirt trail. Every available man—mortar men, cooks, and headquarters personnel—had been thrown in front of the positions and all were fighting desperately. The situation was greatly confused, but the defenders fired their small arms and mortars at point-blank range, effectively holding the enemy off, although he infiltrated around both flanks and continued moving to the rear.

In order to renew the attack that had gotten stuck on the focal point the 277th Volksgrenadier Division entered its 991st Grenadier Regiment, which had been kept in reserve until now, into the fray from the area southwest of Ramscheid in a southwesterly direction. It was expected that the right wing of the 990th Grenadier Regiment would be pulled along in the attack. However, this attack soon was pinned down by enfilading fire from the American positions on the edge of the woods immediately west of the Reichsstrasse or was broken up. During the morning the American artillery fire opened up again; attempts by the 990th and 991st Grenadier Regiments to once again renew the attack from the depth were stopped cold in front of the West Wall by fire concentrations.

SITUATION WITH THE GERMAN ARMY BY THE AFTERNOON OF 16 DECEMBER

By the afternoon of 16 December, the situation in the sector of the 277th Volksgrenadier Division was as follows: both assault parties had managed to break into the American positions and make openings in the forward positions. Only with great difficulty and putting the last immediately available reserves into the fray, the 393rd Infantry averted the collapse of both battalions in the front line. The assault parties of the 277th Volksgrenadier Division had suffered severe losses, especially in officers and NCOs. They no longer had the strength to continue the attack. This was made worse by the lack of support by a promised brigade of assault guns, at least in the first phase of the attack.

With its rightmost assault group the division apparently had reached the Jans Bach, and had therefore penetrated the woods to a depth of about two kilometers, but now was pinned down still 3.5 kilometers from its objective.

The Germans Attack

The leftmost assault group, which had launched its attack from the Udenbreth area, had been able to penetrate the US main defensive positions, which were less deep in this sector, but they were still at least five kilometers from their objective. Even the attack by the reserve regiment had not been able to give new momentum to the attack. The study by the divisional commander gives one the impression that the gained success and the critical situation of the enemy were not recognized in their full measure. Certainly this was partially caused by the fact, that due to poor means of communication, reports came in late and in insufficient number. The divisional commander estimated that the plan, to break through the wooded zone quickly and by surprise and to free the routes of advance for the panzer divisions, had failed.

How had the attacks of both German infantry divisions on the left worked out till the afternoon of 16 December? The 12th Volksgrenadier Division had orders to break through the American positions on both sides of Losheim, to take the important crossroads of Losheimergraben with a reinforced regiment, to attack along the railroad with another reinforced regiment, take Honsfeld and the advance to Hünningen and Büllingen. As their attack progressed, they were to turn north at Malmédy and block the roads leading down from Verviers and cover the right flank of the tank units. The assembly area mainly was in the West Wall; there had been no difficulties; the Americans did not note their movement into position and preparation. At 0600, the division attacked, with the reinforced 48th Grenadier Regiment on the right and the reinforced 27th Fusilier Regiment on the left. The 89th Grenadier Regiment and the 12th Fusilier Battalion remained in Frauenkron as divisional reserve. The antitank units, the assault guns (six were available) with engineers, and a company of the 27th Fusilier Battalion formed an advance detachment and stood by on the road from Kronenburg to Hallschlag to advance via Losheimergraben in the direction of Büllingen as the situation warranted.

The 48th Regiment attacked on both sides of the road from Scheid to Losheimergraben, and the 27th Regiment attacked on both sides of the railroad that ran from Losheim to Honsfeld. The first objective of the attack was the western edge of the state forest of Scheiden and the state forest of Buchholz. At first both assault groups made good progress. The 48th Regiment had entered the woods without running into any opposition; then intense fights developed for individual extended fighting positions, which had been reinforced by wire obstacles, tree obstacles and mines. Considerable losses were suffered. In the afternoon the regiment was pinned down in front of Losheimergraben, which had been built into a strongpoint and which was defended stoutly by the Americans. At 0900, the 27th Regiment reported the taking of Losheim and was continuing its advance on both sides of the railway. In the afternoon, they ran into strong resistance at Buchholz Station (also known as Losheimergraben Station).

On the left of the 12th Volksgrenadier Division, both assault groups of the 3rd Fallschirmjäger Division had become pinned down in minefields west of Ormont at about the height of the Reichstrasse. Two companies of the engineer battalion of the 1st SS Panzer Division were attached to the division to help with mine clearing.

So in the entire corps sector by the afternoon, the American positions had not been broken through, and neither had even one of the advance roads been opened up for the Panzer Divisions. Of the three advance roads assigned to the 12th SS Panzer Division *Hitlerjugend*, only the one from Losheimergraben via Büllingen and Bütgenbach to Malmédy was really good, but it could only be reached via Rocherath-Krinkelt or via Losheimergraben. It was assumed that the road over Losheimergraben was easier to open up than the one that ran to Büllingen via Rocherath-Krinkelt.

In order to take the road via Losheimergraben the 12th SS Panzer Division either had to take the Reich road from Hollerath or the road from Sistig via Hallschlag to Losheim. However, the road from Hallschlag to Losheim was part of the route of advance of the 1st SS Panzer Division and therefore was not available to the 12th SS Panzers. Furthermore, the bridge over the railroad in the road from Losheim to Losheimergraben had been blown up during the withdrawal earlier in 1944 and not been rebuilt since, as well as the bridge across the railroad one kilometer north of Lanzerath. The Reich road from Hollerath to Losheim still for large stretches was in American hands or covered by fire from their light infantry weapons, and it was partially mined, so that it could not be used.

Therefore, by afternoon, corps headquarters ordered that the most advanced panzer grenadier battalion of the right assault party was to be drawn forward and assigned to the 277th Volksgrenadier Division in order to expand the breakin along Advance Road A (Hollerath and Rocherath-Krinkelt) into a breakthrough. The OB West war diary for 1245 hours reads: "12th SS Panzer Division with advanced elements in Hollerath, in 30 minutes to launch an attack to complete the breakthrough." This mission was given to the reinforced 1st Battalion of the 25th SS Panzergrenadier Regiment, one platoon of antitank guns, and a platoon of heavy infantry guns had been attached to it.

In the morning the right assault party had already been ordered out of the assembly area to move forward and exploit a successful breakthrough by the Volksgrenadiers. The war diary of 3rd Battalion, 25th Panzer-

The Germans Attack

grenadier Regiment, the last battalion in the marching order, gives the following activity:

16 December 1944

- 0700 hrs Liaison officer brings orders to assemble, advance and attack
- 0701 hrs Verbal orders to all company commanders: The battalion marches up to the road from Roggendorf to Kall [9.5 kilometers northeast of Hollerath], the point in the area of Strempt [6 kilometers northeast of Kall]; Order of march at start: 10th Company, command element, 12th Company, 9th Company, 11th Company. After marching up advance to the northern exit of Kall, then stop, wait for further orders. Our battalion is last in the advance of the regiment. Attached to it are:
  1. 1 antitank platoon (motorized)
  2. 1 antiaircraft platoon
  3. For the duration of the march 1st Company, 12th Engineer Battalion
- 0725 hrs Gas arrives; divided under the companies
- 0745 hrs Advance of the battalion . . .
- 0820 hrs The Battalion reaches the northern edge of Kall; battalion commander to the regimental HQ . . .
- 1030 hrs Battalion continues the march . . . Order of march now is 10th Company, antitank platoon (motorized), command element, antiaircraft platoon, 12th Company (antitank and mortar platoon), 9th Company, engineer company, and 11th Company
- 1130 hrs The battalion reaches the edge of Sistig [8.5 kilometers northwest of Hollerath]
- 1230 hrs The progress of the march is delayed. Units that are in column of march ahead of us, get mixed up. The battalion stops on the road with the point element in Sistig. On orders from the division (Liaison officer at the starting point) 3rd Battalion, 25th Panzergrenadier Regiment stands down.

The reinforced 1st Battalion, 25th Panzergrenadier Regiment, under Capt. Alfons Ott, after waiting in the area of the bend in the road west of Hollerath, began its attack in the afternoon. During the stand-by period, the first losses had occurred due to artillery harassment fire on the area of the bend in the road. The battalion advanced through the hole made by the 989th Volksgrenadier Regiment south of the forest track from the bend in the road to Rocherath (Advance Road A). By this time the advance elements of the 25th Panzergrenadier Regiment had reached the Jans Bach. The 1st Battalion advanced in arrowhead formation: one company in front, two other companies echeloned to the rear, left and right, the battalion staff behind the front company, the heavy weapons company behind the battalion staff. The heavy weapons, the antitank platoon and the attached platoon of heavy infantry guns followed later, because bridging material for crossing the dragon's teeth of the West Wall was not in place in time. While the grenadier companies advanced through the woods, the heavy weapons had to be drawn after them over the forest track. After a short while they got stuck in the mud. This also happened to the signals, and supply vehicles and the ambulances.

The 1st Battalion made first contact with the Americans when it crossed the Olef Brook south of the forest track (about 500 meters west of the Reich Road). The U.S. unit was a vedette consisting of four men; they were taken prisoner and sent to the rear. In the subsequent advance, the battalion met hardly any resistance worth mentioning. Later in the afternoon, it had reached point 634 at the exit of the Forêt Communal de Rocherath, about 500 meters west of the crossroads (on the 1:25.000 map of 1945, this wood is marked as 'Büllinger Woods'). The advance elements of the 1st Battalion at first received weak rifle and machine gun fire from the direction of Rocherath, probably from cover detachments, which the 393rd Infantry had pushed out between the woods and the villages of Rocherath and Krinkelt, where its headquarters and supply units were located.

Captain Ott reported: "We were at shouting distance of the enemy. I had an English-speaking man shout at the Americans, who were seemingly very surprised by our sudden arrival that they were to surrender, as they had already been bypassed on both sides. I even sent a man to the height in front of us with the same demand. This man arrived there safely but did not return."

These demands had no results. In the meantime, a small column of vehicles came down the road from Krinkelt to the crossroads near point 634. Presumably, these were supply vehicles taking ammunition to the American troops still at the front line. The column was stopped; the men were taken prisoner and led away to the rear.

During its advance through the Dreiherren Woods and the Forêt Communal de Rocherath, the 1st Battalion did not have any contact with units of the 989th Volksgrenadier Regiment; neither had it been able to raise its own regiment on the radio. The Americans experienced similar difficulties in the vast woods as well. Because of the unclear situation, Captain Ott now assumed a defensive position and sent back his adjutant, 2nd Lt. Willi Klein, with a scout party, to report to the 989th Volksgrenadier Regiment and obtain further orders. The battalion received heavy American artillery fire; at the same time during the night the enemy was probing forward on both open flanks of the battalion. Captain Ott gained the impression that the Americans tried to encircle him. As communications were still out, during the night Captain Ott decided to withdraw to his forward troops. It is unclear when this happened; the battalion probably withdraw in the early hours of the morning.

While the reinforced 1st Battalion, 25th Panzergrenadier Regiment, stood by under the orders of the 277th Volksgrenadier Division, and by the afternoon of the sixteenth had advanced through the Dreiherren Woods, the 12th Volksgrenadier Division had continued its attack. By 1600 hours, its 27th Fusilier Regiment stood in front of Buchholz Station (Losheimergraben Station). The 48th Grenadier Regiment to its right was pinned down facing the strongly fortified and defended American strong point of Losheimergraben.

In the meantime, the 3rd Fallschirmjäger Division's 9th Regiment had taken Lanzerath. This freed the Losheim–Lanzerath–Buchholz Station road so that the blown bridges could be bypassed. The 12th Volksgrenadier Division drew up its 89th Grenadier Regiment, which had been in reserve in the Schleiden Forest, just in case the 48th Grenadier Regiment would fail in its attempt to break through at Losheimergraben the next day.

The evening report of OB West for 16 December reads: "Advance detachment of 12th SS Panzer Division advanced towards Honsfeld via Losheimergraben at 1600 hours. Lanzerath and Merlscheid (south of Lanzerath) taken." This report contains several mistakes. The advance detachment was that of the 1st SS Panzer Division. They did not attack via Losheimergraben, but via Buchholz Station, after Lanzerath and Merlscheid had been taken. The day report of 16 December partially corrected these mistakes. While no decisive progress had been made in the attack sector of the 277th Volksgrenadier Division and the 12th Volksgrenadier Division still was pinned down in front of Losheimergraben, the conditions for a breakthrough had been made at the edge of the 12th Volksgrenadier Division and 3rd Fallschirmjäger Division sectors.

THE 3RD BATTALION, 23RD INFANTRY, 2ND INFANTRY DIVISION, COMES TO THE RESCUE

The 3rd Battalion, 23rd Infantry, 2nd Infantry Division, was attached to the 99th Division early in the afternoon of 16 December and received orders to move from their assembly area northwest of Camp Elsenborn to an assembly area on the western edge of the Krinkelter Wald and prepare to counterattack the same night astride a road running northeast through the Wald to regain positions lost by the 393rd Infantry.

The 3rd Battalion, 23rd Infantry, entrucked at 1400 and detrucked at a road junction at the western edge of the Wald at 1630 in order of Companies L, I, K, Headquarters and M Company. L Company went into position east of the road from the junction south to a point about 1,200 yards (covering the Weisserstein Trail), K Company took a position east of the road from the junction north for about 800 yards (they blocked the exit from the forest). I Company stretched along the road from K Company's left flank to a point six hundred yards north (down the Schwarzenbuch Trail). The battalion command post was located two hundred yeards north of the junction. Somewhere in front of these men were the remnants of the 3rd Battalion, 393rd Infantry, 99th Division, and they knew also that close behind these troops the Germans were coming.

K Company, 23rd Infantry, had just detrucked and was assembled in a scrub pine area about four hundred yards northeast of the junction when a heavy concentration of *Nebelwerfers* and 105-millimeter fell in this area, causing K Company twenty-one casualties, two of which were killed. L Company received eight casualties. The organic motors were also caught in this barrage, but they had no losses and returned safely to Krinkelt.

As L Company was organized to dig in, a five-man enemy patrol penetrated the area. Three of the patrol were killed and two taken prisoners. After digging into defensive positions, the battalion was informed it would attack at 0715 the following morning instead of that night, since the commanding officer of the 1st Battalion, 393rd Infantry, thought the situation looked better and there was no immediate need of a night attack. At about 2300, L Company was ordered to move its 3rd Platoon to hold a roadblock in the vicinity of L Company. The removal of this platoon left a gap between L and K Company. During the night, constant *Nebelwerfer* and 105-millimeter barrages fell in the battalion area, especially on K Company. The probable target of these concentrations was the road junction (Ruppenvenn) itself, to deny the use of the only road leading from the 393rd Infantry units back to Krinkelt.

For 17 December, the I SS Panzer Corps ordered the continuation of the attack in order to force a breakthrough on a broad front. The 277th Volksgrenadier Division, after reorganization, could participate in the attack with only its own assets and then not until afternoon. Therefore, the entire reinforced 25th SS Panzergrenadier Regiment was attached to it, in order to

The Germans Attack

expand the deep break-in into the Dreiherrenwald to a breakthrough towards Rocherath.

On the morning of 17 December, all along the International Highway, units of the 3rd Battalion, 393rd Infantry, 99th Infantry Division, were trying to hold off the attacking Germans and find a way back. The battalion had even made plans to launch an counterattack to restore the lines. At around 0800 hours the attack began, moving slowly and carefully. I Company, 394th, had just about reached its line on the left and abreast of the other companies. I Company, 393rd, was almost at its reserve position when the Germans struck the M Company front at about 0930 hours. This cracked the perimeter defense and quickly forced the battalion commander to call off his own counterattack. He shifted his forces swiftly towards the threat. Contacting his companies by radio, he ordered I Company, 394th Infantry, to turn and come south, cutting between M Company's rear and the battalion command post to act as a block there. He then ordered I Company, 393rd, to send back two platoons to go into position immediately behind I Company, 394th, to act as a cushion there as well as to serve as a mobile reserve.

Maj. Siegfried Müller, commander of the 25th Panzergrenadier Regiment sent his 2nd Battalion in on the right of the forest track (Advance Axis A), as this could not be driven over and was blocked by vehicles that had become stuck. This attack was to remove the threat to the flank of the advance elements of the 989th Grenadier Regiment, which stood on the Jans Bach. The 12th Tank Destroyer Battalion was assigned to cooperate

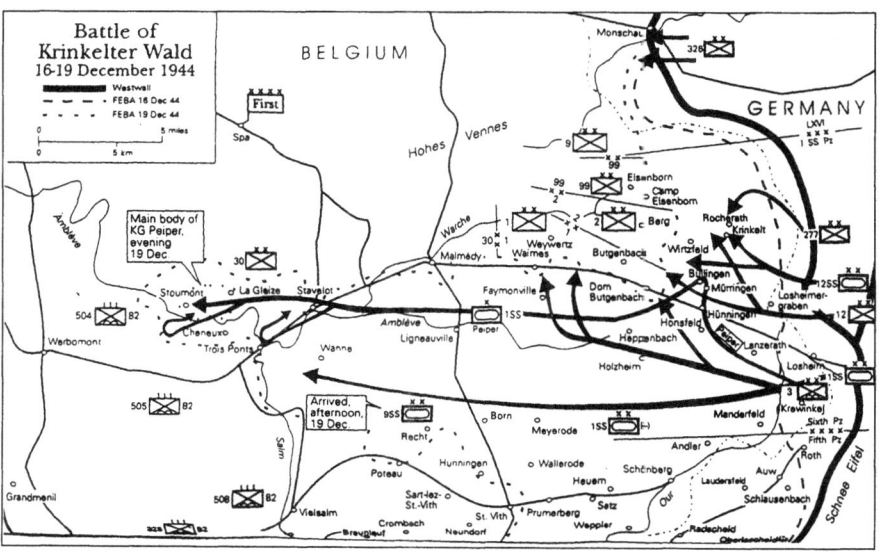

Battle of Krinkelter Wald 16-19 December 1944

with 2nd Battalion, 25th Panzergrenadier Regiment. The 2nd Artillery Battalion and a company of engineers had also been assigned to the regiment. Nothing dependable can be said about the tasks of the 1st and 3rd Battalions. At the outset, 3rd Battalion probably was held back as reserve, while it was assumed that the 1st Battalion was still at the west edge of the woods near the crossroads, which was an intermediate objective of the 2nd Battalion and 12th Tank Destroyer, the latter having to stick to the forest tracks.

Captain Brockschmidt, mentioned earlier, commanded the tank destroyer battalion. Major Neumann commanded the 2nd Artillery Battalion, which took positions in the area of the bend in the road at Hollerath. With the 7th Company leading, the battalion attacked. It had been organized as an assault company and was equipped with extra satchel charges and flamethrowers. The 1st and 2nd Company of the tank destroyer battalion followed the company, the staffs of the 2nd Battalion and the Panzerjäger Battalion. The other two panzergrenadier companies and the support company followed echeloned to the left and the right. The men, who since the afternoon of the sixteenth had sat on their vehicles and had frozen without any winter clothing, were glad that they could move and warm themselves.

The 2nd Battalion, 25th Panzergrenadier Regiment, and the tank destroyer battalion at Olef Brook had curved away in a northwesterly direction along a logging track and ran straight into the attack of the 3rd Battalion, 393rd Infantry Regiment, which was trying to regain its old main line positions.

2nd Lt. Ernst Stuhr led a platoon of the 7th Company and reported about the attack: "The company advanced in a widely dispersed manner. To the left of the forest track was the 1st Platoon, to the right the 2nd Platoon. By the edge of the road, I saw battalion commander Schulze standing up by the edge of the woods. He was using his binoculars. In front of him an armored reconnaissance vehicle had taken position. Its commander, a bearer of the Knight's Cross, stood in the turret and was looking forward through binoculars [this probably was Maj. Gerd Bremer, commander of the Reconnaissance Battalion, bearer of the Oak Leaves]. As we entered the woods there was a loud explosion. A mine had gone off. An NCO lost his right foot and lower leg. The woods were mined, and wires on top of the surface connected the mines. After we entered the woods we ran into scattered members of the army. They were ordered to join us. At first our attack made good progress. The fighting spirit of the men was excellent. The resistance by the enemy increased all the time. All kinds of projectiles exploded, not only on the ground, but in the treetops as well. Via a runner I was ordered to take over the company, as 2nd Lieutenant Hirsch had become a casualty.

The Germans Attack

Ernst Stuhr.

The same applied to the commander of the 2nd Platoon [probably 2nd Lieutenant Lützel]. Shortly afterward, 2nd Lieutenant Stuhr suffered multiple wounds, first in the right armpit so that his right arm largely became useless, afterwards a splinter in the back next to the spinal column, then a wound in the right upper thigh and a few moments later he got a burst of a submachine gun fire in the right leg. He passed out and only in the hospital train regained consciousness. Later his right leg had to be amputated."

As the attack progressed, the 2nd Battalion, 25th Panzergrenadier Regiment ran into the command post of the 3rd Battalion, 393rd Infantry. In its vicinity were the firing positions of 81-millimeter mortars, which can still be made out today, and mined obstacles of felled trees blocked the forest tracks. Well-dug-in antitank guns controlled the road at that point. Captain Brockschmidt had gone forward when he noticed that the attack had stalled, and he ordered 1st Lt. Helmut Zeiner, commander of the 1st Company, to go into the wood with his tank destroyers, to deploy, to drive down the trees and shoot up the resistance nests. This got the attack going again.

The Germans pressed their attack and were successful in forcing M Company, 393rd, to yield about 100 yards, stubbornly and unwillingly. This was regained when two I Company platoons joined with M Company to push the Germans back. But the German pressure continued. They hit first with infantry, and then, about a half-hour after the start of the attack, the first

German tank appeared, coming along the former MSR until it was stopped and, for about fifteen to twenty minutes, fired its machine guns but not its heavier cannon.

There were some casualties from this fire, and the 3rd Battalion tried to put artillery fire on it. This was difficult because of the poor observation and communication. An M Company mortar observer acted as an artillery forward observer; he called back his range readings to battalion headquarters, where the artillery liaison officer relayed it back to the firing batteries. Friendly artillery fire was poured in, but had no effect on the German tank. It did help to dissipate the German infantry accompanying the tank. They were scattered and disorganized, allowing the battalion to bring up four bazooka teams to try to knock out the tank.

However, after the artillery fire came down upon it, the German tank moved on down the road—actually, a dirt trail—almost into M Company's command post and continued to stir up trouble. The bazooka men poured desperate shots at it and finally succeeded in hitting one of its tracks, immobilizing the vehicle. Otherwise it suffered no casualties because the crew continued to fire their machine guns. About this time two more German tanks appeared, coming down the main road from the east, probably from Hollerath. Infantry, too, accompanied them, and, when American artillery fire was brought to bear, they scattered. The bazooka men turned their attention to these tanks and knocked one out. The other stopped behind it and continued to fire its machine guns while standing in the main road. Then, two more enemy tanks appeared—making five in all—and these worked into the network of confused trails in the command post area. One of these was knocked out.

PFC Allan Nelson, bazooka man in the 3rd Squad, 2nd Platoon, I Company, 393rd Infantry: "The next morning [17 December], our company was ordered to withdraw to the area around the battalion command post where we dug in on a defensive perimeter. Colonel Allen, the battalion commander, gave orders for all to withdraw to a position behind the line of defense that the 2nd Division was setting up. Captain McIntyre, the battalion doctor, stayed behind with the wounded. It was later reported that the Germans captured the medics, taking the ones not injured and leaving the wounded for three days unattended in the woods. When we got the command to pull out of the 3rd Battalion headquarters area, I took off on my own, figuring that one person by himself did not present as big a target as a group of guys together. I had not gone far and was still in the woods when a tremendous artillery barrage started landing nearby. I hit the ground and remember the loud explosions and big flashes of white light, and I thought the world was coming to an end. When the barrage stopped, I broke out of the woods and headed across an open field. It was bright and sunny and there were a few small groups of other Americans plodding through a couple feet of snow up to the knees. When I got to the far side of the open field, I reached a dirt road which I think must have gone into Krinkelt. I caught up with some other GIs, and we shortly passed through the line being set up by the 2nd Division. I felt really sorry for them because they were going to have to face the Germans shortly and make their stand. By this time I was back with I Company, and we were directed to leave the road and move into a forest for the night. During the night we heard a terrific firefight going, and as we looked out we could see tracers from German tanks moving in toward Krinkelt. My next clear memory is our company pulling back up the hill to Elsenborn Ridge and digging in."

Finally, at about 1030 hours on this critical morning of the seventeenth, the 393rd Regiment gave permission to the 3rd Battalion to withdraw to the old regimental reserve sector approximately 2,400 yards from Rocherath. Because of the large number of wounded, they were given first priority in the evacuation. All available transportation was used to load as many as possible aboard. When all the vehicles were filled, there still remained twelve to fifteen wounded for whom there was no room and who could not be carried. These were left behind, and Capt. Fredrick J. McIntyre, the battalion surgeon, and some of the aid station personnel remained behind with them. They were not heard from later and were presumed to have been captured.

The report of Captain Brockschmidt illustrates how they fought and led here: "Lieutenant Colonel Schulze put his bag down on the ground and said: 'Here is the battalion command post.' I had a short talk with him about how the attack could be renewed and where we would put the focal point of our attack. A few minutes later, there was an impact and shrapnel in the left knee wounded me . . .

"The grenadiers were held up for a long time by snipers in the trees. Finally the enemy was defeated. In the command post, which was taken, the men found hot drinks, chocolate and all kinds of food. There was a necessary short break. Then the battalion commander renewed his attack."

Lt. Col. Richard Schulze remembered the battle like this: "As the men for the most part had no combat experience, action of the leaders in the foremost lines was of prime importance. In the first hours all the company commanders were either killed or wounded, including the battalion adjutant, 2nd Lieutenant Buchmann, and the technical leader (K). The NCOs took over the companies. I remember the difficult crossing of the Jans Brook very well, because when I was nearly at the brook, snipers in the trees fired on me. And I shammed being dead for a while before I finally gained cover by a sudden jump. The continued attack, which after the assembly of the battalion went south, finally led to success. In the battle in the woods a considerable amount of prisoners were taken and led away to the rear."

Early on the morning of 17 December, Lieutenant Colonel Tuttle of the 3rd Battalion, 23rd Infantry, was informed by the commander of the 3rd Battalion of the 393rd Infantry, Lt. Col. Jack G. Allen, that the 23rd Infantry would not attack as ordered, but would dig in and organize its present position "to hold at all costs." Tuttle was further informed that the Germans—a battalion of the 25th Panzergrenadier Regiment of the 12th SS Panzer Division—had launched a strong attack against the 3rd and 1st Battalions, 393rd Infantry. The battalion command post was then moved 1,000 yards northwest while the companies placed their men in better defensive positions where they started to dig in. Since at this time the troops had only their normal load of ammunition, a request was made for additional ammunition. The battalion S-4 was told that all supply roads in the area had been cut by the enemy, and it was not possible to get ammunition. Lieutenant Koch, however, started to the rear and found a route to Krinkelt where he loaded his trucks and started back to the battalion. By the time he arrived east of Krinkelt, however, he found all routes cut by enemy tanks, and he was unable to reach the battalion. Also, at no time during the morning did the battalion command post have wire communication with the companies, but depended entirely on SCR 300 radios.

At about 1000 hours, Tuttle was informed that the 3rd Battalion, 393rd Infantry, would withdraw through his battalion to reorganize in an area east-northeast of Rocherath. The 1st Battalion, 393rd Infantry, would also withdraw to extend the line on the right of his 3rd Battalion, 23rd Infantry. Lieutenant Eisler, commanding L Company, 23rd Infantry, received permission to draw back his platoon on the road block. As the platoon was withdrawing, they were hit by an artillery concentration and scattered. Simultaneously, a twenty-man enemy patrol hit the gap, which existed between L and K Companies. While the two tanks supporting L Company covered the gap with machine-gun fire, the 3rd Platoon reorganized and got back into position in the gap and drove off the enemy. Six dead were picked up in front of the position, but it is believed that many more casualties were inflicted on the patrol.

At 1100, the 3rd Battalion, 393rd Infantry, began withdrawing through I and K Companies and continued to the west. About the same time, the 1st Battalion, 393rd Infantry, began infiltrating back through L Company in small disorganized groups and continued to the west. Contact was never established with L Company's right flank, which remained exposed throughout the following engagement. As the 393rd Infantry troops withdrew through I and L Companies, 23rd Infantry, positions, they dropped off their ammunition, a considerable amount of small arms ammunition, but few grenades or bazooka rounds.

I Company also had an exposed left flank, and although it had received some of the 393rd Infantry's ammo, it was still very short of antitank ammunition. For its seven bazookas, for example, it had only three rounds. Placing its two 393rd Infantry antitank guns in a position to fire up the road to the north, I Company used the two attached Sherman tanks of C Company, 741st Tank Battalion, to cover a road junction 500 yards to the north. A short time later, however, the tanks moved on their own volition to the right flank platoon of the company (according to the after-action report of the 741st Tank Battalion, Lt. Victor L. Miller received orders to move to a better line of defense).

The unit journal of the 741st Tank Battalion shows Lieutenant Miller attached to the 3rd Battalion, 23rd Infantry Regiment: "Shortly after noon, the left flank platoon leader observed several German tanks on a ridge line about twenty-five hundred yards to the northeast and heard several more in the vicinity. As he called for artillery, which scattered the observed tanks, extremely heavy machine-gun and small-arms fire swept the platoon, the first indication that German infantry was in the immediate vicinity. The infantry hit I Company about 1230 from the front and left flank. Heavy small arms fire and artillery scattered the enemy on the company's front, but it was never adjusted on the Germans to the flank. The left flank platoon repulsed seven attacks on the flank with small arms and mortar fire, but as the Germans were being driven back for the seventh time, a German tank [tank destroyer] approached down the road to within one hundred yards of I Company's position and opened fire. At this time according to Captain MacDonald, commanding I Company, the antitank gun crews abandoned their guns. Captain MacDonald then called for artillery to lay on the tank, but this was ineffective. He then started back to bring up his two Sherman tanks, but found they had withdrawn into K Company's position, and he was unable to reach them. Returning to the left flank platoon, Captain MacDonald found that two more German tanks had approached the position. The 23rd infantrymen, however, maintained strong small-arms fire-keeping the tanks buttoned up and exacting a heavy toll of the German infantry. Due to the snipers in the trees, the panzergrenadiers made only slow progress, the more so because communications with the antitank troops, which had broken through, partially failed."

1st Lt. Helmut Zeiner reported the details of the battle: "We followed along a narrow, partially winding forest track to a point where it split up and fell away. There was a firefight. The enemy had positioned antitank weapons, snipers in the trees and some Shermans (or tank destroyers) in an ambush. Roy, an NCO who had taken over my position at the head of the 1st platoon, but driving behind me, was killed by a shot through the head. Roy had earned the Knight's Cross in the invasion and was a sympathetic young man with a lot of talent and courage. Nothing helped! The death of our comrade roused a great anger in all of us, and I simply drove into them. I took over an American double-barreled antiaircraft gun, and we fired high explosive shells and the double-barreled machine gun to the left and right on fleeing enemies. The forest track led downward; on our right hand there was a valley. On the other slope there was an open space with a fleeing Sherman, which got away in the heat of the pursuit."

Within a short time, the tanks, with German infantry disposed on both sides of each tank, reached positions where they could fire point-blank into the foxholes. A bazookaman fired two rounds at the lead tank, but he missed and was knocked out. A section of heavy machine guns held their positions and took a heavy toll of the enemy infantryman until they ran out of ammunition. As the tanks overran I Company's left-flank platoon, the

Helmut Zeiner on leave at home, with his son. HELMUT ZEINER

The Germans Attack

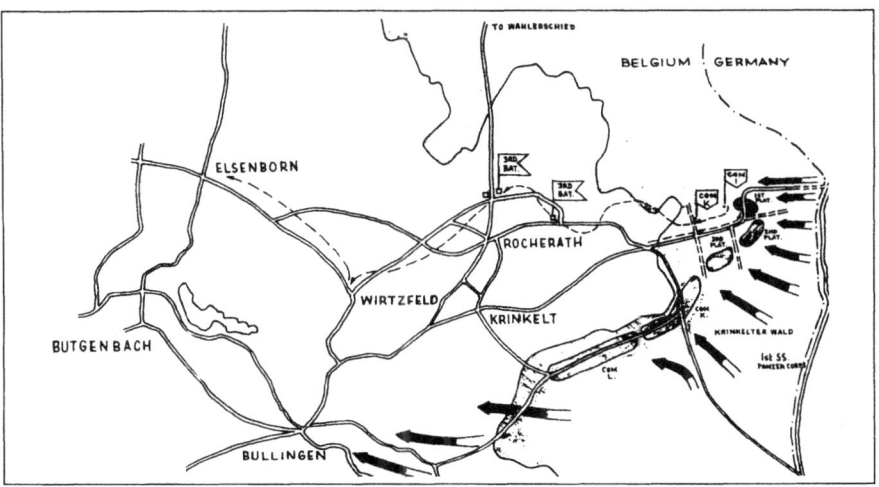

The German advance.

enemy launched strong infantry attacks on both the front and rear of the company's position. Hit from three sides, the 2nd and 3rd Platoons withdrew and tried to form a line on K Company's left flank. They were able to hold there for only a few minutes, and were driven back to the battalion's original command post to the left rear of K Company. Forming along a firebreak there, they held and inflicted heavy casualties on the enemy for about ten minutes before the tanks again appeared and pounded them at pointblank range.

One of the men in MacDonald's group was PFC Richard Cowan, who for his actions received the Medal of Honor. His citation reads: "He was a heavy machine gunner in a section attached to I Company in the vicinity of Krinkelter Wald, Belgium, 17 December 1944, when that company was attacked by a numerically superior force of German infantry and tanks. The first six waves of hostile infantrymen were repulsed with heavy casualties, but a seventh drive with tanks killed or wounded all but three of his section, leaving Private First Class Cowan to man his gun, supported by only fifteen to twenty riflemen of I Company. He maintained his position, holding off the Germans until the rest of the shattered force had set up a new line along a firebreak. Then, unaided, he moved his machine gun and ammunition to the second position. At the approach of a Royal Tiger tank [likely a Jagdpanzer IV tank destroyer; the 12th SS Panzer Division did not have Tiger tanks in their units], he held his fire until about eighty enemy infantrymen supporting the tank appeared at a distance of about 150 yards. His first burst killed or wounded about half of these infantrymen. His position was rocked by an 88-millimeter shell [75-millimeter of the Jagdpanzer IV] when the tank opened fire, but he continued to man his gun, pouring deadly fire into the Germans when they again advanced. He was barely missed by another shell. Fire from three machine guns and innumerable small arms struck all about him; an enemy rocket shook him badly, but did not drive him from his gun. Infiltration by the enemy had by this time made the position untenable, and the order was given to withdraw. Private First Class Cowan was the last man to leave, voluntarily covering the withdrawal of his remaining comrades. His heroic actions were entirely responsible for allowing the remaining men to retire successfully from the scene of their last-ditch stand."

This time, the men scattered in all directions, so Captain MacDonald ordered the radios destroyed and maps burned. As the communications sergeant was burning the maps, he was captured, but later managed to escape when artillery landed in the vicinity and the Germans took cover. On his way back, Captain MacDonald tried to make another stand at the M Company commandp ost but was again forced to withdraw. Later in the day he reported back to Lieutenant Colonel Tuttle while the scattered company

A modern shot of the treeline of the Krinkelter Woods.

The Germans Attack

attached themselves to other units in the vicinity to continue the fight. The company was never reorganized again until 20 December.

Another Medal of Honor winner was nearby, Pvt. Jose M. Lopez. The citation for his medal reads: "On his own initiative, he carried his heavy machine gun from Company K's right flank to its left, in order to protect that flank which was in danger of being overrun by advancing enemy infantry supported by tanks. Occupying a shallow hole offering no protection above his waist, he cut down a group of ten Germans. Ignoring enemy fire from an advancing tank, he held his position and cut down twenty-five more enemy infantry attempting to turn his flank. Glancing to his right, he saw a large number of infantry swarming in from the front. Although dazed and shaken from enemy artillery fire, which had crashed into the ground only a few yards away, he realized that his position soon would be outflanked. Again, alone, he carried his machine gun to a position to the right rear of the sector; enemy tanks and infantry were forcing a withdrawal. Blown over backward by the concussion of enemy fire, he immediately reset his gun and continued his fire. Single-handed, he held off the German horde until he was satisfied his company had effected its retirement. Again he loaded his gun on his back and in a hail of small-arms fire he ran to a point where a few of his comrades were attempting to set up another defense against the onrushing enemy. He fired from this position until his ammunition was exhausted. Still carrying his gun, he fell back with his small group to Krinkelt. Private Lopez's gallantry and intrepidity, on seemingly suicidal missions in which he killed at least 100 of the enemy, were almost solely responsible for allowing Company K to avoid being enveloped, to withdraw successfully and to give other forces coming up in support time to build a line which repelled the enemy drive."

As soon as I Company had been driven from its positions to positions behind K Company, a strong force of enemy infantry hit K Company frontally while infantry and tanks struck from the left flank. Artillery had knocked out wire communication shortly before, and the company had limited observation in the scrub growth where it was dug in. The first K Company unit overrun was the 1st Platoon, dug in on the left flank, which managed to inflict heavy casualties on the German infantry, but were helpless to stop the tanks with only small arms fire. In the absence of an order to withdraw (the platoon leader had become a casualty), the platoon held its ground until it was overrun.

According to Lieutenant Clise, the 2nd Platoon's leader, who was trying to contact the platoon to order them to withdraw, the infantrymen stayed in their holes while the tanks overran their positions, then emerged to fight hand-to-hand with the enemy infantry. The struggle was one of bayonets and clubbed rifles, with one bazookaman swinging his rocket launcher at a German armed with a machine pistol before he was cut down.

Clise returned to his platoon to bring up the three Sherman tanks, which were supposed to be in K Company's area; but he found they had departed outside the forest. As he returned to his platoon, three German tanks approached along the road and hit the left flank of the 2nd Platoon. Clise learned that the company commander had ordered the 2nd and 3rd Platoons to withdraw. The two platoons fought from tree to tree until they reached a wood about four hundred yards northwest of the road junction, where they decided to make a stand. They managed to hold there for about twenty minutes before the tanks again overran them. Again withdrawing in good order, the company was crossing an open field (east of the Lausdell Crossroads) in the deep twilight when an intense nebelwerfer and artillery concentration landed in their midst and scattered the remaining men in all directions. As they pulled back, they could see Lt. Victor Miller's two Sherman tanks burning a few yards from the forest edge where they had engaged the leading Panzerjäger IV emerging from the trees. Miller's tanks had knocked out two of the German Panzerjäger IVs but were destroyed by return fire from the other Panzerjäger IV.

K Company's rearguard fight from early afternoon to dark allowed I and L Companies to withdraw from their positions without heavy casualties and gave battalions from the 9th and 38th Infantry Regiments time to form a defensive line on the high ground east of Krinkelt. The two remaining officers and the scattered men attached themselves to 9th and 38th Infantry units to continue the fight. K Company was not organized again until 20 December.

L Company had little contact with the enemy during the early afternoon, except for artillery concentrations falling in its area a number of times. The first indication that the companies on its left flank were withdrawing was when sixty men from I Company entered the area. Lieutenant Eisler was forming a secondary line behind his company with these men when a number of K Company men came into the area with the word that K Company was withdrawing. A few minutes later a number of men dressed in American combat pants, combat jackets and American helmets approached from the direction of K Company. As they reached the first line of foxholes, they opened fire on the L Company troops. According to the men of that unit, there is no doubt but that they were German troops dressed in American uniforms trying to infiltrate behind L Company's position.

At the same time that the enemy opened fire, strong forces attacked L Company from the front and right and left flanks. The company managed

The German Panzerjäger IV, which was used by the 12th SS Panzer Division when it tried to get through the Krinkelter Woods. American reports often wrongly called it a Tiger tank.

Sherman Corner, with two knocked-out Shermans, one of which belonged to Lieutenant Miller and his men.

Modern view of the Krinkelter Woods. This shows the road used by the tank destroyers of *Kampfgruppe Zeiner*. HANS WIJERS

to hold off the enemy until almost all of the ammunition was expended; at that point Eisler radioed the battalion S-3 that he was going to withdraw. As the 1st Platoon covered the withdrawal, Eisler ordered the 393rd Infantry vehicles and antitank guns in the area destroyed, then led his company back a hundred yards to a position where he could reorganize the company before withdrawing further. At this time he received orders from Tuttle to withdraw all the way into Krinkelt, which he accomplished with the loss of only half a squad.

As the company entered a draw southeast of Krinkelt, a concentration of *Nebelwerfer* and artillery fire landed in the draw, scattering the men. Reaching the eastern edge of the town, Eisler found eighty to ninety L Company men, which he organized into platoons with stragglers from the 9th and 38th Infantry Regiments. At this time, he learned that Colonel Stokes wanted to see him. Colonel Stokes informed him that he was attached to K Company, 38th Infantry, and was to organize his remaining men along the road running southeast from Krinkelt. Picking up ammunition, as well as .30- and .50-caliber machine guns and equipment in the town, Eisler put two platoons in the indicated positions, holding a third platoon in Krinkelt as a reserve force.

Meanwhile, the Germans continued their advance, fated to collide next with the 1st Battalion, 9th Infantry, at the Lausdell Crossroads. 1st Lt. Helmut Zeiner had been ordered by his battalion commander to carry out the attack toward Rocherath with his 1st Tank Destroyer Company and a platoon of the antitank escort company; the 2nd Tank Destroyer Company and 2nd Battalion of the 25th Regiment, would follow. In the meantime, it had become dark.

CHAPTER 5

The Battle at Höfen, 16–18 December

Under the command of Lt. Col. McClernand Butler, the 3rd Battalion of the 395th Infantry took up positions in Höfen about the middle of November. Their single mission was to hold the vital road net leading into the heart of the V Corps supply and command area through the German border town of Monschau and the Belgian town of Mutzenich into Eupen, the V Corps headquarters.

On the night of 11–12 December 1944, the 612th Tank Destroyer Battalion arrived in an assembly area at Sourbrodt with its 3-inch towed guns. At the time of arrival, little was known of its future mission. After closing into the area, the battalion commander reported to headquarters 2nd Infantry Division for instructions, and upon returning, immediately ordered a meeting of the staff and unit commanders. At this meeting, the 2nd Division's plan of attack was carefully outlined. A Company would be in direct support of 9th Infantry Regiment (2nd Division) and, from a previously occupied position in Höfen, would be prepared to support the regiment's attack by direct fire on Rohren. A Company's commander, the 612th Tank Destroyer Battalion's commander, and the battalion S-3 proceeded to Höfen. The commander of the 3rd Battalion of the 395th was very happy to see them, especially in view of the fact that this area of responsibility was quite large, and that his troops were green, never having been battle-tested. He felt that, in addition to providing additional fire power, the presence of the 612th's A Company would probably tend to have a steadying influence on his inexperienced men.

The town of Höfen, situated on a ridge overlooking the town of Rohren, controlled access to the Eupen Highway. The terrain surrounding the town was hilly, and generally open immediately around the town. Two main avenues of approach by road led into the town. One came up the main road leading northwest from Neuhof, through Wahlerscheid to Höfen. The other came down from the northwest from the town of Rohren. A wooded draw and trail led into the central part of the town from a branch of the Kluck River.

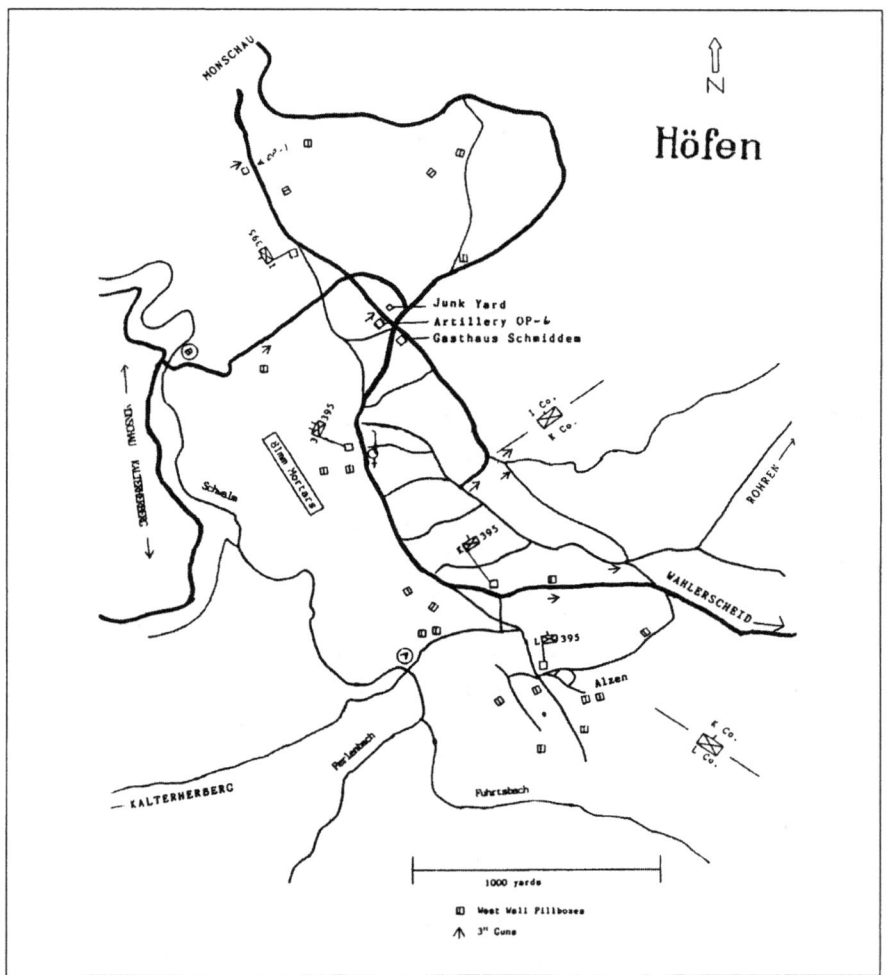

Höfen and vicinity. THOR RONNINGEN

On December 13 the commander of A Company, 612th Tank Destroyer Battalion, with his platoon leaders and gun commanders, made a daylight reconnaissance of the area. Exact positions for the guns were selected, primarily to afford direct fire into Rohren; and routes into the positions were selected. Gun positions having been selected, the company moved in that night, driving so slowly and quietly that many of the infantry troops were unaware that the tank destroyers were in the area.

Since one battalion of infantry was far from sufficient to protect the area, it had, of necessity, been spread rather thinly. The line consisted of a series of strongpoints. Some of the twelve tank destroyer guns were placed

The Battle at Höfen, 16–18 December 297

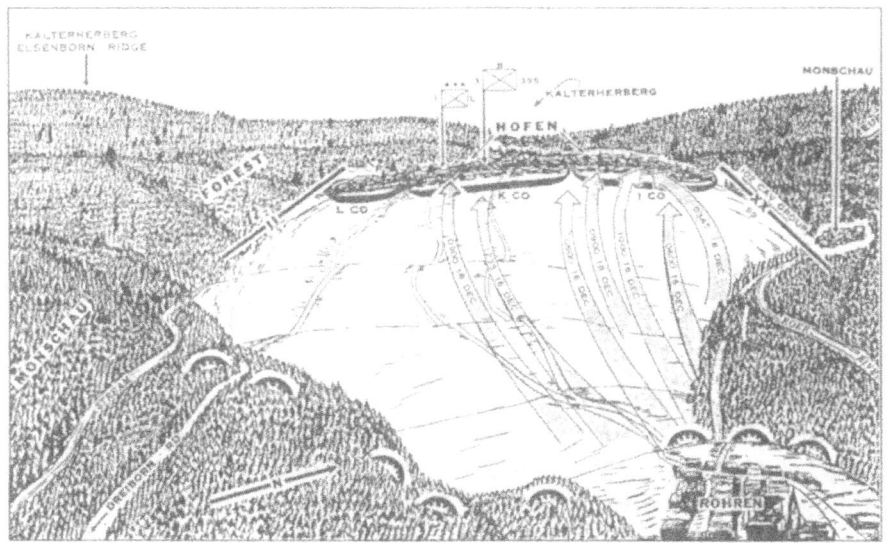

The assault on Höfen.

practically within the front lines. In order to give some degree of flexibility to the defense, the battalion had constituted a reserve of one platoon, which was located near the tank destroyer company's command post. On the fifteenth, the gun commanders of A Company, 612th Tank Destroyer Battalion, briefed the crews; gun positions were prepared, sand-bagged, and covered with logs. Snow was falling and the weather was bitterly cold. In view of the heavy snow, it became necessary to camouflage the gun positions with sheets furnished by battalion supply. The communications section tied in wire lines to the 395th's 3rd Battalion command post.

Rationing of ammunition had been in effect for two months, and as a result, the 612th Tank Destroyer battalion had no more than its prescribed basic load of ammunition. Supply was of no particular problem for the forthcoming mission (support of the 2nd Infantry Division's attack). Combat suits had been issued, but the battalion was short of a few boots of hard-to-get sizes. The battle-tested procedure would govern supply and evacuation. The battalion command post moved to Wirtzfeld, closing into the area at 0900. The night of the fifteenth found the battalion bedded down with a secure feeling that it was up to strength and prepared to capably perform its mission.

Prior to the German attack, the 3rd Battalion, 395th Infantry had spent most of its time digging in deep. The well-prepared defensive positions enabled the battalion to call friendly fire from the supporting 196th Field Artillery Battalion, right down on their frontline positions, with little damage to friendly personnel, but with devastating effect upon attacking German forces.

Thornton Piersall, a member of I Company, 395th Infantry, remembers: "In our first early days up on the front we were in an old house—there were two or three of us—and we had a sound powered telephone. We were awake, someone was on guard, when we saw the telephone moving toward the wall. We were sure there were German soldiers outside trying to pull our phone out or cut the lines. I'm not sure how many holes in the wall there were, but I feel confident there were some bullets fired. On investigation, however, it turned out to be a cow. A loose cow had gotten its legs tangled up in our phone wire and pulled the phone all the way across the floor. Quite an introduction to the front lines!"

There was no prior indication that an attack of was coming. Some reports had been received from prisoners captured on patrols during the second week of December, that SS troops were seen in the towns just east of the German lines, but this was thought simply to mean that these SS troops were merely at rest centers.

The German artillery served as an alarm clock all up and down the entire front. At 0525 hours on 16 December, a tremendous barrage of artillery, mortar and rocket fire fell along the area occupied by the 3rd Battalion, 395th Infantry Regiment, and A Company, 612th Tank Destroyer Battalion. The barrage included a great number of rockets that were nine or more inches in diameter, and about four feet in length. A large number of buildings were set afire, and many were crumbled. The executive officer of A Company, 612th Tank Destroyer Battalion, roused his company commander telling him that the schoolhouse, fifty feet away, had been hit by artillery and had caught fire, along with other buildings in the area. This barrage accomplished a tremendous amount of damage within the town. All wire lines were immediately severed. Casualties among the men of the 3rd Battalion were light because the unit had several weeks of preparation; the position was well dug in and ready for such an emergency.

George W. Neill of 3rd Battalion headquarters, 395th Infantry, tells his story: "I woke up in my dugout at 0525 hours to a thunderous storm of shells bursting into and near our positions. The sound was terrifying. I had never heard anything so much like the end of the world—and of me. The earth trembled; so did I. I expected to be crushed at any moment; I tried to get closer to the ground, but couldn't—I was already there. I held my steel helmet over my head, expecting my treasured dugout to blow into a thousand pieces. The shells falling around me were among the first the Germans hurled in the Battle of the Bulge.

The Battle at Höfen, 16–18 December

George Neill.

"I lay there alone, trapped. I couldn't dash for my much safer foxhole; I'd be cut to ribbons before I got halfway. The only thing to do was to lie still and pray that the logs over my head were thick enough to stop the hail of shell fragments. Despite my fear, I remained remarkably clearheaded.

"The storm eased, but did not stop. I made a split-second decision to dash to my foxhole. I had been sleeping, as usual, fully dressed with shoes on, ready for just such a moment. I grabbed the M1 rifle belt of the man who was on guard with my BAR in his foxhole, and crawled backwards through my hanging-blanket door. Grabbing the guide rope attached to the trees, I slid down the icy hill to my empty foxhole. During those few seconds, two shells landed in our area, but far enough away to leave me unscratched.

"The artillery storm returned to the intensity of the first five minutes, accompanied by ear-splitting *Nebelwerfer* rockets, appropriately named 'screaming meemies.' Some big shells going over our position, heading farther west, sounded like speeding trains, one after the other. After pummeling us for about thirty-five minutes (rated one of the heavier barrages of World War II), the apocalyptic bombardment of screaming, whistling, whining and crashing ceased."

At 0550, the entire front was glowing with artificial moonlight produced by high-powered searchlights employed by the Germans. As the Germans played these powerful lights against the low hanging clouds, the men in the front lines were set for the attack. Visibility was increased to a few hundred yards.

At 0600 hours, the German grenadiers of the assault companies of the 1st Battalion, 751st Regiment, and the 1st Battalion, 753rd Regiment, of the 326th Volksgrenadier Division, under the command of Maj. Gen. Dr. Erwin Kaschner (from accounts of the 326th's attack on Höfen on 16 December, Kaschner had only three battalions for his attack), seemed to rise from the haze in front of Höfen and approached the town in that slow, determined walk which had become so characteristic. They attacked in strength at five different points, with the main effort located at the boundary between I and K Companies of the 3rd Battalion, 395th Infantry, while another force tried to penetrate the Monschau area on the extreme left flank (L Company, 3rd Battalion, 395th Infantry).

PFC Bruce Waterman and member of L Company had one of the best views of the German attack from the south end of the 3rd Battalion's front. He was on two-hour guard at a second-story window of L Company's command post. He was looking out to the east and northeast toward the German lines. "Suddenly, as far as I could see, there was an instantaneous flash of artillery, mortar, and tank fire along the entire German line. In seconds, shells began exploding just to the north of us in Höfen and on the 3rd Battalion foxholes defending the village along its eastern edge. No shells hit near us, so I could continue watching the fireworks without ducking. After a short pause, I heard lots of rifle and machine gun fire coming from our front foxholes."

At this time only radio communication existed between 3rd Battalion headquarters and front line and heavy weapons companies. As communication between the artillery liaison officer and the 196th Field Artillery guns was out until 0650, the attack was repulsed by the 3rd Battalion's own machine guns, small arms, and mortar fire, including hand-to-hand fighting. This was the 3rd Battalion's first major engagement against the enemy. The 81-millimeter mortar platoon took over the concentrations, placing effective fire on the enemy while they themselves were receiving heavy counterbattery fire. The rifle platoons withheld their fire until the enemy was completely exposed, and then opened fire with such devastation that the Germans were completely repulsed, at all but one point of the line.

Capt. William S. Groff, commander of A Company, 612th Tank Destroyer Battalion, recalls: "To me it was immediately apparent that the tank destroyers in front of us were in trouble; all communications were out. I dispatched some of our runners to the platoon positions in a effort to determine the situation. At this time a messenger came running from the 3rd Platoon, which was located immediately in front of the company command post, to report that this platoon needed more machine gun ammunition. By this time German machine-gun fire began hitting the company command post. I then, accompanied by my first sergeant, headed for the 3rd Platoon. I told the messenger to stay at the command post and try to get as much ammunition as needed.

"When we arrived at the platoon command post, the platoon leader reported that the Germans had overrun the infantry front and had penetrated to a position a few yards in front of their platoon. Here the withering fire of automatic weapons, which were carefully positioned to protect the tank destroyer guns, had met the Germans. Here the Germans were stopped, temporarily at least, and had taken up positions in a house previously occupied by our own infantry. I decided to attack this position by fire. The .30- and .50-caliber machine guns were turned on the house and began pouring their devastating fire through the windows and doors. Some of the 3-inch tank destroyer guns fired high explosive also. It was now decided to attack the position in order to restore the main line of resistance. Some of the infantry and the tank destroyer men, by use of walking fire and supported by the direct fire of the machine guns and 3-inch tank destroyers, were able to drive the Germans out."

The attack at the boundary between I and K Companies of the 395th Regiment raged on, and thirty or more Germans succeeded in penetrating the line and got into houses in Höfen. S/Sgt. Robert L. Craft had half of his squad from the first platoon of I Company in a house with a barn attached. They had been there since arriving in Höfen on 9 November and had built up quite a large supply of ammunition (rifle and machine-gun rounds, grenades, and bazooka rounds), which they stored in the barn. The barn had a thatched roof, like many of the buildings, which had been set afire by the German artillery. When the flames began to get near the stockpile of ammunition, they felt it was no longer safe to stay in their positions.

Craft and one of his men, Robert E. Crist, dove out a back window only to discover about a platoon of enemy soldiers aiming at them from across the street. Realizing they had no other options, the two men surrendered to the Germans. There were a number of German wounded lying in the intersection to the south, and machine guns from the 612th Tank Destroyer Battalion firing down this street. A German NCO tried to tell Craft and Crist to go into the intersection to retrieve the wounded men. Both of the Americans pretended they could not understand what they were being told to do. As a German officer called the NCO over to ask him something, Craft told Crist to get ready to run, as he felt they had a better chance running from the Germans than they did going into that intersection. Crist asked, "What?"—so loudly that the Germans realized something was afoot.

About this time the NCO realized that Craft had hand grenades hanging from his lapels and came over and snatched them off. As he turned to throw the grenades down a hole, Craft pushed Crist through the door of a house, grabbed a burp gun and both men ran through the house and leaped out a back window. They were now exposed to machine gun fire from the tank destroyer men, but fortunately, the machine gun jammed. Craft yelled to identify himself, and the machine-gun crew held off firing at them.

Captain Groff continues his story: "Amid the groans of the dying and wounded, the Germans could be seen withdrawing. The 3-inch guns began peppering them with high explosive, which completely demoralized them as they withdrew in confusion toward Rohren, leaving many dead and wounded. In their confused withdrawal, they left the previously captured men of the 395th Regiment. It can be positively stated that these men were very happy to be liberated so soon."

By 0745, the enemy had withdrawn except for a single penetration in the center of the battalion position (boundary between I and K Company). The enemy making this penetration, although carrying automatic weapons, rocket launchers, and rifle grenades, was liquidated by 0845 hours by the men from the front line. The front line units at this time fought so effectively that the battalion was not forced to commit its reserve. The attack on the extreme left flank (left flank of I Company) was repulsed by artillery and mortar fire.

Results of the days fighting were as follows: 19 prisoners captured, 104 German dead in an area 50 yards in front of the lines to 100 yards behind the lines at one point, and approximately 100 German dead along the battalion front. Enemy wounded could not be determined. The 3rd Battalion's casualties were four killed, seven wounded, four missing in action. Captured Germans stated that their mission was to take Höfen at all costs. Enemy artillery fire continued throughout the day, with heavy concentrations from 1028 to 1033 hours. All troops were on the alert for the remainder of that day.

Lt. Col. McClernand Butler, commander of the 3rd Battalion, 395th Infantry, and Capt. William S. Groff, commander of A Company, 612th Tank Destroyer Battalion, got together to ensure effective coordination. Everyone was elated over the temporary success, but realized that more action was to come. The tank destroyer platoons were tied in by wire with the infantry, and the radios of A Company, 612th Tank Destroyer Battalion, were distributed throughout the area to ensure an alternate means of communication. All effort was concentrated on improving the positions.

At 1235, the Germans made another effort. This time an attack was launched of company size. The Germans apparently wanted the road to use

The Battle at Höfen, 16–18 December

as a means of approach into the area. The infantry, in coordination with terrific artillery and mortar fire, beat off this attack very quickly.

This was the last attack on the sixteenth, but rest for the weary soldiers was not to be had. Supplies had to be replenished, dead removed and some of the debris cleared to permit the vehicles to move around on their supply missions. Minefields were laid and guns were shifted in an effort to prevent further penetrations.

Throughout the seventeenth, the men in Höfen were subjected to heavy artillery fire, with German planes strafing and bombing the town again and again. Material damage was heavy. Information at this time was received that German paratroopers had been dropped behind the lines, that two companies of infantry had penetrated the unit on the left flank, that the enemy was in position to the left rear, and that heavy fighting was going on to the south, on the right of the 99th Division's front.

THE LAST GERMAN ATTACK, 18 DECEMBER

There was no sleep for the men of the units during the night of 17–18 December. The Germans continued to pour in artillery and *Nebelwerfer* fire. At 0330 hours, Capt. William S. Groff went to the battalion command post in Höfen to learn of conditions elsewhere along the front and to await further developments. At 0345 hours on 18 December, the enemy again launched an attack against the battalion's positions. The main effort was directed at I Company. Despite heavy concentrations of mortar and artillery fire, the enemy successfully infiltrated the lines and surrounded the battalion observation post which was located in the I Company area. One of the tank destroyer gun crews, in a house located well forward and offered mutual support to a section of infantry, was captured. I Company attacked the infiltrating force at daylight and, after considerable close-quarter fighting, succeeded in killing or capturing the entire German platoon.

Beginning at 0830 hours, the 3rd Battalion received another artillery, mortar, and rocket concentration which was more intense than the proceeding attack on the sixteenth. At 0900 hours, the concentration lifted and the Germans attacked, striking the I and K Company fronts, using assault guns and armored cars against K Company. The fighting which took place was very bloody. During the attack, one of the gun positions of the 612th Tank Destroyer Battalion, which was located in a old convent was surrounded. The fight became so desperate that mortar fire was called on the position.

On the K Company front the German infantry moved in front of the tanks and shouting like wild men, charged the company positions. Machine guns, 81-millimeter mortars, 105-millimeter artillery, and 155-millimeter howitzers inflicted heavy casualties on the Germans, but they continued to advance and succeeded in effecting a penetration in the K Company line about 100 yards long. The infantry lines were breeched again and again, and the tank destroyers, fighting as infantry, met the attacking Germans with a hail of lead. Light machine guns were fired from the hip by the keyed up Americans whe were determined to halt the advance of the fanatical Germans. The additional firepower and battle experience of the tank destroyer men served them well.

The commander of the 3rd Battalion, 395th Infantry, immediately called for mortar and artillery fires on the penetrated area. The Germans withdrew from the K Company area in disorder, and riflemen took a heavy toll as the enemy retreated. The tank destroyers were firing on the German assault guns and armored cars but could not hit them because a small ridge to the front gave the German armor ample defilade. However, the German armor did not attempt to move into firing positions, and once the German infantry broke, they hastily withdrew. The 155-millimeter howitzers eventually brought them under fire and two armored cars were abandoned by the Germans.

While this fighting was taking place the German forces that were attacking the I Company front succeeded in making a small penetration, but could not hold it, and withdrew. The entire battalion front had been cleared by 0930 hours, but only for a short time. At 1000 hours, a force consisting of approximately a battalion of infantry attacked the center of I Company and drove a penetration about 100 yards deep and 400 yards wide. The battalion observation post was surrounded and approximately 100 German infantrymen who had moved into four large stone houses in the penetrated area were firing from the windows and doorways. Concentration of heavy artillery and mortars were placed on the occupied houses, but as they were constructed of stone, results were negligible.

At this time the artillery sealed the entrance of the penetration with planned concentrations, and the battalion commander ordered the battalion reserve, which consisted of one rifle platoon, to move into positions to contain the penetrating force. Two 57-millimeter antitank guns which were in position near the penetrated zone were ordered to fire armor-piercing ammunition into the buildings occupied by the Germans.

Within a few minutes, the 57-millimeter guns opened fire and methodically shattered the stone walls. Riflemen of the reserve platoon fired into the windows to prevent the Germans from firing on the 57-millimeter gun crews. The fire from the 57-millimeter guns proved effective, but the Germans did not surrender until the riflemen attacked the buildings with white phosphorus grenades and forced the Germans out. Twenty-five badly shaken Germans were taken prisoner, and inside the buildings were found the

The Battle at Höfen, 16–18 December

remains of approximately seventy-five Germans who had been killed by the fire of the 57-millimeter antitank guns.

This was the Germans final attempt to take Höfen; however, during the period from 19 to 24 December 1944, constant pressure was maintained on the battalion front by German raiding patrols. These forays were usually beaten off by mortar and artillery fire. The battalion prepared for another full-scale attack against the position, but none developed. News of the German break through to the south of Monschau finally filtered down to the 3rd Battalion, 395th Infantry, and only then did everyone fully realize the magnitude of the German effort.

OPERATION *STÖSSER*

The paratroopers were part of Operation *Stösser*. The German command's intent was to drop a number of paratroopers well behind American lines on the night of 15 December. Von der Heydte and his paratroopers were to have dropped fifteen miles in front of the 6th Panzer Army early on the morning of 16 December to seize a key crossroads for Dietrich's panzers, but the trucks needed to take the parachutists from their barracks to the airfield thirty miles away never arrived. The jump was rescheduled for before dawn on the seventeenth; but even before the transport planes took off, the schedule for Operation *Wacht am Rhein* indicated that by then the 6th Panzer Army would be well past the drop zone The Germans were to seize the crossroads at the Hohen Venn area at Mont Rigi (roads leading from Malmédy, Sourbrodt-Elsenborn/Robertville to Eupen). Their commander, Col. Freiherr Friedrich-August von der Heydte, was one of the most experienced paratroopers among the group. 120 Ju 52 planes of the 3rd Transport Wing were ready to fly these men to the designated area. But only one pilot, who flew the lead plane, had flown such an operation before. To help keep their formation, they flew with their navigation lights on which made them targets for antiaircraft fire. Von der Heydte's paratroopers executed their operation on the morning of 17 December, but things soon went askew.

The pilots of the 120 Ju 52 transport aircraft—half of whom were just out of flight school and had never seen action—were unable to stay in formation. Only eleven planes successfully negotiated U.S. antiaircraft fire and found their way through the darkness and strong wind gusts to reach the marshy, heavily wooded landed zone. Some men came down in Holland, and 200 of the paratroopers were actually dropped thirty miles to the east behind German lines by hopelessly disoriented pilots. Many of the untrained paratroopers who landed in the proper location were killed or injured by the high winds or rough ground; von der Heydte, who already had a broken arm, was knocked unconscious upon landing.

Because of all this confusion, troopers and supplies were dropped all the way from the Rhine River to the intended drop area near Eupen. Some were dropped as far away as Aachen. The original von der Heydte group consisted of 1,200 men, of whom 150 were left behind at the time of the drop. These latter troops, mainly service and supply personnel were to go forward with the ground forces. Because of the bad drop, approximately 1,000 men were widely scattered and only about 300 men were assembled around the road junction south of Eupen.

On the morning of 17 December, immediately following the drop, von der Heydte actually had only about twenty-five men with him; the rest of the 300 filtered in during the day. Because he had such a small force, von der Heydte did not attempt to block the road leading from Eupen to Malmédy, but sent out small reconnaissance groups instead. The small groups went into Stavelot, Malmédy, Verviers, and even as far as Werbomont, and were successful in bringing back very valuable information concerning American troop movements. Von der Heydte, however, was unable to communicate this information to 6th SS Panzer Army because his radio had been smashed in the drop. He had asked Dietrich for carrier pigeons to relay messages, as he had seen the American paratroops use them in Normandy. Dietrich only laughed at the suggestion, however, and said that a radio would be sufficient.

Von der Heydte stated that he addressed a message to Maj. Gen. Maxwell Taylor of the U.S. 101st Airborne Division because he was the only American general whom von der Heydte could recall at the time and because his patrols had informed him that American paratroops were moving into the area near Werbomont. In view of this, von der Heydte felt that Taylor's troops might also be in the area, and hoping to surrender some of his wounded men, he addressed the message to Taylor. Because he knew that the plans for the attack called for the capture of Monschau on the first day, von der Heydte himself went to Monschau about four days after the drop. Although he saw American artillery units west of the town, he entered it anyway and was captured. He later learned that about 150 of his men were successful in escaping back through the American lines.

CHAPTER 6

The Withdrawal of the 2nd Infantry Division Begins

On the seventeenth, General Robertson ordered the withdrawal of the 9th and 38th Regiments of the 2nd Infantry Division and directed that they move south as fast as they could get started, placing Colonel Hirschfelder, the senior regimental commander on the spot, in charge of the disengagement and withdrawal from the Wahlerscheid area. General Robertson also issued orders to the remaining battalion of the 23rd Infantry, plus a tank destroyer company of the 644th Tank Destroyer Battalion under the command of Capt. Harlow F. Lenon and a company of medium tanks (A Company, 741st Tank Battalion) to move south immediately toward Rocherath, Krinkelt, and Wirtzfeld.

There was a high ridge to the southeast of Wirtzfeld, and General Robertson directed Col. P. D. Ginder, the spare combat team commander, to take such forces as could be sent him and coordinate the defense of that sector. General Robertson ordered Colonel Stokes to take charge of the Rocherath-Krinkelt area and organize it as units became available to him. The headquarters commandant was also ordered to alert the headquarters personnel and organize close-in-positions for the defense of the division command post. This was already set up as standard operating procedure and was done accordingly.

THE 1ST BATTALION, 9TH INFANTRY, 2ND INFANTRY DIVISION, TAKES UP DEFENSIVE POSITIONS NORTHEAST OF ROCHERATH AT THE LAUSDELL CROSSROADS

At 0955 on 17 December, completely unexpected orders came to the battalion commander, Lt. Col. William D. McKinley, to evacuate the positions so dearly won and withdraw in the direction of initial forward assembly areas of 12 December. These orders subsequently were learned as being incident to and required by the German counteroffensive, which began on 16 December. The orders to McKinley included instructions for clearing the area of all fighting gear and every possible bit of equipment, and they were augmented

William McKinley.
EDWIN NORRIS/U.S. ARMY

by the knowledge that further instructions relative to the future mission of the battalion would be given later in the progress to the south.

The problem of breaking contact and withdrawing over the route, which the battalion had come, was made difficult since the battalion was still in continuous contact with the enemy, and had been since dark on the evening of the sixteenth. The problem, however, was solved happily by a continuous normal barrage called to cover the withdrawal, and also by the movement of two reinforced rifle platoons through three consecutive delaying positions on the tail of the battalion column. Under the circumstances, company commanders exercised almost unbelievable control, both in the movement of their men and the taking of all equipment and transportation with them. The battalion regrouped in the low ground about 1,200 yards southwest of Wahlerscheid by 1500 hours and proceeded south on the main road toward Rocherath.

About 4,000 yards north of Rocherath, the division commander, General Robertson, personally intercepted McKinley and gave him instructions as to his future mission, apprising him of as much information available regarding the German counteroffensive and the imminent threat to the division's main supply road running north of Rocherath and along which the division still had elements of another infantry regiment and much road-bound material. He directed McKinley to move his battalion to seize and secure the road net—the Lausdell Crossroads—northeast of Rocherath against enemy infil-

Edwin Norris.

tration from the east. He directed McKinley to take command of all friendly troops in the area that might be found withdrawing from the east toward this road crossing, and to stabilize a line to protect the east flank of the division. He also told him that he could call on his usual supporting artillery battalion, the 15th Field Artillery Battalion, as well as on the 924th Field Artillery Battalion (99th Division), which had been supporting the Wahlerscheid attack from positions just northeast of the Rocherath Barracks.

He stated that he had previously committed, at this same crossroad, K Company, 9th Infantry; the 1st Platoon of M Company; and the Ammunition and Pioneer Platoon of the 3rd Battalion, under Lt. Wesley Knutsen. He also stated that elements of the 23rd Infantry and 393rd Infantry of the 99th Division, would be in the area, falling back against the German thrust in this area and to stabilize them if possible. The commanding general punctuated the urgency of this situation by personally leading elements of the battalion in commandeered two-and-a-half-ton vehicles and leading them within 1,000 yards of the road net position.

Wesley Knutsen recalls: "When, at about 1500, I reported to Lt. Jack Garvey, the K Company commander, he placed the A&P Platoon in position securing the right rear of K Company. At this time there had been enemy activity in the sector, but General Robertson had said that he expected enemy attacks momentarily. At the same time, elements of the 99th Division and of the 23rd Infantry were coming out of the woods to the east of the K positions in groups of twos and threes and in various states of disorganization."

T/ Sgt. Edwin Norris of K Company, 9th Infantry, remembers: "On the morning of 17 December, we got word of the German attack, which would be called the "Battle of the Bulge" by Americans. Orders came for the 9th Regiment to pull back and set up a defense line south of Wirtzfeld. Some of the men of my 1st Platoon did drift back during the night. Also some of the 2nd, 3rd, and Weapons Platoons came back. K Company ended up with about one 100 men out of almost 200. After we had started back to Wirtzfeld, General Robertson came in a jeep and pulled K Company out of the line of march and told Lieutenant Garvey, the commanding officer, to move the company to the crossroads near Rocherath and Krinkelt. The crossroads was known as Lausdell Crossroads. He was to set up a defense line. General Robertson said he would have the 1st Battalion join K Company and we would be under command of its commander, Lieutenant Colonel McKinley."

PFC Frank E. Royer, K Company, 9th Infantry, who at that time was close to Garvey and the general, remembers this clearly today. He writes: "Then on 17 December, we were told to pull back and give all these pillboxes back, which we'd lost quite a few people getting them. We had to go back, and we marched all day. Probably in the middle of the afternoon, I saw a general-in-chief over there by the side of a road, a crossroad. I'd never seen a general before over there. He was a two-star general, Robinson was his name, General Robinson [Robertson], I think it was. He called my company commander, I could hear him. He said, 'Hey, Jack'—he called him Jack. His name was Jack Garvey. Of course, I didn't call him Jack, but he came over there. I could hear him tell my commander, he was talking loud and we could all hear. We were just standing there waiting. He said 'Well, I want you to go down this road. There's supposed to be some action down there'—some of the divisions or some outfit, the 99th Division maybe. 'You're going to be a division reserve.' And division reserve is way back. There was supposed to be the 99th Division in front of us. So we just happened to be unlucky. As he drove up, we were marching by and he stopped. So our company—it was just our company—went down this road, and the rest of the guys kept retreating back to wherever they were supposed to be going."

According to Lawrence Shoemaker, a runner in the 2nd Platoon of K Company, 9th Infantry, 2nd Division, "K Company left Wahlerscheid the morning of 17 December, arriving at Lausdell Crossroads at 3:30 P.M. General Robertson was there and told Captain Garvey to have his men dig in and defend the Lausdell Crossroads and the road in front of the farmhouse (Palm House). The men were dug in along the road headed east toward

The Withdrawal of the 2nd Infantry Division Begins

Modern view of the Lausdell Crossroads looking toward the Krinkelter Woods. This is what McKinley's men saw when the Germans came out of the woods. HANS WIJERS

Germany. Company headquarters moved into the basement of the farm house. I was with the company headquarters as a runner for the 2nd Platoon. When we arrived at the crossroads the Germans were firing artillery mortar and small arms at our position. Tanks and ground troops moved closer to the crossroads."

Utilizing the transportation at hand, the 1st Battalion moved to its objective and closed by 1700 hours. The leading elements of the battalion, A and B Companies, arrived just in time to get in position astride the road net facing southeast before darkness fell. Contact with K Company was improved to give depth to the battalion position. C Company, whose effectives numbered less than fifty men, was moved into a reserve position on the high ground on the north flank. A detachment of C Company, 644th Tank Destroyer Battalion, was located in the area with three guns in positions to cover the cross roads. The commanding officer of this detachment was contacted by Lieutenant Colonel McKinley, ordered under command, and told to remain in position until further orders. All of this time the battalion was moving in and consolidating positions in the midst of a scene of wild confusion. Heavy small-arms and machine-gun fire was coming from the wooded high ground to the east, and friendly vehicles and personnel, out of control and unable to be contacted in many cases, were streaming to the west. While Lieutenant Colonel McKinley was circulating through the area assuming command of the troops that were there, elements of the 99th Division were streaming through toward the rear in a very disorganized state. Many of the men had thrown their weapons away and were inquiring of all they met, 'Where is the escape gap?'"

Frank Royer continues his story: "We didn't have to go too far down the road. The officers always had maps for some reason. The whole time, I never saw a map as a private. Nobody ever showed me, and I always just went wherever they told me. But we got to a point on our map where we were supposed to hold this road. There were some crossroads, and there was a farmhouse up on one side. The rest were all fields. By that time, we were getting a little snow. So we started to dig our foxholes, and while we were digging that afternoon there were stragglers coming back along the road in front of us here. Some of them with no guns or helmets, they were really kind of retreating. They looked bad, they were from another division, the 99th I guess. We'd see them, and they'd say, 'Oh, you can't stop them,' or 'They're terrible,' or something. I suppose they had it bad, but . . . so we just kept digging, 'cause we didn't see a sign of a German yet, so it wasn't nothing critical."

Against this demoralizing picture the battalion moved in with orders to hold. Heavy machine guns were emplaced on the high ground and along the road net to cover the routes of enemy foot troops along the main road running to the southeast. Because the battalion had cleared its original area in the morning, and of necessity had to leave in position all of its antitank mines, the area was without name. However, the detachment commander of the 644th Tank Destroyer Battalion had some mines with him, and arrangements were made for him to hand carry them to the crossroads area to be picked up by B Company. Just at dark with the companies just in position, the battalion commander contacted the commander of the 3rd Battalion, 23rd Infantry, and made plans for him to extend the right flank along the high ground leading toward Rocherath, as soon as he was able to regain control of his scattered elements which were falling back to the west in front of the German attack. At that time, Charles MacDonald, the commanding officer of I Company, 23rd Infantry, arrived without men; he was shown on the ground where he would place his company to extend the right flank of the battalion position, if and when he was able to gain control.

S/Sgt. Norman Bernstein recalls: "At 1800, a meeting was held at the battalion command post, 300 yards northeast of the road net at which all company commanders were given further instructions and information as to the situation. The weather at this time was very foggy. There was snow on the ground and the visibility was limited to about 100 yards. Darkness fell at approximately 1800. The night was absolute black."

Everything indicated how critical the situation was, and company commanders were informed to tell their men again of the absolute necessity of

The Withdrawal of the 2nd Infantry Division Begins 313

holding the position. Measures were taken to counteract an immediate attack by the enemy on the position. The company commander of B Company arranged with the commander of the 644th Tank Destroyer Battalion to get his mines in position in front of him. The battalion artillery liaison officer, having worked feverishly on his communications which had been out of contact through faulty action for some two hours, regained communication and planned his defensive fires along the roads in front of the positions. With these counter measures in effect, the company commanders returned to their companies; then with dark came the first enemy attack.

At 1830, communication with the world outside of the battalion was nonexistent. The wires were out, and the radio wouldn't reach regiment. Lt. John C. Granville, the artillery liaison officer, had been struggling for a half-hour with his SCR 610 radio that had stopped functioning. At about 1835, he finally got his radio working, and just in time, for B Company called in at that moment and reported they could hear tanks approaching.

According to 1st Lt. Roy Allen of B Company, 1st Battalion, 9th Infantry, "At 1930 hours it was reported by the 1st Platoon, B Company, that three tanks were approaching our position. It was reported that there were other tanks, and that with each tank were about thirty Germans. The three tanks were allowed to go by owing to the fact that we were not prepared for tanks."

At about 1930 hours, three tank destroyers with about one platoon of escorting infantry broke through the 1st Battalion's positions down by the road. This was the small combat group of 1st Lieutenant Zeiner. Half an hour later further Panzers with infantry loomed up out of the darkness. B Company was instructed to hold their fire until positive identification could be made. About three tank destroyers passed through the position, moved 400 yards toward Rocherath, and stopped. These were assumed to be U.S. tanks until they opened fire on the Americans.

At the same time, heavy concentrations of enemy artillery fell in the area. U.S. artillery was brought to bear on the enemy tanks setting one of them on fire. This lit the surrounding country so that the defenders could see to an extent what was transpiring. Two panzers were knocked out by mines, another two by bazookas. Finally the remaining five or six panzers with their escorting infantry managed to break into the 1st Battalion positions; but then the attack was stopped cold by the massed fire of seven artillery battalions from Elsenborn Camp. These were the following elements of the tank destroyer battalion and the 2nd Battalion of the 25th SS Panzergrenadier Regiment, for which 1st Lieutenant Zeiner waited in vain in Rocherath. He assumed they had taken the wrong direction.

Roy Allen resumes his story: "At approximately 0200 hours, we again heard tanks approaching our position. Sgt. Ted Rickerstaff and I immediately prepared to place antitank mines in front of the oncoming tanks. As we armed the eight mines, the German tanks were 400 yards away. A bazooka was then placed in a position to cover the mines. The mines stopped two tanks and the other proceeded to go around them through the fields. Two tanks were knocked out with bazooka."

Captain Brockschmidt remembers: "The mass of the 2nd Battalion of the 25th SS Panzergrenadier Regiment and the 12th Anti-Tank Battalion had followed 1st Lieutenant Zeiner, after they had driven the enemy out of the Forest of Krinkelt. They followed him closely down the forest road that ran down to Rocherath. Shortly after they left the woods they ran into the prepared defenses of the enemy in the dark, but were able to drive him back, effectively supported by our own artillery. Just east of Rocherath, at the Lausdell Crossroads, they again ran into superior American troops. The attack was pinned down by very strong artillery fire. Also an attempt to outflank the enemy by going north, failed in the face of his superior strength with the loss of some tank destroyers. It is suspected that the commander of the 2nd Anti-Tank Company, 1st Lieutenant Wachter, and the commander of the 3rd Platoon, Bitau, were killed in this action."

T/ Sgt. Edwin Norris resumes his account: "No sooner than our units got in place, the Germans infantry, tanks and artillery hit us. We did get some antitank mines in place and this helped stop the tanks; our artillery played a major roll. The 12th and 15th Artillery Battalions turned one battery each around to fire on enemy tanks and infantry within 800 yards of the command post and still kept us covered. A few tanks and infantrymen got through, but were taken care of by antitank guns and a few of our tanks. We also had a few half-tracks with four .50-caliber machine guns mounted on them. There were the 462nd Anti-Aircraft Unit firing at the tanks and infantry, and also bazookas."

When the attack on Wahlerscheid was planned, McKinley, realizing that the ground there was unsuitable for the emplacement of the 57-millimeter antitank guns, had organized five bazooka teams in each rifle company making a total of twenty-two teams in the battalion. There were also five "daisy chains" or "necklaces" of antitank mines in the battalion, each chain having six mines in it.

As stated before, the enemy tank blazing at the crossroad in the center of the battalion position lighted up the surrounding countryside. Lt. Roy Allen, who had prepared one of the mine necklaces, went toward the direction from which the enemy tanks were coming. He put the necklaces across the route of approach of a second group of tanks. The first two tanks in line were disabled by the mines and blocked the road. The remaining tanks

The Withdrawal of the 2nd Infantry Division Begins 315

caught on to the situation, detoured around their knocked-out fellows and continued toward Rocherath. This occurred between 1900 and 2000. At about this time, Lt. John Melesnick, the commadner of B Company, notified Major Hancock that another column of enemy armor with approximately a platoon of infantry accompanying each tank was moving down the road past B Company. This column was a long one and appeared to extend 1,000 yards east to the woods in front of B Company. The artillery, under direction of the liaison officer, started to search the road with fire, starting close to B Company and working back toward the wood. This fire continued for about ten minutes while B Company raked the infantry with machine gun fire. The enemy tanks stopped when the artillery came in on them, and the defenders could hear the screams of enemy wounded.

At the same time that this action was taking place, A Company saw and reported another column of seven tanks with accompanying infantry.

The artillery was shifted to this second column at the end of the ten-minute concentration on the first. The artillery fire knocked out four of the seven enemy tanks, so that only three of them got into Rocherath. The artillery was instructed to continue interdicting the road until told to stop and the fire continued throughout the night. The first column reported by B Company dispersed into the field around the crossroad, apparently with the mission of protecting the flanks of the following armor.

The commanders of A and B Companies reported that an undetermined number of enemy tanks were in the company areas and within fifty yards of the company command posts. Bazooka teams were sent out and disposed of at least three tanks. American riflemen picked off the crews. The enemy infantry that had accompanied the tanks was scattered by the artillery and machine gun fire and did not reappear.

At about 2230, A Company reported that there were enemy tanks deploying in the forward edge of the woods in front of them. These tanks approached the battalion from three different directions. The enemy had been using the artillery liaison officer's frequency, so that his calls for fire had to be made in the intervals between enemy messages.

When the enemy tanks approached and seemed to be in a fair way to overrunning the positions, Lieutenant Granville screamed into his radio for fire on the three routes used by the enemy. He gave the coordinates to be fired on and added, "if you don't get it [artillery] out right now, it'll be too goddam late." Granville couldn't get a receipt for the message and "reached out for God to take him by the hand." Three minutes after the call, heavy effective artillery fell on the enemy, and at 2315, the attack seemed to bog down. The enemy apparently decided to wait until daylight to determine what was opposing them. Of all the enemy tanks that had participated in the attack, only three—from *Kampfgruppe Zeiner*—got through into Rocherath.

At about 2330, McKinley sent a message to the regimental commander, "We have been strenuously engaged, but everything is under control at present."

At about 2400, Lt. Col. Jack Allen, commanding officer of the 3rd Battalion of the 393rd Infantry, came to the battalion command post and was told that he was to tie in on the left flank of the battalion. Allen was shown the left flank positions on the ground and departed for his own unit. From 2400 until daylight, there was no fighting. Major Hancock said the silence was "almost frightening."

At about 0100 on 18 December, telephone communication was established with the 38th Infantry. Sometime before dawn, the battalion received instructions to withdraw at first light, or whenever Lt. Col. Jack Norris's 2nd Battalion of the 38th Infantry was in positions behind them. The occupation of defensive positions by Norris's battalion was to govern the withdrawal of McKinley's men, and the 1st Battalion of the 9th Infantry was to hold in positions until instructed by the 2nd Battalion of the 38th that the time for withdrawal was ripe.

About an hour before dawn, an incident occurred, humorous in itself but indicative of the impossibility of close coordination between even adjacent squads. A messenger from K's right-flank platoon crawled up to Lt. Wesley Knutsen and asked, "Did you know there were two tanks in rear of you?" Startled, Knutsen said, "No, where?" The informant pointed to the next row of bushes, thirty yards away, "There," he said. "Why don't you knock them out?" demanded Knutsen. When the man answered, "They're ours," Knutsen breathed a deep sigh of relief, because of both the unexpected potential support and of gratitude for not having to fight an enemy tank in his very own command post. Knutsen said that at any time during the night, he could read a newspaper by the light of the burning buildings and from tracers overhead. He tried it at about 0200 when, after he had issued orders to the men to destroy all letters, one of his men brought an important personal letter to be checked.

T/Sgt. Edwin Norris continues: "It is important that the units that gave K Company and 1st Battalion support be recognized. They are the 12th Field Artillery Battalion, 15th Field Artillery Battalion, 2nd Engineer Combat Battalion, 2nd Medical Battalion, 644th Tank Destroyer Battalion, 2nd Signal Company, 741st Tank Battalion, and the 462nd Anti-Aircraft Battalion. These units gave us the very best support. When the platoon leaders called for artillery fire, it was there and on target. When a telephone line was

The Withdrawal of the 2nd Infantry Division Begins

cut by fire, it was replaced or repaired immediately. Due to cold and foggy conditions, our men were suffering badly from hypothermia (below normal body temperature). Our clothes, socks and shoes were wet. We had taken winter training in Wisconsin and northern Michigan before going overseas, and the temperature would drop to 35 and 40 degrees below zero, but, we had the best winter clothes, and we had no bad problems. But, not so here in Belgium; our clothes were just normal wool with no over shoes, and the cold conditions was our worst enemy, this and being out-numbered. Also, the enemy had most of the best equipment. I think it can be said that we had the best soldiers, best trained and able to use the weapons that we did have and improvise when we had to just to survive.

"This battle at Lausdell Crossroads in defense of the twin villages was as close to the Battle of Armageddon as it will ever come. It was pure hell, and I think the Germans will also agree."

CHAPTER 7

The Fight for Krinkelt-Rocherath, 17 December

THE ORGANIZATION OF THE DEFENSE OF KRINKELT-ROCHERATH
At about 0745 on the morning of the seventeenth, Captain Love received a written message, signed by Col. Francis Boos, the regimental commander, to the effect that approximately thirty tanks and a battalion of enemy infantry were in the vicinity of Büllingen. The message ordered Captain Love to organize and defend Krinkelt-Rocherath with the antitank company in the positions then held. (They had been in the area since 15 December.) Love sent Lt. Irving Ratner, the company reconnaissance officer, to regiment to obtain a clarification of the message. When Ratner returned, he had no further information except that the 3rd Battalion of the 38th was moving south on tanks to defend Krinkelt from the south.

Captain Love immediately sent the 1st Gun Platoon (three 57-millimeter antitank guns) under Lt. Lewis Silver to defensive positions to the south and west of the town, the 2nd Gun Platoon (three 57-millimeter antitank guns) to the east, and the 3rd Platoon (three 57-millimeter antitank guns) to the north and northeast. The mine platoon (under the command of 1st Lt. George W. Stewart) was to form as a rifle platoon and organize forward of and between the 1st and 2nd Platoons. Capt. Stratton F. Callier Jr., the commander of the service company, received orders that his company was to occupy the crossroads to the east of the command post (Route Vers Udenbreth) and prepare to defend it assuming an infantry-rifle role. The orders were that the company was to occupy the roadblock position and to hold at all costs until relieved. The positions were occupied as ordered.

At about that time, Captain Love began to notice confusion among the 99th Division's attached and supporting elements in the area. Rumors were rife: "The 99th is in full retreat," "The 99th is counterattacking," "We're pulling out," "We're holding at all costs," "Retire—the whole position is about to be overrun." The parts of the 99th that were withdrawing had

The Fight for Krinkelt-Rocherath, 17 December

James Love.

apparently no semblance of order in their movements, probably because they were from frontline outposts 100 to 200 yards apart, consisting of six men or less.

1st Lieutenant Stewart of the mine platoon made a reconnaissance of the area, and at about 1030 put his platoon into position. The positions that were occupied by the mine platoon were abandoned antiaircraft artillery positions, and there were large quantities of abandoned 20-millimeter and 40-millimeter ammunition in the area. In the positions where the mine platoon had been placed to act as infantry, the men dug in and improved their positions. The were told that there were no troops on the left, and the troops that were supposed to be on the right were never contacted.

THE 3RD BATTALION, 38TH INFANTRY, TAKES UP ITS POSITIONS

At about 0800 on 17 December, Colonel Barsanti received an order from Colonel Boos, regimental commander, that the 3rd Battalion was to move to Krinkelt and that Barsanti was to go ahead and contact Colonel Stokes, the asstant division commander. Boos said that the mission of the battalion would be to act under the instructions of Stokes and prepare to attack and retake Büllingen, which by this time was in enemy hands. The enemy situation as Boos knew it was simply that enemy tanks and armored infantry had taken Büllingen and were in the town.

Immediately upon receipt of the regimental commander's order, Barsanti issued orders to get the battalion on the road south for the four-and-a-half-mile march back to Krinkelt. The heavy machine guns were ordered loaded on transportation to go immediately to Krinkelt. As soon as he had issued the order, Barsanti, with his reconnaissance party consisting of the battalion S-3, the communications officer and the heavy weapons commander, proceeded on jeeps to Krinkelt. This little party went through Krinkelt at about 0845, but was unable to locate the assistant division commander. Barsanti decided to continue his reconnaissance on his own, going to the high ground overlooking Büllingen, the town that Barsanti had been told to take. Colonel Barsanti's little party arrived at the base of Hill 629, which was the commanding ground in the vicinity, and went toward the west, passing five American tank destroyers that were heading in the direction of Büllingen. As the head of the reconnaissance party reached and rounded a turn in the road, the leading tank destroyers and the first jeep in line were fired upon by enemy tanks from the high ground to the south of them. The men left the vehicles and jumped into the ditches on the sides of the road. Barsanti looked the situation over, satisfied himself as to the terrain, and with the rest of his party, backed the jeeps out of the enemy observed area and returned to Krinkelt.

According to Harold L. Hoffer, a company commander in the 644th Tank Destroyer Battalion, "At about 1500 hours on 17 December 1944, as commander of Reconnaissance Company, 644th Tank Destroyer Battalion, attached to the 2nd Infantry Division, I noticed a motorized column moving from east to west through the town of Büllingen. Our command post was located at the south edge of Krinkelt, some two miles from the column which appeared to contain U.S. Army and German vehicles."

Colonel Barsanti returned to Krinkelt where he met Colonel Stokes at about 0930 hours. Stokes ordered the 3rd Battalion commander to set up a defense on the south side of Krinkelt with L Company facing south out of the town; its mission was to hold any attempt of the enemy to thrust from Büllingen or Mürringen. L Company arrived in Krinkelt at about 1000 hours and went into positions ordered.

Overhead, American planes and enemy planes were engaged in dogfights. Two enemy planes strafed L Company positions while that company was going into position. A P-47 was forced to jettison its bombs in order to engage enemy aircraft. The bombs fell in the L Company position, causing twelve casualties. I Company followed L Company into position after about half an hour and went into position on the east of Krinkelt, facing east with a two-fold mission. The company was to pull through their position any 99th

The Fight for Krinkelt-Rocherath, 17 December

Jack Norris (center). ALFRED PRICE

Division men who were withdrawing back through the lines, and to defend from the south and east against any enemy coming into Krinkelt.

K Company came into position immediately following I Company with the mission of protecting the north flank of I Company along a line 800 yards long in the gap between Krinkelt and Rocherath, and along the southern portion of the latter, including a line to the east of Rocherath.

Arnold B. Parish of the 2nd Platoon, K Company, 38th Infantry, remembers: "We were moving up to relieve part of the 9th Infantry Regiment. The ground was covered with ice and snow as we moved toward Wahlerscheid. The 9th had been successful but had lost so many men that some of their squads were less than half strength. As we moved through the snow everyone was quiet as we all knew that in a short time we would be engaged with the enemy. The column stopped and we waited to move on. Lieutenant Lahner, our platoon leader, was called away to meet with the company commander and the other platoon leaders. We had hopes that maybe something better was planned for us. We began to talk among ourselves guessing what our next move may be. In about twenty minutes, Lieutenant Lahner returned. He talked briefly to Sergeant Ward, our platoon sergeant. I wasn't close enough to hear the conversation. Immediately our company turned and started moving in almost the opposite direction. We took the road that ran from Wahlerscheid to Rocherath and Krinkelt."

The whole battalion was in position by 1130 hours on the seventeenth and represented the first troops from the 2nd Infantry Division in the area. Colonel Stokes attached to the 3rd Battalion all tanks and tank destroyers in the Krinkelt-Rocherath area with orders to cut every road leading from the east and south into the twin towns. By 1230, there was at least one tank or one tank destroyer on each road leading into the defensive position. Elements of the 99th Division began pulling through the battalion positions at about 1300 hours. These were in groups of twenty to thirty men which were fed back towards the rear where they were picked up as stragglers.

Sometime during the afternoon, L Company was attacked by a force of about forty Germans. All of this force was killed or driven off by the 81-millimeter mortars firing in the draw to the south of L Company. At about 1330 hours, the battalion position started to receive medium to heavy artillery fire from the enemy held area. This artillery was varying in intensity from light to heavy. At about 1400, Boos called Barsanti to say that the 1st and 2nd Battalions would be on their way south as soon as they could extricate themselves from the fight at Wahlerscheid.

During the afternoon, B Company of the 741st Tank Battalion (Col. Leland Skagg) and a full company of the 644th Tank Destroyer Battalion (self-propelled), plus a platoon of tank destroyers from C Company of the

Members of HQ Company, 741st Tank Battalion: Smith, Rockwell, Styles, and Boyd.
JESS STYLES

644th under the company commander, Capt. Harlow F. Lenon, went into positions that were considered to be critical. At that time, there was still in the town most of C Company of the 801st Tank Destroyer Battalion (towed 3-inch guns) that had been attached to the 99th Division. The 38th Regimental Headquarters Company (Capt. Ralph H. Stallworth) moved in sometime during the afternoon, so that at dusk, there was some semblance of a defensive force already organized and in position in the town.

THE 2ND BATTALION, 38TH INFANTRY, MOVES INTO ITS POSITIONS

While in positions in the vicinity of Wahlerscheid, after making an attack to the north, the 2nd Battalion was ordered to hold up the attack. On 16 December at about 2135 hours, Lt. Col. Jack Norris, battalion commander, received a warning order from Col. Francis Boos, the 38th regimental commander. The warning order contained no specific information. Boos simply stated that the whole front was in a chaotic state, and that Norris should not be surprised at any order that he might receive. Boos further ordered the battalion to remain static until orders to the contrary were received. At 1025, Boos directed that Norris make preparations for a withdrawal, and at 1230, the battalion received instructions to break contact with the enemy and withdraw to an assembly area. The battalion withdrew behind the 1st Battalion of the 38th in the following order: F, G, E. The two companies in direct contact with the enemy, G and E, disengaged under cover of an artillery barrage in front of their positions.

Some confusion resulted when the move to new positions was attempted. Three times orders were changed, and three times reconnaissance parties were dispatched to get information about the new area. The difficulty was that usually encountered when command communication is poor, or slow, and there exists two logical choices.

John B. Savard of G Company, 38th Infantry, recalls: "Late on the sixteenth, my company was ordered to hold what we had, but be prepared to continue the attack on the seventeenth. As more information was received, it became apparent that the fighting we could hear was not just a local counterattack, and we were told to be ready to withdraw all our men and equipment back down the single road toward the Belgium towns of Rocherath and Krinkelt, for we faced the danger of being cut off. When the withdrawal orders were given, the 38th Regiment was leading the advance and my battalion was assigned the mission of protecting the regiment's withdrawal."

At 1600 hours, G Company was told to move to an area where it would set up and defend a roadblock along the route to the south. At 1630 hours,

John Savard.

Harold Barkley.

the command post personnel were sent to a temporary command post that was set up for HQ Company. F Company led the battalion south. G Company stopped off at the roadblock as ordered. E Company broke with the enemy at 1700 hours and under cover of the confusion that existed as to what position to occupy, a spot decision was required. Because there was artillery fire coming close to the column, Captain Erwin decided to go into one of the disputed positions. Upon reaching this area it was found that the 1st Battalion of the 9th Infantry was already there, but Erwin decided to set about organizing a defense.

PFC Harold G. Barkley, the first scout for G Company, tells his story: "It was just getting dark, when we received orders to fall back. It was a bitter pill to swallow since we had to relinquish our hard earned gains without a fight, and in time the battle for the pillboxes at Wahlerscheid would be referred to as 'Heartbreak Crossroads.' Fierce fighting erupted all about as we made our way back down the road we had advanced over on the previous days—

tree bursts and machine guns. After a while, our lieutenant called a brief halt and ordered us to shed our overcoats so we could move faster, as the coats were wet and heavy. Although I didn't know what was happening at the time, our company was told to dig in at a firebreak and await the passing of E Company, which had been left behind as the rear guard. E Company passed through and we were now the rearguard, the last unit to leave the forest."

As he was preparing to execute the plan, at 1900 hours Boos arrived and ordered the battalion to move into the alternatively selected position. At about 2100, F Company went into the final position.

At 2130 hours on 17 December, E Company, on the way south from Wahlerscheid, arrived at the temporary command post. On orders from the regimental commander, E Company sent the 2nd Platoon under Lt. Melhorn P. Binns to assist the service company of the 38th that was maintaining a roadblock. Immediately after the 2nd Platoon left, the remainder of E Company was sent by Boos to join them and to reorganize their positions. E Company got into the positions as ordered, improved the positions, and evacuated some wounded who were found there.

Meanwhile, on 17 December at 2000 hours, the regimental commander ordered G Company to move from the road block they had been holding and organize a defensive position around the regimental command post. G Company, on its way south, reached the 2nd Battalion's command post on 17 December at 2230 hours when Capt. Edward Farrell, the battalion S-3, led the company off on its mission. G Company, along with some tank destroyers in support, assumed position along the main supply route on the east and west sides of the road.

At about 2200 hours, F Company moved into an assembly area at the crossroad where heavy enemy artillery and mortar fire fell on the company. F Company remained in this position at the crossroad with both its left and right flanks cutting the main supply route. E Company continued south along the main supply route and set up a defense between the main supply route and the road on its right flank. Captain Farrell returned to the G Company road block at about 2015 to relieve G Company from that mission and to place it in a perimeter defensive position around the regimental command post.

G Company moved out from the road block in a column of twos behind Captain Farrell on one side of the road, and Capt. Joseph E. Skaggs, the G Company commander on the other. Along the route of advance, the column passed the C Company position, and a voice from the C Company area yelled, "Get out of there or be cut to ribbons." No second warning was required, and the men hit the ditches on both sides of the road. Farrell and Skaggs made a quick reconnaissance, and determining that the route was not safe to travel, set off with G Company following across country to a road junction just north of regiment. Here was a fight in the dark with a force of enemy set up against the defense around the regimental command post.

John B. Savard of G Company, 38th Infantry, recalls: "The night of the seventeenth was the beginning of a nightmare. I can vividly recall our withdrawal and our attempts to block the enemy advance. At one point, in pitch darkness, we set up a defense along a firebreak protecting our line of withdrawal. The ground was frozen and only shallow holes could be dug. The forest around us was filled with artillery bursts and tracer fire. Luckily, the enemy forces facing us were not able to get much armor forward, and the pair of Sherman tanks which were supporting our position kept the enemy from overrunning our line. After things settled down a little, the tanks withdrew down the road to Rocherath and we were ordered to follow."

THE 1ST BATTALION, 38TH INFANTRY, MOVES INTO THE KRINKELT-ROCHERATH AREA

After the 9th Infantry Regiment of the 2nd Infantry Division had withdrawn out of the operational area at Wahlerscheid under cover of artillery fire and fog, the 1st Battalion of the 38th Infantry was pulled out as well and assembled, while the 2nd Battalion covered the withdrawal. Capt Rumsey was at the head of the column with instructions to go straight down the road and meet guides, which would be posted at the road junction in Rocherath.

At the Rocherather Baracken Crossroads, about one kilometer north of the village, the battalion came under strong fire from artillery and rockets, just as A Company passed. It was "the heaviest fire that this old, combat proven battalion had ever run into." C Company suffered the most losses and was scattered. In the midst of all this, the head of the battalion entered the town at about dark. The guides from the battalion had been instructed to meet at the road junction, but when the head of the battalion led by Captain Rumsey reached the above road junction, the only member of the guide detail present was Lt. Robert O. English, the guide for the command post group who had never seen the area the rifle companies were to occupy and could offer nothing in the way of assistance.

Joseph Jan Kiss Jr. of C Company, 38th Infantry, describes his experience: "Someone yelled, 'Pull back. We're pulling out.' Under artillery fire, in broad daylight, we pulled back about seven or eight miles from near Wahlerscheid to the twin towns of Krinkelt and Rocherath in Belgium. I hit the ground near a German foxhole, afraid to get in it as it may be booby-trapped. A

The Fight for Krinkelt-Rocherath, 17 December 327

machine gun burst over me, tearing black bark off trees, exposing the white wood underneath, causing me to dive in the foxhole anyway. We walked into Krinkelt at dark with German tanks on the horizon firing point blank at us. (We could see them on account of light from the burning buildings.)

"We were walking along the road in a ditch two feet deep filled with water. The wounded were falling on the road and into the ditch. We had orders to help no one. 'Leave them for the medics. Keep moving.' The dead or wounded that fell on the road were mashed by trucks, tanks and jeeps, bumper to bumper trying to escape. I saw men smashed flat as a pancake. You could see outlines of helmets through bodies twice a normal size smashed flat. I had to stare at some for a while to figure out that it was once a human being. Some animals in a burning barn across the road were crying, and it sounded like the crying of human babies."

Slowly, the battalion column moved straight down the road, always under the artillery. It continued, still meeting no guides until, after passing the crossroads, Captain Rumsey realized that they were wrong when they received small arms fire from the front. He doubled the column back on itself, and turning southeast of the above crossroad, continued to the crossroads. Here the road made a decided bend toward the south in the direction from which the column had just received small arms fire. Rumsey strongly suspected that the battalion would run into trouble if it continued in that direction, so leaving the column where it was, he and Lieutenant English set out on a reconnaissance on foot. They met the battalion executive who told them where they might find the guides, and doubling the column back on itself a second time, finally found the officer guides at the road junction where they had mistakenly been waiting for the column. Several things caused trouble within the unit. Some tank outfit (designation unknown) was in the process of turning around at one of the road junctions passed, and mixed with, and blocked the column.

When they came back down the road in the dark, they ran over several men who had been wounded by the enemy artillery on the road. A two-and-a-half-ton truck also slid off the bank on the side of the road and pinned four men to the tank. To add the confusion they learned that the C Company guide had been wounded and was unavailable. A Company and its attached machine gun platoon was still in fairly good shape and immediately started moving into its assigned positions.

1st Lt. James Sturwold, the executive officer of A Company, 38th Infantry, remembers: "At about dusk, the head of the column reached the rendezvous point and halted. I took the platoon leaders and their platoons to the selected positions. I also took the command post group to the selected command post and put them in position in the basement and ground floor of the buildings. No one in the group knew anything about the situation except that there was a counterattack in progress. The move into position was made in the cold foggy evening through the foot-deep snow that laid on the muddy ground. The infantry started digging in immediately upon reaching the assigned positions. Their digging was accelerated by the sound of heavy small arms and automatic weapons fire in the distance. During the digging process, reports arrived from all platoons that flares of all colors were being observed in portions of the sector to the north and northeast. As the reports of the flares continued to come in, it was indicated that the flares were coming closer, until after about an hour the spent flares were landing in the left flank of the company area."

At about 1930 hours, Major Coopersmith went back down the route to pick up B Company, which had become separated from the column during an especially heavy artillery concentration. Captain Rumsey stayed at the road junction where he had met the guides, while A Company moved past him into position in a southeasterly direction. B Company went straight east to tie into the left flank of A Company. Colonel Mildren hadn't been heard from for some time, so that left Coopersmith in charge. At this time, the condition of the battalion was only fair. A Company was still in pretty good shape. B, C, D, and HQ Companies had suffered heavy casualties. C Company, having been harder hit, was disorganized and, to a certain extent, demoralized. The B Company officer guide volunteered to lead C Company, whose guide had become a casualty, into their positions. As it turned out, C Company was never to occupy these positions.

Lt. George Adams, leader of the 2nd Platoon of C Company, 38th Infantry, recollects: "Along the road moving south from Wahlerscheid, on the night of 17 December, C Company came under heavy artillery and *Nebelwerfer* fire. We lost seventeen men. I stopped with the wounded men seeing to it that they were taken care of, and by the time I was finished making the men comfortable, the rest of C Company had gone and was out of sight. With my own platoon, a machine gun section from D Company and a part of Headquarters Company attached, I took the wrong turn, and we met enemy small arms fire along the way. I decided that we were off the proper route and retraced our steps. Back at the road junction where I took the last turn, there was a U.S. tank in position. I asked the tank commander were the proper route was, and so we caught up finally with the rest of C Company."

At about 1630, the 3rd Platoon, under the command of Lt. Robert Everly of C Company, 38th Infantry, was pulled out of the C Company column that was still on the march for its positions, and was sent to establish a

The Fight for Krinkelt-Rocherath, 17 December

roadblock at the road junction with elements of the service company, which, at that moment, was already under heavy enemy fire.

The remainder of C Company (1st, 2nd, and 4th Platoons), plus Lt. William Trumbley's machine-gun platoon from D Company, waited in houses in town for about an hour in expectation of meeting a guide from battalion. While they were waiting, some men from the 3rd Platoon of C Company and the company headquarters who had been sent to the service company road block reported that they had been attacked by tanks and forced to withdraw. These men remained with the 2nd Platoon.

PFC James Branch of HQ Company, 1st Battalion, 38th Infantry, recalls: "We got orders not to eat any food we might have nor to expend any ammunition needlessly and to wait until dark to move back into Rocherath-Krinkelt where we were cut off. We were to get in groups of ten to twelve men with one machine gun, one bazooka and one radio. We were to take a house and wait for further orders. This is where the chaos began. On our way back machine gun fire ripped through our columns at several points. Tracer bullets were flying everywhere. It was so bad we had to stop and hit the ditches and return fire before we could continue on. Somewhere along the road back my captain, Boyd E. Arrandale, was hit by a shell fragment and was left behind in a barn."

The headquarters column entered the town, and as they made a sharp left turn, they came in the full view of an enemy tank. By the light of a blazing Sherman tank that apparently had been set afire by the enemy tank, the head of the column received a heavy volume of accurate fire from the weapons of the enemy armor: machine gun and tank-mounted high-velocity cannon. When the leading vehicle was fired upon, the column stopped behind a building and the personnel from the headquarters crawled into the new command post building through ditches. There were enemy infantry around the building that had been selected; a patrol of clerks was formed, and the enemy were routed out of the area so that the command post could be set up. The command post was established in the basement, and all the headquarters personnel that could be spared were organized into defense groups and put into position around the command post building.

THE FIRST ATTACK ON KRINKELT, 17 DECEMBER

At the service company's positions, at about 1600, Captain Callier could see some U.S. soldiers running toward the southwest out of the Krinkelter Woods. They seemed to be making for the draw to the southeast of the service company's positions. Enemy artillery, tank, and small-arms fire fell on the men; they reached the draw and the service company people could see some of them fall. The riflemen in the service company were then ordered to open fire on the woods from which the enemy fire was coming.

After opening fire on the enemy-held woods, the road block force pulled back 100 yards to the west of its position. It had no sooner withdrawn than the enemy placed a heavy concentration of artillery and tank fire on the position that had been vacated. The hedgerow that the men had been holding was completely erased as if it had never existed. Immediately following this heavy enemy barrage, Captain Callier drove back to the regimental rear headquarters in his jeep to request some aid at the roadblock. At about 1615 hours, Captain Callier called the forward command post and was assured that the 2nd Battalion was on the way south, and that he was to hold at all costs until relieved.

At about 1800 hours, the enemy attack started with the most intense concentration of artillery and mortar fire that Capt. James Love had so far experienced. The enemy artillery preparation was closely followed by the approach of tanks from the northeast. The farthest advance of the northern most branch of the enemy tank attack was to the north-south road through Krinkelt and Rocherath, but the southern branch of the tanks (*Kampfgruppe Zeiner*) got into Krinkelt and milled around the town generally raising hell. Apparently, the tanks had expected no organized resistance since they had penetrated the thin outpost lines of the 99th Infantry Division. The tanks and the infantry riding them were engaged by small arms fire as soon as they got into the town, and the enemy infantry dismounted and got into the houses.

THE NORTHEAST ATTACK ON ROCHERATH

As the attack started, the 1st Battalion moved into town through the heavy artillery and mortar fire, and part of the battalion got broken up by the fire. At about 1900 hours, Captain Love got word from regiment that C Company was to be attached to the antitank company on its arrival in the town. With a total of about seventy men and officers, C Company arrived in the town at about 1930 hours under the command of Capt. Edward C. Rollings and was positioned in the town.

Joseph Jan Kiss Jr. of C Company relates: "At the crossroads someone tapped me on the shoulder and said, 'What outfit, son?' I said, 'Charlie Company, 38th Regiment, 2nd Division.' I saw two stars on his helmet, but I knew from pictures that he was Gen. Walter Robertson, our division commander. He said, 'Down this road to the left about two blocks to a brown brick house on the end.' I said, 'Yes, sir,' called to my squad and took off. I heard later that he was all over the area trying to build up a good strong line and gather up stragglers. I got into the brick house just as a German tank shot an 88 shell above the door, killing one GI. (The money from his wallet was shredded.) The Germans were calling, 'Hey, Charlie Company,' but we had orders long ago never to answer, as they only wanted to locate you. Although 99th Division and 106th Division GIs who were shot up badly kept coming through our lines for days and yelling to us (especially wounded), we wouldn't answer until we positively identified them."

When Captain Rollings joined the antitank company's defensive position, he told Captain Love that he had a platoon wiped out at the service company roadblock. Rollings's troops went into position to the south of the antitank company in time to break up a tank-infantry attack. C Company was in three houses to the south of the antitank company's command post and had part of a platoon in a house to the north of the command post. In these positions, C Company, the service company, and the two platoons of the antitank company (a three-gun platoon and the mine platoon) held off at least fifteen enemy tanks and about 250 enemy infantry.

Joseph W. Ferron, a loader with the antitank company: "When it was just about dark, a German tank came up the road we were covering. We tried to fire on this tank, but our 57-millimeter antitank gun would not fire. We opened the breechblock very quiet-like and put in another round. They were British shells. The problem was, someone handed the same damned shell back to us three times! Next morning, we looked, and one shell had three firing pin marks in the primer. I was the loader and John W. Manley (now deceased) was the gunner."

At about this time, stragglers from all units of the 2nd and 99th Infantry Divisions were filtering through the positions. Adams's 2nd Platoon of C Company was joined in the house by the crews of two half-tracks, one of which was sitting across the road next to the now enemy-occupied house, and the other parked in the street in front of the platoon defensive position. These men seemed decided to spend the night with C Company, and Adams was glad to have reinforcement of any kind.

About fifteen minutes after the crews of the half-tracks entered the buildings, a German tank pulled up the crossroad, and began firing into the 1st Platoon (C Company) positions which was to the rear of the 2nd Platoon (C Company) house. Adams immediately went to a tank destroyer that he knew to be within easy reach and within firing distance of the tank and attempted to get it to fire on the enemy armor. The tank destroyer's commander said that it would be impossible fo fire on the tank as he could not see it through his telescopic sights in the dark. Adams made the suggestion that he might be able to see the enemy and would try at once, but the tank destroyer commander refused. A compromise was finally reached in which it was decided that the infantry would fire an illuminating shell in the general direction of the tank and the tank destroyer would try its luck.

Sgt. Andrew Paul from C Company had followed Adams out of the house. He became impatient at this palavering and, removing a .30-caliber light machine gun from its mount on a jeep that was stopped outside the platoon position, draped a belt of ammunition around his neck and walked toward the enemy tank firing his machine gun from the hip. Lieutenant Trumbley appeared just then, and as Paul's gun jammed, took the gun from Paul, cleared the stoppage and took up the assault fire himself. A German infantryman from somewhere in the vicinity fired what was thought to be a rifle grenade at Trumbley; it hit the wall of a house about six feet from the lieutenant, wounding him in the right leg with a fragment. The enemy tank, unaffected by all this, fired about six more rounds at the house and moved away. At this time, the American tank destroyer pulled out and was not seen again. During the next ten minutes, Adams posted his platoon and attached units to more advantageous positions. One of the guards in the windows reported a column of two's marching north along the road in front of the platoon positions, which they didn't know it at the time, was probably E Company of the 38th.

All during this attack, in which it appeared that the Germans had difficulty in getting their fire to lift, the enemy artillery was falling heavily all over the whole area, including where their own infantry was operating. Their method of attack seemed to be to illuminate the targets and blind the American gunners with momentary flashes from floodlights that were mounted on the tanks. The effect of the floodlights was terrifying, according to Captain Love. The blinding light followed by the inky blackness of the night, in which no one could see anything, made the battle seem as uncoordinated as if it had been fought in a pit. The enemy seemed to depend heavily on the effect on morale by using a high percentage of tracers in his ammunition; Love estimated most of the firing that was done the first night to be about one-third ball ammunition and the rest tracer.

There was one thing that operated heavily in the favor of the defenders. The enemy seemed to be as confused as the Americans. Most of the action around the antitank company's position was by split groups of Americans fighting equally split-up groups of Germans. For example, at one stage of the fight, there was a group of Germans holding a house that was between two American-held houses. One group of the enemy set up positions in the house directly across from the antitank company's command post.

At about 2000 hours on the night of the seventeenth, Captain Love pulled his men out of the house they had been occupying and into which the enemy was firing antitank grenades, and put them into a field to the north and a little west of the command post, keeping them there until the attack was repulsed. The only men remaining in the house were those of a machine gun crew that remained at their gun on the second floor of the building.

At about 2030 hours, Captain Love got a call from regiment that the 2nd Battalion was on the way down, and that E Company would be the first company in line and would be attached to Love and under his control. Love was ordered to get a guide on the road, meet E Company and place them as he saw fit. When the guide got out to the road, E Company was already there and deployed generally to the east of the antitank position and toward the service company's road block. While E Company was moving into position, Love was busy supervising operations in his own area.

There was a severe attack against his positions, and he had no chance to check E Company. By 2130 hours, the worst part of the attack in the antitank areas was over, perhaps forty-five minutes after it had ended in E Company's area. It was in this attack that the 9th Squad lost its gun (3rd Platoon). While the enemy attack was in progress, the defenders from C Company were firing antitank grenades, throwing hand grenades, and even rocks at the infantry riding the enemy tanks. At the end of the fight in C Company's area, one side of the road was occupied by C Company, the other by the Germans.

The antitank company's command post after the battle. JAMES LOVE

Lt. Ulrich W. Crow of E Company, 38th Infantry, remembers: "We entered a house in the town (Rocherath) to try to warm up. I have never been so cold in my life. The trees would freeze and crack; it sounded like a rifle shot and would scare hell out of you. I had set the machine gun up on a little road that ran down from the house we were in. Later that night I walked down the road to see how the men with the machine gun were doing. I approached my men and asked if everything was all right; they replied that the place was crawling with krauts. We had a sign of 'hammer' and the cosign was 'anvil.' When the machine gunners would hear something they would yell 'hammer,' and whoever was out in the darkness had better reply with 'anvil.' At times during the night I would hear the machine gun go off. At daylight there were a few dead krauts on the road."

Lt. George Adams, leader of the 2nd Platoon of C Company, remembers: "The house across the street that had been abandoned by the squad from the second platoon had been occupied by a small force of the enemy. Hard on the heels of the withdrawal of the enemy tanks, loud voices started to call in German, from the now German-held building across the street. The hailing continued for about five minutes in German then when the enemy realized the calls were achieving nothing, changed. The occupants began calling out in heavily accented English for the C Company men to surrender. The words, as nearly as they could be made out were, 'You Americans had better surrender before we come and kill you; we'll give you five minutes to give up.' No one answered the summons, and at the end of five minutes, the Germans called, 'Are you surrendering?' Again we didn't respond to it."

All those within the 2nd Platoon position who could observe without being seen from the outside were watching the street for futher developments. Following a lapse of several minutes after the calls in English, the platoon could see three or four American uniformed men in the street with shadowy figures behind them. It was immediately deduced that the Germans were using Americans they had captured as shields. One of the men in the street said, 'I'm from B Company, 38th Infantry,' the other said he was from D Company. Adams ordered his riflemen who were posted in the windows of the house to shoot at the shadowy figures behind the Americans in the street, and the whole group pulled back. One of the American riflemen said, 'We don't believe you.' One of the captured Americans answered, 'Captain MacArter (B Company) has been captured and B Company has been captured,' and pled with the little garrison to surrender saying, 'If you don't come out in five minutes, they're going to kill all of us.'

Lieutenant Adams's platoon took a vote and decided to remain where they were until killed or overrun; so the pleas of the Americans or Germans,

The Fight for Krinkelt-Rocherath, 17 December 335

whichever they were, just angered them and didn't persuade them to surrender. In a further attempt to induce the little garrison to give up, a man came out into the street saying, "I'm from B, 38th Infantry," stumbling over the word "infantry." He was shot for his lack of proficiency in English. Adams adds that conversation with the captured men, after they had been retaken by the Americans, indicated that most of the conversation in English was done by Americans, and for the most part, all the Germans said was 'Come out.' The reports indicated that the prisoners were well treated by the Germans.

After the scrap, Love put the company command post group back in the building they had been occupying, set up a guard, and operating on a relief system, got the men to get some sleep. At about 2230 hours, Lt. Edward Sweeny, the assistant reconnaissance officer, went to check the E Company positions and coordinate the defense with the 2nd Battalion. G Company was to go into position to aid in the defense of the regimental headquarters on the right of the antitank company's area. The guard outside the door of the antitank company's command post stopped the G Company column just in time to save them from walking down the road between the C Company positions and the enemy houses across the street. Capt. Edward Farrell, the 2nd Battalion's S-3, and Capt. Joseph E. Skaggs, commander of G Company, were with the company, and Love guided them to the regimental command post.

According to John B. Savard of G Company, "As G Company fought its way into Rocherath, it seemed like the whole town was on fire. The town was being defended by service troops of the 38th Regiment, and it seemed that enemy forces occupied half the houses. Regimental headquarters was under attack, and our first mission was to secure the area around this headquarters."

PFC Harold G. Barkley recalls: "As we proceeded toward the twin villages Rocherath and Krinkelt, we passed a long line of abandoned U.S. vehicles. Intense fighting was taking place off to our left, and tracers streaked the dark sky. Artillery fell everywhere. Rocherath-Krinkelt was under massive tank and infantry assaults. When we reached Rocherath, our company was ordered into the center of town to defend the Regimental command post which was under attack. Fighting seemed to be everywhere. No one knew just where the front line was, for in fact, there wasn't one at that time."

On 17 December, Barkley's commander directed Sergeant Imbody to go up and check the 2nd Platoon. While en route he was surrounded by approximately fifteen of the enemy and told to drop his weapon, which he did. Two of the Germans were standing in front of him and one on either side. The sergeant, thinking he was just about done for, decided he would make a break for freedom. He hit the two German soldiers in front of him, took a swing at a third, and ran for cover, yelling to the 2nd Platoon, a short distance away, to open fire. As a result Imbody gained his freedom, and the fifteen Germans were either killed or captured. For this heroic incident, the sergeant was awarded the Silver Star by Maj. Gen. Walter M. Robertson, the commander of the 2nd Division at that time.

After leaving the command post, Love went toward the E Company positions to check on them, and on the way met two men, both badly wounded, one of whom was practically carrying the other. They said they had been overrun, and with another member of their group, lined up against a wall and shot. They had both feigned death, and when the Germans moved on had started back to try to find the American lines.

Love continued to the E Company position, where he talked to 1st Lt. Allan A. McElroy, commander of E Company, ordered a slight change in E's lines, and over the telephone told the 2nd Battalion's commander, Lt. Col. Jack K. Norris, that E was now under his control. Norris had not been acquainted with the fact at that time. Love's next stop was the service company's position, where he found them getting ready to withdraw, on orders from regiment, to a new service train bivouac area after having been relieved by units of the 2nd Battalion. Love now checked with the 3rd and 4th Gun Squads for casualties, checked the security of the position, and went to bed at about 0100 hours.

At about this time, a bit earlier around midnight, Pvt. Aloysius F. Perkowski, the company commander's radio operator of C Company, arrived at the platoon position of 1st Lieutenant Adams with word that enemy tanks had fired into the building occupied by the 1st Platoon, C Company. He also reported that Captain Rollings, who had been with the first platoon until the tanks started firing, had left them and hadn't been heard from since. Perkowski had gone out to look for the captain but couldn't find him, so stayed in the house with the 2nd Platoon group.

During the rest of the night there was no action except for the everpresent artillery which kept houses blazing; and smoke billowing over the town added to the confusion caused by the mist and light rain that fell intermittently throughout the battle.

THE EASTERN ATTACK ON ROCHERATH
At about 2015 hours, 17 December, while B Company was moving into its position, the battalion commander arrived at the command post to take over. He brought information that Norris perhaps expected to have to fight

The Fight for Krinkelt-Rocherath, 17 December

for Krinkelt-Rocherath. About thirty minutes after the commander came into the command post, the vehicles started to arrive. The vehicle-carried weapons got into A Company in good shape. B Company's weapons had been routed toward their positions and were on their way. C Company—less the platoon that was on the roadblock—was moving northeast along the road toward its assigned positions. Leading C Company were the jeeps loaded with the company's weapons.

At about 2100 hours on 17 December, while the 1st Battalion of the 38th was pulling into Krinkelt to take up defensive positions on the left of 3rd Battalion, K Company received an attack by about five enemy tanks accompanied by eighty infantry (these German troops were breaking out of the Krinkelter Woods and through McKinley's positions at the Lausdell Crossroads). Just prior to the attack, more men from the 99th Division had been pulling back through K Company, men who escaped the heavy fighting in the Krinkelter Woods. K Company had been ordered by Colonel Barsanti to hold its fire until anyone who approached the front was positively identified as enemy. K Company reported a force of tanks and infantry approaching, and Barsanti reiterated the order to hold the fire until the company was positive of the identity of the approaching troops.

The enemy got into the company positions before they were positively identified. Because of this, K Company's left flank was forced back 150 yards. The two leading enemy tanks had their bright spotlights on, and blinded the men in the defensive positions. Capt. Davney D. Rogers of K Company called for artillery fire on his left flank, and the leading enemy tank was hit and put out of action. K Company's support platoon was committed and regained the ground lost to the tank-infantry combination.

A bazooka team polished off the second enemy tank in line, and heavy American artillery fire forced the rest to withdraw. When the enemy was allowed to get close to the K Company positions because they could not be identified, the battle resolved into hand-to-hand fighting. After the fight, K Company found that it had accounted for fifty-two enemy dead on the battlefield. One enemy soldier came so close to the position that he grabbed the barrel of a light machine gun; the gunner was forced to finish him off with a .45 pistol.

The mass of the 2nd Battalion of the 25th and the 12th Anti-Tank Battalion had followed 1st Lieutenant Zeiner after they had driven the Americans out of the Forest of Krinkelt. They followed him closely down the forest road that ran down to Rocherath. Shortly after they left the woods, they ran into the prepared defenses of the Americans in the dark, who, effectively supported by artillery, were able to drive them back. Just east of Rocherath

Members of the 12th Anti-Tank Battalion of the 12th SS Panzer Division *Hitlerjugend*. At left is 1st Lieutenant Wachter, commander of the 2nd Anti-Tank Company, who was killed in action. HELMUT ZEINER

they again ran into superior American troops. The attack was pinned down by very strong artillery fire. Also an attempt to outflank the Americans by going north failed in the face of superior strength with the loss of some tank destroyers. It is suspected that the commander of the 2nd Anti-Tank Company, 1st Lieutenant Wachter, and the commander of the 3rd Platoon, Bitau, were killed in this action. At this time, an estimated two platoons of enemy infantry supported by three tanks hit between A and B Companies from the east (*Kampfgruppe Zeiner*).

1st Lt. James Sturwold, the executive officer of A Company, 38th Infantry, offers this account: "A tank destroyer from a friendly unit had been on the road to the left flank of the company and was expected to withdraw through the company, and the men had been so warned. At about the time the men expected a friendly tank destroyer, approximately 2230, an enemy tank attack developed on the left flank about where the tank destroyer had been reported to be coming in. Lt. Robert Duckart, platoon leader of the 1st Platoon, had gone to the adjacent area on his left flank to contact the platoon of K Company that was there in order to coordinate his platoon's defense with them. Because they had been expecting friendly armor to enter the position, A Co let the enemy tank get into the defensive area without firing on it. When Lieutenant Duckert saw the tank in the lead, and recognized it as enemy, he opened fire with his automatic carbine on the infantry accompanying it. He estimated that there was about a platoon with the tank. There were fifteen dead the next morning in the area where Duckert had fired on them.

"The tank continued to advance, firing its machine gun and its 88-millimeter. It got very close, and Duckert, who all this time was edging closer to the K Company commandp ost foxhole, jumped into it when the tank got too close. The tank ran over the command post with Duckert and several others in it. Fortunately for all concerned, the tread of the tank passed along the longitudinal edge of the hole, pushing dirt in on its occupants. The only injury sustained in this close squeak was Duckert's hand. It was bruised."

S/Sgt. Kenneth Ramago, B Company's communications sergeant, came to B Company's command post to tie in the 2nd Platoon by wire in order to improve and maintain control. He wanted to know where the platoon command post was located, so Sturwold undertook to lead him to it. On the way down, they sweated out being shot by their own men whom they thought might mistake them for enemy. The sentry, who challenged them, recognized them immediately and let them pass. Ramago was left at the platoon command post to carry out his mission.

Sturwold next went to the 1st Platoon to check on them and found that the platoon leader, Lieutenant Duckert, was not in the vicinity. The men indicated that Duckert had not returned from his excursion to the K Company positions. At about 2330, Sturwold placed one squad on the left of the company position to close the gap that existed on the road to the left of A Company, where A was to tie in with K. The 1st Platoon closed to its right to form a more solid position and left its left flank open. After placing this squad in position, Sturwold returned to the company command post where he learned that heavy fighting was in progress on the left flank of the 1st Platoon in the area he just left.

2nd Lt. Carl G. Patterson, leader of the 1st Platoon, remembers: "The 1st Platoon had been hardest hit by enemy artillery on the way south from Wahlerscheid and did not move as a unit. In any case, the 1st Platoon had only just arrived in position when the enemy launched his first tank attack. B Company as a whole, although they had started to organize their positions, had had no time to get holes dug when the enemy tanks arrived."

Patterson had just put the machine gun section into position when the attack hit. The enemy attack, as B Company saw it, divided into two prongs. One of these attempts struck the left flank of the company where the 3rd

Platoon was in position, with the road as the axis of the enemy advance. The second thrust, a frontal assault against the company, struck at the junction of the 2nd and 3rd Platoons, achieved a penetration there, and separated the 2nd Platoon on the right from the rest of the company. The 2nd Platoon leader, Lt. Lloyd Crusius, had worked his way to the left of the company to check with the 3rd Platoon as to their locations, plans of fire and disposition of weapons. He was at the 3rd Platoon command post when the enemy attack started and immediately made his way back to his own platoon to supervise their activity. Crusius reached his platoon, and with them, he fought his way back to G Company of the 2nd Battalion where he stayed for the remainder of the action.

This attack was again repulsed. At about the same time, word was received from battalion that some enemy infantry and a least one tank was heading toward the company position from the direction of the battalion command post to the rear of A Company. The 3rd Platoon already had some men in a house in the northwest of the company. This little force was covering the northwestern approaches to the company positions and acting as a reserve in the position. Lieutenant Sturwold took several of their men and S/Sgt. Milton Bird of the weapons platoon and organized a guard in positions facing the battalion commandp ost on the road along the left (north) flank of the company. The rest of the 3rd Platoon were in houses and took positions in the windows to assist in the defense by covering the approaches with rifle fire. The enemy tanks never got as far as the A Company positions although they fired in its direction.

The 3rd Platoon, with the exception of about seven men, was wiped out as a fighting force; all but the seven are listed as either killed or missing. The little group, including the platoon leader, Lt. John Dailey, were not heard from again. The machine gun section that had been placed by Patterson on the left (east) flank of the company, moved north to the road near the mortar section position at the rear of the 1st Platoon positions. The 1st Platoon fell back in confusion, overrun on all sides by enemy. Part of the 1st Platoon was captured and held in Krinkelt until retaken by a platoon of C Company (Adams). At about 2100 hours, most of the weapons platoon, several D Company men who were without their weapons, two squads from the 1st Platoon, and parts of the 2nd and 3rd Battalions (about forty riflemen), plus about twenty medics from the 2nd Medical Battalion under Sergeant Peterson, formed a defensive position along the line (mixed platoon).

1st Lieutenant Zeiner reported about the attack: "In night and snowstorm I went off with my companions—slowly, so that the infantrymen could keep up with us. Then we came to a fork in the road. We took the left road

The Fight for Krinkelt-Rocherath, 17 December   341

and after about one kilometer we ended up at the edge of Rocherath. Silence! With engines switched off we listened to the night. Nothing! I sent some infantrymen forward as scouts to ascertain whether the village was occupied or had been abandoned. In the meantime I tried to establish radio communications with the following guns, as well as with the commander. Final result: the enemy held the village, and I only had three Panzerjäger IVs behind me. Presumably the others in the snowstorm had taken the right road at the fork."

Immediately after the American line was formed by the composite group of 2nd and 3rd Battalion men, an estimated platoon of enemy infantry attacked the position. The little force held off the enemy attacks, so that the Germans brought up tanks for support. When the presence of enemy tanks became known to Patterson, because there were no anti-tank weapons in the group of Americans, he pulled back to the church to their immediate rear. Here they found two US tanks which they tried to get into position to counter the enemy threat. One of the tanks (741st Tank Battalion), beside which Sergeant Patterson was attempting to lead to a more advantageous position, was hit and put out of action before it could move from the position in which Patterson had found it. Patterson lost track of the second tank and didn't see it again. The crewman of the damaged American tank were injured when their vehicle was hit and were evacuated into the church. Lt. Robert Campbell, the weapons platoon leader who had been wounded earlier, was brought into the shelter of the church also.

Zeiner continues: "Now it came down to taking on the unsuspecting enemy (as the scouting party had reported) and to take the village. From the map I gained an impression of a small village with a church, cemetery and a few houses. Only in front of the church there was some enemy activity visible. Infantry fire. I drove up to the church, right behind me the remaining guns. I had ordered the infantry escort platoon to search all houses and bring any soldiers found down to the street disarmed. Now, however, a dramatic event took place. I stopped my tank destroyer at the crossroads next to the church and ordered the motor stopped in order to orient myself acoustically. Then I heard random shots behind me, and then suddenly to the right of me, seemingly behind the church, the howl of a heavy engine. I only saw the side of the church looming out of the snowcovered churchyard, but suspected an enemy tank was moving behind the church, restarted my engine, pivoted my tank destroyer ninety degrees to the right and in this position I saw a Sherman backing out from behind the church about eight to ten meters away from me. I ordered armor-piercing shell lowered the barrel and when the giant was right in front of my gun, I closed my hatch, and we

Entering Krinkelt from the Lausdell Crossroads—the same direction from which Zeiner entered the town.
HANS WIJERS

Aerial view of Krinkelt. Zeiner approached on the road at bottom-center.

fired at the tank. It immediately caught flame and for a long time it illuminated the scene of the battle and the churchyard. Two men, limping out of the tank, managed to take cover in the church. We left them untouched. In the meantime, I again heard tank noise behind the church, and on the other end of the church square we caught another Sherman. Then a third Sherman was made combat incapable by a following tank destroyer that pivoted to the right."

Cpl. Kelly Layman of B Company, 741st Tank Battalion, tells his story: "At about 10:30 that night, Jerry sent a big combat patrol into town, and we decided we'd better do something about the tanks outside. Ours wouldn't run, so Slod and one of the other tank commanders took off to see what should be done. Just about that time we heard Jerry tanks coming down the road with their doughs. That's when we started to sweat. My tank wouldn't go, so I climbed into A Company's dozer—I mean I tried to—but he had a full crew and was moving out. I then decided to go over to the other tank. The sergeant (Sladkowski) had gone, so I climbed in the turret and wound up in the bow gunner's seat. The A Company tank had moved out and hadn't gone fifty yards, when they set him on fire, and the crew bailed out. In our tank, we didn't know that there was a Jerry tank only thirty yards to the right rear of us, but we did know about the one directly in front of us. It was the one on our right that hit us!

"We had only backed up about ten feet, when they let go with an HE, and blew our right track off. We sat there for a couple of seconds trying to move, but it was no good. They hit us again with another HE, in the turret, and still we sat there! But when they put an armor piercing through our motor compartment and set us on fire, it was time to bail out, which we did. An A Company man and I ran into the church, and a medic put some shaving cream on our burns, it's the only thing he had; he said he was sorry he couldn't do more, but it sure felt soothing."

The church was set up as a fort, and by the light of burning vehicles and houses, Patterson's little command kept the enemy away from the position with small arms fire. The enemy in this engagement could do little damage to the church. There was too much light in the neighborhood, and as Paterson found out later, some firing came from the vicinity of the 1st Battalion command post which was just across the street.

1st Lt. James Sturwold resumes his account: "There had been contact men outposts sent out to the front to intercept any enemy attempts to infiltrate. Of the Germans accompanying the tank, all were not killed or driven to cover; the portion in line with the left flank of the left platoon continued to advance aggressively. Some of these troops were of the SS and hit Duckert's platoon, machine gunning the area heavily and throwing potato masher grenades. The contact men, having seen that the attack was a massed one rather than just infiltration, withdrew to the platoon proper. Here they too took up fighting positions with better cover.

A Jagdpanzer IV as seen during the Normandy campaign. HELMUT ZEINER

The command post of Col. Frank T. Mildren's 1st Battalion, 38th Infantry.
DAN STYLES

The 38th Infantry's 1st Battalion's command post in Krinkelt.

"During the action, one of the SS men, trying or using an American soldier as a shield and firing the American's sub-machine gun, tried to get into the company positions. Two outposts passed the pair when the captive American answered their challenges. The third had a nervous trigger finger, and seeing two men advancing from what he knew to be the enemy direction shot them both. All through this hot action, there was little artillery or mortar fire, and the right flank of the company was quiet. The German attempt to get through was frustrated."

During this fighting, several soldiers from the 99th Division and from the 23rd Infantry came into the company area along the road. Fortunately for the men concerned, the A Company men who saw them first held their fire and didn't shoot. Sturwold remained in the positions that he had set up with the 3rd Platoon until about 0330 on the eighteenth, and then again returned to the company command post.

After the enemy attacks described above were repulsed, there was no further activity along the company front until about 0200 or 0300 when the 2nd Platoon reported noise of shouting and tanks on the hill to their front. Capt. Roy White, the company commander, called for artillery fire on the hill which was delivered first as a heavy concentration and then as harassing fire which continued through the night and next morning.

A destroyed Sherman of the 741st Tank Battalion, which fell victim to *Kampfgruppe Zeiner*.
JESS STYLES

The comamand of Col Frank T. Mildren's battalion. JESS STYLES

Joseph Jan Kiss Jr. of C Company, 38th Infantry remembers: "Three German tanks knocked out three of our tanks by the church which looked like a tank graveyard. German artillery and *Nebelwerfer* (six-barrel rockets) poured it on. The night of the seventeenth, Captain Rollings had another guy and me hook antitank mines to telephone wires across the road in a ditch. We hid in the cellar across the street. If enemy tanks came down the road we were to pull the wire and drag the mines onto the road in front of them. None came."

1st Lieutenant Zeiner continues his story: "Now there was silence. I dismounted and saw a whole mass of freezing Negroes, partially in pajamas or similar clothing about 100 meters behind me between both tank destroyers that followed me, pressed together on the street, guarded by our infantry. I was really sorry for the guys and ordered to assemble all prisoners into a house and then block the house from the outside. This spared me the guarding of the prisoners, which probably had not been necessary, as the prisoners were completely demoralized, shocked by the events of the night. A white American officer assured me that all his men no longer had any weapons and would do all I required of them. He then also stayed in the aforementioned house.

After a short discussion of the situation with the infantry commanders and my gun commanders I wanted to know how much fuel and ammunition we still had. I now went down to my AFV and unsuspectingly suddenly was fired at from a house. It was armor-piercing ammunition, probably from an anti-tank rifle. I pivoted my gun towards the firing, and after about half an hour, nothing moved there anymore. By firing high-explosive shells at the firing we seemingly had established quiet. Then the reports of the gun commanders arrived, and on the basis of this catastrophic situation, I radioed for resupply of fuel and ammunition".

Cpl. Kelly Layman remembers: "We lay in the church all night listening to the guns firing, and the krauts hollering, and all that stuff just raising cain. It started to quiet down about five in the morning, and at seven or eight I found K.V., and we started to look for the command post. We had gone about fifty yards, and were talking with some doughboys, asking if they knew where our command post was. They didn't know and just then it started again. Somebody shouted, 'Here come some Panther tanks!' We headed for a house and tried to find a cellar but couldn't, so we just sat there and waited. In the same house there were some antitank boys from the 23rd Regiment, and they loaded up three bazookas and were waiting."

Harold L. Hoffer, commander of the reconnaissance company of the 644th Tank Destroyer Battalion, recounts: "In the early evening hours of 17 December, several German tanks moved in to the south edge of Krinkelt, halted at the church which appeared to be a key artery some 100 yards from our command post, a typical two story rural dwelling. The tanks proceeded to shoot up our exposed reconnaissance vehicles and knock out communications. Although several of our men jumped into our M20s and attempted to fire their .50-caliber machine guns at the tanks, I ordered them out of the vehicles just before the 75s destroyed the vehicles."

B Company, which arrived around 2130 hours, entered the action on the left of it. Before they could dig in, both companies were hit by an attack by tanks [tank destroyers] and infantry from a northeasterly direction. A Company let the tank destroyers roll through, opened fire on the following infantry and could hold it off; B Company was broken, and only one platoon managed to escape. The survivors together with the remains of C Company withdrew toward the regimental command post in Rocherath and joined the anti-tank company in the battle for the village.

Joel Martinez of the 1st Battalion of the 38th Infantry describes his actions: "We got into a basement (battalion headquarters) in a house about 100 yards from the only church there at a forkroad. Soon it got pretty dark. The situation outside was a mess. There were bullets flying almost everywhere. Suddenly, a tank pulled up outside and the Germans were hollering, 'Surrender yanks, surrender yanks.' Well, some of the guys must have scared them because they pulled away. There were a couple of guys, a lieutenant and a Sergeant Baker, I believe from HQ Company, whom to me were truly brave. They scouted around outside and picked up a couple of machine guns and some ammo. An infantry major came to me and told me I was going on an outpost, and I told him I was not an infantryman; he said, 'You are now,' and out I went. I was put out next to a wall. Bullets hitting it made a scary thud. Somehow I made out a shadow coming toward me and I whispered, 'Claw'— no answer. I did it again, no answer. I was about to squeeze the trigger, when the word 'Hammer' came from the shadow. I told the lieutenant he'd been just thirty seconds from death. Sometime in the night, I was relieved from this post, and then again still dark. A young guy and I were put on behind a machine gun, behind the corner of the command post house. The gun was atop of a jeep hood (no tripod available). A few Germans tried coming in calling out, '*Kamerad, Kamerad.*' I opened up on them."

Harold L. Hoffer continues: "So went the night, the quiet winter coldness, the uncertainty, the Germans strolling the streets from house to house. The company was divided, half in the small dwelling mentioned and half in a similar dwelling just across the narrow street. We saw no other American soldiers, and our battalion commander, Lt. Col. Ephriam F. Graham Jr., informed me that we were pretty much alone in Krinkelt. Colonel Graham ordered that we not expose ourselves during the night but to await the morning. No one slept. I spent most of the night on the second floor of the command post with Cpl. Monroe S. Block as my runner. Several German soldiers entered the house across the street where half of our company was located, but our troops remained concealed, and the Germans shortly came back into the street. Sometime during the night, a tank shot the corner off the room in which I was standing. I was hit in the mouth with a piece of brick or stone, but no one was otherwise injured. At about 0500 hours, the Germans noisily prepared and ate their breakfast, seemingly confident that no American GIs were anywhere near. Then they climbed in their tanks and moved back east."

Harold's twin brother, Capt. Gerald L. Hoffer, the battalion's motor officer, who was in Sourbrodt during the fighting in Krinkelt, writes: "At the time of Hof's excitement in Krinkelt-Rocherath, I was the battalion motor officer in Sourbrodt, several miles west of Krinkelt. I was living in a nice three-story home. The twenty mechanics were replacing M10 engines, when required, in freezing cold outdoors. I still do not know how they did it. On the morning of 17 December, I was nonchalantly delivering a vehicle to our company in Krinkelt. Just west of town, I was unable to proceed as GI vehicles clogged the road as far as I could see to the east. The drivers were all prone with weapons pointed toward Krinkelt, and for the first time, I knew that the Germans had broken through and that Harold was surrounded. It was a terrible fear as I returned to the battalion headquarters to inform the colonel. The next morning in Berg, who walked in with a puffed lip? Harold—Thank God! What an experience he had. I will always have a high regard for all of those 644 heroes who were eyeball to eyeball with the Krauts, fighting for their lives, and their buddies lives during those terrible days."

Colonel Barsanti of the 3rd Battalion was ordered to send a platoon from I Company (south of Krinkelt) to the north end of Rocherath to aid the regimental antitank company (Captain Love) that was engaged in a desperate fight. When this platoon reached the church in the center of Krinkelt, it was fired on by direct fire from three German tanks. Lt. John L. Kennedy, the battalion S-2, was leading the platoon up to the town and to the antitank company's positions, and the men were dispersed when the tank fired on them. The platoon was fully reorganized and continued on its assigned mission leaving no reserve in the company.

The unit journal of the 9th Infantry recorded the following for 17 December:

> 2100 hours: "Artillery radio has received notice that tanks have broken through our red battalion in westerly direction toward Rocherath."
> 2240 hours: "Colonel Graham says that the Krauts with strong forces are in Rocherath and Krinkelt."
> 2245 hours: "One enemy tank spotted in the village; others heard outside the village to the east and northeast. 'Krauts' are in the village in some strength. C Company of the tank destroyers tries to ascertain where they are in order to destroy them . . ."

The journal of the 38th Infantry gives the following details:

> 1630 hours: "Tiger tanks are coming from the woods towards the service company. The 23rd withdraws from the wood. Our tanks have disappeared."
> 1633 hours: "Two of our tanks are reported as having been killed by the Jerries."
> 1650 hours: "The enemy has broken through Tuttle's battalion. Tuttle's battalion is severely disrupted. A platoon of tank destroyers is on its way to us."

2145 hours: "B and C Companies are still trying to reach the positions they were ordered to. Are being shelled. Enemy Panzers and infantry have broken into the village from the east. Have advanced up to the command post. Staff members killed numerous infantrymen, forced a Panzer to withdraw, after it had fired three 88-millimeter rounds into the house that contained the command post, after ramming the house previously."

2315 hours: "Sergeant Buckenby observed three Tiger tanks, five groups of enemy infantry of each 150, 20, 20, 20, 18 and 20 men penetrate into Rocherath to the vicinity of the church, while he himself was hidden in an hole on the north-south street through Rocherath. He also saw 27 U.S. prisoners march towards the church."

As the evening wore on, the staff of the 38th Infantry Regiment reached Rocherath. The houses planned to be used by the command post were occupied by German grenadiers and had to be retaken first.

SUMMARY

At 2100 hours, a German attack from the east on Krinkelt was reported. In one sector it was beaten off by fire of artillery, mortars and small arms. In another sector three panzers and a company of infantry advanced up to the rear area positions, from where they finally were forced back by units of the 3rd Battalion. It is possible that the attack on Krinkelt, which was launched farther to the south, was carried out by elements of the 1st Battalion, 25th Regiment. The three panzers and the accompanying grenadiers certainly were the small combat group of 1st Lieutenant Zeiner.

The combat area of the villages of Krinkelt-Rocherath by the late evening yields the following image: The 1st and 3rd Battalions of the 393rd Infantry had been destroyed by the attacks on 16 and 17 December. Their remains withdrew in a chaotic manner leaving behind material, were reassembled and brought back to Elsenborn for reformation and defense.

The 1st Battalion, 38th Infantry, had been followed by the 2nd Battalion. At 1900 hours, it took positions about 400 meters north of Rocherath, forming up on the 2nd Battalion, 9th Infantry. There it was subjected to lively artillery and machine-gun fire. G Company was detached to protect the regimental command post.

The situation of the weak forces that had been broken through into Rocherath and Krinkelt had worsened over the night of 17–18 December. In the face of the great enemy superiority, which here consisted of three battalions of infantry, anti-tank guns, tanks and tank-destroyers, this was not a surprise.

Zeiner reported on this: "It was about 0200 hours at night (18 December 1944). We try at intervals to reestablish radio contact with our own tank destroyer battalion. Then we very briefly made contact with the signals of a Waffen-SS panzer regiment. The talk was inconclusive as we were jammed continuously. Ammunition, fuel and hot coffee would have done the trick for us. We took up an all-round defense. According to the infantry scouts the small village was a lot larger than we originally had assumed. In the western most sector the enemy infantry still held out; at dawn we heard track and engine noises. It was about six o'clock in the morning when I had to take a very hard decision. I still had no radio contact with battalion, had no motorcycle despatch riders, didn't know where our battalion was, probably two to three kilometers behind us in the woods, which we had penetrated the day before. I only had about forty men infantry left and my tank destroyers only had about ten high-explosive shells left. We only had a small supply of fuel as well. And then we had made about eighty prisoners. Tactically our situation in the center of the village would be hopeless when confronted with an infantry attack. Was I to lose my men, the tank destroyers—they were all operational—and the prisoners, when the enemy would show the true strength of this ridiculous enemy in the morning light? So the all-round defense was abolished. A new pocket was formed, but with the prisoners in the middle and the tank destroyers out in front and to the rear. In the meantime visibility had increased. I hoped to make visible contact with German units at the edge of the woods where they were according to the map. So we leave our old positions in Rocherath and take up positions about 300 meters east of the eastern edge. Hardly had we arrived there, a dense hail of enemy projectiles began. But we also felt another sensation. We see the edge of the woods, and there in a broad formation one tank after another shows up. They are German ones. We wave cloths to prevent us being shot by our own comrades and in the process forget to take care of the phosphorus shells that are exploding all around us. Our prisoners crawled under the tank destroyers to take cover. Our infantry did likewise."

The confused situation around Krinkelt-Rocherath is also illustrated by the report of the medic of the tank destroyer company, Benno Zoll. He wrote: "The village was still partially occupied by the Americans. At the edge of the village there was a ruin with a large Red Cross flag. I thought that the cellar would be empty and went down into it. To my amazement I saw that there were still five Americans there. One of the Americans spoke perfectly German. He enquired of me how things would be in German captivity. They gave me cigarettes, chocolate and their medical material, as they certainly would be relieved of this in German captivity. They told me that all of them were conscientious objectors, but had been trained as medics and now had to prove themselves in the front lines. I then again went up to the street, to look for our men. To my horror I noted that the village still was full of Americans and people fired from all cellar holes. Our tank destroyers had vanished. Luckily I spotted some men from our infantry escort and asked them what was going on. They said: 'Get the hell out of here or the Yanks will get you!' I joined up with them. After a while we reached our own troops. What would the American medics have thought?"

CHAPTER 8

The Second Attempt to Seize Krinkelt-Rocherath, 18 December

During the night, all the German tanks in the town of Krinkelt except one had been finished off. The last one, a lone Panzer IV, was in front of the church firing at the 3rd Battalion's command post and was causing a lot of discomfort with its machine gun as well as its tank fire. Colonel Barsanti, the commander of the 3rd Battalion ordered five bazooka teams sent out to get to the tank and stop its firing. Two of the teams got direct hits on the tank but didn't knock it out. Apparently, the attempts to finish it off worried the tank crew so that they decided to make a run for it. The tank came full speed in the direction of Krinkelt. At that moment, Maj. Vivian G. Paul, regimental S-4, left the command post, and got into his jeep to go to regiment. As he got into his vehicle, the enemy tank rounded the corner going at high speed. Major Paul and his driver left the jeep and rolled into the ditch on the side of the road. The tank rolled over the jeep mashing it flat. As the tank hit the jeep, one of the 57-millimeter guns belonging to the 3rd Bn hit the tank and broke its traversing mechanism. The tank continued on its way with the turret swinging wildly, completely out of control. Lt. Fred Sutton, the battalion's assistant S-3, was in the street. He got an American tank to open fire on the enemy tank, but it missed.

At the command post, and facing Büllingen, Barsanti had a tank destroyer for protection. The tank destroyer put three rounds into the tail of the tank as it passed in front of L Company's command post. L Company personnel, with rifle and small-arms fire, picked off all of the enemy tank crew as they attempted to leave the tank; none escaped.

About midnight on 17 December, A Company of the 38th Infantry received word from the battalion that elements of the 99th Division and the 23rd Infantry would probably withdraw through the company area and that they should on the lookout for them. Shortly after the call was received, the right (second) platoon reported a convoy of vehicles approaching from the enemy direction. The guards on the road halted the convoy which was immediately indentified as belonging to the 99th Division. The head of the

The Second Attempt to Seize Krinkelt-Rocherath, 18 December

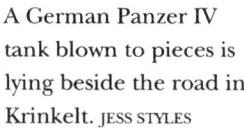
A German Panzer IV tank blown to pieces is lying beside the road in Krinkelt. JESS STYLES

column stopped at the company command post, and two majors from the outfit came in to make inquiries as to the condition of the routes of withdrawal toward Elsenborn, the location of the enemy, and the positions of friendly units. They were given all the information at hand; that the enemy were all around and in Krinkelt-Rocherath, and that there was an enemy tank in the vicinity of the command post firing across the only route of egress left open. The two majors hesitated in view of the danger and sent a bazooka team after the enemy tank. They left to make a reconnaisance of the route.

Colonel Riley, the regimental commander, came into the company command post soon after the two majors departed and also requested information. Captain White repeated what he had told the two majors. The colonel, hearing the report of the enemy tank, decided to dismount the men and, leaving the vehicles where they were, to proceed to Elsenborn on foot cross country. He tried to persuade White to release the only map in the company to him, which White refused to do. While the colonel was talking to White, the two majors, apparently having completed the reconnaisance to their satisfaction, returned to the column, gave the men the order to mount and move off. The column started and continued moving through the positions all during the night. In all, there were about 100 vehicles in the column, of which only about four (Sturwold wasn't sure of the number, but thought four was about correct) were lost to the enemy.

On 18 December, the I SS Panzer Corps ordered the continuation of the attack on Krinkelt-Rocherath using the 1st Panzer Battalion under command of the 12th SS Panzer Division. Between Neuhof and Losheimergraben, the Reich Road was to be cleared as soon as possible from mines and other obstacles, so that the axis of advance C could be used. The 12th Volksgrenadier Division was ordered to take Mürringen and Hünningen, to continue the attack on Wirtzfeld and to advance on Bütgenbach from Büllingen. On its left flank, the 3rd Fallschirmjäger Division was to advance in the Faymonville area. The 1st SS Panzer Division was ordered to follow *Kampfgruppe Peiper* on two of the axes of advance and to join up with it; Peiper was to take Stavelot and and then break through to the Meuse.

During the night of 17 December, the 1st Panzer Battalion, consisting of the 1st and 3rd Panther Companies and the 5th and 6th Panzer IV Companies, was to move from the Blumenthal area (2 kilometers northeast of Hellenthal) over the Reich Road via Hellenthal, Hollerath, and Miescheider Heide to the fork in the roads west of Udenbreth, or via the bend in the road at Hollerath. Then, over the forest track leading to the northwest to the assembly area in the Fôret Communale de Rocherath. The battalion was ordered to destroy the enemy in Rocherath and Krinkelt in co-operation with the reinforced 25th Regiment and the 12th Tank Destroyer Battalion operating with it, and subsequently to advance on Elsenborn. The reconnaissance battalion was to support the attack on Krinkelt from the south as soon as Mürringen had been taken by the 12th Volksgrenadier Division. The 560th Heavy Tank Destroyer Battalion, the 3rd Half-Track Battalion of the 26th Regiment, and the marching group of the bulk of the 26th Regiment, were to stand by to advance down the Advance Route C as soon as the obstacles were removed and Mürringen and Hünningen were taken. The 12th Artillery Regiment and 12th Rocket Battalion were to support the attack from their positions. The division established an advanced command post in a western wall bunker directly north of the bend in the road west of Hollerath.

The small combat group of 1st Lieutenant Zeiner could not accompany the attack of the panzer battalion; they had to refill their tanks, replenish their ammunition and catch some sleep. To do this the group was withdrawn, and the escorted prisoners were marched off to a prisoner collection point. The attack of the 1st Panzer Battalion began shortly before it got bright. The battalion had to make use of the improvised road from Point 634 to Rocherath, as minefields had been reported on both sides of the track. They drove in single file with the 1st Company leading, followed by the 3rd, 5th, and 6th Companies.

At about 0100 on 18 December, Colonel McKinley, at the Lausdell Crossroads, succeeded in establishing telephone communication with the 38th Infantry. Sometime before dawn, the battalion received instructions to withdraw at first light, or whenever Lt. Col. Jack Norris's 2nd Battalion, 38th Infantry, was in position behind them. The occupation of defensive positions by Norris's battalion was to govern the withdrawal of McKinley's men, and the 1st Battalion, 9th Infantry, was to hold position until instructed by the 2nd Battalion, 38th Infantry, that the time was right for withdrawal.

The Second Attempt to Seize Krinkelt-Rocherath, 18 December

At first light, the enemy renewed his tank-infantry attacks with about twelve tanks and the usual platoon of infantry with each tank. The weather, hazy and drizzly, was ideal from the German point of view. The visibility was practically nil. Normal barrages were fired by the US artillery, and the enemy attack was again halted. At about 0800 hours, enemy tanks completely overran the front line companies. The infantry accompanying the tanks fanned out, and in the melée following, enemy tanks came to within twenty feet of American infantry; the fighting then resolved into hand-to-hand fighting and grenade battles. At this time the only communication with B Company, 1st Battalion, 9th Infantry, was by runner, so that control was poor. The left platoon of B was out of antitank ammunition; perhaps because of this six or seven men from that platoon broke and started to run toward the rear. This was reported via C Company; McKinley personally met and stopped these men and sent them back to the platoon.

Capt. Götz Grossjohann, commander of the 6th Company, reported: "When the fog lifted at dawn the attack was launched. In front of us the Panther companies entered the village of Rocherath. My company was at the end of the battalion. I thought I spotted movement at the edge of the woods halfway to the right in front of us, and suspected an enemy anti-tank gun. In order to have a better view, I opened my turret hatch and aimed my binoculars at the edge of the wood. At this moment an infantry projectile hit me. Via radio I transferred command of the company to 2nd Lieutenant Pucher."

1st Lt. Roy Allen of B Company, 1st Battalion, 9th Infantry, recalls: "The tanks started to approach our position at about 0700 hours on 18 December. As they approached the mines (we laid there the evening before), they could see the other two tanks which had been knocked out, and they proceeded to go through the field. The leading tank was hit by a bazooka and stopped. However, it kept on firing both its machine guns and a large turret gun. Lieutenant Milesnick of B Company went forward, brought other bazookas into position and fired four rounds at the tank. These did not penetrate. During the time the bazooka was being fired the tank was firing its machine guns and turret gun in the general direction of our company. Milesnick was hit in the leg. Sgt. Odie Bone of B Company and a group of about four others obtained gasoline from a broken half-track, poured it on the tank, and set it afire. During this time the machine gunners of D Company were returning fire at the tank. As the tank occupants opened the hatch of the tank, they were shot by the machine gunners.

"I saw one heavy machine gun of D Company knocked out by the tank before the Germans left it. The men who had been firing the machine gun immediately got another set up in position and continued to fire. Sgt. Earlie W. Moncrief of B Company (MIA) and myself placed mines on another small road we thought may possibly used by the Germans for their tanks. During this time we were receiving fire from enemy machine guns. The riflemen of B Company fired at the turret men of the enemy tanks as they proceeded to come down the road. One American tank, which was operated by Germans, was stopped by the unit on B Company's right flank. Two Germans left this tank. One was shot by D Company, and I shot the other. I personally searched this man to be positive he was German. The men of B Company next to the road our tanks were defending did not leave their position until they were ordered to do so, although they were receiving much fire from enemy tanks and infantrymen."

T/Sgt. Edwin Norris of K Company, 9th Infantry, remembers: "Throughout the night of 17 December and the day of 18 December, the Germans came with their big tanks, artillery, rockets, mortars, hand grenades and waves of infantry. Only one time did any Americans start to run, and only after they ran out of ammunition and rockets for their bazookas. Colonel McKinley stopped them, and they fought them hand to hand with rifle butts and bayonets. The Germans were tough people. They were jumping over their dead and kept coming, but were stopped by Americans that would not give up and held off the 6th Panzer Army and destroyed a big part of it. I was taken off the line sometime on 18 December 1944, unconscious and diagnosed with hypothermia."

At about 0900 hours, A Company reported themselves completely overrun by tanks and infantry. The company commander, Lt. Stephen E. Truppner said that his men had holes and that he wanted the artillery poured in on his own position, because the situation was hopeless anyway. He said they would duck into their holes and sweat it out. This was the last that was ever heard from Truppner. With the concentration as called for by Truppner, an artillery battalion for thirty minutes, the German attack in that sector was stopped. Twelve men from A Company's machine-gun section was all that got through to the American lines; for that company, it was all over.

According to PFC Frank E. Royer of K Company, 9th Infantry, "On 18 December, morning came and there were more German tanks, and the artillery got bad. In books I read that the lieutenant called for our own artillery on our position, because they were libel to get more tanks or Germans than they would us. Because we were in our holes, and the Germans weren't so much. So we had real bad artillery fire of our own American artillery. And we also had chemical mortars that make a kind of smoke, when it gets on your clothes it kind of burns a hole. It doesn't stop until it gets to the skin, then it burns; they're kind of bad. But some of those they were shooting were close to us, but they didn't hit us or nothing. I guess. I ended up with some on my clothes later on, because at dark, they glow."

At about 1000 hours, orders were received that the withdrawal would begin at 1300 hours. McKinley's estimate of the situation was that he would be unable to get his troops out from very close contact with the enemy. Fate, however, intervened. Lt. Eugene Hinski, the antitank platoon leader saw four tanks from A Company, 741st Tank Battalion, moving down the road, intercepted them and asked them if they would like to do some fighting. The tank platoon leader said, "Hell yes," and Hinski directed him to the battalion commander.

McKinley was very pleasantly surprised to see the four tanks, for in them he saw salvation. With his S-3, Captain Harvey, McKinley planned a tank counterattack and withdrawal of the battalion under its cover. It was known that there were four enemy tanks covering the withdrawal route. Lieutenant Barcaloni, the tank platoon leader, was to split his platoon pulling it in, two tanks from the right and two from the left on either side of the route to withdrawal. The tanks on the right were to act as decoys and attract the attention of the German tanks. The plan worked. The left section got three hits on one enemy tank and two in a second one. The other two enemy tanks took off toward Rocherath and a shot in the rear of one of them disabled. The last one "ran like hell toward Rocherath."

Somewhere in the vicinity of Lausdell, the German 2nd Battalion of the 25th joined up, which had been left lying there since the previous night; to the left of the road presumably the 1st of the 25th was advancing. The attack in the fog first hit the 1st Battalion, 9th Infantry, which had been dug in at Lausdell facing east and south. The first tanks could roll on into the village of Rocherath. While American artillery was fiercely bombarding the field road, the grenadiers attacked and penetrated the American positions. Bitter man-to-man fighting ensued. For the time being the grenadiers did not manage to create a breakthrough. When the fog lifted at about 0830 hours, more tanks rolled down the field road and fired their machineguns at the American holes along the road. The grenadiers stormed forward, and A Company was overrrun. They requested artillery suppport; for half an hour an artillery battalion fired on this sector. Also G Company, which was attached to the 1st Battalion, 9th Infantry, was broken up. Only one officer and twenty-two men escaped from the two companies; both other companies managed to hold their positions.

The 2nd Battalion, 38th Infantry, pulled over to the east from its position north of Rocherath in order to establish a back-up position behind the 1st Battalion, 9th Infantry, and allow it to withdraw. A platoon of Sherman tanks of the 741st Tank Battalion showed up unexpectedly and killed two tanks, but could not break through to the encircled company. Under then tanks' protective fire, the remains of the company withdrew, but followed closely by the grenadiers. The tanks and grenadiers that had broken into the northern part of Rocherath were engaged in heavy fighting with the 1st and 2nd Battalions, 38th Infantry, which lasted the entire morning.

One of the men in McKinley's group was PFC William A. Soderman, who for his actions received the Medal of Honor. His citation reads: "Armed with a bazooka, he defended a key road junction near Rocherath, Belgium, on 17 December 1944, during the German Ardennes counteroffensive. After a heavy artillery barrage had wounded and forced the withdrawal of his assistant, he heard enemy tanks approaching the position where he calmly waited in the gathering darkness of early evening until the five Mark V tanks which made up the hostile force were within point-blank range. He then stood up, completely disregarding the firepower that could be brought to bear upon him, and launched a rocket into the lead tank, setting it afire and forcing its crew to abandon it as the other tanks pressed on before Pfc Soderman could reload. The daring bazooka man remained at his post all night under severe artillery, mortar, and machine-gun fire, awaiting the next onslaught, which was made shortly after dawn by five more tanks. Running along a ditch to meet them, he reached an advantageous point and there leaped to the road in full view of the tank gunners, deliberately aimed his weapon and disabled the lead tank. The other vehicles, thwarted by a deep ditch in their attempt to go around the crippled machine, withdrew. While returning to his post Private First Class Soderman, braving heavy fire to attack an enemy infantry platoon from close range, killed at least three Germans and wounded several others with a round from his bazooka. By this time, enemy pressure had made Company K's position untenable. Orders were issued for withdrawal to an assembly area, where Private First Class Soderman was located when he once more heard enemy tanks approaching. Knowing that elements of the company had not completed their disengaging maneuver and were consequently extremely vulnerable to an armored attack, he hurried from his comparatively safe position to meet the tanks. Once more he disabled the lead tank with a single rocket, his last; but before he could reach cover, machine gun bullets from the tank ripped into his right shoulder. Unarmed and seriously wounded he dragged himself along a ditch to the American lines and was evacuated. Through his unfaltering courage against overwhelming odds, Private First Class Soderman contributed in great measure to the defense of Rocherath, exhibiting to a superlative degree the intrepidity and heroism with which American soldiers met and smashed the savage power of the last great German offensive."

The Second Attempt to Seize Krinkelt-Rocherath, 18 December

1st Lt. Roy Allen, B Company, 1st Battalion, 9th Infantry, remembers: "Before we withdrew from the position, it was impossible to communicate with the artillery so as to instruct them where to place their fire. This was due to the Germans jamming our radio set. I stayed in position with approximately fourteen men of B Company and fired back at German infantrymen who turned to cross the road to our front. None of the men hesitated to comply with orders, and although a German tank did cut off our escape to the rear, the men stayed in position and returned fire until ordered back by the battalion commander. We pulled back 200 yards to higher ground and again set up a defensive position, where as it grew light, we were to cover the road by fire. This could not be done by night. From this position we could prevent German infantrymen from crossing the road; however, it was impossible for us to stop the tanks. During the hours of darkness the men did return fire although it meant death for many of them because they gave away their position. Sergeant Lindquist of B Company was twelve feet from a German tank. He saw a German approaching the hedgerow, behind which he was stationed, and very near other men of B Company. Although Lindquist had to expose himself to the tank, he shot this German. At the same time, the machine gun on the tank opened up and killed Lindquist."

When the enemy tanks left, the battalion started its withdrawal, which was completed in twenty minutes. The battalion commander and S-3 were the last to leave the area, and according to McKinley, "The Heinies were literally screaming 'Hände Hoch' from the hedgerows as they withdrew."

When noses were counted, A Company had three men, B had twenty-seven, C had forty or more, D got out with sixty, and K, which was attached, had twelve. Under cover of darkness that night seven more men from A Company came back with reports of having seen a column of American prisoners of war being marched back toward the German rear. When the battalion assembled in Rocherath, it was found that of the total battalion strength of 600 men that began the fight, 197 were left, including attachments. There was only enough to organize six rifle squads from the entire battalion.

PFC Frank E. Royer resumes his story: "There was a quite a few guys killed then. It was around 1230 hours. The German tanks went up to the only house there was. That was where the captain (Capt. Jack Garvey) had his company command post, and that was a bad move on his, but he didn't know it was going to be like this. So the German tanks went right up to the door. The captain and a couple of guys came out. By then they had us where you hardly couldn't shoot. Our ammunition, by that time we were low. There were a couple of guys that got out of their hole, and the Germans didn't shoot them. I was with a guy named E. J. 'Sandy' Sanders. He was from South

Carolina. He was a private like me. We said, 'Well, what do we do?' You know? So we just decided, 'Well, OK, they didn't shoot them,' so we got up. I think there was about ten of us altogether that got captured with the captain and the lieutenant. So we started walking. The Germans, they always looked for wristwatches, but I had slid mine up my arm up above mu shirt. I showed my elbow. It looked there wasn't one on, but I had my watch up above my elbow. So I saved my watch, I brought it home, I still got it!"

Lawrence Shoemaker, a runner in the 2nd Platoon of K Company, 9th Infantry, observes: "I saw American soldiers being captured on the morning of the eighteenth. Some of these men were wounded. The were a team of artillery forward observers and spotters. They were about fifty yards from the farmhouse. The enemy had completely surrounded K Company during the night, we were out of ammo. A German tank moved up in front of the farmhouse as asked that we surrender or they would blow the farmhouse down. Trying to save the lives of his men, Captain Garvey asked for a German officer in which to surrender. A storm troopers officer and his troops came to the house around 1330 hours and asked for the officer in charge. Capt. Jack Garvey surrendered K Company, 9th Infantry, to the Germans."

At about 1900 hours on 18 December, after following a circuituous route, the battalion assembled in Krinkelt in one house. General Robertson told McKinley to see the men got all possible sleep; since it was the only reserve left in the division, it would probably have to launch a counterattack the next morning. The reminder of the men who stayed had hot chow and slept there. The A&P Platoon joined the 3rd Battalion in Wirtzfeld at about 0800 hours on 19 December.

The men who did get back hadn't expected ever to get out, and knowing they had orders to hold at all costs, considered themselves fortunate still to have their lives. At dawn on the eighteenth, the American riflemen in the windows of the building, that Adams and his men had occupied all night, started the battle with shots at two or three Germans who appeared incautiously in the windows across the way.

1st Lt. James Sturwold, executive officer of A Company, 38th Infantry, recounts: "At about 0600, an American medic from a unit (unidentified) of the 99th Division came into the lines of the company. A sentinal, suspecting a ruse, sent him under guard to the company command post, where he was questioned until his indentity as an American soldier was established beyond doubt. His indentity was raffirmed by some 99th men who had been at the command post for the whole evening, and whose identity had been proved. This medic had come into the American positions from locations behind the German lines. He brought the story that about 200 Germans and some 150 Americans were in the area that was being shelled, and that the Ger-

The Second Attempt to Seize Krinkelt-Rocherath, 18 December

mans had sent him to the U.S. positions to try to get them to surrender on threat of annhilation of the GI prisoners if the defenders didn't capitulate. The man said that the Germans were not mistreating the prisoners. His report was that the 200 enemy were on their own without tank or other support. I said they were armed with two flamethrowers, four machine guns, six bazookas and rifles and machine pistols.

"It appeared the enemy had sent the medic into the U.S. lines after having taken a liking to him. The Germans tried to extract from the man a promise that he would return. He refused to give the required promise, but in spite of this they had let him come to the U.S. lines on his mission. Since the medic was the only aid man near the company at the time and wanted to stay with them, they kept him. The battalion was notified by radio of the 200 enemy and the U.S. artillery fire was increased. Shortly after the increased firing, screams could be heard coming from the enemy-held hill, followed immediately by the sounds of industrious digging and chopping as the Germans dug in."

It was foggy and still dark; as the fog lifted and daylight came, the woods became visible. Under direction from Captain White, the fire was shifted north, repeated, shifted and fired again. Some other artillery unit picked up the firing, and the close support artillery resumed harassing missions on the company front.

Captain Love, who went to bed at 0100 hours, was not awakened until about 0700 hours. When it was just getting light, C Company detected Germans in a house directly across the street from them. Hearing American voices coming from the house, they suspected that some American soldiers were being held prisoner in the house. Sometime between 0830 and 0900 hours, Captain Rollings and his runner came dashing in the front door, and he immediately ordered the building across the street retaken.

Lieutenant Adams sent his second squad across the street to retake the building in question. The men in Adams's house covered the attackers with rifle fire from the windows as the attack started. Captain Rollings, standing in the doorway better to observe the action, was struck in the leg by a ricocheting rifle bullet. The attack proceeded auccessfully, but a German Waffen-SS officer who had been wounded in the leg, and was in the basement of the enemy occupied house, almost interrupted the attack when he threw a potato masher into the street wounding two of the attacking infantrymen. At about the same time, he ordered two red flares to be fired, apparently a signal for tanks to attack, because shortly after the flares had been fired, enemy tanks came into the position for the first time that day. Two of the remaining men from the second squad threw three grenades into the enemyoccupied building and went inside. The Germans surrendered, and the squad took about thirty Germans prisoner, found eleven more dead in the house and its environs, and released about thirty-five Americans. Two were S/Sgt. Ronald Mayer and PFC Henry Mills, machine gunners from the antitank company's 9th Ssquad who had been captured the night before while manning a machine-gun post in a house near the service company's road block. Also in the group was one officer, Lt. Ralph L. Schmidt from B Company. At this point, the Americans, who were from B and D Companies of the 38th, gave the information that they had been well treated, although they had been forced at the point of a pistol to go into the street and request the surrender of the platoon of C Company that eventually rescued them. Rollings and his runner took away the German prisoners and the recaptured Armericans and came to the house where Adams was set up and stayed for a short time to aid in the defense.

The Americans remaining with Adams replenished their ammunition supply from a U.S. half-track that had been beside the enemy held house. The tank destroyer and half-track men that had spent the night with them left to go to the rear and find their outfits. The retaken men from B and D Companies set out on their own, looking for any weapon that they could find. Just at daylight around the command post was seen a lot of abandoned American equipment that had not been there the night before. All of the equipment belonged to the retreating troops of the 393rd Infantry, 99th Division, and attached troops that came out of the Krinkelter Woods. There were several two-and-a-half-ton trucks, two 3-inch towed tank destroyer guns, and about 300 yards away, there was a quadruple .50-caliber antiaircraft gun that the Germans were firing in the general direction of the American positions. This gun soon ran out of ammunition. Also about the same time, E Company was detached and returned to the control of the 2nd Battalion.

About 0730 hours, an unknown number of enemy tanks without infantry support started coming in from the north along the same route used by the tanks the previous night. Captain Love couldn't understand how these tanks were getting past the 5th Squad, who at least should have fired at the enemy as they passed the squad positions. He called regiment, notified them of the new attack by these tanks, and called for three platoons on the radio. Lt. Marc H. Schowalter, platoon leader of the 2nd Platoon, reported that the 5th Squad was not accounted for and could not be located. The complete squad became officially missing in action.

Lt. Ulrich W. Crow, a member of E Company, 38th Infantry, remembers: "Later that morning, the soldiers manning the machine gun came running back up the road and told me there were three German tanks coming toward us. I'm not sure what kind they were. We pulled back into the house and let the tanks pass. As the tanks pulled through, there was a U.S. tank

The Second Attempt to Seize Krinkelt-Rocherath, 18 December 363

destroyer that pulled in behind them and fired on the back tank, stopping it. When the krauts bailed out of the tank, my riflemen had a field day on them. The tank destroyer fired again and disabled the second tank. Again my riflemen dispatched the tank crew. The tank destroyer could disable a German tank from the rear but not from the front.

"The lead tank by this time had realized what was happening and turned and opened fire on the tank destroyer. Standing beside the tank destroyer was an American soldier. A tank round must have hit him square in the chest because he exploded from the waist up. I can close my eyes and see it happen just like it was yesterday. All that fell were his legs. It was one of the most horrific sights I saw during combat. The tank fired again hitting the tank destroyer putting it out of action. I was standing in the door of the house, watching it all when the tank fired and hit the house I was in. I was hit in the right side of my head with pieces of shrapnel and the concussion knocked me unconscious. I was evacuated to an aid station. I'll never forget what I saw on the way to the aid station. The Germans had shelled us all night with artillery. There were dead soldiers and body parts strewn along the road. I was eventually evacuated to a field hospital in France and then to a hospital in England."

After about eight tanks had passed the crossroads going too fast and having appeared too suddenly for the garrison to do anything about it (there was no bazooka ammunition and no 57-millimeter antitank guns in the vicinity), the enemy tank column started to "accordion"—i.e., the vehicles at the head of the column slowed or stopped and the remainder of them closed up and halted. One of the enemy Panther tanks stopped about 50 yards from the crossroads and about 200 yards from the command post. Captain Love found two self-propelled tank destroyers of the 644th Tank Destroyer Battalion in position for good shots at the enemy tanks, if the tank destroyers would but move a few yards. The crew of the tank destroyers said they had orders to remain where they were, covering critical positions, and wouldn't move to firing positions. Captain Love then went to an American M4 Sherman tank and led him into position about 75 yards from the Panther. The M4 finished it off with two rounds, beautiful flanking shots into the right side of the hull. The Americans in the windows of Captain Love's command post enjoyed picking off the tank crew as they abandoned their vehicle.

A detail was sent to the regimental ammunition depot in Krinkelt for bazooka rounds and K rations, and by 0900 hours there was enough ammunition in the position. About this time, another Panther moved along the road that seemed to be the main route of approach for the Germans in the assault. It moved along the road toward the other tank that had just been knocked out by the Sherman. As the Panther got behind the already been disabled German tank, Pvt. Isabel Salazar picked up a bazooka, went to the second-story window of the command post, and at a range of about 200 yards, knocking out the moving enemy tank with one round. The momentum of the tank carried it into position beside the one that was already there. There were now side by side, two out of action German tanks that formed a very effective road block. About an hour later, Salazar gave a repeat performance by knocking out a 75-millimeter German assault gun on a Mark IV chassis (Panzerjäger IV) that pulled up behind the two finished tanks.

At about 0800, Colonel Barsanti received orders from Colonel Boos that L Company was to report to the 2nd Battalion, as the situation was critical there and the battalion needed reinforcements. L Company's vacated position was occupied by Task Force Brakel, a small group of stragglers plus a platoon of heavy machine guns under Capt. Frank Brakel, M Company's commander. In addition to the platoon of machine guns that had been attached to L Company, there were about seventy stragglers from the 99th Division.

L Company proceeded to join Lt. Col. Jack K. Norris, commander of the 2nd Battalion. Shortly after L Company left the control of the 3rd Battalion, Task Force Brakel was attacked by a force of sixty to seventy-five Germans from the south. All but fifteen or twenty were wiped out by heavy machine guns and mortars. Immediately after the tank episode, L Company received an order to move out. The company passed to the northeast through Krinkelt into Rocherath; there the company commander got in touch with the S-2 of the 2nd Battalion and was instructed to contact Capt. Edward L. Farrell, battalion S-3.

At the time, Farrell was the acting commander of E Company, whose commander was a casualty. L Company was instructed to move to the right of E, closing the gap between E and the regimental antitank company under Love. L's move forward from its original position was under intermittent enemy artillery fire. The head of the company got to within about 200 yards of the 2nd Battalion's lines. Captain Murphy found the E Company command post dugout where he reported to Captain Farrell and told him that L was attached to him and gave him the rest of his instructions. The situation as outlined by Farrell was that the position had been under almost continuous counter attack, and all that was required of the supporting company was to go into position on the open right flank of E Company.

In company with his runner, radio operator, a bazooka team and the platoon leader of the leading platoon, Murphy crawled on his belly on a reconnaissance of the positions to be occupied. The position was under intermittent enemy artillery fire all during this time. Under cover of a light fog and the heavy pall of smoke from the burning building in the town, the

The Second Attempt to Seize Krinkelt-Rocherath, 18 December

John Murphy (right).
JAMES WRIGHT

little party crawled forward toward the positions assigned to the company. After about 100 yards of creeping and crawling, they reached the positions and looked them over. In a nearby field there were five German tanks hub to hub, but the little force had nothing effective to use against them, so returned to the company. Instructions were issued to infiltrate forward to positions. The plan adopted and followed was to use the cellars of artillery-shattered houses as strong points along a line from the left of the regimental antitank company to the right of E Company. The positions occupied were along about a 200 or 250 yard front with the flanks of the company cutting two roads which the enemy had been using as his main tank approach into the town.

Immediately upon arrival into the positions, at about 1100 hours, the mortars of the company, plus an extra one that had been salvaged from the 99th Division's abandoned material were set up in position. Immediately after the positions were occupied, the enemy launched an attack with between sixty and seventy-five infantry supported by heavy tanks (Mark IV and Mark V). The tanks approached to within about 200 yards of the positions and fired into the buildings occupied by the company while the enemy infantry moved up. The weapons platoon leader, Lieutenant Thompson, brought the fire of all four of the mortars to bear on the enemy infantry killing or wounding an estimated half of them and driving the rest of them off. Murphy brought the artillery fire to bear on the tanks, disabling one of them which was later destroyed by tank destroyer fire. The other enemy tank withdrew. All during this time, the positions were under heavy small arms and machine gun fire. The defenders from L Company held these positions the rest of the afternoon during which time there were no further enemy attacks although several enemy tanks appeared in view out of range. These tanks didn't attempt to break through the company.

About the fight in Rocherath, a tank commander in the 2nd Platoon of the 3rd Company, Willi Fischer, reported: "On 18 December 1944, the fateful attack on Krinkelt-Rocherath was carried out. A perfect 'tank graveyard.' The tanks of the 1st Company had the lead, followed by our company under company commander Brödel. I was lined up behind Beutelhauser, my platoon commander. When I got to the vicinity of the church I saw a theater of horror. Beutelhauser was shot in front of me. Both of us already had crossed the second crossroads. When Beutelhauser was shot I could more or less make out the position of the enemy double-barreled antitank gun. Beutelhauser could jump out of his tank and get himself to safety. Under the cover of a house, I positioned my tank, without knowing at this moment what I was to do. Next to me stood Brödel's vehicle, the cart was burning slightly, Brödel was sitting in the turret lifeless; he had been killed. In front of me along the rest of the street all tanks had been knocked out and four at this time were still burning. One tank still was moving—I think it was Freier's tank—and under my covering fire it was able to withdraw towards the later battalion command post.

"This opportunity also was used by a part of our crews, which had holed up in a shed; under protection of the tank they also withdrew. In this way they barely averted being taken prisoner by the encircling American infantry. Behind me Jürgensen showed up with his tank. I had to see to it that I gave up my hopeless position and wanted to withdraw myself behind the cross-

The mortar section of L Company, 38th Infantry.
JAMES WRIGHT

roads. It was clear to me that the American antitank gun would have recognized this plan and hold the crossroads under fire. They actually did so. The first round missed, the second hit the track and the hull from the side; luckily no loss of life; radio destroyed, track almost gone. I just was able to follow Jürgensen's instruction when the track slipped down and the road wheels on one side were standing in the mud, which later froze up strongly. Next to our new position (after all the entire attack had been brought to a standstill), we discovered about twenty Americans in a hole in the earth underneath a tent cover, which then surrendered. Likewise, Americans still held out in various houses in the part of the village we had occupied. These also killed our unsuspecting comrade Bandow with a shot through the heart from an ambush, when he wanted to camouflage Jauch's tank with planks. This occurred in my direct vicinity in front of my eyes."

After the wounding of Captain Grossjohann, gunner Max Söllner reported: "After the wounding of our boss, we took part in the attack with our tank. It was very difficult for us as without a commander we were handicapped with regard to sight. Despite several exhortations none of the platoon commanders reported to switch over to us. So I merely passed on all orders that came to our tank from battalion. Nevertheless things worked out quite well, as our company got to Krinkelt without any losses and took up positions there. There I also met Untersturmführer Pucher, who wanted to switch over to our tank."

Loader Hannes Simon reported: "Shortly afterwards, we carried out a tank attack towards the church. About ten high-explosive shells were fired, two of them were tracers. I had a discussion with 2nd Lieutenant Pücher; with the second tracer I was to open the breech prematurely. While we were talking the shell ignited. With the last high-explosive shell, the casing got stuck in the barrel. Under cover of the wall of a house, but under fire, we managed to free the jammed casing using a sponge from the outside."

At about 0945 hours, a group of German tanks came down the road on the left of the C Company position. The first group of approximately eleven tanks with infantry riding them got by the little strongpoint that Adams was holding without being spotted, but there was no time to get the anti-tank weapons into action. Sgt. Richard Shinefelt, in command of the squad in the recaptured house, fired two or three antitank rifle grenades at the enemy tanks without any apparent damage, but the riflemen in both of the positions did a very through job of eliminating almost all the infantry that was riding the backs of the tanks. The first group of tanks continued down the road.

Adams's group assembled two bazooka teams using one weapon that had been with the group from the beginning and getting another from a jeep in front of the house. As the enemy tanks continued to pass the house,

Willi Fischer.

the bazooka teams scored many direct hits on the tanks but as far as was observed, no tanks were disabled. However one of the tanks in the second group was finished off by personnel in the company command post.

The command post personel in the top floors of the building were firing every weapon at hand on the enemy infantry that came in on the tanks, and few of them got out alive. The fourth tank in line (three got through) was knocked out by a bazooka from G Company, which had come into position early in the morning and organized a line across the street to the east of the regimental comand post and at the road junction to the northeast of the command post. The last remaining tank turned around and moved to the northeast where it remained hidden between some buildings.

PFC James Branch with HQ Company, 1st Battalion, 38th Infantry, remembers: "There were eleven men in my group. We had one machine gun, one bazooka, one radio, our rifles and pistols, and one rifle with a grenade launcher. Immediatly after we had taken our house which was not occupied by the anyone, a German tank drove down the road. Red, the red-headed sergeant, had the bazooka. He used it on the tank and set it on fire."

Behind the second group of tanks came three more that stopped at the crossroads, one pointing south, one west and one north at the men from C Company. This last tank, probably having seen the firing coming from the little group of men, fired a 75-millimeter round into the second story of the house, with no effect except to get rid of more plaster and brick that formed the ceilings and walls of the building.

The Second Attempt to Seize Krinkelt-Rocherath, 18 December

The action died down for the next hour or so, and through a back window the men could see American tanks and tank destroyers moving into position to the north of them. Someone came up to the house and told Adams to pull out because a large tank battle was expected to take place in the immediate vicinity almost at once. The little group of the 2nd Platoon men pulled back to the company command post taking the weapon platoon with them. The German tank that had gone into position with the three mentioned above and was pointing to the north, had fired one round into the house that the company command post had occupied the night before and set it afire. The command post group pulled out and set up another command post next door to the antitank company's command post (Captain Love).

At about 1100 hours, Lt. Robert F. Welch from G Company, plus one platoon and a heavy machine gun squad, reported to the company command post for instructions. They were acting on orders from battalion to go into positions on the left flank of the platoon of K Company that was along the road to the left of 1st Platoon. The left flank of the G Company platoon was to rest on the road to the north and its right was to contact the right of K. While the platoon from G was going into position, heavy firing was heard from what seemed to be enemy machine guns on its left front. Along the road on the left flank of G, there were six knocked-out enemy tanks, one of which was immobilized, but still firing. As soon as the platoon from G got in, Sturwold returned to the A Company command post, got a company runner, and led him back to the G platoon, with a wire line. The wire was connected to the platoon's sound-powered telephone; then Sturwold and his wireman returned to his company.

John B. Savard of G Company recalls: "When we finally forced the enemy out of the buildings around the regimental command post, I found myself as a temporary guard in a barn-like building attached to regimental headquarters. The radio equipment was in operation, and I could hear operators sending and receiving messages. Few people seemed to know what was going on. When the situation in our part of town had stabilized, G Company was given a new mission. We were to fight our way back to the outskirts of town and defend a road junction which friendly troops might use to get into town."

During the morning of 18 December, there was not much activity in A Company's sector. The only enemy activity was in the form of spasmodic artillery fire, mostly in the area of the right platoon.

In the southern village of Krinkelt, the Panthers of the 1st and 3rd Companies were fighting. Several attempts to penetrate deeper into the village failed in the enemy artillery fire. Still some tanks managed to advance up to the road that led from the southernmost exit of the village to Wirtzfeld; but they were knocked out by tanks, tank destroyers and bazookas. In Rocherath, tanks and grenadiers advanced up to the command post of the 38th Infantry Regiment, but were not able to hold there. In the afternoon the German troops managed to push back the 2nd Battalion, 38th Infantry, into the northern part of the village.

Joel Martinez of the 1st Battalion, 38th Infantry, tells his story: "Me and Lieutenant Baker stayed there until daylight, when we saw about seven tanks approaching on the road behind the church. A friendly quad machine-gun half-track pulled in across the street from us and started firing at the tanks, and so did we (.30 caliber). We saw no enemy infantry, just tanks. When the tanks got a direct hit on the tracks we went to the basement. A lot of guys went after the tanks including me. Having found a sharp charge in the basement, I didn't make it, somebody else got him first. Along about 1300 hours a sniper on the church steeple was taking shots at us, so again I became part of a squad to get the sniper, and we did. The other two artillery men on my liaison section were Captain Shamoon and Tech 5 Bishop. Private First Class Cheek did not get caught with us, he got killed after the Battle of the Bulge."

At about daylight on the eighteenth, Lt. Sidney P. Dane, S-2 of the 1st Battalion, 38th Infantry, came to the outside of the building, and thinking that there were Germans in the church, he called in German for them to give up. Of course, the outfit did nothing, and finally, Dane realized the men weren't German and told them who he was. They came out of the church and under the guidance of Dane, reported to Major Coopersmith at the 1st Battalion to aid in the defense of the east and northeast sides of the command post. The men got some antitank weapons, bazookas, and all through the eighteenth, kept up the tank and infantry battle. Patterson was hazy on the rest of the engagement saying that the fighting on the eighteenth was not so heavy as on the previous night.

At about 1300 hours at the 2nd Platoon command post of B Company (under Lt. Lloyd L. Crusius), an officer from E Company came in and conveyed instructions that the platoon was to become attached to F. Acting on these instructions the platoon went into position. E Company of the 38th was on the right of the platoon, and some other element (Crusius didn't know which) of the 2nd Battalion were on the left of the platoon.

The occupation of the assigned positions began as ordered. At about 1330 hours, the platoon had reached a point about 200 yards south of the proposed positions when it was fired upon by an enemy tank, part of a group that had been operating in the northeast part of Rocherath during the day. The tank fire pinned down Crusius's platoon for a short time. His men stayed in position for ten to fifteen minutes, and during a lull in the firing, they moved in and occupied the assigned positions. They remained there until just after dark.

The Second Attempt to Seize Krinkelt-Rocherath, 18 December

At about 1300 hours, when the tank battle appeared to be over, Captain Rollings of C Company returned from the battalion aid station where he had gone to get patched up, and sent the platoon back to its original house where they had fought so hard during the night. Some one, Adams didn't know who, reported at this time that fifteen enemy tanks were knocked out in the course of the battle.

The German tank that had sat on the crossroads with its gun pointing north was still in position. It was hidden by a shed from view of C Company's position, but the men knew it was still there from the occasional sound of its motor warming up. From the window of the house that the 2nd Platoon occupied, and for which they had conceived a sort of affection, the men could see through a gap in a hedge German infantry or tankers running to and from the vicinity of the tank. After watching this performance for a couple of minutes, Adams got his carbine. It had been modified to make it fully automatic when desired, and he rested it on a window sill pointing at the gap in the hedge through which he and the others had seen the parade of Germans. Every time a German appeared across the opening, he would get a burst from the carbine.

During these hours, although by comparison there was little activity, the artillery fire, both enemy and friendly, never ceased. At about 1600 hours, a German tank pulled up into a hull defilade position and fired about three rounds into the 2nd Platoon building. About four more enemy tanks passed along the same road. One of them was put out of action by a bazooka round from the company command post. It was firing from a position just behind the first one that had been knocked out by the command post group. The last tank in line stopped at the corner, fired a couple of rounds into the already heavily pounded building occupied by Lieutenant Adams and his men, and collapsed into the basement the stairs that led to the second floor and some of the wall of the building. The tanks, less the one that had been put out of action, pulled off down the road toward the southwest in the direction of the church in Krinkelt, and stopped along the left side of the road where they stayed for a short time.

On the afternoon of 18 December, 2nd Lieutenant Engel reached Krinkelt with two tanks from the company which arrived late. He describes what he found there: "Because of the soft soil, the repair crews could not repair my tank on the spot. It had to be hauled off to the repair company. In the meantime Captain Bellmer, a former infantryman, has met up with a tank in order to gain experience in tank combat. The leaderless tank 325, the platoon command tank of the 2nd Platoon, had joined up with us in the meantime, after a breakdown had been fixed. Immediately I take over this tank and drive, followed by Captain Bellmer, to Krinkelt.

"After a easy drive we reached the village of Rocherath. Even the first houses show the marks of the fighting that had gone before. From the middle of the village the noise of battle is audible. Captain Jungbluth, liaison officer with the regimental staff, takes the point and gives us signs to keep us going in the right direction. However, I somehow sense trouble, as here I am to act contrary to the basic rules of armored warfare, which indicate that without any infantry escort, villages are to be bypassed if possible. In the fraction of a second I therefore turn left and order the tank that is escorting me to follow me. Hardly thirty minutes later, I obtain proof of the correctness of my actions. I drive along the slope, along the backs of the houses, turning our turrets towards cellars and windows, reaching an open place at the church. I allow Bellmer to overtake me and drive both tanks in the 3 o'clock position, so that the front is towards the enemy and the wall of a house covers one side always. Our open flanks are facing one another. Our arms cover two roads that lead straight into the American held part of the village.

"Straight in front of us is the main road, over which the company has attacked and which we avoided. On the other side, in an administrative building, I recognize the battalion command post. Next to its entrance is the command tank of Major Jürgensen, next to him the commander in conversation with some officers and men of the battalion staff. I report to him. His face shows depression and resignation. The failed attack and the painful losses, especially in the 1st and 3rd Companies, obviously depress him. He orders me not to change my position for the time being, as I can enter battle from there in the best possible manner. Now I also can view down the main road. The killed tanks of the company offer a shattering sight. At this moment a single tank approaches the command post, which, only about a 100 meters distant, suddenly changes into a burning torch. Shortly afterwards the commander of this tank, Freiberg, shows up at the command post with a bandage round his head and he reports the following: 'In the doorway of a house I saw a woman, who was waving a white cloth. While I was still focusing on that and wondering what it meant, I was shot. My tank burned straightaway.'

"Later it became clear that a Sherman tank, which had been immobilised but was intact and crewed, had fired this hit. I certainly would have suffered the same fate if I had followed indications at the entrance to the village. The fighting in Krinkelt flares up again and again. Both sides fight with great determination and bitterness."

Because of the dust and smoke from the falling stairs and walls, Adams found it necessary to get his little group out of the house they had held so long and get into a ditch along the road just behind the damaged building.

The Second Attempt to Seize Krinkelt-Rocherath, 18 December

Visibility was nil in the clouds of stifling smoke that rose from the partiallly demolished strongpoint, and the men could not have breathed in it. Adams went to Captain Rollings who still was on the go in spite of having been hit in the back by a piece of falling timber and a leg wound. Adams tried to secure permission to abandon the house on the grounds that it was no longer tenable. Rollings told Adams, "Hell no! Get back there, that is a key position."

The little group returned to the house as soon as the dust had settled enough to allow them to breathe; they re-established their defense of the house with their machine gun in the window and the riflemen as guards. The enemy tanks had set afire a half-track that was in front of the platoon, and it continued to burn most of the night. Because there were so few men in this little group split between two houses, and because the house on the east side of the road was impossible to defend at night, with its blind spot to the east, Adams pulled the men from the indefensible house and reinforced his little group with them. At about 1800 hours, the American artillery opened fire in a target area that seemed to enclose Adams and his group within a semicircular wall of fire, interposed between him and the enemy. This fire kept up all during the night, and the men derived a great deal of comfort from it.

Between 2200 and 2300, a group af four enemy tanks led by a captured German-manned Sherman came past C Company's command post with their lights on. The men were deceived by the Sherman in the lead and thought the group was friendly armor. They hailed the tanks in English, and when there was no answer, opened fire on them. Unaffected, the four tanks continued north and weren't seen again. During the remainder of the night, things remained quiet except for enemy artillery fire on the positions. Adams was told that G Company was to work in on the left (north) flank of the position during the night, but none of the men from G were contacted.

G Company's John B. Savard recalls: "We had had little food and no sleep for about thrity-six hours and when we finally reached our objective; it was completely dark. We spent the evening of the eighteenth preparing our defensive position at a junction where two roads met on their way into Rocherath. After the position around some farm buildings was secured, a patrol was sent out to attempt contact with any friendly troops still heading for Rocherath. None of the patrol returned, and all were listed as killed in action. As the night passed, metallic sounds were heard in front of my platoon and reported to the captain. We were told there was at least one knocked-out German tank at the edge of a farm field, and perhaps the enemy was trying to retrieve it. We called for artillery fire, and the noise stopped.

"Soon after, under cover of darkness, a group of men approached our position walking down one of the roads. Our outposts believed it was our returning patrol, but before they could react, an enemy force of about a dozen men were inside our perimeter spraying the area with automatic fire. First Sergeant Embody gathered some company headquarters men and began to clean out the enemy. We had already heard that the SS troops we were facing were killing American prisoners, and therefore none of the attackers were taken prisoner. The burp gun fire by the original enemy force must have been a sign, for the whole line erupted in battle.

"My foxhole buddy Norman Martz was hit in the head and was dead in the foxhole. Others along the line suffered similar fates, but with mortar and machine gun fire we held our position. As the Germans pressed forward Captain Skagg called for artillery fire on our position which probably turned the tide of battle. When the Germans withdrew, my squad was down to five men. The rest of the company was about the same. As daylight came, a relief column reached us, and we withdrew into town where we formed teams to hunt down the German tanks which had forced their way into town under cover of darkness."

SUMMARY

By the evening, it became clear that German tanks and panzer grenadiers had penetrated into both villages—Rocherath and Krinkelt—and pressed the far superior American troops, but they were unable to take the entire villages. The attack cost a high toll in tank crews, tanks and grenadiers. Among the infantry the main load was borne by the 1st and 2nd Battalions of the 25th Panzer Grenadier Regiment, whose 3rd Battalion probably had become pinned down by American artillery fire shortly after leaving the woods east of Krinkelt. The 990th Volksgrenadier Regiment of the 277th Volksgrenadier Division pushed back the 3rd Battalion, 393rd Infantry, 99th Division, behind the Rocherath-Wahlerscheid road, but was unable to rupture its front. On its right flank were two battalions of the 395th Infantry, 99th Division.

The opponents also suffered serious losses. The brave American infantry were strongly supported by a tank battalion (741st), a tank destroyer battalion (644th), and an antitank company (801st). In the street fighting, they defended in depth. It has to be stressed that, contrary to American reports, no Tiger tanks were used on the German side, and that there were not two battalions of tanks, but one. Against the American tanks and tank destroyers, the German side especially felt the lack of grenadiers, which are indispensable in a street fight. Both panzer grenadier battalions were facing more than four American infantry battalions.

The Second Attempt to Seize Krinkelt-Rocherath, 18 December

The situation had developed more advantageously with the neighbours to the south. To this, the fact that the 12th SS Panzer Division *Hitlerjugend* bound strong American forces and threatened others in the flank, certainly contributed. The 394th Infantry, which was left only the retreat route through Krinkelt, evacuated its positions in Mürringen at two o'clock in the morning of 18 December, as did the 1st Battalion, 23rd Infantry, in Hünningen. They thought they were authorized to do this by a radio message from the 99th Infantry Division. They formed a motorized column and a foot column. When the motorized column approached Krinkelt, they heard the noise of battle and the sound of tanks. This was the small combat group of Zeiner.

The motor column dismounted, for the commander thought that the road to Wirtzfeld, running through Krinkelt, could not be used. On foot the troops marched on to Elsenborn. The foot column, which began a little later, found the abandoned vehicles. They made sure that a part of Krinkelt still was in American hands, and manned the vehicles. They reached Elsenborn without any problems.

An American artillery battalion, the 371st Field Artillery Battalion, had taken up positions near Mürringen. When they had to withdraw, they abandoned the majority of their guns. At 0740, the 3rd Battalion, 38th Infantry, reported the passing of elements of the 394th Infantry. About one hour earlier, *Kampfgruppe Zeiner* had withdrawn from Krinkelt, and the 1st Panzer Battalion had not advanced that far.

While the 1st Battalion, 23rd Infantry, was preparing to withdraw from Hünningen, elements of the 27th Fusilier Regiment of the 12th Volksgrenadier Division managed to penetrate into the village at several spots. The American battalion had to fight to keep its withdrawal route open. The fusiliers took Hünningen, and the 48th Volksgrenadier Regiment of the 12th Volksgrenadier Division, took the abandoned village of Mürringen. The road from Losheimergraben to Büllingen was open. Presumably now, only the advance battalion of the 12th Volksgrenadier Division moved on Büllingen. It consisted of the antitank company, an assault gun battalion with six operational assault guns, and a company of fusiliers and engineers.

After the breakthrough of *Kampfgruppe Peiper*, Büllingen had been reoccupied by the Americans with weak forces. Now it was retaken and cleared. The 12th Volksgrenadier forbade any further advance on Bütgenbach, as the right flank was fully open. The advance detachment of Holz assumed defensive positions on the northwest and western edge of Büllingen. This is confirmed by the daily report of OB West on 18 December, which states: "The 12th Volksgrenadier Division took Büllingen and captured sixteen airplanes and seven antitank guns, and since 1400 hours is advancing on Wirtzfeld and

Bütgenbach." Major Holz's report, however, shows that the command to attack the Domäne Bütgenbach "was cancelled at the last minute."

At 1000 hours, *Kampfgruppe Peiper* took Stavelot; a report by Horch stated they were southwest of the town by 1500 hours. By evening, they had reached the vicinity of Stoumont. At 1430, other elements of the 1st SS Panzer Division took Recht (four kilometers to the south of Engelsdorf-Ligneuville). The 3rd Fallschirmjäger Division advanced northward from the area northeast of Heppenbach.

For the 6th SS Panzer Army, it was of decisive importance to open up the road that led to Spa via Malmedy in order to protect the right flank of *Kampfgruppe Peiper* and create room to bring up fuel and ammunition. Therefore, they ordered that the attacks of the 12th SS Panzer Division on Rocherath and Krinkelt were to be stopped. On 19 December, this sector was to be taken over by the 3rd Panzer Grenadier Division. The units of the 12th SS Panzer Division that had not been in combat were to move to Büllingen as quickly as possible to open up the road to Bütgenbach from there. The elements that were fighting in Krinkelt-Rocherath had to follow. Units earmarked for the attack on Bütgenbach were attached to the II SS Panzer Corps.

CHAPTER 9

Withdrawal toward Elsenborn

On 18 December, when all efforts of the 12th SS Panzer Division of the German 6th SS Panzer Army to penetrate the enemy lines had come to naught, the 3rd Panzer Grenadier Division was given the order to take the Krinkelt-Rocherath area and continue the attack in the direction of Elsenborn. But soon it became clear that the 3rd had been given an impossible task. The division had to advance across terrain that was unsuited for motorized units in the face of an American defense in a dominant position, forcefully supported by strong artillery. For more than a week the division wallowed in the mud before the crests of Elsenborn Ridge, trying in vain to break through.

THE MISSION OF THE 3RD PANZER GRENADIER DIVISION
On 16 December, the 3rd Panzer Grenadier Division, commanded by Maj. Gen. Walther Denkert, was taken out of OKW reserve at the express request of Field Marshal Model in order to be put into action on the Ardennes front in the sector of the 6th SS Panzer Army. At the time, the division was resting in an area near Zülpich, ten kilometers northwest of Euskirchen. On 30 November, the division had been withdrawn from the Aachen front, where it had fought without pause since the middle of October, and where it had suffered severe losses. Within the division, the hope that they would not be sent back in action lived for a while. After a very short rest period, the units prepared for training the new replacement troops and receiving the weapons, vehicles and other things necessary to participate in the coming operations. Orders for this had already been given, and the new material was due to arrive, among which were fifteen Jagdpanzer IV/L70 tank destroyers. These, however, would not arrive before the end of the year, when the division would be engaged in the Bastogne sector.

The breakthrough was to be realized by the infantry divisions while the SS panzer divisions of the 6th SS Panzer Army were kept in reserve to be launched toward the Meuse through the gaps in the American defenses the infantry created. The northern flank of the breakthrough was covered by the LXVII Corps, composed of five divisions, among which was the 3rd Panzer Grenadier Division.

Denkert had to assemble his division in the Kall area, west of Schleiden, in order to take part in the battles that would develop later. During the briefing, Model enquired as to the state in which the division found itself, being especially worried about the fuel situation. Beginning on 17 December, the 3rd Panzer Grenadier Division moved toward the zone to which it had been assigned.

The strength of the 3rd Panzer Grenadier Division, according to the report of the inspector general of panzer troops in the west on 8 December, was 80 percent of the normal strength; it contained 337 officers and 11,905 other ranks. A report from 1 December, drawn up when the division was relieved from the Aachen front, reveals that the three companies of the 103rd Panzer Battalion possessed twenty-five assault guns, and the 3rd Tank Destroyer Battalion had only six Jagdpanzer IV/L70s. According to General Denkert, at this time the division was fit for only limited attacks.

THE 3RD PANZER GRENADIER DIVISION GOES INTO LINE

As the attack of the 6th SS Panzer Army was not progressing according to plan, Generalfeldmarschall Model on 17 December envisaged using 3rd Panzer Grenadier Division south of Monschau and launching towards Hautes Fagnes, via Kalterherberg, Elsenborn and Sourbrodt. Finally, Model decided to assemble the 3rd Panzer Grenadier Division behind the 12th SS Panzer Division and put it into battle on the heels of the latter as soon as it had achieved some confidence.

On 18 December, when it became clear that the attacks by the 12th SS Panzer Division had become bogged down, the 3rd Panzer Grenadier Division received orders to relieve the panzer division from the next morning. The 3rd Panzer Grenadier Division was to continue the diversionary attack and push forward toward Elsenborn and its military camp, then change direction toward the northeast, toward Verviers. After having given his combat units orders to advance next night to the area of Hellenthal-Hollerath, General Denckert immediately made for the LXVII Corps headquarters at Dalbenden, near Urft. Having been brought up to scratch on the current situation and having gotten additional information, Denkert returned toward the front in the early afternoon and he went forward to reconnoiter his new operational area.

The reconnaissance carried out by Denkert led him through Hellenthal and Hollerath, towards the Dreiherrenwald Forest where he went as far as the edge of the Krinkelt forest. The reconnaissance took place at grey light and without intervention by Allied aircraft, but it made the difficulties the

Smoke and dust rise from the blast as infantrymen prepare dugouts somewhere in Belgium.

3rd Panzer Grenadier Division was to encounter during its advance amply clear. The route chosen for the march was completely blocked by convoys that slowed, and even stopped the small car of General Denkert completely. He nevertheless concluded that the first half of the road was navigable in comparison with the forest tracks farther west. Bomb or shell craters on the roads had to be filled in or bypassed by the military convoys. Vehicles damaged or partially destroyed by air attacks, torched or left behind due to technical problems posed further obstacles. In any case, the advance to the front of the 3rd Panzer Grenadier Division over narrow one-way roads, with short or long distances between the vehicles, would necessitate a traffic organization and properly functioning radio communications.

In the wooded and hilly terrain of the Dreiherrenwald, the road conditions were catastrophic. The forest track leading through the two woods (Dreiherrenwald and Krinkelterwald) toward the villages of Rocherath and Krinkelt was in terrain formerly occupied by Americans. The road had turned into a veritable bog, a mud bath, especially in the deep valleys where passage had been completely blocked by vehicles that had bogged down to the middle of the wheels. Mines, which had been placed along the shoulders by the enemy, made by passing of obstacles, such as backed-up trucks, impossible.

General Denkert gives the following account: "The crossing of the first valley already was difficult for me. After a while it became impossible to proceed by vehicle and the reconnaissance continued on foot. It took me several hours to reach the west edge of the Krinkelterwald. One noted, especially in the narrow valleys, the traces of heavy fighting and especially the mines, which, on explosion, had caused numerous losses. The idea of abandoning the muddy road and continuing the march on the green moss of the forest was very alluring, but impossible because of the danger. A small car with a sergeant of the 12th SS Panzer Division which had passed us and strayed slightly from the track, ran over a mine and blew up in a violent explosion. This march, in gray and cold weather, in which we wallowed in mud up to our ankles, passing vehicles and other equipment which had been destroyed, bogged down in mud or broken down and abandoned, with the view, each time a terrible view, of bodies which the majority had been horribly mutilated, remains my worst memory of the war.

"At the crossroads, on the western edge of the Krinkelterwald, there were several knocked-out Sherman remains. This crossroads later was known as 'Sherman Corner.' I enquired after the situation with an tank officer of the 12th SS Panzer Division, and I learned that the attack had carried our troops as far as Krinkelt and Rocherath. I don't remember exactly, but I think it was at this time I learned of the rearwards movement of the 12th SS Panzer Division, toward the south of the sector. At that particular moment the noise of the fighting and the activity of the American artillery was relatively low."

En route, Denkert noted a large number of American soldiers who had fallen in the woods and close to the road he was using. A cursory inspection identified the men's unit as the 99th Infantry Division of the United States Army. On the way back, at nightfall, General Denkert rejoined his advance headquarters, situated on the western approaches of Hollerath, where he installed himself in the casement of a large bunker of the Siegfried Line. Shortly after arrival at his forward headquarters, Denkert briefed his unit commanders on the results of his reconnaissance. Therefore the division had to move as soon as possible and, especially, prevent the enemy from reestablishing his front.

The next day, 19 December, the 3rd Panzer Grenadier Division moved toward the firing line. The worst fears of its commander were soon realized, as the advance was difficult and slow. The road conditions and bottlenecks presented almost insurmountable problems, but "luckily," as Denkert wrote after the war, "the skies remained closed throughout the journey, because otherwise the division's movement would surely have ended in a catastrophe." The commanders were hard put to reach the Krinkelterwald before dawn on 20 December and to cross it with vigor on foot. Starting zones were assigned to each unit and an O-group of the commanding officers was convened for the next morning before dawn, at seven o'clock at Sherman Corner to get their last briefings and their orders for the attack.

RENEWED ATTACK ON KRINKELT-ROCHERATH, 19 DECEMBER

At about 2200 hours on 18 December, I Company, 38th Infantry, stopped an attack by about twenty Germans and one self-propelled gun. The self-propelled gun was knocked out, but the enemy casualties were unknown to the defenders. In the meantime, all hell had broken loose in the north of the town, and heavy firing could be heard in that vicinity. The 2nd Platoon from K Company and one platoon from I Company were sent to the regimental antitank company to aid its commander, Captain Love, in his defense of the area to the east of Krinkelt-Rocherath. The strength of K Company at this time was about 340 men; its overstrength resulted from reinforcements from 99th Division stragglers and about seventy men from I Company, 23rd Infantry, including its commander, Charles MacDonald, who had escaped from the Krinkelter Woods. There were plenty of men for the defense.

At about 0100 hours, 19 December, K Company was attacked on its left flank by five German tanks and about 100 infantry. The enemy infantry were screaming wildly, and the enemy tanks had very bright spotlights mounted on them. The attack was stopped entirely by the artillery. The 38th Field Artillery Battalion, plus several battalions of attached artillery, effectively fired on the enemy force and stopped it, knocking out two of the tanks and forcing the others to withdrew.

At about 0500 hours, Task Force Brakel on the south end of Krinkelt reported forty or fifty enemy infantry in the draw to the front working toward their position. The 81-millimeter mortars from the battalion fired 250 rounds in this area and either killed the entire force or made it withdraw. The accuracy of the fire, which Captain Brakel himself adjusted by sound, was attested to by the screams of the enemy wounded—the more screams, the more mortar fire was poured on them.

Meanwhile, some enemy snipers that were still in the town began sniping at the mortar positions from the rear. M Company headquarters personnel plus about twenty men from the 81-millimeter mortar squads were send out to eliminate the snipers. They methodically went about cleaning up the houses in their rear area, killing about nine Germans and taking seven others prisoner. They then returned to their own jobs and continued the firing mortars on the enemy.

At about 0200 hours on 19 December, after a comparatively quiet period, an enemy tank followed by several armored half-tracks ran down the road to the front of L Company's positions, apparently with the object of turning down the road on the right of the company. Two men of a bazooka team that had been placed along the road got two hits on the enemy tank. It wasn't knocked out, but it backed off and pulled out taking the armored vehicles with it. There were no further armored attacks during the rest of the early morning.

At 0500 hours, enemy infantry of about company strength attacked F Company's position. F repulsed the attack. Apparently, the enemy had located F's positions the day before and had determined at that time that F's left flank was open. Acting on this, they tried an attack on the position held by G Company. A machine gun from G that had been placed in front of the company position held its fire until the Germans were within fifteen or twenty yards of it, then opened fire. There were twenty or thirty enemy dead counted in front of this position when the action was over.

At about 0900 hours, an estimated platoon of enemy sneaked in behind the house that had been taken and abandoned the day before by the men of Adams's platoon. Captain Rollings had a tank destroyer fire three rounds into the rear of the house through the front of it. The enemy were carrying out casualties for the next three quarters of an hour. During the evacuation of the enemy casualties, a German tank pulled up within 200 yards of Adams now thoroughly battered ruins. Adams heard the tank commander say, "Range, 200." Behind the tank, an estimated reduced-strength company of enemy infantry worked up to and into the buildings across the street from C Company's command post.

The command post personnel engaged the enemy in a heavy fire-fight with all the weapons at hand. The tank now opened fire in the direction of the American tank destroyer but couldn't hit it because of intervening buildings, and giving it up as a bad job, changed targets and opened fire on the company command post. Rollings yelled to Adams to get a bazooka and finish off the enemy tank that was harassing him. Adams grabbed a bazooka himself, climbed into what was left of the attic. Sgt. Rudolph Kraft, second in command of the squad that was manning the house, got the second bazooka and joined Adams in the attic. Wanting to get increased effectiveness from a volume of fire, the officer and the sergeant decided to fire a volley at the tank. They loaded and aimed and at the count of three, attempted to fire. Kraft's weapon discharged, but Adams's misfired. The sergeant's round hit the bogies of the tank. Adams, discarding his useless weapon, took over as loader for Kraft. The second round entered the top of the turret and burst against the inside.

Adams bent over to load a third round, which probably saved his life when a high-velocity shell hit the wall of the house, and was quickly followed by a second. The first round piled wall, ceiling, and rubble on top of the two men, so that the second, which entered the attic and burst, did no damage to either of them. The two then went quickly to the basement of the house to better cover. The enemy tank continued firing. Every time the enemy tank fired a round, all the men ducked into the cellar. When the tank ceased fire, they all ran back upstairs and manned the defense positions. This queer fighting continued until about noon when two more enemy tanks pulled up to the crossroad marked on the sketch. One of these fired several rounds into one of the unoccupied houses in the vicinity, and one or two into the one occupied by Adams and his men. Next they opened up with machine-gun fire on the barn adjacent to the building. The barn's thatched roof was set on fire by the tracers from the machine gun.

Then something happened, and according to Capt. James Love, who saw something from his command post he had never heard of having been done before. The German tank commander opened the hatch in the top of the tank. He took a *Faustpatrone* out of the inside of the tank and fired it at the command post building, caving in the whole top. The tank withdrew. Only one man was injured in the collapse of the roof. The only reason Captain Love could give for the tank commander bringing his whole upper body out of the turret without being shot, was that those who saw it were so surprised, they didn't do anything. In any case, he got away scotfree.

At about the same time, men from C Company and the antitank company command post found an enemy tank in a wooden barn about sixty yards north of the command post. It apparently was waiting in concealment for a likely target. It was well inside the barn, but unfortunately for its crew, its gun was too long to hide inside the building, and someone saw it. One of the tank destroyers in the vicinity was able to fire on the building without moving. Several rounds brought the building crashing down on the enemy tank, and the tank destroyer finished it off.

Adams went to the command post to report to Rollings on the situation. He had been wounded slightly when the wall of the house fell on him. Adams needed medical attention, and told one of the men nearby to get a jeep from in front of the company command post. One man was injured by rifle fire trying to get the jeep out, so Adams decided to go on foot. The fact that they had fought so long in the house that has been destroyed, prompted Adams later to ask what happened after he left. He learned that one of the company officers, Lieutenant Mode, had tried to put out the fire in the barn with ten gallons of water but was unsuccessful, and because Adams house was so close to the conflagration, the position was abandoned.

At about 1100 hours, an American soldier was hit badly while trying to move between two buildings nearby. An aid man tried three times to get to

A destroyed M10 tank destroyer of the 644th Tank Destroyer Battalion at Krinkelt.
KARL-HEINZ HECK

An M4 Sherman tank of the 741st Tank Battalion on one of the roads into Krinkelt. KARL-HEINZ HECK

the injured man, and was shot at by the enemy although his Red Cross armband was plainly visible. Finally a man from another house went out and took the injured man to shelter.

At about 1300 hours the commander of the self-propelled tank destroyers in the vicinity gave Love permission to employ the tank destroyers as he saw fit, thus countermanding the order that held them in position, and under which they were acting. At about 1500 hours, a Mark IV got to about half way between the antitank company and the regimental command post and "started shelling hell out of us." It hit a tank destroyer and wounded the whole crew. In improving the defensive positions, Love had worked another tank destroyer to the north side of the command post house, and after immobilizing the Mark IV with a bazooka, Captain Love sent for another tank destroyer. The bazooka round evidently got the Mark IV's motor, for it had difficulty traversing its gun. Because of the locations of buildings, the tank destroyer had to come up with its gun pointing to the rear, and while the Mark IV was traversing slowly as if by hand through ninety degrees, the tank destroyer traversed his gun through about 200 degrees, got off three rounds and took the turret right off the Mark IV. Another Mark IV that was moving in near the first one apparently saw what was happening, for he pulled out.

On the morning of the nineteenth at about 1000 hours, the position of L Company was again attacked by sixty or seventy-five enemy infantry supported by two or three tanks. The 3rd Platoon positions apparently had been located, and the enemy concentrated his attacks on them, leveling the houses they occupied around their ears. Captain Farrell called for artillery on the enemy tanks, getting a direct hit on one of them. The others took off. Machine guns, mortars and the artillery got the rest of the enemy infantry, or drove them off. After the attack was beaten off, the company received artillery fire from the Germans causing some casualties, but there were no further attacks for the remainder of the day.

When daylight came, the enemy attacks on the 3rd Battalion positions decreased. The battalion kitchens were in the area, and a hot meal, the first in some forty-eight hours, was served to the men under the noses of the enemy. The companies were resupplied with ammunition and water and "spirits were damn high." The roads leading into the area were so littered with knocked-out enemy tanks that the routes of approach for future enemy attempts of penetration were effectively blocked.

At about 1630 hours, Colonel Barsanti received orders from Colonel Boos that the entire defensive force would begin a withdrawal at about 1730 hours as dusk began to fall. The withdrawal of the troops was in the order they were positioned from north to south: 2nd, 1st, and 3rd (minus L Company) Battalions, with the 3rd Battalion acting as the rear guard. I and K Companies were behind with part of Task Force Brakel, two squads each to form the rear guard. They were to initiate their own withdrawal after the last company had departed. These squads were instructed to meet Colonel Barsanti on their way out. In addition to the above instructions, I and K Companies were to send eight men to meet Colonel Barsanti at the above crossroad. M Company was instructed to send two bazooka teams to this point. Colonel Barsanti, assuming command of the little composite rear guard, set a 200-yard semicircular line around the crossroad. The withdrawal started according to plan, but as the 2nd Battalion pulled out, the Germans followed close behind them. The enemy set up a machine gun about 200 yards north of Colonel Barsanti's crossroads and interdicted the crossroad with fire. Because of the inability of the enemy effectively to aim their guns in the dark, and because of the cover afforded the withdrawal by the slope of the terrain, the enemy fire passed over the heads of the American troops. The men were able to pass the crossroads unhurt by moving in a low crouch.

K Company was to start the withdrawal with the 3rd Battalion, but as the move started, they were attacked by about five enemy tanks and 100 infantry. K Company was ordered to stay and fight off the enemy attack, and I Company was withdrawn first. Task Force Brakel followed I Company out while K Company brought about ten battalions of artillery to bear on the German attackers. K Company began their withdrawal by squads at about 1915 hours to the vicinity of the Battalion command post. The artillery fire was so effective that the attack on K Company stopped completely. Four of the five tanks were finished off, three by artillery and the fourth one by a bazooka team from K Company that didn't have to move from its position to hit the enemy armor.

While this tank action was in progress, Barsanti and his little group were at the crossroad holding it open for the last of K Company. The enemy had occupied the vacated battalion command post and were milling around the area about 300 yards away. At last, K Company showed up, and on orders from the colonel, went past the crossroad "at a dead run." A platoon of tanks and a platoon of tank destroyers which had remained behind were ordered down the road toward Wirtzfeld.

Colonel Barsanti and his little covering force held the crossroad open while the last elements of the division withdrew through them. The colonel was at this time convinced that he and his men would not get out of the place alive. At last everything cleared, including the engineer demolition platoon that had stayed behind to destroy abandoned equipment. The last daisy chain of mines was put on the road. There were Germans all around the crossroad, and none of the force dared to fire any more for fear of being completely cut off. The order to withdraw was given, and the men moved at the double toward Wirtzfeld.

One of the men in the engineer demolition platoon was Truman Kimbro, who received the Medal of Honor. His citation reads: "Truman Kimbro, C Company, 2nd Engineer Combat Battalion, 2nd Infantry Division. On 19 December 1944, as scout, he led a squad assigned to the mission of mining a vital crossroads near Rocherath, Belgium. At the first attempt to reach the objective, he discovered it was occupied by an enemy tank and at least twenty infantrymen. Driven back by withering fire, Tech 4 Kimbro made two more attempts to lead his squad to the crossroads but all approaches were covered by intense enemy fire.

"Although warned by our own infantrymen of the great danger involved, he left his squad in a protected place and, laden with mines, crawled alone toward the crossroads. When nearing his objective he was severely wounded, but he continued to drag himself forward and laid his mines across the road. As he tried to crawl from the objective his body was riddled with rifle and machine gun fire. The mines laid by his act of indomitable courage delayed the advance of enemy armor and prevented the rear of our withdrawing columns from being attacked by the enemy."

The withdrawal began under heavy artillery and small-arms fire. Contact with the enemy was successfully broken however, and under the cover of darkness, the company withdrew and started back towards the high ground north of Wirtzfeld. The leading elements of L Company had passed through Wirtzfeld when a heavy concentration of *Nebelwerfer* fire fell on the 3rd Platoon, last in the column. The heavy casualties which were caused by this fire were evacuated without disturbing the progress of the column.

The U.S. V Corps decided to abandon the exposed positions in Krinkelt-Rocherath, which were also threatened in the south, as soon as the last elements of the 99th Infantry Division, withdrawing east of the line Mürringen-Rocherath, had passed. The positions around Wirtzfeld were also to be evacuated as soon as the troops that were coming from Krinkelt-Rocherath had passed the village. The plan was for a new defensive front northwest of Wirtzfeld with the 2nd Infantry Division and the remains of the 99th Infantry Division. The withdrawal was to be covered by the 741st Tank Battalion, the 644th Tank Destroyer Battalion, and the engineers of the division. The withdrawal began from the left flank so that the road from Krinkelt to Wirtzfeld could be kept open.

The Americans began to withdraw gradually and fell back to the western part of the village.

2nd Lieutenant Engel of the 3rd Panzer Company remembers: "Under threat of court martial Jürgensen had handed me the responsibility for the defense of my tank, another Panther of the 1st Company with a three men crew and an un-crewed Panzer IV. It was a nice feeling: the Americans in one half of the village, and we on the other side with eight men and three tanks that could not fight. It was good that the Americans did not suspect this. Before the break of dawn and before assault guns of the 3rd Panzer Grenadier Division occupied the village, they had withdrawn far beyond the edge of the village".

Until relief arrived, there were still losses among the remaining tanks which secured the part of the village taken the previous days. To cover the preparation for the withdrawal, the American artillery time and again bombarded the eastern part of the village.

Max Sülner, gunner of the company commander's tank of the 6th Company, writes: "During a bombardment in Krinkelt, we got a shell in front of the turret which tore a one-meter-wide hole in our armor. With this, our driver, Karl-Heinz von Elm, was completely torn apart. Our radioman, Gottfried Opitz, lost his left arm. He had at least been partially covered by the radio apparatus; Hannes Simon got his legs full of shrapnel. I was sitting in the cupola and had put my legs on the bar next to the barrel; so I got off with a fright. I was able to give Hannes and Gottfried a place in a halftrack which drove to the first aid post. Our tank was towed to the repair company in Losheimergraben where we buried Karl-Heinz."

On 19 December, the 3rd Panzer Grenadier Division attacked Krinkelt from the south and the southeast with the 103rd Tank Battalion, equipped exclusively with assault guns, while a panzer grenadier battalion (the 2nd of the 8th Regiment) attacked Wirtzfeld with the 89th Grenadier Regiment of the 12th Volksgrenadier Division. The 1st Battalion of the 8th, after assembly in the Rocherath woods, was to bypass Rocherath to the north and take the high ground immediately to the north of it. The afternoon report of OB West for 19 December reports: "277th Division, with a combat group via the Rocherath Barracks, is held up while going to the north; is ordered toward Elsenborn. Point element currently south-west of Hollerath. Start is planned for 1300 hours."

The result of the fighting by the 38th Infantry is reported in their unit journal:

> 1150 hours: Tanks at 983051 behind Flak turret. 'Jerries' in flak turret.
> 1237 hours: About an hour ago two tanks showed up and fired on the area of the command post (possibly Panzer IVs).
> 1305 hours: Another tank on the road, where five have been killed, is on the left flank of A Company, is firing straight at A Company.
> 1316 hours: German tank brought men up and unloaded them in a killed tank from where they're firing machine guns at the area of the church.
> 1345 hours: Colonel Stokes orders: at 1730 hours withdrawal to the positions indicated on the map. The 395th with the attached 2nd battalion of the 393rd is to move over the road. . . . All other units under command of the 38th Infantry . . . road towards Wirtzfeld . . . destroy all American and German equipment simultaneously. Leave no equipment behind that the Germans can use!
> 1340 hours: Tank activity. We put artillery fire there. One tank hit, crew bails out.
> 1345 hours: Do we fire on the church tower? Yes.
> 1355 hours: Start withdrawal now, the important vehicles straightaway.

1610 hours: Twelve Panzers are coming up the street, where other Panzers have been reported as well (with the 3rd Battalion, 38th Infantry, in the village of Krinkelt).
1650 hours: 1st Battalion reports that the artillery killed three tanks, damaged two, the others are scattered; one tank killed by tank destroyers.
1737 hours: Use own covering forces to protect the withdrawal.
1835 hours: I Company reports that enemy tanks are entering the village.
1930 hours: Ready to march off.
2215 hours: All units here by 2200 hours.

PFC James F. Fleming, a BAR man in the 1st Platoon, C Company, 1st Battalion, 9th Infantry, 2nd Infantry Division, recounts: "I have vivid memories of the four days in particular, 16 through 19 December 1944. The weather conditions were snow, fog and miserably bitter wet cold. The foxholes we occupied were widely spaced out on a defensive line at the edge of a forest. Our division was recently moved northward toward the Roer River dams with our previous positions being taken over by the newly arrived 106th Infantry Division and parts of the 99th Infantry Division. The weather continued to get colder with more snow falling. Unfortunately, we were not issued the white camouflage suits and continued to wear the khaki overcoats as outerwear. The utter chaos, confusion and weather made these four days the most miserable and unforgettable time of my three campaigns with the 2nd Infantry Division in World War II. Our C Company suffered many casualties during this time. When we were able to regroup again as an organized unit on 21 December at Camp Elsenborn, Belgium, it was determined that we had lost approximately three-fourths of our company to killed, wounded or prisoners of war. The fighting was intense, close range, at time by fixing bayonets and counterattacking German infantry and tanks with bazookas. This was essential to our survival and to avoid being taken prisoners during our withdrawal toward where we hoped to find our battalion and Division.

"One of the toughest and most memorable fights against the advancing Germans occurred near Rocherath at a place which was commonly referred to by the GIs of the 1st Battalion, 9th Regiment, as the Purple Heart Crossroads. We suffered extremely heavy casualties, but the unit held up the German offensive enough to allow units to reorganize better defensive positions and was awarded the Presidential Citation for their efforts.

"Due to our disorganized and confused state, most of the fighting was carried out by small individual units of the 1st Battalion. Despite the

deplorable weather conditions of snow, sleet, bitter cold and fog, and very high casualties, the three infantry companies of the 1st Battalion were able to delay the German advance long enough for the 2nd Division to form a new defensive position around Elsenborn, Belgium.

"The weather grew colder day by day, and after we rejoined our unit on 20 December we had to use sticks of dynamite to start our foxholes as the ground was frozen to a depth of three to four inches. Until completion of our foxholes on a more permanent line of defense, we slept by forming a pyramid of three or four men and dozed standing upright and moving your feet to avoid frostbite. The next morning in order to operate our weapons, in my case the BAR, we resorted to urinating on the firing mechanism to get it started. The cold, reported to be the worst in fifty years, made conditions so miserable that a few members of my squad actually said that being killed was better than living in these unbearable conditions. Fortunately, I never got that desperate. On many occasions men who got wounded fell in the snow and couldn't move, so they froze to death before the medics could find them.

"After we resumed the offensive from Camp Elsenborn, every ten to fourteen days units were withdrawn from the line so the medics could examine our feet. While I was okay on the initial inspection, on the next inspection the medics determined my feet were frozen. I was initially evacuated to

Withdrawal towards Elsenborn

After the battle for Krinkelt-Rocherath, destroyed equipment littered the area.
JESS STYLES

Eupen, then to Verviers and on to Liege, Belgium, then finally to Paris, France, where I was told my combat days were over. On hearing this, I breathed a big sigh of relief."

Paul Thomson of the 12th Field Artillery remembers: "We left our fox holes on 10 December 1944 as the 106th Division took up our gun slots. We moved out in the bad snow storm; it took six days to reach Elsenborn.

"On 13 December, the attacking regiments' orders were to breach the Seigfried Line. They didn't make it that night as they ran into big pill boxes. We had to bust them with artillery; the guys in the attack had some of the hardest hand to hand fighting.

"On 16 December, a lot of heavy shelling fell on Elsenborn. Early on the morning of the 17th we had the first indication of the seriousness. When German parachutes landed in the rear and were approaching from the south and east. Elsenborn was shelled again heavier using 380-millimeter shells. I measured the butt of one, and it measured 380 millimeters.

"The seventeenth was so cold and still snowing, wind blowing. My feet, hands and face were almost frozen. I was told then that there might be a kitchen truck in the woods. I went looking for it and found it had been blown up. I hurried back to the gun and field phone to report to fire direction that someone was firing on us from the rear. We had to turn our gun around, and it took ten to twelve men to do it. As we fired about 400 rounds, the ground began to thaw from the heat of the gun where the shells came out of the barrel; the trails and the jacks were stuck in the mud. We were allowed 400 rounds for each gun, which weighed six and a half tons.

"The 12th Field Artillery at Elsenborn, six kilometers north and west, sent three bazookas out to south and east approaches to the city. The Germans' goal was to reach the rich gasoline and food dumps at Liege and Namur, without which the panzer army couldn't move. They got no closer than Rocherath.

"On the morning of the eighteenth, they renewed their assault. We fought hard; the artillery fired in all directions, and again the attacks stopped. The snow was red with American blood.

"On the nineteenth, another heavy attack was thrown at Rocherath; again we stopped them with our guns. Then we participated against the 12th SS Panzer Division. It was so cold and still snowing, raw winds and freezing temperatures, we figured about twenty below.

"Later in the afternoon and night of the nineteenth, we moved six miles to Sourbrodt where we spent six weeks.

"The minute we moved to a new location, I dug my foxhole; I never slept in a building during the war. I always dug the hole wide and deep enough for me and God. I never changed my clothes from the time I went in on Omaha Beach until the war was over. We got new clothes at an old army post north east of Paris. My underwear looked like lace curtains, and at my boot tops I had a ring of hair from my legs. The artillery fire whipped my pant legs and wore it off. Smooth legs. I never had a bath. Stinky—all of us!

"I was scared every minute of the day and night. We won."

CHAPTER 10

Conclusion to Book Two

Prior to 13 December, the twenty-two-mile southern portion of the V Corps' front from Monschau southward toward Losheim was held by the 99th Infantry Division on the high ground along the west side of the German-Belgian border. The 18th Cavalry Squadron of the 14th Cavalry Group was on the right (south) flank of the 99th in the Manderfeld area, screening the five-mile gap between the 99th and the 106th Infantry Division to the south in the VIII Corps. On the left (north) flank of the 99th, the 38th Cavalry Squadron maintained contact and screened the flank.

On 13 December, two regimental combat teams of the 2nd Infantry Division and one of the 99th Infantry Division attacked north from the vicinity of Krinkelt-Rocherath through the center of the 99th's front along the axis of the Rocherath-Wahlerscheid road with the seizure of the road junction at Wahlerscheid as the initial objective and, ultimately, the Roer River dams. On the night of 15–16 December, the 9th Infantry took the Wahlerscheid Crossroad, and the 38th Infantry passed through the 9th and started to move toward Dreiborn, Germany, the regiment's objective. The 23rd Infantry was in the vicinity of Camp Elsenborn in the assembly area. The 395th Regimental Combat Team of the 99th Division, attacking on the right of the 2nd Division, captured several pillboxes in the Siegfried Line the first two days.

The German attack began before dawn on 16 December, and by nightfall, the Germans had reached only the Losheimergraben Crossroads. The two regiments of the 99th Division, maintaining defensive positions east of Krinkelt, became heavily engaged, as did the 3rd Battalion of the 395th Regiment at Höfen, the north end of the division line, but they held fast. The attacking regiments of the two divisions were not the target of the German attack, but ultimately, they could have become surrounded and pinched off.

During the day on 16 December, the 1st and 3rd Battalions of the 23rd Infantry were attached to the 99th Division to reinforce them in their defense, the 1st Battalion moving to Mürringen and the 3rd to the east of

Rocherath. At the end of 16 December, the 9th and 38th Regiments and the 2nd Battalion of the 23rd Infantry were in the vicinity of Wahlerscheid.

On the morning of 17 December, the Germans overran the American positions to the southeast of Büllingen, which were held by the 393rd and 394th Regiments of the 99th Division and the 18th Cavalry. Before 0800 hours, enemy tanks of the 1st SS Panzer Division *Leibstandarte Adolf Hitler* appeared in Büllingen where the 2nd Quartermaster and 2nd Signal Companies, the supply installation of the 2nd Division, the medical supply dump, B Company of the 2nd Engineer Battalion, and the kitchens of the 3rd Battalion, 23rd Infantry, were located. Most of the troops defending the town were soldiers of the 107th Engineer Battalion.

Also in the vicinity were the 99th and 2nd Infantry Divisions' airstrips; the spotter planes of the 2nd Division were destroyed, but except for one, the planes of the 99th Division were flown out, escaping destruction. 17 December saw the heaviest air activity by the enemy that the 2nd Division had experienced. During that day, the enemy lost sixteen or seventeen planes to friendly aircraft and to antiaircraft weapons in the vicinity. At one time, supporting fighter-bombers had to jettison their bombs so that they could fight off enemy aircraft.

About five enemy tanks turned north from Büllingen toward Wirtzfeld, where they were destroyed by self-propelled tank destroyers of the 644th Tank Destroyer Battalion and 57-millimeter antitank guns of the 2nd Division's headquarters defense platoon.

The German unit in Büllingen did not press the move to the north from Büllingen but moved to the west and southwest, conforming to its assigned route of advance, their right (north) boundary running in a line about through Büllingen. While this was happening, the 12th SS Panzer Division and the 277th Volksgrenadier Division were vigorously attacking the 393rd Infantry, 99th Division, and the 23rd Infantry, 2nd Division, toward Krinkelt and Rocherath. The 9th and 38th Regiments withdrew from Wahlerscheid and set up defensive positions at Krinkelt and Rocherath. The 2nd Battalion of the 23rd moved to Wirtzfeld to protect the town from the south. They remained in these positions for about three days until the 99th Division and other V Corps units could be consolidated along Elsenborn Ridge.

The German attacks from the east continued for about three days and nights. On the night of the seventeenth, four tank destroyers from *Kampfgruppe Zeiner* were in Rocherath, having come through the lines at the Lausdell Crossroads, heavily engaged by the men of Colonel McKinley's 9th Regiment. The enemy repeatedly attacked with armor and infantry, but the American troops effectively repelled them. The U.S. troops in Krinkelt-Rocherath and Wirtzfeld withdrew during the night of 19–20 December to

Conclusion to Book Two   395

prepared positions in the high ground just east and northeast of Wirtzfeld. These positions had been prepared under the direction of Major Hoke, the division's special service officer.

Captured enemy maps showed there were four routes through the 99th-2nd Division area that Hitler planned to use in his attack by the I SS Panzer Corps to the west. The plan, however, did not anticipate the presence of the 2nd Division. In conditions of cold, wet, snowy weather, with fog, mist, rain, and smoke from burning buildings making the visibility next to impossible, the defense of Rocherath and Krinkelt—and later Elsenborn by the 2nd and 99th Divisions and other V Corps units—completely stopped the I SS Panzer Corps, whose mission was the seizure of Elsenborn Ridge and the road net leading to Liege and the Meuse River.

Sources

BOOK ONE: THE LOSHEIM GAP

German

Der Vergangenheit auf der Spur: Geschichte der 3. Fallschirmjäger Division by Fritz Roppelt
7. Panzerkompanie: Chronik der Siebten Panzerkompanie der 1. SS-Panzerdivision "Leibstandarte" by Hans Behrendt.
Gefährten unsere Jugend, Die Flakabteilung der 1. SS-Panzerdivision "Leibstandarte" by Karl Wortmann
Meine Ehre heißt Treue by Oswald Siegmund
Lützows wilde verwegende Schar: das mecklenburgische Grenadier Regiment 89 in beiden Weltkriegen by Biblio Verlag
Einsatz des 14./Rgt 89, 12. VGD in die Ardennen-Offensive by Hans Zeplien
Alte Kameraden: verschiedene Beiträge Angehörigen der ehem. 12. VGD
Einsatz der 12. VGD während die Ardennen-Offensive by Gerhard Engel
Die Vorausabteilung Holz by Major Holz
Berichte zum Einsatz des Füsilier Rgt. 27 by Hubert Eggert
Die Ardennenoffensive in der Zeit von 16 Dezember bis 29 Dezember by Gerhard Engel
MS B-733, Neustadt, 1947
Chronik der 277. Volksgrenadier Division by Wingolf Scherer
ETHINT 10: 7 September 1945, an interview with Joachim Peiper
ETHINT 11: 18 September 1945, an interview with Joachim Peiper (ML 752)
ETHINT 12: 12 August 1945, an interview with Otto Skorzeny
ETHINT 15: 8–9 August 1945, an interview with "Sepp" Dietrich
ETHINT 16: 10 July 1945, an interview with "Sepp" Dietrich
ETHINT 21: 11–15 August 1945, an interview with Fritz Krämer
ETHINT 62: 11 August 1945, an interview with Walter Staudinger

United States

Battle Babies: The Story of the 99th U.S. Infantry Division in World War II by Walter E. Lauer
Hey Mac: A Combat Infantryman's Story by William F. McMurdy
Combat Engineer: The History of the 107th Engineering Battalion by Frederick Stonehouse
World War II Operations Reports of the 254th (C) Engineer Battalion
Combat Interviews of the 99th Infantry Division
After-Action Reports, 394th Infantry Regt (99th Infantry Division), December 1944

Sources 397

After-Action Reports, 393rd Infantry Regt (99th Infantry Division), December 1944
After-Action Reports, 23rd Infantry Regt (2nd Infantry Division), December 1944
After-Action Report, 801st Tank Destroyer Battalion
After-Action Report, 14th Cavalry Group
After-Action Report, 612th Tank Destroyer Battalion
Lyle Bouck's presentation file
Story of the I&R Platoon by G. Vernon Leopold
Video of the 99th Infantry Division
Checkerboard, the newspaper of the 99th Infantry Division Association

BOOK TWO: HOLDING THE LINE

German
Die 3. Kompanie by Willie Engel
Die 12. SS Pz. Division (Teil I und Teil II) by Kurt Meyer
Lützows wilde verwegende Schar: das mecklenburgische Grenadier Regiment 89 in beiden Weltkriegen by Biblio Verlag
Einsatz des 14./Rgt 89, 12. VGD in die Ardennen-Offensive by Hans Zeplien
Berichte zum Einsatz des Füsilier Rgt. 27 by Hubert Eggert
Chronik der 277. Volksgrenadier Division by Wingolf Scherer
ETHINT 15: 8–9 August 1945, an interview with "Sepp" Dietrich
ETHINT 16: 10 July 1945, an interview with "Sepp" Dietrich
ETHINT 21: 11–15 August 1945, an interview with Fritz Krämer
ETHINT 62: 11 August 1945, an interview with Walter Staudinger

United States
Infantry Soldier by George W. Neill
How a Ninety-Day Wonder Survived the War by Charles D. Curley Jr.
Battle Babies: The Story of the 99th U.S. Infantry Division in World War II by Walter Lauer
"We'll Never Go Overseas": History of the 741st Tank Battalion
Butler's Battlin' Blue Bastards by Thor Ronningen
Against the Panzers by Allyn R. Vannoy and Jay Karamales
Combat Interviews of the 2nd Infantry Division
After-Action Report, 38th Infantry Regt (2nd Infantry Division), December 1944
After-Action Report, 23rd Infantry Regt (2nd Infantry Division), December 1944
After-Action Report, 9th Infantry Regt. (2nd Infantry Division), December 1944
After-Action Report, 393rd Infantry Regt (99th Infantry Division), December 1944
After-Action Report, 395th Infantry Regt (99th Infantry Division), December 1944
After-Action Report, 394th Infantry Regt (99th Infantry Division), December 1944
After-Action Report, 801st Tank Destroyer Battalion
After-Action Report, 644 Tank Destroyer Battalion
After-Action Report, 612 Tank Destroyer Battalion
After-Action Report, 741st Tank Battalion
Checkerboard, the newspaper of the 99th Infantry Division Association
The Defense of Höfen: A Historical Monograph by the U.S. Army
99th Infantry Division video

Acknowledgments

BOOK ONE: THE LOSHEIM GAP

When I was about twelve years old, I asked my dad to take me to the Ardennes for a tour of the places I had read about in books on the Battle of the Bulge. We never knew then that it would result in what you see here. Thanks, Dad, for all your time; I'm sorry you can't be here to see this book.

Numerous people helped me with this, my first book on the Ardennes. My intention was not to present a historical overview of the battle, but primarily to let the veterans speak in a chronological way. It is nearly impossible to list all the people who helped with the book, and forgetting only one is unforgivable, but to all the veterans, relatives, historians, and others, I give thanks with all of my heart for their help.

I want to thank a few very special friends, without whose help I would never have been able to write the book. Karl-Heinz Heck was my guide in Belgium and took me to places hardly anyone else could have found, and his wife made me the most wonderful pea soup you can have in the Ardennes. B. O. Wilkins (K Company, 393rd Infantry) checked every single line in this book, getting my text correct and trying to understand what I meant when I wrote down my thoughts in Dutch and English. Dick Byers (C Company, 371st Field Artillery) is no longer with us, but without his help in finding stories and pictures and putting me in contact with many veterans, this book would never have been possible. Wingolf Scherer (277th Volksgrenadier Division) found the information on the 277th Volksgrenadier Division. Frank van de Bergh, my Dutch colleague and friend, did all the German-to-English translations and went with me to the Ardennes in the winter of 1999, where—in inches of snow—we took all kinds of measurements without getting off the road (he will never forget that experience!). Thank you all.

BOOK TWO: HOLDING THE LINE

In addition to those listed above, I would like to thank Frank Rieser for his wonderful drawings; Daniel P. Huseman, who believed in this project from

Acknowledgments

the very beginning and who helped contact those involved with the 2nd Infantry Division; Col. W. Stockwell for his maps; Walter Schüle, who found Helmut Zeiner, whose account provided great insight into the fighting in Krinkelt; Günther Burdack, who provided everything he could find on the 12th SS Panzer Division; and Daniel Styles for letting me use the pictures his father, Jess Styles (HQ Company, 741st Tank Battalion), took after the battle in Krinkelt-Rocherath.

www.ingramcontent.com/pod-product-compliance
Lightning Source LLC
Chambersburg PA
CBHW071851290426
44110CB00013B/1109